HOUGHTON MIFFLIN

Math

MATHEMATICS

Cover Activity: *Understanding multiplication through arrays is the subject as students design an egg carton to hold Yolks for 24 Folks (Module 4, Investigation, pages 156–157). Students (shown here clockwise from upper left): Salena Davila, Evan Mahoney, Aaron Coggins, Stephanie Ozawa, Emelia March.*

HOUGHTON MIFFLIN Math MATHEMATICS

Program Authors
Harry Bohan
Gerlena Clark
Heather J. Kelleher
Charles S. Thompson

Contributing Authors
Nadine S. Bezuk
Jean M. Shaw
Lucia Vega-Garcia

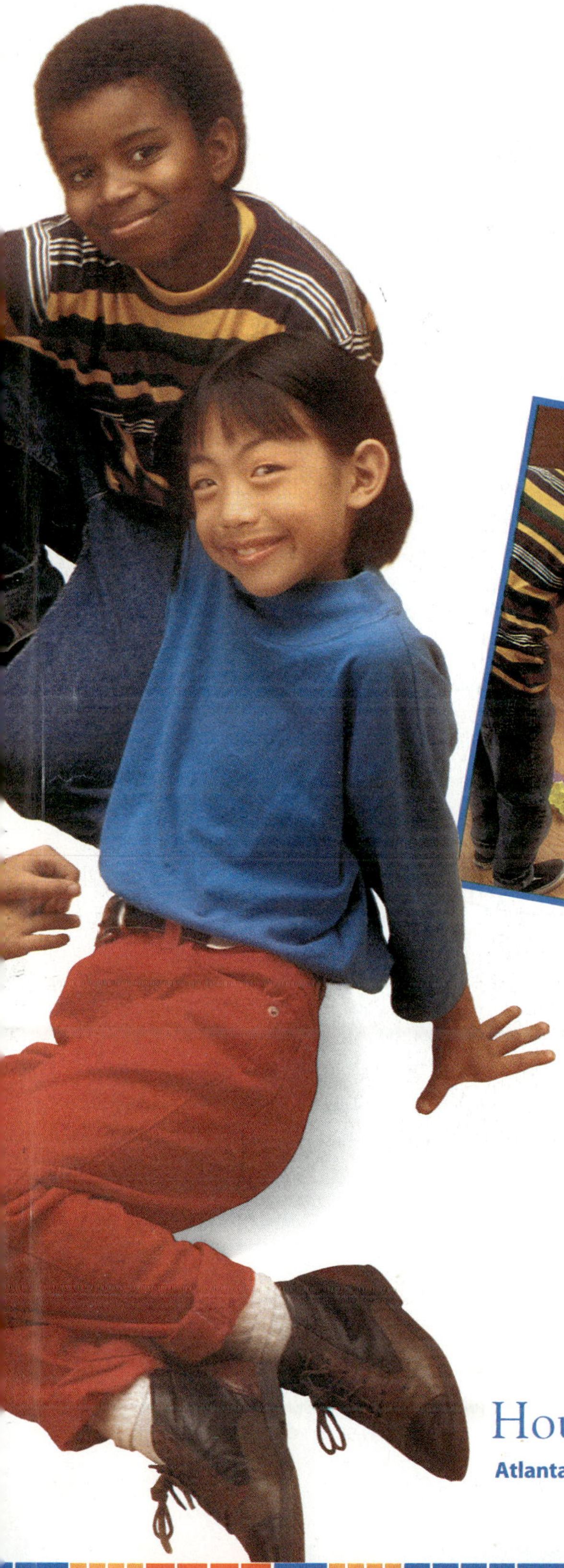

Houghton Mifflin Company • Boston
Atlanta • Dallas • Geneva, Illinois • Princeton, New Jersey • Palo Alto

nd Contributors

Nadine S. Bezuk
Associate Professor of Mathematics Education
San Diego State University
San Diego, CA

Contributing Author, Developer of Concept and Materials for Math to Go

Harry Bohan
Professor of Mathematics Education
Sam Houston State University
Huntsville, TX

Program Author, Developer of Philosophy and Grades 3-6

Gerlena Clark
Los Angeles County Mathematics Consultant
Los Angeles, CA

Program Author, Developer of Philosophy and Teacher Training Materials

Heather J. Kelleher
Former Classroom Teacher and Doctoral Student
University of British Columbia
Vancouver, BC, Canada

Program Author, Developer of Philosophy and Grades 1–2

Jean M. Shaw
Professor of Elementary Education
University of Mississippi
University, MS

Contributing Author, Developer of Kindergarten Level

Charles S. Thompson
Professor of Education
University of Louisville
Louisville, KY

Program Author, Developer of Philosophy and Grades 3–6

Lucia Vega-Garcia
Bilingual Education Director
Santa Clara County Office of Education
San Jose, CA

Contributing Author, Developer of Teacher Support for Students Acquiring English

Acknowledgments

Grateful acknowledgment is made for the use of the following material: **16** From the book *How to Count Sheep without Falling Asleep,* by Ralph Leighton and Carl Feynman, illustrated by George Ulrich.

—Continued on page 460

Printed in the U.S.A. ISBN: 0-395-67910-9
3456789-VH-98 97 96 95

Developed and produced by Ligature

Specialists

Brenda Gentry-Norton
Research Associate
Program for Complex Instruction
Stanford University
Palo Alto, CA

Consultant for Assessment Philosophy and Materials

Brenda Glen
Classroom Teacher
Balderas Elementary School
Fresno, CA

Field Test Coordinator and Developer of Teacher's Edition Notes, Grades 5–6

Joan L. Hopkins
Classroom Teacher
Escondido Elementary School
Palo Alto, CA

Field Test Coordinator and Developer of Teacher's Edition Notes, Grades K–2

Betty Iehl
Educational Consultant
San Gabriel, CA

Developer of Teacher's Edition Notes, Grades 4 and 6

National Center to Improve the Tools of Educators
Douglas Carnine, Director
Edward Kameenui, Associate Director
University of Oregon
Eugene, OR

Developer of Alternate Strategies Materials, Grades 2–6

Mary Anne O'Neal
Educational Consultant
Carson, CA

Developer of Teacher's Edition Notes, Grades 3 and 5

Annie Podesto
Staff Development Specialist
Stockton Unified School District
Stockton, CA

Consultant for Assessment Philosophy and Materials

Sally Y. Wong
Title VII Adviser
Los Angeles Unified School District
Los Angeles, CA

Developer of Teacher's Edition Notes, Grades 3–6

Field Test Teachers

Kindergarten Modules **Traci Assad,** Fall River Summer School Program, Fall River, MA • **Susanne Burke,** Holmes School, Dorchester, MA • **Leland Clarke,** Holmes School, Dorchester, MA • **Beverly Letendre,** Fall River Summer School Program, Fall River, MA • **Sarah Outten,** Slade Regional Catholic School, Glen Burnie, MD • **Debbie L. Rea,** Escondido School, Stanford, CA • **Pat Robinson,** Escondido School, Stanford, CA

Grade 1 Modules **Robin Crawley,** Holmes School, Dorchester, MA • **Suraya Driscoll,** River Heights School, East Grand Forks, MN • **Nancy Matthews,** Douglas School, Douglas, MA • **Mary Miller,** Holmes School, Dorchester, MA • **Johanna Roses,** Baker School, Chestnut Hill, MA • **Elaine Kuritani Tsumura,** Marrama School, Denver, CO

Grade 2 Modules **Najwa Abdul-Tawwab,** Holmes School, Dorchester, MA • **Mary Jane Brown,** Forwood School, Wilmington, DE • **Joan L. Hopkins,** Escondido School, Stanford, CA • **Dorene Odom,** Holmes School, Dorchester, MA • **Ida R. Wellington,** Washington School, Oakland, CA

Grade 3 Modules **Robin Burstein,** Greenwood School, Des Moines, IA • **Joanne Castelano,** Slade Regional Catholic School, Glen Burnie, MD • **Diane Rezek Fator,** Emerson School, Berwyn, IL • **Linda Griffiths,** Kennedy School, San Diego, CA • **Michele Hilbing,** Slade Regional Catholic School, Glen Burnie, MD • **Sharnell Jackson** Decatur School, Chicago, IL • **Janet M. Laws,** Lombardy School, Wilmington, DE • **Patricia Y. Lynch,** Lombardy School, Wilmington, DE • **Efraín Meléndez,** Dacotah Street School, Los Angeles, CA • **Doris Miles,** Sandburg School, Wheaton, IL • **Ricki Raymond,** Piper School, Berwyn, IL • **Deb Schantzen,** River Heights School, East Grand Forks, MN • **Bonnie Schindler,** Kennedy School, San Diego, CA • **Theresa Sievers,** Komensky School, Berwyn, IL • **Kimberly Bassett Whitehead,** Lombardy School, Wilmington, DE

Grade 4 Modules **Lynda Alexander,** St. Elizabeth School, Chicago, IL • **Betty Coleman,** Parkman School, Chicago, IL • **Karen DeRon-Head,** Armour School, Chicago, IL • **Keith Libert,** Escondido School, Stanford, CA • **Joe Montoya,** Horace Mann School, Rapid City, SD • **Robert Poncé,** Niños Heroes School, Chicago, IL

Grade 5 Modules **Lynnise H. Akinkunle-Gool,** Niños Heroes School, Chicago, IL • **Doris Buffo,** Balderas School, Fresno, CA • **Ronni K. Cohen,** Burnett School, Wilmington, DE • **Valerie De George,** Greeley School, Chicago, IL • **Brenda Glen,** Balderas School, Fresno, CA • **Brenda Leigh,** River Heights School, East Grand Forks, MN • **Cynthia L. Lew,** Madison School, Pomona, CA • **Lisa Palacios,** Pleasant Hill School, Carol Stream, IL • **Kathryn Peecher,** Revere School, Chicago, IL • **Cindy Sardo,** Burnett School, Wilmington, DE • **Henry A. Simmons,** Balderas School, Fresno, CA • **Delorise Singley,** Oakwood Windsor School, Aiken, SC • **Cecilia Maria Vasquez,** Balderas School, Fresno, CA • **Michelle Wilson,** Jefferson School, Fresno, CA

Grade 6 Module **Dorothy Cooper Jones,** Banneker Achievement Center, Gary, IN • **Albert Martinez,** Marianna Avenue School, Los Angeles, CA • **Sharon Oechsel,** Hiawatha School, Berwyn, IL • **Christopher G. Reising,** Kennedy School, San Diego, CA • **Lee Wirth,** Pershing School, Berwyn, IL

Reviewers

Kathryn A. Alexander, Macon Middle School, Brunswick, GA (Grade 6 modules) • **Sherry Bailey,** Richland School District #2, Columbia, SC (Grade 5 modules) • **Elsbeth G. Bellemere,** Scarborough School District, Scarborough, ME (Grade 5 modules) • **Sharon L. Cannon,** Myrtle Beach Middle School, Myrtle Beach, SC (Grade 6 modules) • **Cleo Charging,** White Shield School, Roseglen, ND (Grade K modules) • **Judy C. Curtis,** Colfax School, Denver, CO (Grade 3 modules) • **Myra S. Dietz,** Carroll School #46, Rochester, NY (Grade 6 modules) • **W. L. Duncker,** Midland School District, Midland, TX (Grade 5 modules) • **Donna Marie Falat,** Longfellow School, Bridgeport, CT (Grade 2 modules) • **Linda Gojak,** Hawken School, Lyndhurst, OH (Grade 6 modules) • **Annette D. Ham,** Waltersville School, Bridgeport, CT (Grade 5 modules) • **Feliciano Mendoza,** Miles Avenue School, Huntington Park, CA (Grades 5 and 6 modules) • **Kenneth Millett,** Department of Mathematics, University of California, Santa Barbara, CA (Grade 6 modules) • **Rita Nappi,** Read School, Bridgeport, CT (Grade 4 modules) • **Mahesh Sharma,** Cambridge College, Cambridge, MA (Grades K and 6 modules) • **Patricia E. Smith,** Crosswell School, Easley, SC (Grades 3 and 4 modules) • **Bonnie Townzen,** Lubin School, Sacramento, CA (Grade 1 modules) • **Angelia W. Whiting,** Beardsley School, Bridgeport, CT (Grade 1 modules) • **Pamela Yoka,** Covedale School, Cincinnati, OH (Grade K modules)

Contents

Page		
xii	Math Power	
xiv	Ongoing Investigation	How Do We Grow?

Module 1

1	**Who Needs Numbers?**	
4	**Section A**	**Time and Temperature**
4	Lesson 1	Build a Year
8	Lesson 2	Clock Time!
12	Lesson 3	High or Low?
14	**Section B**	**Organize Numbers**
14	Lesson 4	Group Count
20	Lesson 5	Rounding Rally
24	Cumulative Review	Number Power Without Numbers
26	**Section C**	**Money, Money, Money**
26	Lesson 6	Choices, Choices
29	Lesson 7	Money Fun
33	Investigation	Make Money
34	**Section D**	**Seeing with Numbers**
34	Lesson 8	First or Last
39	Lesson 9	How Many?
44	Cumulative Review	Looking Back
46	Investigations	Number Show

Module 2

49	**How Big Is Big?**	
52	**Section A**	**Exploring Length**
52	Lesson 1	Sizing Spiders
55	Lesson 2	Large Leaps!
59	Lesson 3	Lots of Addends
62	Investigation	Stairstep Sums

64	**Section B**	**Inches, Feet, and Yards**
64	Lesson 4	How Long Is It?
68	Lesson 5	Take It Away
74	**Cumulative Review**	**Amazing Facts**
76	**Section C**	**Comparing Weights**
76	Lesson 6	Light Weights
78	Lesson 7	Balancing Act
81	Lesson 8	Big Eaters
84	**Section D**	**Filling It Up**
84	Lesson 9	Hold It!
88	Lesson 10	Growth Patterns
92	**Cumulative Review**	**Looking Back**
94	Investigations	Measure Hunt

MODULE 3

97 **Have a Party**

100	**Section A**	**Exploring Addition**
100	Lesson 1	Add 'em Up
105	Lesson 2	Numbers, Please
110	**Section B**	**Exploring Subtraction**
110	Lesson 3	It's a Party
114	Lesson 4	Party Games
120	Investigation	WOW
122	**Cumulative Review**	**Party Pro**
124	**Section C**	**Metrics**
124	Lesson 5	Party-Metrics
128	Lesson 6	Spills and Chills

Contents

132	**Section D**	**Using Thousands**
132	Lesson 7	Elephant Party
135	Lesson 8	Party Guests
140	**Cumulative Review**	**Looking Back**
142	Investigations	Showing Ten Thousand

MODULE 4

145 **Multiply!**

148	**Section A**	**Exploring Groups and Arrays**
148	Lesson 1	Sizing Up Groups!
152	Lesson 2	What's an Array?
156	Investigation	Yolks for 24 Folks
158	**Section B**	**Connecting Arrays to Multiplication**
158	Lesson 3	Factors and Times
160	Lesson 4	The Great Array Game
163	Lesson 5	Gathering the Facts
166	**Cumulative Review**	**Stamps**
168	**Section C**	**Multiplication Strategies**
168	Lesson 6	Multiplying with Jacob Two-Two
173	Lesson 7	Five, Ten, Fifteen. . .
176	Lesson 8	Keeping Count
178	**Section D**	**Choosing Multiplication Strategies**
178	Lesson 9	Multiply Your Way
182	Lesson 10	Combination Lunch
184	Lesson 11	On a Roll!
188	**Cumulative Review**	**Looking Back**
190	Investigations	Plan a Perfect Playground

MODULE 5

193 **Facts on Parade**

196	**Section A**	**Multiplication Facts and Strategies**
196	Lesson 1	Facts to Know
200	Lesson 2	The Final Ten
206	Investigation	Number Design
208	**Section B**	**Parts of a Whole**
208	Lesson 3	Multiplication Parade
212	Lesson 4	Shaping Multiplication
216	**Cumulative Review**	**Freedom Festival**
218	**Section C**	**Setting Up Division**
218	Lesson 5	Equal Sets
224	Lesson 6	Division Stories
228	**Section D**	**Dividing Shapes**
228	Lesson 8	Spare Parts
232	Lesson 9	Shape Faces
236	**Cumulative Review**	**Looking Back**
238	Investigations	March to Your Own Beat

MODULE 6

241 **Crafty Fractions**

244	**Section A**	**Discovering Fractions**
244	Lesson 1	Every Part Counts
248	Lesson 2	Number the Parts
254	**Section B**	**Comparing Fractions**
254	Lesson 3	Size Them Up
260	Lesson 4	In Between
264	**Cumulative Review**	**Craft Corner**

Contents

266 **Section C** — **Adding and Subtracting Fractions**
266 Lesson 5 — Paper Chain
268 Lesson 6 — Fractions in Action
274 Investigation — Weaving Fun

276 **Section D** — **Fractions in Sets and Probability**
276 Lesson 7 — Fair Share
280 Lesson 8 — Chances and Choices
284 **Cumulative Review** — **Looking Back**
286 Investigations — Facts and Fiction

MODULE 7
289 **Food for Your Life**

292 **Section A** — **Multiplication Count**
292 Lesson 1 — How Many Tens?
296 Lesson 2 — Graphing to Estimate
300 Investigation — Multiply Three Ways

302 **Section B** — **Understanding Multiplication**
302 Lesson 3 — Trading Tens
308 Lesson 4 — Trading Hundreds
312 **Cumulative Review** — **Floating Markets**

314 **Section C** — **Exploring Decimals**
314 Lesson 5 — What's a Tenth?
322 Lesson 6 — The Next Place

Contents

324 **Section D** — **Using Money**
324 Lesson 7 — More Money
328 Lesson 8 — Making Change
332 **Cumulative Review** — **Looking Back**
334 Investigations — Pack a Picnic

MODULE 8

337 ***Puzzles, Shapes and Games***

340 **Section A** — **Points, Lines, and Angles**
340 Lesson 1 — What's Your Line?
346 Lesson 2 — Angles Everywhere

348 **Section B** — **Figure It Out**
348 Lesson 3 — Open or Closed
350 Lesson 4 — How Many Sides?
356 Lesson 5 — Getting Around
358 **Cumulative Review** — **Field of Shapes**

360 **Section C** — **Division Is Sharing**
360 Lesson 6 — Even Shares
365 Lesson 7 — Write It!
369 Investigation — The Lost Key

370 **Section D** — **Congruence and Symmetry**
370 Lesson 8 — Shapes That Match
374 Lesson 9 — Parts That Match
380 **Cumulative Review** — **Looking Back**
382 Investigations — Puzzle Pictures

385 Tool Kit
409 Extra Practice
441 Glossary
449 Index
460 Acknowledgments

Math Power

The goal of this book is to help you build your **math power.** Math power means being able to understand and use math.

REASONING AND PROBLEM SOLVING

You will learn how to think about math and how to solve problems. These are important parts of building math power.

CONNECT AND COMMUNICATE

Talking and writing about math will help you understand it. Try to connect new math ideas to math you already know.

As your math power grows, you'll use math more and more every day. Math power can help you in shopping or planning things to do. It can even help you in your play.

Math power can also help people in their jobs. No matter what you want to be, math can help you do your job. Discuss with your class some ways that firefighters or teachers or doctors use math in their work.

These students are showing some keys to math power. When you see one of these keys in your book, you will know that it can help you build math power.

Some math problems you can work in your head. For others you will need a computer or a calculator. Math power helps you choose the best way.

Sometimes drawing can help you understand a problem or show others what you think. Drawing helps you build math power too.

Ongoing Investigation

How Do We Grow?

First of all, what *is* an investigation? It's a special kind of math problem that does not have just one answer. In fact, an investigation can lead you to many answers.

Investigations take time. Some take hours or days. Others take a week or more. The one that begins on this page is called an ongoing investigation. You'll work on it all year long.

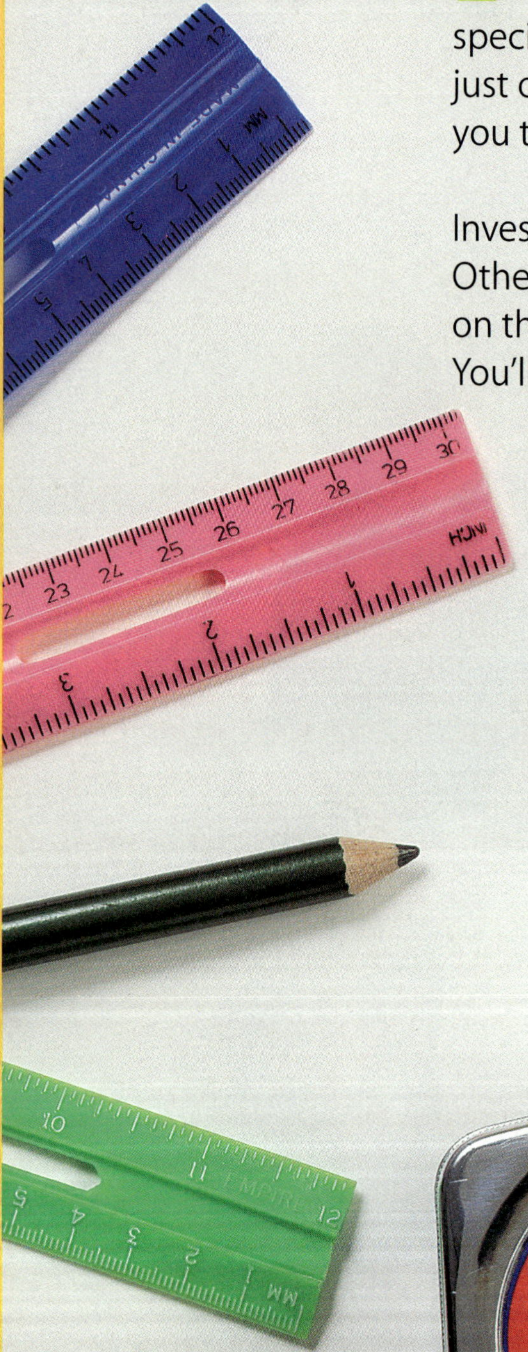

1 Goal

This year investigate "how we grow" with your class. Measure everyone today. Then predict how many inches your whole class will grow by the end of the school year.

2 Measure

Work with a partner to measure yourself. Measure these two things:

- how tall you are
- how high your reach is

3 Inch by Inch

Here are some steps you can follow for measuring.

a. Stand in front of a long strip of paper.

b. Have your partner put a pencil mark at the top of your head. This shows your height.

c. Hold up your arm. Your partner should put another pencil mark at your fingertips. This shows your reach.

d. With your partner, measure how long it is to each mark. Write the length *in inches.*

e. Also write today's date beside each mark. Sign your name at the bottom.

Did You Know?

- ***The deep-sea clam takes about 100 years to grow the length of a pencil tip.***
- ***Baby blue whales grow about 200 pounds a day.***
- ***It takes two months for your hair to grow an inch.***

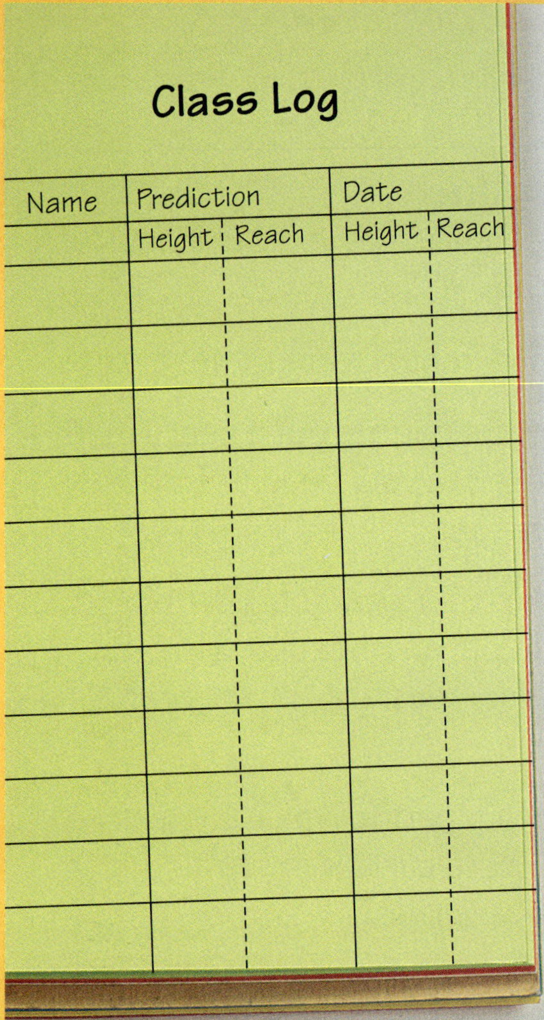

4 Take a Guess

Think about how much you might grow this year. Then predict the *total number of inches* your class will grow. Make two predictions: one for height and one for reach.

5 Talk It Over

Talk with your classmates about how you can make good predictions. Can you think of ways to figure out how tall you might be at the end of the year? How can you use your calculators?

6 Looking Ahead

During the year, you will measure yourself several more times. Each time, you will put new marks on the paper. You might change your predictions as you learn more about how you grow. At the end of the year, you will know the real answers!

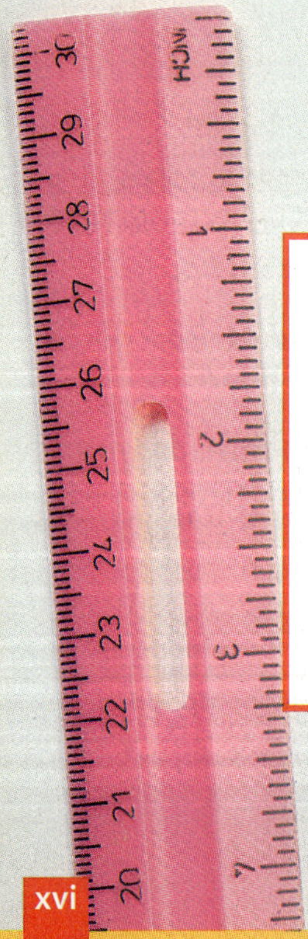

Keep in Mind

Think about these things when you make your prediction:

- ☐ Write down the number of inches your class might *grow.* Don't write the height.
- ☐ Be sure your prediction is for your *whole class*, not just one person.

MODULE 1

Who Needs Numbers?

What is wrong with this picture? Something is missing. Think about how you would use the calculator or telephone. There are no numbers to help you. Who needs numbers? You will explore that question in this module.

SECTION A
Time and Temperature

SECTION B
Organize Numbers

SECTION C
Money, Money, Money

SECTION D
Seeing with Numbers

Number Hunt!

1 Around the Town

All the numbers are missing! Go on a number hunt and find all the places where numbers are missing. Be able to tell your class why the numbers are important.

2 Around Your Class

Hunt for numbers in your classroom. Where do you find numbers? What are they for? Find as many as you can.

Word Bank

- A.M. and P.M.
- bar graph
- degrees Fahrenheit
- picture graph
- place-value chart
- rounding

Investigations Preview

Learn about time, graphs, numbers, and money. These subjects can help you design a new money system or invent your own way to show numbers.

Make Money (page 33)

How would you change the money used in the United States to make it easier to identify and use?

Number Show (pages 46–48)

Use what you know about place value to make your own system for showing numbers from 0 to 9,999.

SECTION A Time and Temperature

LESSON 1

Build a Year!

What You'll Need

- *Fraction Tool or ruler*

ACTIVITY 1 Making Months

With Your Class A calendar is full of numbers! Add numbers to a blank month. Then use your month to help make a class calendar for the whole year.

1. Divide into 12 groups. Start with January and take turns naming months in order. Each group should have a different month.

Choose a special date in your month. Find out what day of the week that date falls on.

Where could you look for information about your month?

CONNECT AND COMMUNICATE

Does your birthday always fall on the same day of the week? Can you explain why that happens?

2. Show the name of your group's month on your calendar.
3. What do you need to know to put numbers on your month?
4. Start with a day and date you already know. Write it on the calendar.
5. Fill in your calendar with a date for each day.

TOOLS AND TECHNIQUES

Thirty days has
September,
April, June, and November.
All the rest have thirty-one,
Except February which
has twenty-eight
Until leap year comes and
makes it twenty-nine.

How many days are in your month?

How can you put the dates in order?

What holidays are in your month?

✔ **Self-Check** *Can you tell what day of the week and date it is today?*

Activity 2 Class Calendar

With Your Class Make your months into a year! Put your month with the months other groups have made.

What order do the months go in?

What month comes before your month?

What month comes after your month?

Activity 3 Find the Date

With Your Group Stump your group. Pick a secret date in your month. Write the date down.

1. Group members try to find out the secret date. They ask questions that can be answered yes or no.
2. Don't just guess the date! Some questions let you cross out more dates than others.

CONNECT AND COMMUNICATE

In Your Journal *Write about how you think a calendar can help you organize your time.*

ACTIVITY 4 Spin It!

With Your Group Now use what you have learned about months and dates. Play Spin It!

What You'll Need
- *spinner*
- *game pieces*

1 Start with your game piece on the fifteenth day of your month. Spin to move.

2 Move your game piece. Say the day of the week and the date where you land.

3 The winner is the one who moves off the month first. You can move off either end of the month.

Do You Remember? Try It!

Fill in the blanks.

1. There are __?__ months in a year.
2. __?__ comes after Tuesday.
3. __?__ is the first month.
4. __?__ comes after May.
5. __?__ comes after Friday.
6. __?__ comes before July.

Write the next number in each group.

7. 7, 8, 9, __?__
8. 8, 10, 12, 14, __?__
9. 5, 10, 15, __?__
10. 1, 8, 15, __?__
11. 1, 4, 7, __?__
12. 30, 27, 24, __?__

Think About It

13. Does a month always have 30 days? Explain.

LESSON 2 Clock Time!

What You'll Need
- *paper plates*
- *crayons or markers*
- *scissors*
- *winged paper fasteners*

ACTIVITY 1 Build a Clock

On Your Own Use numbers to help you make a clock. Start with a paper plate.

1

Fold your paper plate twice to divide it into quarters. Mark the fold lines with 12, 3, 6, and 9. Use a clock to help you.

2

Divide each quarter of the circle into three equal parts. Number your new lines.

3 Look at your clock.

a. Name two numbers that mark the beginning and end of a quarter hour. Can you show other quarter hours on your clock?

b. How long does the minute hand take to go one quarter of the way around the clock?

c. How long does the minute hand take to go all the way around the clock?

60 minutes = __?__ hour

Draw the minute marks on your clock. How many marks are between each pair of numbers?

Trace and cut out clock hands. Use a winged fastener to attach them to the center of your clock.

DRAWING TO LEARN

Drawing things can help you learn about them. What did making a clock teach you about telling time?

6 **a.** Use your clock to show 12:15. Move the clock to show a time 3 minutes later. What time does your clock show now?

b. Choose another time and set your clock to show it. Swap clocks with a partner. Say the time.

c. Set your clock to show a time that is 7 minutes earlier than the time you showed in b. Say the time your clock shows.

What time does this clock show?

1

2

3

ACTIVITY 2

Clock Talk

On Your Own

1. Look at the clocks 1 through 6 above.
   a. What is the time shown on each clock?
   b. What is the time 1 hour before and 1 hour after each time shown?
   c. Tell something that happens at the times shown.

2. Times in the morning are called **A.M.** Times after noon are called **P.M.** Label the times you wrote about either A.M. or P.M.

3. What is the time 15 minutes after the time shown on the clock above?

4. The clock above shows 10:45. Another way to read the time is 15 minutes before 11:00. Tell the times before the hour for clocks 1 through 6.

REASONING AND PROBLEM SOLVING

Look at clocks 2, 5, and 6. How can you tell the time by counting how many minutes before the hour it is?

4

5

6

Activity 3 Clock Swap

With Your Group Write four different times on a sheet of paper. Then swap papers with a partner. Move the hands on your clock to match the times.

Self-Check *Are some times easier for you to read than others? Work on the times that are hard for you.*

Do You Remember?

Try It!

Write the time shown.

1. 

2. 

3. 

4. 

5. Write the time before the hour for each clock above.

Name the place value of the digit on the left. Then count back 3 from each number.

6. 57 7. 124 8. 5 9. 289 10. 82

Think About It

11. Why is the A.M. and P.M. system useful? Write your answer.

LESSON 3

High or Low?

ACTIVITY 1 Hot and Cold

On Your Own You can tell hot and cold on a thermometer without numbers.

1 Draw your own thermometer. Make a list of six hot and cold things.

2 Draw pictures on your thermometer that show the hot and cold things.

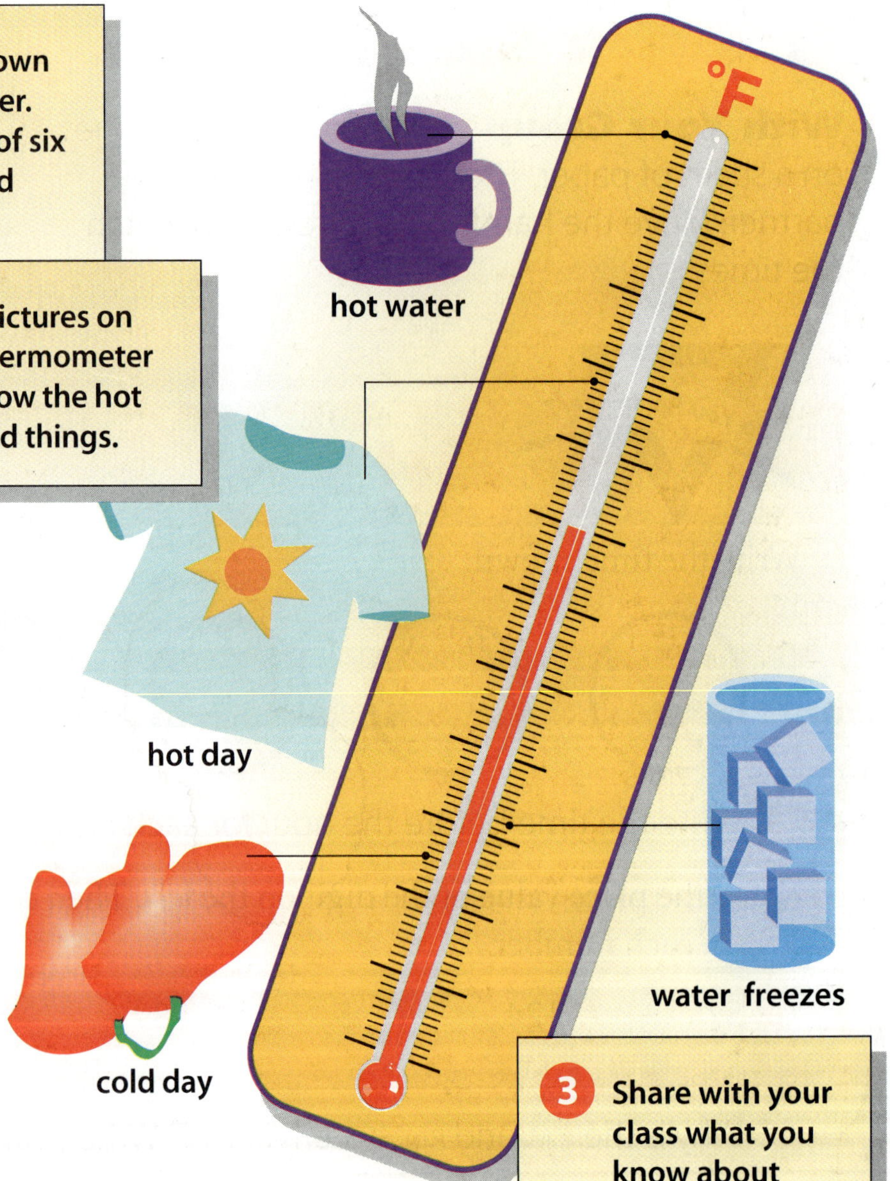

3 Share with your class what you know about temperature.

REASONING AND PROBLEM SOLVING

What do you learn by looking at the thermometer with no numbers?

ACTIVITY 2 Degree Power!

With Your Group Degrees are a way of measuring temperature. On this thermometer every mark shows 1 **degree Fahrenheit.**

1. What is the temperature? Line up the top of the red fluid with the scale.
2. What is the weather like at 88°F? at 40°F?
3. Draw a picture that shows hot or cold. Trade with a partner. Draw a thermometer with a temperature that matches the picture.

Do You Remember?

Try It!

Choose the temperature that matches best.

1. swimming	a. 38°F	b. 85°F
2. a chilly day	a. 40°F	b. 80°F
3. walking barefoot	a. 75°F	b. 35°F

Write in words a number between each pair.

4. 27 and 34
5. 98 and 105
6. 349 and 356

Describe the weather at each temperature.

7. 32°F 8. 75°F 9. 107°F 10. 50°F

Think About It

11. How might the temperature change between 3 A.M. and 3 P.M.? Explain.

CONNECT AND COMMUNICATE

Degrees Fahrenheit is one way to measure temperature. There are many other temperature scales. The Fahrenheit scale is the most common in the United States.

SECTION B Organize Numbers

LESSON 4 Group Count

What You'll Need

- *scissors*
- *bulletin board or large sheet of paper*

ACTIVITY 1 Picture Graph

With Your Class Some graphs don't even use numbers. What pets does your class like best? Make a graph without numbers to find out.

1. Choose four or five kinds of pets to show.
2. Now draw your favorite pet. All students should use a quarter sheet of paper for their drawings. The drawing below shows one way to use simple shapes to draw a pet.

How to Draw a Pet Fish

TOOLS AND TECHNIQUES

Fold your paper as the picture below shows. Cut your paper into four pieces along the folds.

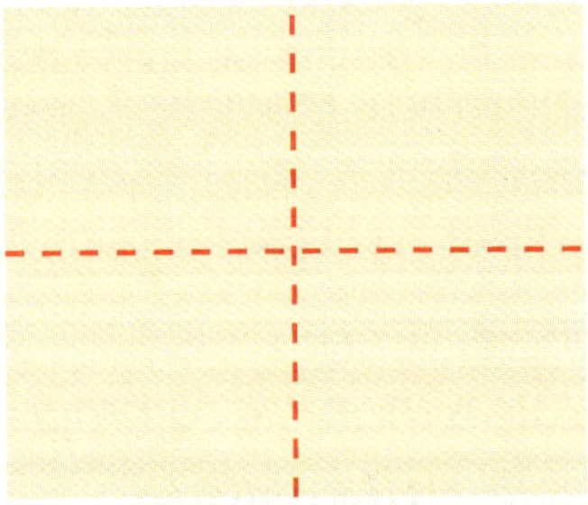

DRAWING TO LEARN

Your graph would not work if each student used a different-sized piece of paper. Explain why.

3. Use the **pictograph** shown to help you build your graph.
4. What does the graph tell you about favorite pets? How does the graph show your results? Tell why you think the graph did not need numbers.
5. Discuss other questions your class graph can answer.

What You'll Need
- *bucket of counters*

ACTIVITY 2 Count Big Numbers

With Your Class Your graph used one picture to count as one pet. A shepherd long, long ago used one small rock to show one sheep.

LITERATURE

Think about how the shepherd uses the black rocks. What if his herd grew so big that his sack was again too heavy to carry? What could he do?

Then he tried counting his sheep by putting small rocks in a sack, one rock for each sheep.

But when his herd got bigger, he couldn't carry the sack anymore.

So he used a black rock ● to replace ○○○○○○○○○○. So ●●○○○ was the same as ○○○○○○○○○○○○○○○○○○○○○○○, except that it weighed less.

From *How to Count Sheep Without Falling Asleep*
by Ralph Leighton and Carl Feynman

1. Make a plan to find how many counters are in a bucket.

REASONING AND PROBLEM SOLVING

How would knowing the number of counters in a handful help you estimate the number of counters in a bucket?

2 How can everyone help with the counting?

3 Does grouping help you count more easily?

4 How can you keep track of your count? The shepherd made groups of ten. Did you?

Activity 3 Show the Number

With Your Group One class used base ten blocks to keep track of their counting. How many counters did the class count?

1 Now use base ten blocks. Show what happens if you add 5 tens' blocks to the blocks in the picture. Do you need to trade for a hundreds' block? Explain.

2 A thousand is ten hundreds. Add 5 hundreds' flats to your blocks. Do you have enough hundreds to trade for a thousand? Explain.

3 We can write numbers in thousands like this.

2,406 say two thousand, four hundred six

Write the total number of base ten blocks you now have. Read the number aloud.

What You'll Need

- *base ten blocks*

What You'll Need
- *10 blank cards*

ACTIVITY OPTION

You could also roll number cubes to choose numbers for the Place Value Game.

CONNECT AND COMMUNICATE

In Your Journal *Could you help another student understand place value? What would you say?*

ACTIVITY 4 Place-Value Game

With Your Partner Make a **place-value** chart. Include thousands. Now play a game.

1. Write the ten digits below on separate cards.

   0, 1, 2, 3, 4, 5, 6, 7, 8, 9

2. Put the cards face down.
3. Choose three cards and put them on your place-value chart. Say the number. Now make a new number. Which is larger? What are the least and greatest numbers you can make?
4. How does the order of the cards on the place-value chart change the number? Write other numbers you can make with your three cards.
5. Choose four cards. How many different numbers can you make on your place-value chart? List your numbers.
6. Choose four new cards. Who can make the greatest number? Who can make the least?

ACTIVITY 5

Calculator Place

With Your Partner You can explore place value with your calculator.

1. Tell your partner a digit and its place value. You might say the number has 2 tens.
2. Have your partner enter a four-digit number with your digit in the right place.
3. Your partner should make the digit one greater. Which works–adding 10, 100, or 1,000?
4. Read the new number. Is your partner right? Switch roles.

Does the example have a 2 in the tens' place?

The digits in the other three places can be anything you want.

CONNECT AND COMMUNICATE

In Your Journal *Write why you think 10 is an easy number to work with. Would you pick another number?*

Do You Remember?

Try It!

Make the greatest possible number.

1. 3, 5, 6, 7 2. 6, 9, 0, 8 3. 4, 7, 7, 6 4. 9, 1, 2, 0

Write in words a number between the following.

5. 674 and 680	6. 49 and 54
7. 296 and 330	8. 450 and 461
9. 93 and 104	10. 6 and 20

Think About It

11. Make a three-digit number. Put its digits in a new order. Why does its value change?

LESSON 5

Rounding Rally

What You'll Need
- *gameboard*
- *spinner*
- *game pieces*

ACTIVITY 1 Play the Game

With Your Group To play this game, find the nearest ten when you land on special places.

24 Rounds to **20**

If you are halfway between two tens, move to the greater ten.

25 Rounds to **30**

Make a spinner. Follow the rules below.

1

Put your game pieces on Start. Spin a number to get off Start. Spin again if you spin Round.

TOOLS AND TECHNIQUES

Need help? *Look up rounding in the Tool Kit.*

2

Move the number of spaces you spin. If you land on a Round space or spin a Round, move forward or backward to the nearest ten.

3

If you spin Round when you are already on a ten, spin again. The first person across the finish line is the winner.

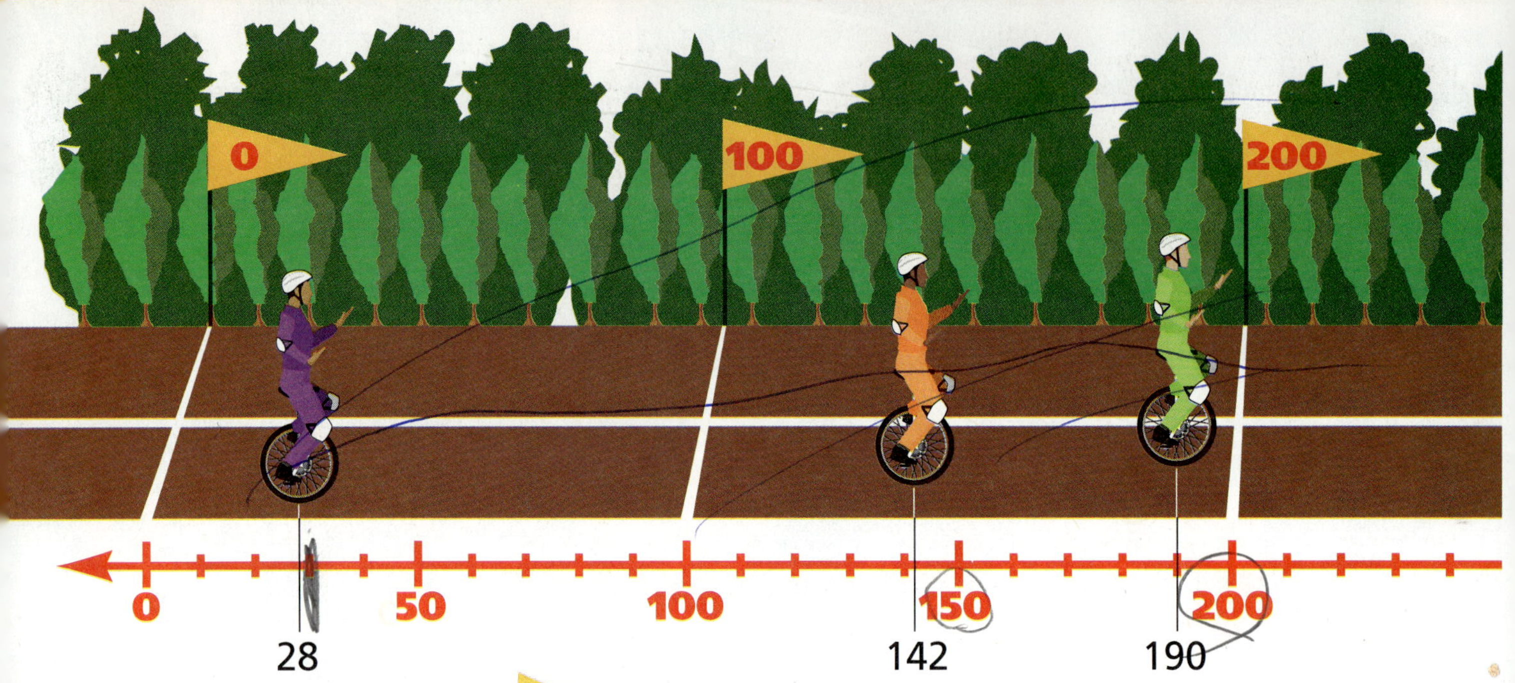

When a number is at the halfway point, round to the higher number. For example, 5 rounds to 10. Likewise, 50 rounds to 100.

ACTIVITY 2 Number Lines

With Your Group The people riding the unicycles get a point for each hundred mark they come near. The judges **round** the distance to the nearest hundred.

1. Look at the person at the 316 mark. Which hundred is he nearer, 300 or 400?
2. Find the person at the 190 mark. Is she closer to 100 or to 200? How many points does she get so far?

3. Round each person's place to the nearest hundred.
4. Suppose the person at 378 falls. How many points does he get?
5. If you fall somewhere between 300 and 400, where are the better places to fall? Why?

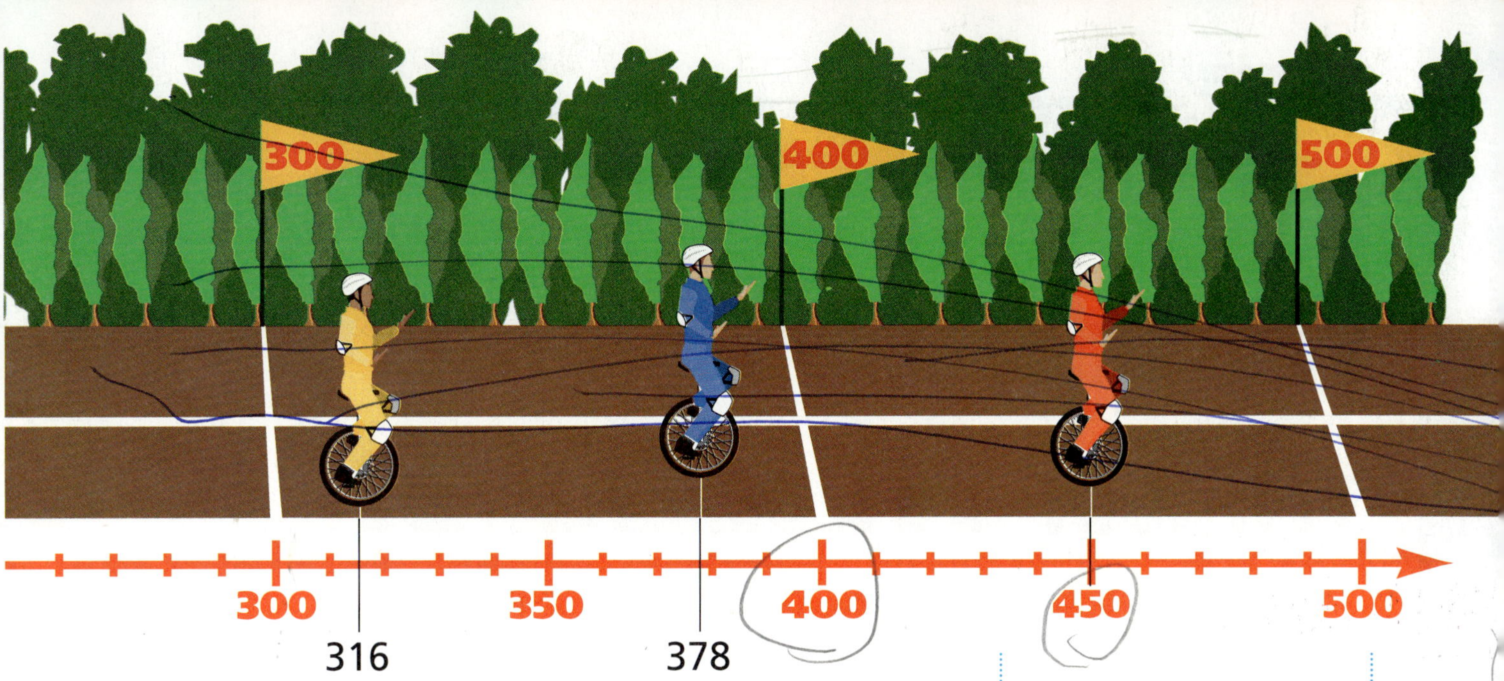

6 The person at 450 is halfway between 400 and 500. The judges had a hard time deciding how many points to give. Why?

7 Halfway numbers usually round up. The judges decided to follow that rule. How many points does the person get so far?

Do You Remember?

Try It!

How many points do the riders get so far? Round.

1. 210 2. 387 3. 468 4. 506
5. 792 6. 121 7. 350 8. 250

Round to the nearest ten.

9. 17 10. 21 11. 62 12. 58 13. 65

Think About It

14. Explain in writing how you can round to the nearest hundred.

Do You Remember?

Cumulative Review

Number Power Without Numbers!

An **abacus** is a very old computing tool. People used a tool like an abacus more than 2,000 years ago. The abacus with beads that move on rods probably came from China. Read the tan boxes about the abacus before you answer any questions.

To show a number on an abacus, you move beads to the lower bar. This shows nine ones.

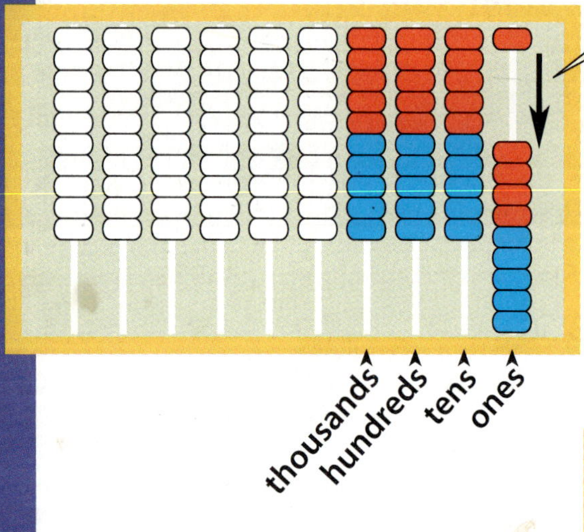

After ten ones move down, a tens' bead moves down. The ones move back up.

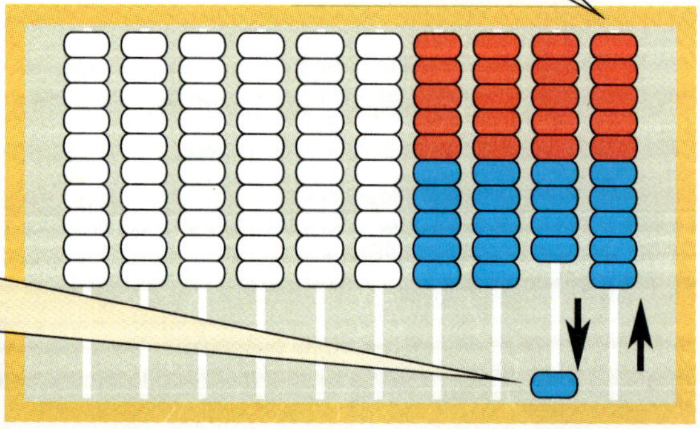

Ten beads on the ones' rod equals one bead on the tens' rod.

1. Look at the large abacus.
   a. How many beads are at the lower bar on the ones' rod?
   b. What number does the ones' column show?

2. What number does the tens' column show?

3. Look at abacus A. What number does it show?

4. Add 2 to the number. What is the sum?

5. Does abacus A or abacus B show the greater number?

6. Look again at the large abacus. What number does it show?

7. Which beads would you move to make the number 200 more?

8. Draw an abacus that shows the sum of 30 + 10.

9. Draw an abacus that shows 3,425.

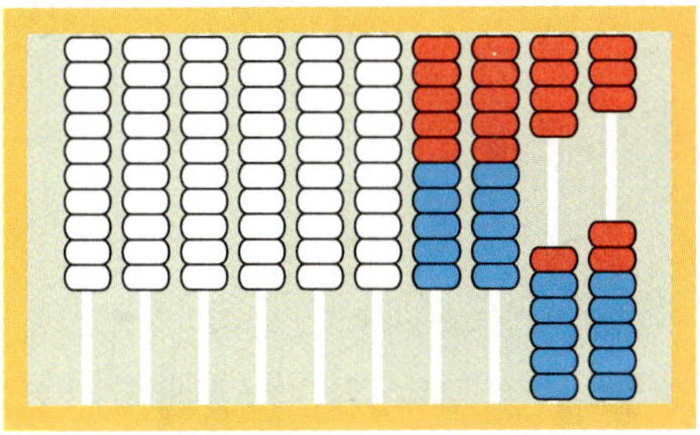

A

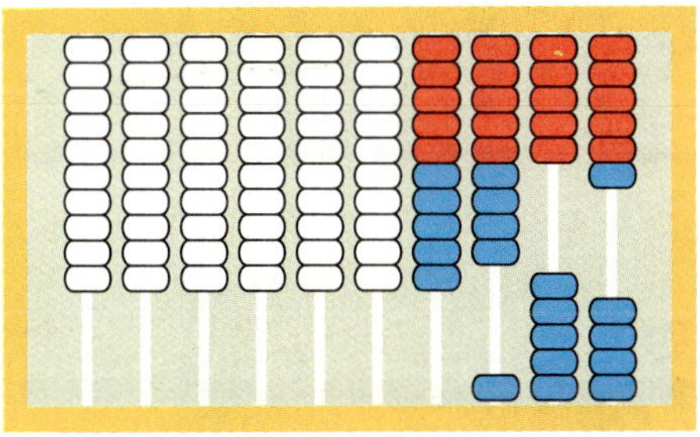

B

Check Your Math Power

10. Suppose you could make an abacus with only 5 beads on a rod. Explain how you think it could work.

LESSON 6 Choices, Choices

What You'll Need
- *grid paper*

ACTIVITY 1 Graph Your Choices

With Your Class Each student can have one of these items. Which one does the class like most? Take a survey to find out. You will need some numbers to graph your survey results.

With Your Group Show how your class voted. Make a **bar graph.** The graph below shows votes from a third-grade class. You can use it as a model to make your graph.

You might want to make other graphs. Topics might include favorite foods, sports, or books.

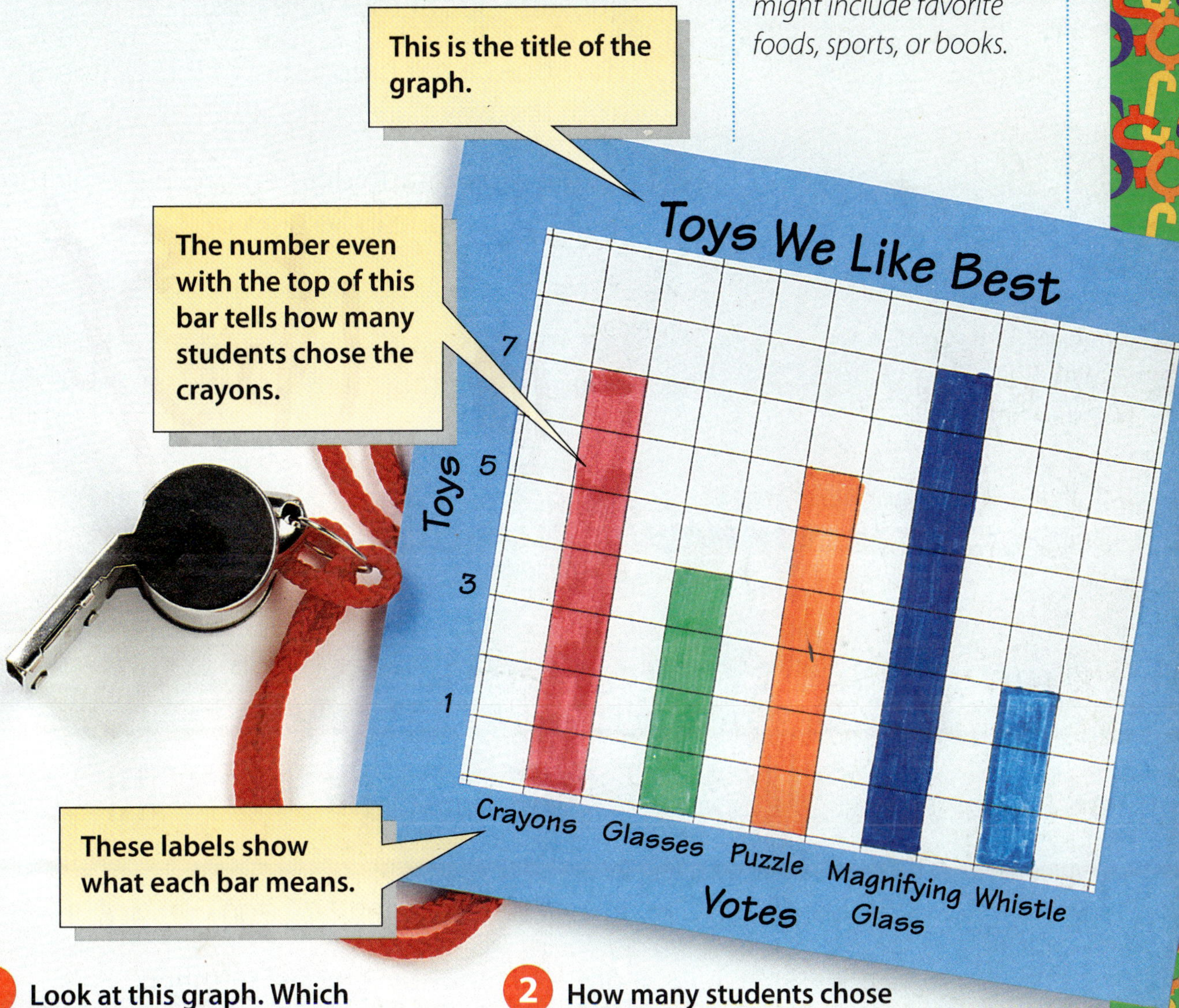

1. Look at this graph. Which item does this class like best?
2. How many students chose the puzzle?
3. How many students voted in this survey?
4. Why are all of the bars even with the numbers at the left of the graph?
5. Now look at your graph. Answer Exercises 1, 2, and 3 using your class graph.

✔ **Self-Check** *How do the title and the words along the sides of a bar graph help you understand the information?*

Activity 2

A Closer Look

With Your Class Think about the way a bar graph shows facts.

1. How does a bar graph help you answer the question about toys your class likes?
2. How does a bar graph show facts differently from the way tally marks do?
3. How is a bar graph different from the picture graph you made in Section B?

Do You Remember?

Try It!

Write a number for each set of tally marks.

1. ||| **2.** 卌 **3.** 卌 || **4.** ||||

Insert the missing numbers.

5. 80, 90, __?__, 110 **6.** 1,000, 900, __?__, 700 **7.** 4, 6, 8, __?__

Put the digits in order to make the greatest number.

8. 6, 4, 8 **9.** 4, 0, 3 **10.** 9, 1, 5 **11.** 7, 6, 7 **12.** 4, 8, 1

Think About It

13. If Exercises 1 through 4 were made into a bar graph, which would be the longest and shortest bars?

Money Fun

LESSON 7

ACTIVITY 1 Write the Amount

With Your Partner How do you need numbers when you use money?

1. Remember what you know about coins and bills. How many pennies are there in a dollar? How many dimes in a dollar? How many nickels equal a quarter?
2. Use play coins and bills to show an amount of money to your partner. Your partner writes the amount of money. Three ways to write amounts are shown here.
3. Take turns. Use more coins and bills to make larger amounts for your partner to write.

What You'll Need

- *play money*

REASONING AND PROBLEM SOLVING

What is your plan for playing the money game? Will you count bills or coins first?

What You'll Need
- *play money*

ACTIVITY 2 Buy What You Like

With Your Group You need to count money when you buy things. To count money, start with larger coins or bills. Then count smaller coins up to the exact amount. You will see how below.

1. An item costs $3.72. How many dollar bills do you pay?
2. How many quarters could you use? How many dimes?

3. Which coins do you need to go from $3.70 to $3.72?
4. What if you pay 3 dollar bills and 3 quarters? Do you get change?

5. Now buy an item for $.65. What coins can you use to pay for it?

You can use a calculator to add your money.

Kids Corner

Visit Kids Corner. Choose items you would like to own. Take turns being buyers and clerks.

6 A buyer picks a baseball. What bills and coins can she give the clerk?

7 A buyer pays for sunglasses with 2 dollar bills, 3 quarters, and a dime. What other coins should she pay?

8 A buyer pays for a $2.15 item with 2 one-dollar bills and 2 dimes. Is this the right amount?

9 Now tell what coins and bills to pay for these. Check your answers with a classmate.

Cost

a. 67¢	**b.** $2.14
c. 47¢	**d.** $4.27
e. $1.52	**f.** $2.48
g. $2.98	**h.** $3.60

ACTIVITY 3 Puzzle Questions

With Your Group Use your skill to solve these money puzzles.

1. List four ways to make $10 using only bills.
2. You have four coins worth 30¢. What coins do you have?
3. List four groups of coins that total 50¢.
4. Make up five money puzzles. Swap with another group. Solve their puzzles.

Do You Remember? Try It!

Write the number of quarters, dimes, nickels, or pennies to make the following amounts.

1. $.67 **2.** 29¢ **3.** $.45 **4.** 72¢ **5.** $.35

Add or subtract. Solve only problems whose answers are even numbers.

6. $10 - 9 = ■$ **7.** $5 + 7 = ■$ **8.** $3 + 3 = ■$
9. $9 + 3 = ■$ **10.** $8 - 3 = ■$ **11.** $9 - 7 = ■$

Think About It

12. Write a rule about how you count money.

Investigation

Make Money

Lucky for you the money you use has numbers. Still, bills can be hard to tell apart. So can some coins. Create money that's easier to use!

- Should coins that are worth more be larger?
- Should all bills be the same size?
- Should all bills be the same color?
- Should all coins be round?

Now make coins and bills that are easier to tell apart.

Ask your family about money from other countries.

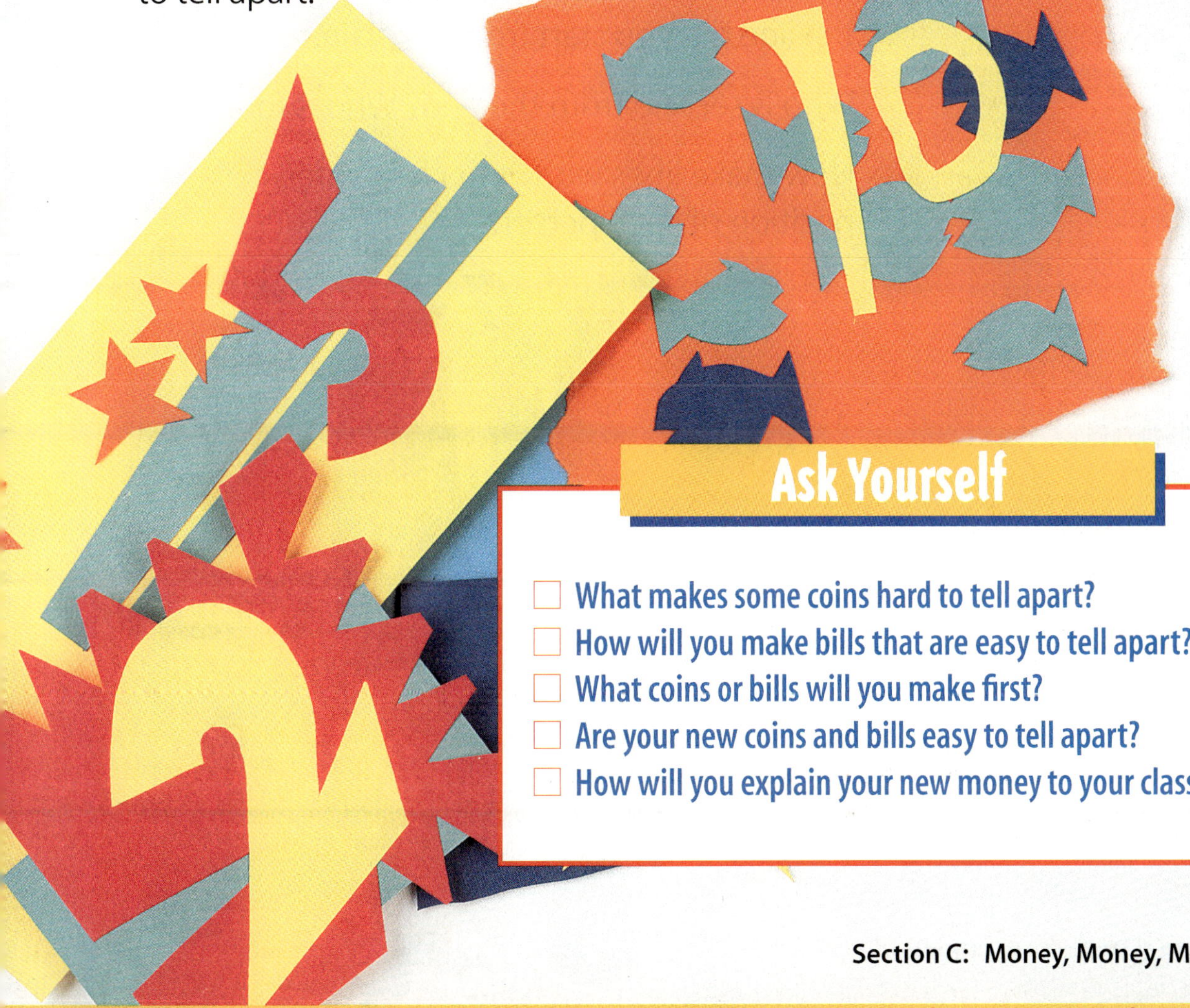

Ask Yourself

- ☐ What makes some coins hard to tell apart?
- ☐ How will you make bills that are easy to tell apart?
- ☐ What coins or bills will you make first?
- ☐ Are your new coins and bills easy to tell apart?
- ☐ How will you explain your new money to your class?

Lesson 8 First or Last?

Think about numbers. Do all numbers tell about amounts?

Activity 1 Hanging Out

With Your Class Words like *first* or *fifth* tell about the way things are arranged in a line.

1. Which student is third in line? Which end of the line did you start from? Explain.
2. Who is second from the end? Who is fourth?
3. Now make lines with your classmates. Tell the position of each person.

CONNECT AND COMMUNICATE

Make a class list of times when you use words like first, second, *or* third.

ACTIVITY 2

The Cube Tube

With Your Group Try the cube tube.

What You'll Need
- *paper towel tube*
- *ones' cubes*

1 **Put in three cubes. Now tilt the tube. Describe the order in which the cubes come out.**

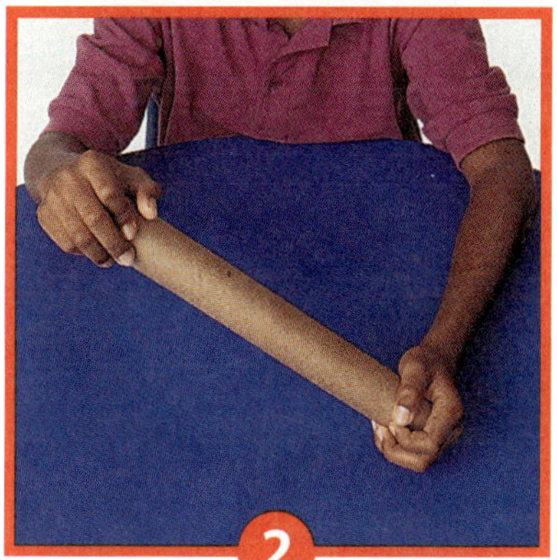

2 **What happens if you tilt the tube the opposite way? Describe the new order.**

3. Switch the order of the cubes. Which cube comes out first?
4. Add more cubes, even five or six. Does adding more cubes change how you think about order?

5. Start with the purple bead below. Use words like *second* or *third* to tell a classmate about the beads.

REASONING AND PROBLEM SOLVING

How can you tell the positions of items in a circle?

ACTIVITY OPTION

Try doing this same lesson with bigger numbers. Choose any nine numbers greater than 10.

ACTIVITY 3

Graph Math

With Your Class Graphing helps you tell the greatest and the least amounts. Graphs help to compare things. Numbers are the key.

1. Use these numbers: 1, 2, 3, 4, 5, 6, 7, 8, 9. Write your favorite one on a slip of paper. Collect the slips. Tally the class results.

2. Use the chalkboard to graph the class results.

3. Which number was the class favorite? Explain how you know.

4. Now write the order for all the numbers. Start with the number that came in first, the number the class liked best.

5. How do you think your graph compares with graphs made by other classes? Explain.

DRAWING TO LEARN

Graphing is a useful way of showing information. What other kinds of graphs can your class draw?

What You'll Need

- *grid paper*

ACTIVITY 4 Graph Again

With Your Group

1. Write the numbers 1, 2, 3, 4, 5, 6, 7, 8, 9 on slips of paper. Put them in a box.
2. Pick one number and tally it on the chalkboard. Put the number back in the box.
3. Pick a number for each student in the class. Use grid paper to graph the class results.
4. How are the results of this graph different from the favorite numbers graph? Explain.

Do You Remember?

Try It!

Fill in the blanks. Use number words to tell the positions.

1. The orange bead is ___?___. **2.** The blue bead is ___?___.
3. The red bead is ___?___ to last. **4.** The last bead is ___?___.

What unit of measurement would you use for the following?

5. the weight of a dog
6. the height of a bicycle
7. the length of a necklace
8. the juice in a glass
9. the weight of an elephant
10. the height of an elephant

Think About It

11. How are bar graphs different from pictographs?

How Many?

LESSON 9

Estimation helps tell *about how many*. Sometimes you estimate when an exact answer is impossible to find. Estimation also helps when an exact answer is not needed.

ACTIVITY 1 Estimate and See

On Your Own Write estimates for each.

1. **Are there 200 buttons in this picture? Are there 5? Count the buttons to check your estimate.**

2. **How did you estimate how many jellybeans are in this bag? Would it be easier if the jellybeans were out of the bag?**

TOOLS AND TECHNIQUES

When you estimate, think about ranges of numbers. For example, ask yourself, is the number greater than 5 but less than 20?

What You'll Need
- *cubes or counters*

ACTIVITY 2

Quick, Estimate!

With Your Group See how quickly you and your group can think of reasonable estimates.

1. **Spill** a cupful of cubes. After five seconds, cover the cubes.
2. **Have** each member write an estimate.
3. **Count** the cubes. Any player who is within five of the actual number gets a point.
4. **Change** the number of cubes. Play until one player has five points.

ACTIVITY 3 A Handful

With Your Group Make an estimate without counting all the beans in the jar.

1. Use the containers for help. Use your sense for numbers!
2. About how many beans are in a handful?
3. About how many handfuls fill the small jars?
4. About how many small jars fill the big jar?

What You'll Need

- *beans or other counters*
- *1 large jar*
- *1 or 2 small jars*

CONNECT AND COMMUNICATE

Share how you estimated with your class. What ideas did your classmates think of?

The Jellybean Jar

There are too many jellybeans to count. Your goal is to make estimates of the number of jellybeans in the jar. Use the questions to help you.

1. **How many jellybeans are in the jar? Make your first estimate.**

2. **Are there 100 jellybeans? Are there 500? 1,000? Are there a million jellybeans in the jar? Explain your estimation strategy.**

3. **Would you like to change the estimate you made? Write a second estimate.**

4. **The jellybeans that are not in the jar fill one scoopful. How many jellybeans fill a scoop?**

5 Now you know how many jellybeans are in a scoop. How does this help you estimate the number in the jar?

6 Make your third estimate. Is it more or less than your first and second estimates?

7 Write your last estimate. How is it different from your other estimates? Explain.

8 Would 10 scoops fill the jar? 30 scoops? How many scoops would fill the jar?

9 There are 500 jellybeans up to the blue arrows. How does that help you make an estimate?

10 Would a bar graph showing the estimates of your classmates help you make an estimate? How?

Looking Back

Choose the right answer. Write *a, b, c,* or *d* for each exercise.

Use this calendar page to answer Exercises 1 and 2.

AUGUST 2000

S	M	T	W	T	F	S
		1	2	3	4	5
6	7	8	9	10	11	12
13	14	15	16	17	18	19
20	21	22	23	24	25	26
27	28	29	30	31		

1. What is the date of the third Wednesday?

   a. August 9 b. August 23
   c. August 17 d. August 16

2. Which date is during the third week of the month?

   a. August 9 b. August 23
   c. August 17 d. August 28

3. Which number rounds to 30?

   a. 22 b. 34 c. 40 d. 21

4. A number has a 2 in the thousands' place, a 4 in the tens' place, a 0 in the hundreds' place, and a 5 in the ones' place. What is the number?

   a. 2,405 b. 2,504
   c. 2,054 d. 2,045

5. About how many students would fit in a school bus?

   a. 3 b. 30
   c. 300 d. 3,000

6. You buy a book for $3.27. You pay three one-dollar bills. What additional coins would *not* be enough to buy the book?

   a. 2 quarters b. 3 dimes
   c. 5 nickels d. 27 pennies

7. How much money is shown here?

a. $5.50
b. $5.75
c. $5.80
d. $5.40

8. Which number word is between *eighth* and *twelfth?*

a. fifth
b. tenth
c. fourteenth
d. twentieth

9. What is true about the time?

a. It is 1:20.
b. It is 20 minutes before 2:00.
c. In one hour it will be 3:30.
d. In 10 minutes it will be 1:45.

10. What number does this group of base ten blocks show?

a. 3,172
b. 2,137
c. 2,317
d. 1,327

Check Your Math Power

Use this graph to answer Exercises 11 and 12.

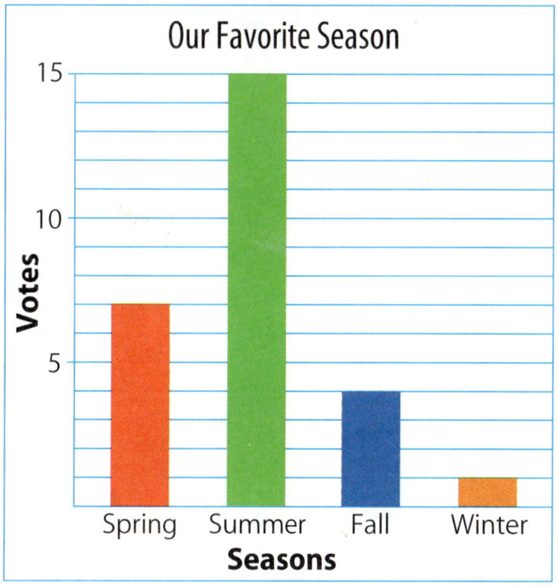

11. Write three facts you can learn from the graph above. Use the title and labels to give you information, too.

12. Explain in writing how you learned your facts from the graph.

13. Explain in writing how you can estimate the number of people in the school assembly hall or in a movie theater.

14. What are the next three numbers in this pattern?
1, 3, 5, 7, __, __, __
Explain your reasons for your answer.

Module 1 Investigations

Number Show

How can you show the number 6,539 without using any digits? You can use a few simple things to show numbers up to four digits.

Investigation A Lots of Ideas

1. Start by thinking about what you know about the number system. Can what you know about an abacus help you?
2. Everything in the picture can help you! What can you use? Of course, you can use any items you want for this investigation.
3. Plan to make at least two ways to show 6,539 without digits.
4. Use words and pictures to tell and show how your idea works.

How can a place-value chart help you?

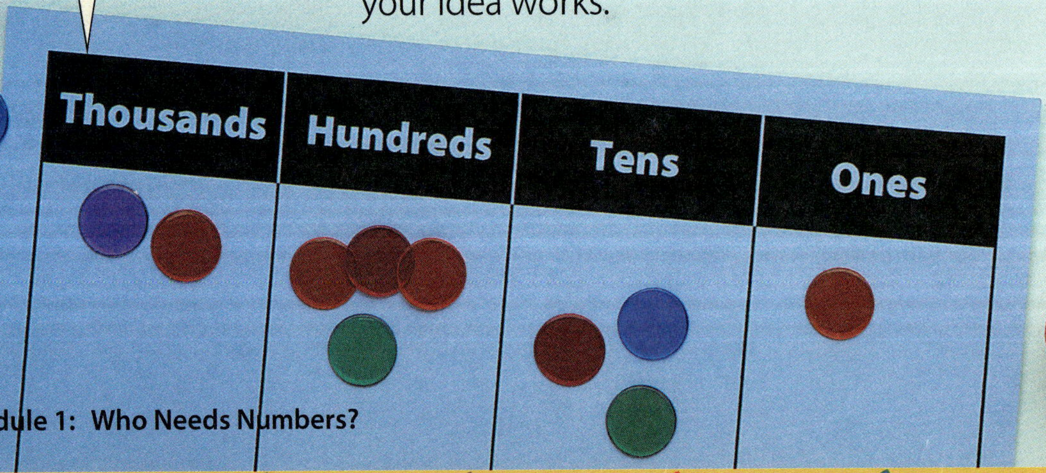

Keep in Mind

Your report will be judged by how well you do the following things.

- ☐ Use what you know about the place-value system to think through the problem.
- ☐ Use materials or drawings to show your idea.
- ☐ Use clear language to describe your idea.

Investigation B: Times Ten

Calculators make trades among ones, tens, hundreds, and thousands. Think about a clock like the one below. How might it make trades?

11:55

Investigate how a calculator and a clock make trades. How are they alike? How are they different? Write a report or present your findings to the class. Use drawings or make models to help you explain.

Investigation C: You Choose How!

These are symbols from ancient Egypt.

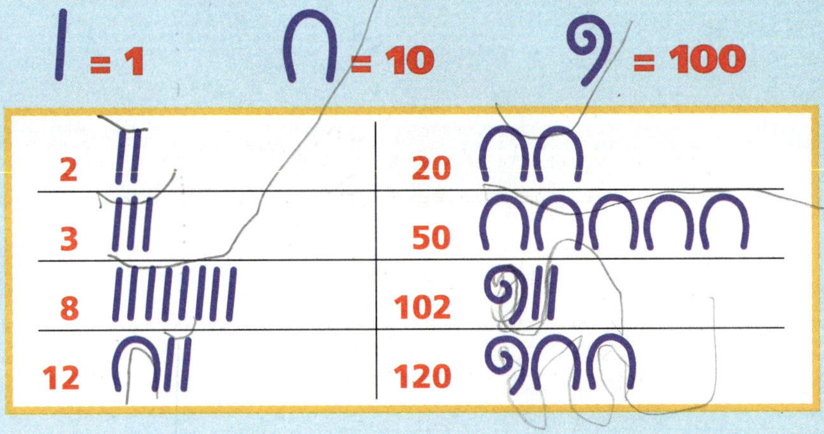

Can you make your own symbol for thousands? Explain to your class how the system works.

Computer Option If you have a computer, you can use a drawing program for this investigation. The cut-and-paste feature will help.

MODULE 2

How Big Is Big?

You know what size a chicken egg is. Have you ever seen an ostrich egg? It's as big as a honeydew melon! What about the ovenbird egg? How does it compare to the bigger eggs? In this module you will measure things that are huge and things that are tiny.

SECTION A — Exploring Length

SECTION B — Inches, Feet, and Yards

SECTION C — Comparing Weights

SECTION D — Filling It Up

MODULE 2 How Big Is Big?

Think Big!

Where can you find really big or small things? What do you like? Imagine dinosaurs and mosquitoes. What about tall buildings and doll houses?

1 **Look** for big and small things around you. Cut pictures of them out of magazines. Take a walk.

2 **Write** down what you find. Then compare. You might trace a big shoe and a small one. Do any big things look small when you compare them to something else?

3 Share notes with a friend. What big and small things did both of you find? What are the biggest and smallest things your friend wrote down?

Word Bank

- addend
- cup (c)
- difference
- gallon (gal)
- ounce (oz)
- pint (pt)
- pound (lb)
- quart (qt)
- sum

Investigations Preview

Where can you find patterns? Addition and subtraction can help. They also will help you compare objects of many sizes.

Stairstep Sums (pages 62–63)

How can you arrange tiles to make stairstep designs? Use your designs to make sums of consecutive numbers.

Measure Hunt (pages 94–96)

Find out about some big and small things that interest you. Math will help you look for patterns in your information.

LESSON 1 Sizing Spiders

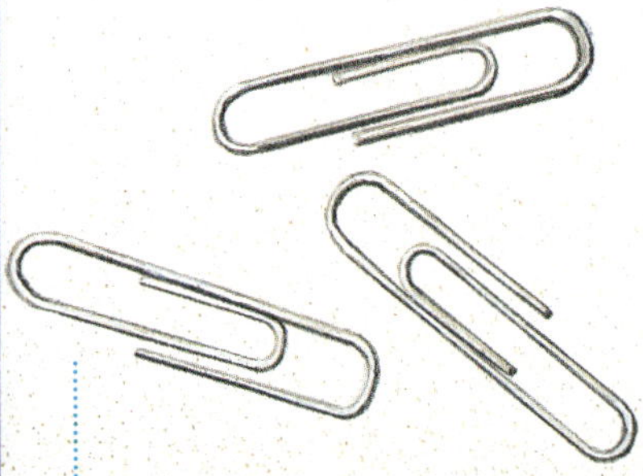

Did you know there is a spider as long as ten of these paper clips? It is the Goliath spider, and it lives in rain forests around the world. Have you ever seen a spider that big?

What You'll Need
- *small paper clips*

ACTIVITY 1 Creeping Along

With Your Partner Study the spiders on these pages.

1. **Look at the spiders. Which one looks the longest? Which one looks the shortest?**
2. **How many paper clips long is each spider? Write the name of the spider and record its length.**

Mexican red knee spider

Fishing spider

3 Look at your answers to Exercise 1. Did you guess the right spiders?

Wolf spider

Huntsman spider

DRAWING TO LEARN

Which is longer, the Mexican red knee spider or the desert tarantula? Use tracing paper to help you find the answer.

Wandering spider

4 Compare the spider lengths. Write three number sentences such as the ones below.

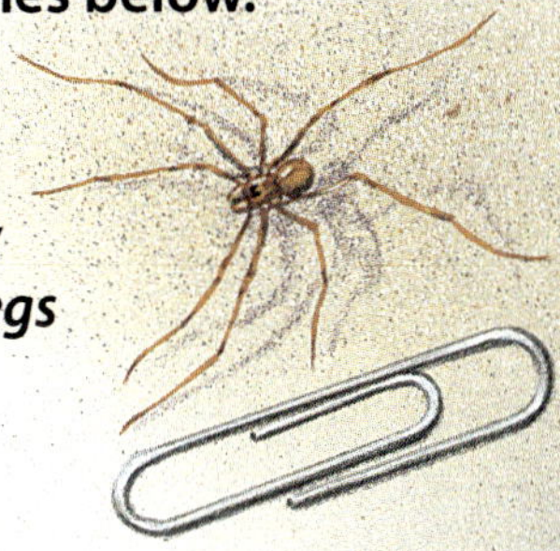

Daddy long legs

1 < 3
1 is less than 3

3 > 1
3 is greater than 1

Desert tarantula

5 Measure a marker and an eraser with paper clips. Write two number sentences using > and <.

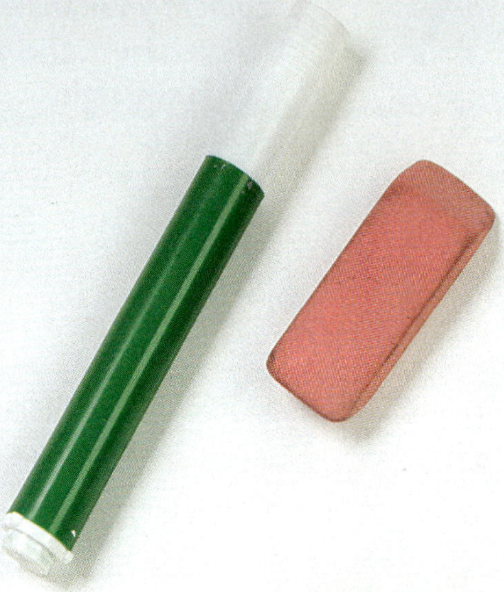

6 Find other objects in the classroom to compare. Measure in paper clips. Write number sentences using > and <.

Do You Remember?

Try It!

Compare the numbers. Write > or <.

1. 3 ● 5
2. 6 ● 10
3. 17 ● 12
4. 5 ● 15
5. 90 ● 40
6. 80 ● 60

Compare the numbers. Write > or <.

7. 19 ● 2 tens
8. 8 ● 1 ten
9. 6 ones ● 5 tens
10. 2 tens ● 12
11. 10 ones ● 11
12. 1 ten ● 1 hundred

Think About It

13. Write a story problem for Exercise 1 and another for Exercise 3. Explain how they are alike and different.

Large Leaps!

LESSON 2

Frogs are amazing jumpers! At one frog-jumping contest, a frog leaped as far as 20 of your shoes placed end to end.

ACTIVITY 1 Ordering Addends

On Your Own Suppose a frog jumps 4 shoe lengths. In a second jump, it leaps 5 shoe lengths.

1. Find the total shoe lengths the frog jumped. Record the number sentence.
2. Change the order of the **addends.** Do you always get the same **sum?**

The Commutative Property says that the order of the addends does not change the sum.

CONNECT AND COMMUNICATE

In Your Journal In your own words write the definitions of addend *and* sum.

ACTIVITY 2 Leaping into Facts

With Your Partner How many shoe lengths can you leap in two jumps?

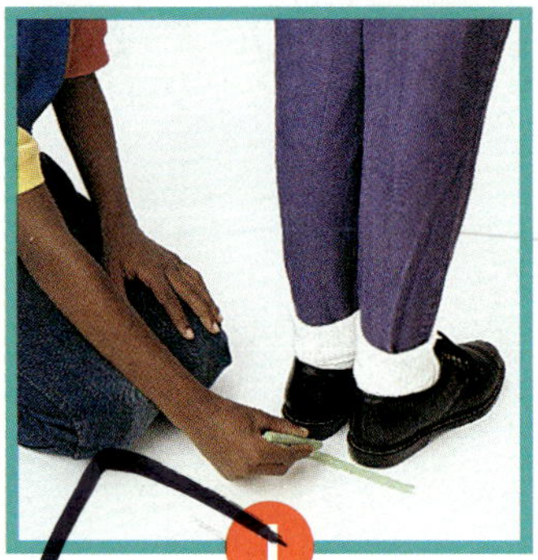

1 Have your partner mark with chalk where your heels are.

2 Jump like a frog. Ask your partner to mark where your heels are.

3 Jump again. Your partner should mark the second jump.

4 Find the number of shoe lengths for each jump. Write a number sentence to show the total for both jumps.

5 Have your partner do two frog jumps. Find the total shoe lengths for the jumps.

6 Do you need to use the same shoe to find the lengths for both jumps? Explain.

7 Compare your number sentences to the ones others wrote. Did anyone get the same sum using different addends?

Activity 3 Remember Your Facts

With Your Group Look at the hints to help you add. Answer the questions.

Helpful Hints

Counting On
$4 + 3 = ?$
Count 3 more
4 . . . 5, 6, 7

Making a Ten
$7 + 4 = ?$
$7 + 3 = 10$
so $7 + 4 = 11$

Using Doubles
$6 + 7 = ?$
$6 + 6 = 12$
so $6 + 7 = 13$

1 Suppose you want to add 3 and 8. Is it easier for you to start with 8 or with 3? Explain.

2 Tell how making a ten can help you find the sum of $9 + 5$.

3 How can using doubles help you find the sum of $7 + 8$?

Tools and Techniques

Think of a ten-frame to help you find the sum of $9 + 5$.

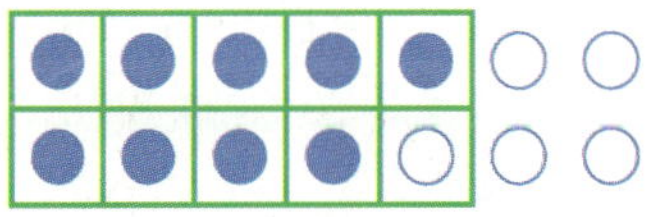

6 + 8 | 8 + 9 | 50 + 60 | 2 + 0

20 + 90 | 9 + 7 | 9 + 8

50 + 40 | 0 + 7 | 5 + 8 | 4 + 8

8 + 8

4 Choose five cards above and find the sums. How did you find each sum?

5 Think of other hints for adding. How can you add 9 to any number? How can you add 0? Explain.

Do You Remember?

Try It!

Find the sum. Use the hints.

1. 6 + 4
2. 7 + 5
3. 8 + 7
4. 4 + 4
5. 7 + 7
6. 8 + 9
7. 5 + 6
8. 7 + 9

Write <, >, or =.

9. 50 + 3 ● 60
10. 74 ● 70 + 8
11. 40 ● 30 + 9
12. 20 ● 9 + 9

Think About It

13. Explain how you added a sum above.

ACTIVITY OPTION

You can practice addition using cards. Write two addends on one side. Write the sum on the back.

Lots of Addends

LESSON 3

Sloths are animals that can sleep as much as 18 hours a day. They hang upside down while they sleep.

ACTIVITY 1 Counting Zzzs

On Your Own Suppose a sloth sleeps 7 hours. It eats, then it sleeps 6 more hours. It eats again and sleeps 4 hours. How long does it sleep?

1. How many addends do you add? Find the total number of hours the sloth sleeps.

2. Here are two ways to group three addends. Which way did you use?

$$\begin{array}{r} 7 \\ 6 \\ +4 \\ \hline \end{array} \quad \begin{array}{r} 7 \\ 6 \\ +4 \\ \hline \end{array}$$

(In the first, 7 and 6 are grouped with a brace and ?; in the second, 6 and 4 are grouped with a brace and ?.)

The Associative Property says that changing the grouping of the addends doesn't change the sum.

3. What is the sum of 1, 3, 7, and 5? Which numbers did you group? Why?

Sloths live and sleep in jungle trees in Central and South America.

Activity 2 Adding It Up

With Your Group Discover different ways you can add these numbers.

1. Add the five numbers above. Then add them in a different order. Do you get the same answer?
2. Choose any three numbers from above. Find the greatest sum you can.
3. Find the least sum of any three numbers above.
4. What numbers above can you add to get the sum 15? Complete these number sentences.

REASONING AND PROBLEM SOLVING

How would you arrange the addends, 1 + 2 + 3 + 4 + 5 + 6 + 7 + 8 + 9, to make them easier to add? What is the sum?

ACTIVITY 3 One, Two, Three

With Your Partner Take turns playing this game. Group the numbers to add.

1. When it is your turn, roll three cubes. Find the sum of the numbers.
2. Write a number sentence that shows the three addends and their sum.
3. Now your partner takes a turn. The person with the greater sum scores a point.
4. The first person to reach ten points wins.

What You'll Need

- *3 number cubes labeled 1–6*

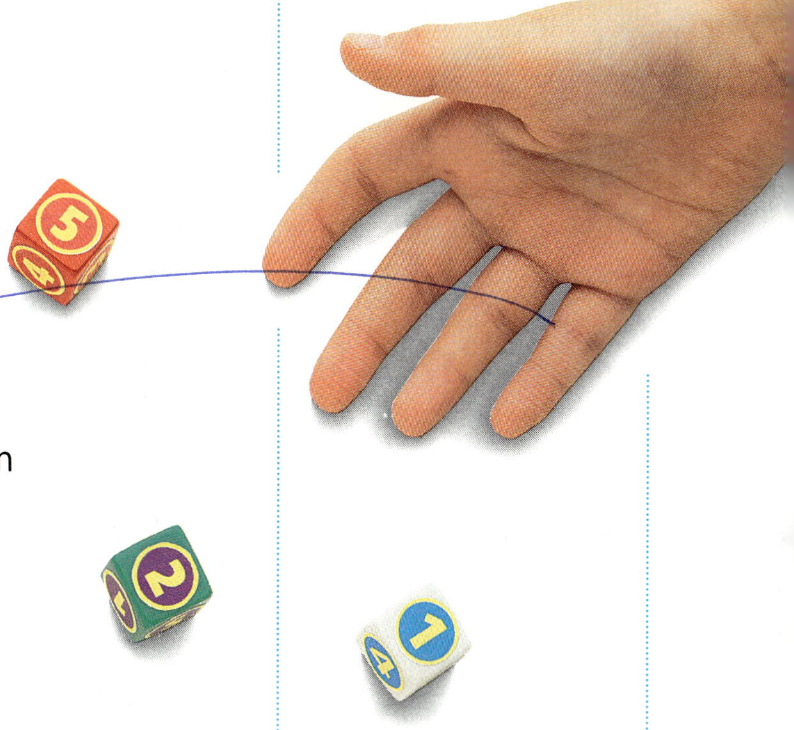

Do You Remember? Try It!

Add. Use sums of ten to help you.

1. 7 + 3 + 1
2. 5 + 4 + 5
3. 6 + 7 + 4
4. 1 + 8 + 9
5. 6 + 3 + 1
6. 2 + 9 + 8

Write the date.

7. 4 days after April 8
8. 6 days before July 8
9. 3 days before June 6
10. 5 days after May 6

Think About It

11. For Exercise 3, find three other numbers that will give you the same sum.

Self-Check *Change the order of the addends for each number sentence you wrote. Do you get the same sum?*

Investigation

Stairstep Sums

You have seen consecutive numbers before. The numbers 2 and 3 are consecutive. So are 7, 8, and 9. They follow in order. What consecutive numbers does this stairstep design show?

Consecutive numbers have a difference of one.

1. Choose 3 to 20 tiles. Can you make a stairstep design that uses all the tiles? If you can, write the consecutive numbers that make the design.

1, 2, 3, **4, 5, 6,** **7, 8, 9,** **10, 11, 12,**

2. Try making designs with other numbers 20 or less. Can you always make a stairstep design with the tiles? Record your work.

3. Look back at your addends. What do you notice about odd and even addends and their sums? Describe any patterns you see.

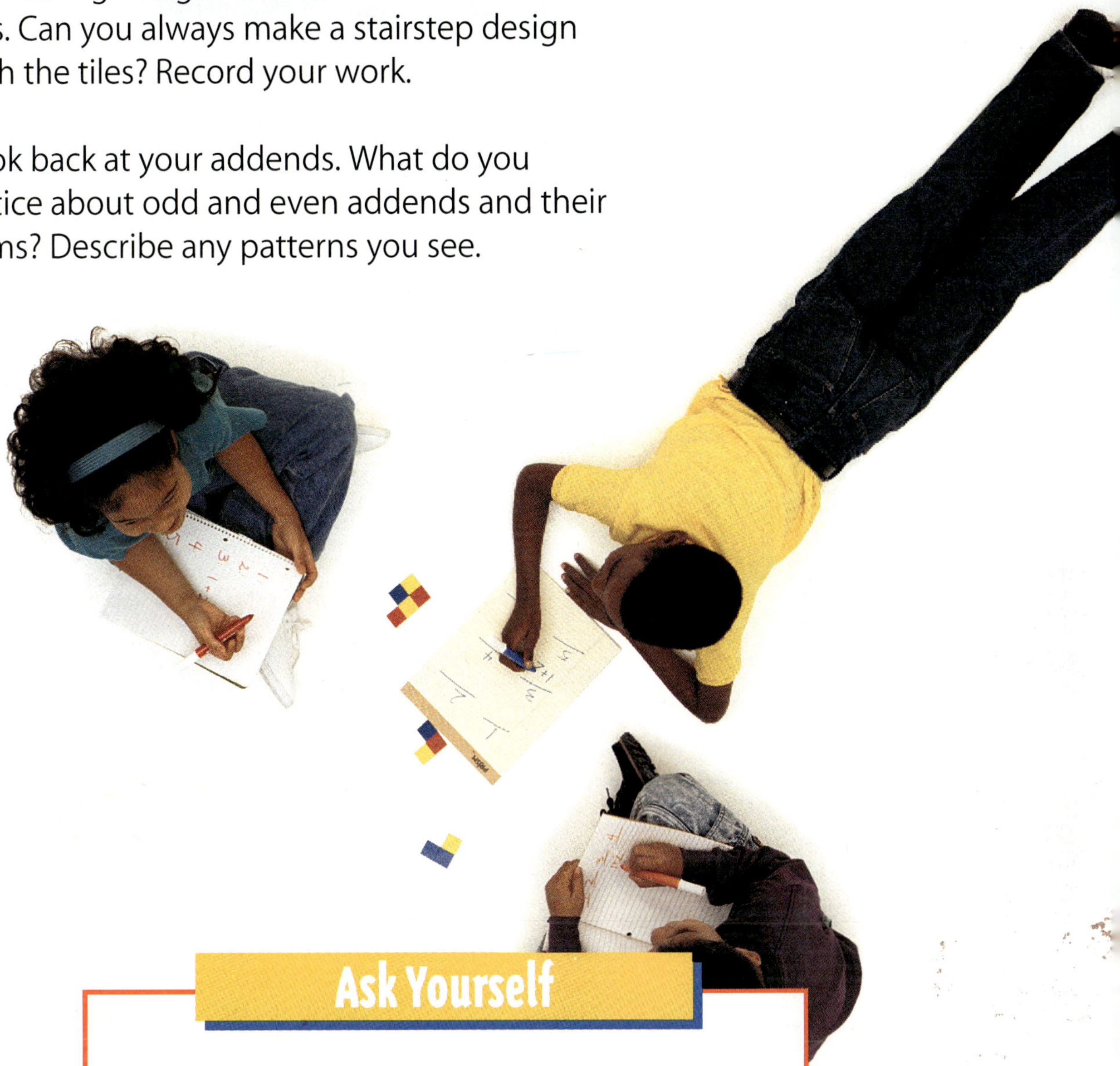

Ask Yourself

- ☐ How does a stairstep design show consecutive numbers?
- ☐ How can I find out which numbers have consecutive addends?
- ☐ How will I organize my work?
- ☐ Do some numbers make more than one stairstep design?
- ☐ Which sums did I write that other students didn't?

SECTION B Inches, Feet, and Yards

LESSON 4 How Long Is It?

People like to grow big fruits and vegetables. A lima bean is about an **inch (in.)** long. One lima bean pod from a garden was 14 in. long! How big is that?

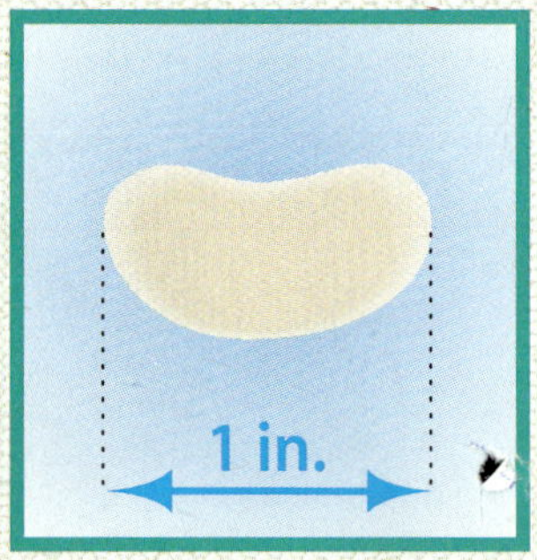

ACTIVITY 1 Make a Ruler

What You'll Need
- *inch ruler*
- *scissors*

On Your Own A paper ruler can help you measure different vegetables.

1. Make a 12-in. strip. Mark and number the inches.
2. Measure the green bean with your strip. How long is it?
3. Why is measuring with a strip easier than lining up lima beans?

ACTIVITY 2 Things to Measure

With Your Partner

What You'll Need
- *inch ruler*

1. Copy the chart. Estimate how many inches long each vegetable is. Record your estimates.
2. Measure each vegetable with an inch ruler. Record the length.
3. Compare the lengths of two vegetables. Write two number sentences using > and <.

Vegetable	Estimate	Actual
Jalapeño		
Green bean	3 in.	4 in.
Snow pea	2 in.	3 in.
Asparagus		
Okra		
Habañero		
Endive		

Green bean Snow pea
4 in. > 3 in.

DRAWING TO LEARN

Draw the actual size of your favorite vegetable. Measure its length. Which is longer, the snow pea or your favorite vegetable?

What You'll Need
- *inch ruler*
- *yardstick*

ACTIVITY OPTION

Make a list of items that are about 1 in. long, 1 ft long, and 1 yd long.

ACTIVITY 3 Larger than Inches

With Your Partner The largest carrot ever recorded was about 192 in. long. For really big objects, you can use other units of measure.

1. Look at the pictures below. How many inches are in a **foot (ft)**?
2. What things can you find in the classroom that are about a foot long?
3. How many feet are in a **yard (yd)**? How many inches are in 1 yd?

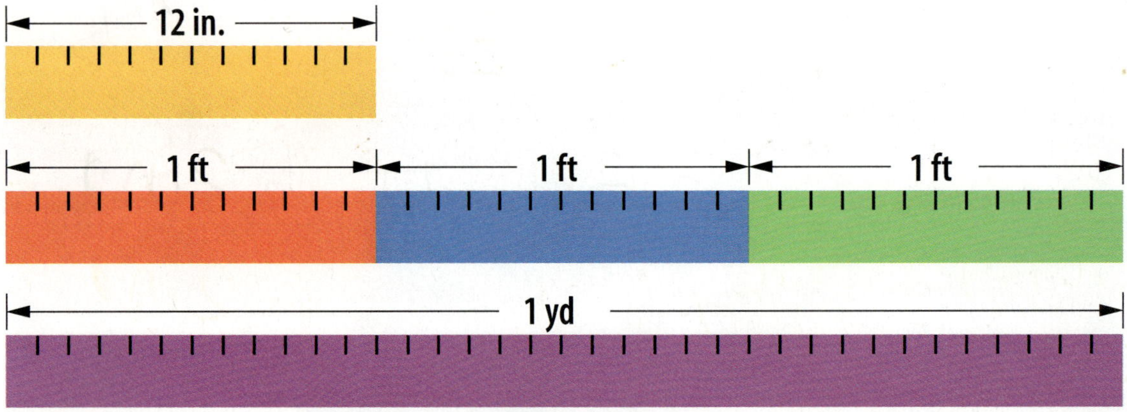

Measuring in Yards

4 Which objects shown here are longer than a yard?

5 Which objects in your classroom are longer than a yard? How many yards is the longest object you measured?

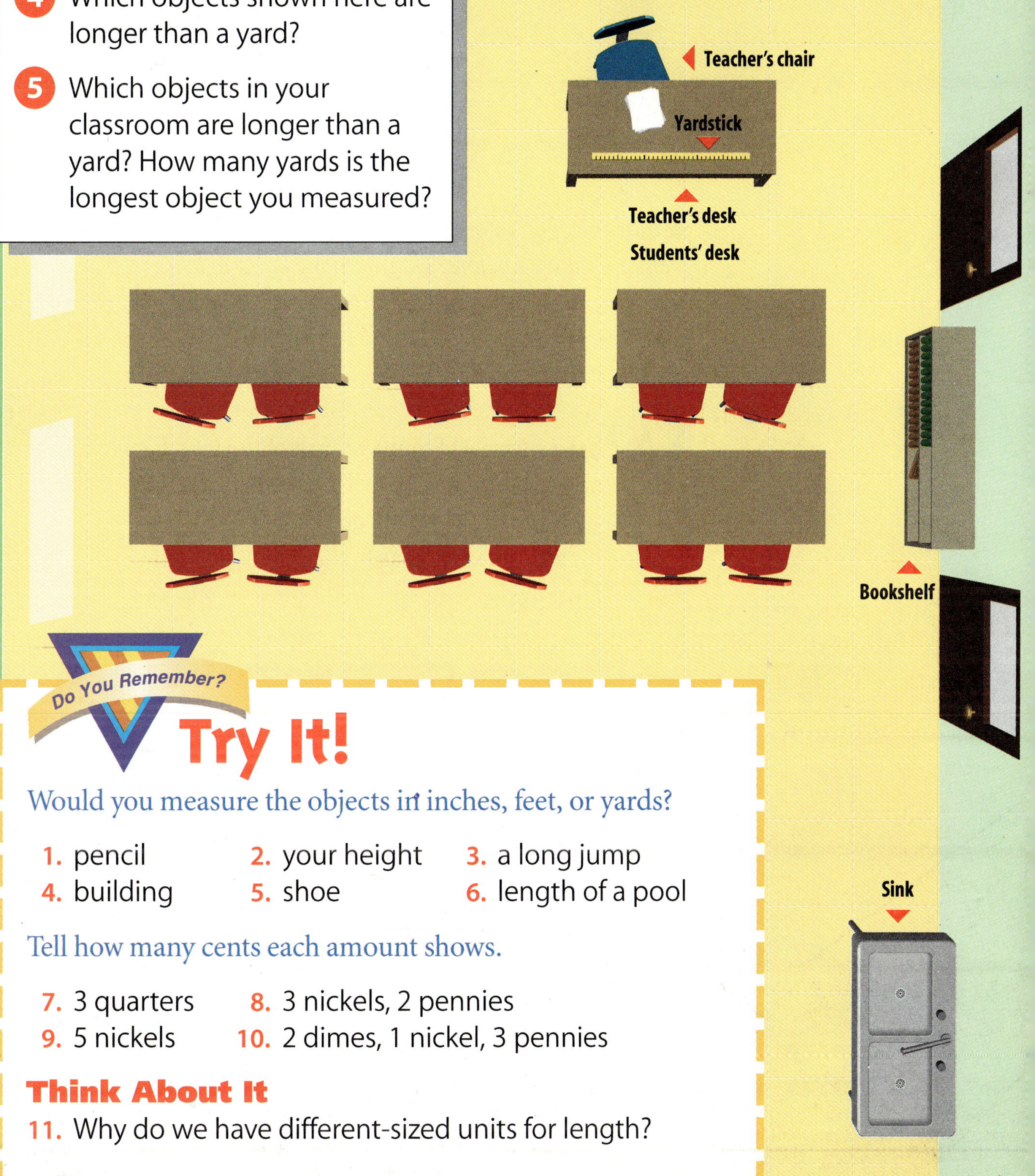

Do You Remember?

Try It!

Would you measure the objects in inches, feet, or yards?

1. pencil
2. your height
3. a long jump
4. building
5. shoe
6. length of a pool

Tell how many cents each amount shows.

7. 3 quarters
8. 3 nickels, 2 pennies
9. 5 nickels
10. 2 dimes, 1 nickel, 3 pennies

Think About It

11. Why do we have different-sized units for length?

LESSON 5 Take It Away

LITERATURE

At the time of this story, some people in Sri Lanka had never seen an umbrella before. They used big banana leaves to keep dry in the rain. One day, Kiri Mama brought an umbrella to his village. A monkey stole it. Kiri Mama brought more. The thief took them, too. Finally, Kiri Mama found his umbrellas.

What a surprise! From a branch of the tree, hanging neatly in a row, were all the umbrellas he had lost. Kiri Mama clambered joyfully up the tree.

He dropped the umbrellas to the ground; all but one which he kindly decided to leave for the umbrella thief.

The next day Kiri Mama opened an umbrella shop.

. . . Soon the news spread throughout the village, and everyone rushed to see this new and marvelous thing called an umbrella.

From *The Umbrella Thief*
by Sybil Wettasinghe

ACTIVITY 1

At the Umbrella Shop

With Your Partner Imagine Kiri Mama at his umbrella shop. Use the chart to answer the questions.

Umbrellas at the Shop

Color	Start of Day	Number Sold	End of Day
Blue	15	9	?
Red	11	2	?
Black	9	2	?
Yellow	12	3	?
Green	13	8	?

1. How many red umbrellas were left at the end of the day? Find the difference between 11 and 2.

$$11 - 2 = ?$$

↑ difference

$$\begin{array}{r} 11 \\ -\ 2 \\ \hline ? \end{array}$$

difference → ?

Helpful Hint

Counting Back

11 – 2 = ?

11 . . . 10, ?

2. Thinking of parts and wholes can also help you subtract. Look at the numbers at the right. Write two addition and two subtraction sentences using 11, 9, and 2.

3. Choose an umbrella color besides red. Find the number of umbrellas left at the end of the day. What four number sentences can you write?

4. Copy and complete the chart above. Which differences did you find by counting back? What other hints did you use to subtract?

What You'll Need

- *inch ruler*

REASONING AND PROBLEM SOLVING

How are 15 – 8 = 7 and 15 – 7 = 8 alike? How are they different?

ACTIVITY 2 A Long Apple Peel

With Your Partner Can you imagine an apple peel more than 172 ft long? That's the longest apple peel ever recorded. It took almost 12 hours to peel!

1 These apple peels are much smaller. How much longer is the second peel than the first? How can you tell?

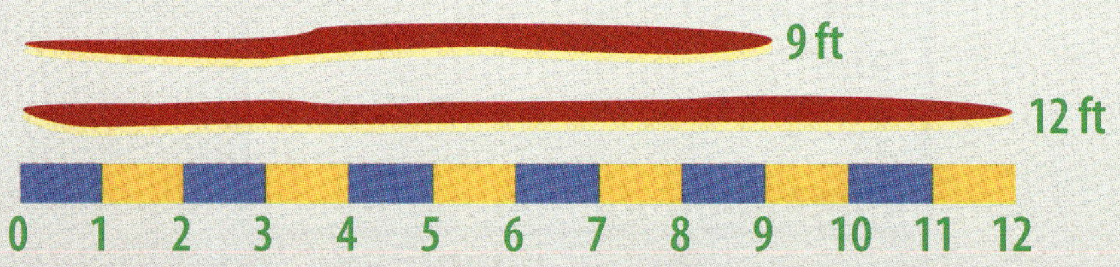

2 Could counting from 9 to 12 help you find the difference? Explain.

3 You have 9 apples. You need 16. How many more do you need? Think of making a ten.

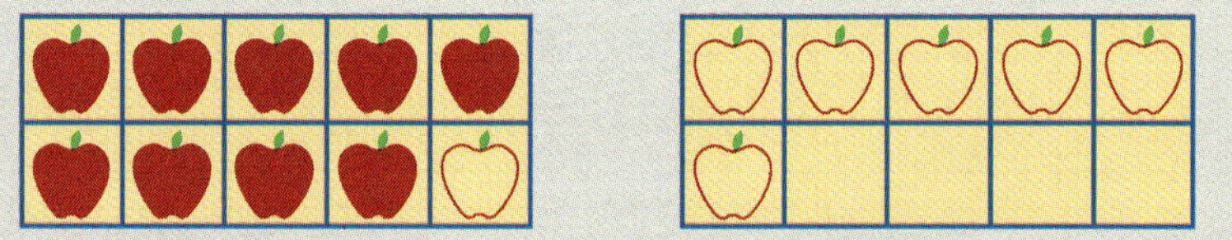

1 more | **6 more**

16 – 9 = ?

4 Find each difference. Did you use counting up, counting back, or making a ten? Explain your way.

12 – 8 = ?

11 – 2 = ?

15 – 9 = ?

10 – 7 = ?

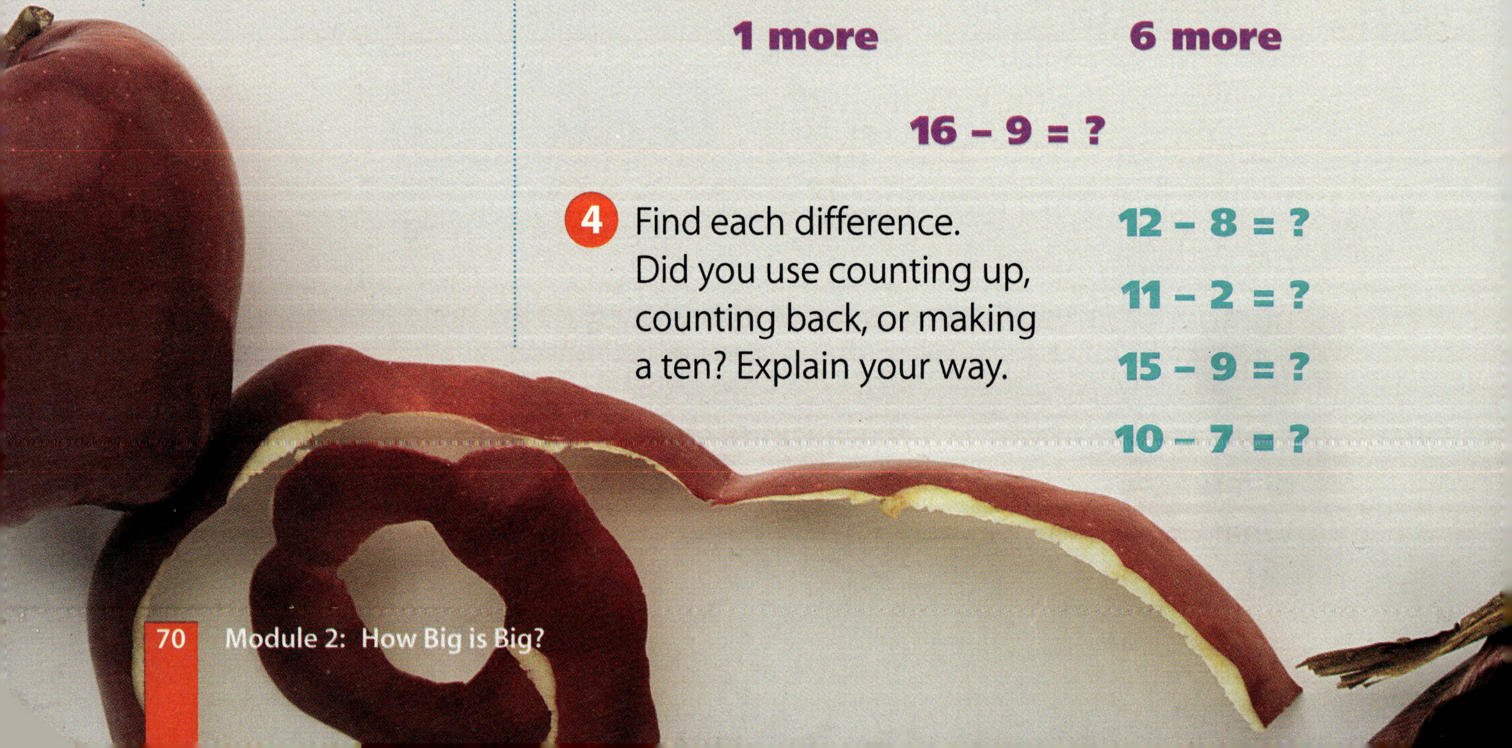

5. Measure the green bean and peanut shell shown below. Copy and complete the chart.

6. Choose two items in the chart. Find the difference in length. How did you find the difference?

	Length (in.)
Banana peel	9
Corn husk	13
Green bean	?
Peanut shell	?

7. Write a story problem that matches this number sentence. Use numbers from your chart.

■ − ▲ = 7

8. Look at Exercises 6 and 7. Which one was easier for you? Why?

CONNECT AND COMMUNICATE

In Your Journal *Write a story problem about comparing the sizes of two objects. Show how to find the answer.*

APPLE PEEL

What You'll Need

- *gameboard*
- *cube labeled 1–6*
- *8-section spinner labeled 2–9*
- *game pieces*
- *counters*

Self-Check *Use addition to check your answer.*

ACTIVITY 3 Peel Appeal

With Your Group In this game, you will try to reach the end of a long apple peel.

1 Start the Game
Roll a number cube. Move a game piece that number of spaces.

2 Find the Difference
Spin the spinner. Subtract the number you spun from the number on your space.

3 Collect Counters
The difference is the number of counters you receive.

4 **Explain Your Answer**
How did you subtract? Tell which subtraction hint you used and why.

12 − 8 = 4
I subtracted by counting up 8 . . . 9, 10, 11, 12.

5 **Take Turns**
Repeat Steps 1 through 4. Play until all players reach the end of the peel. The person with the most counters wins the game.

TOOLS AND TECHNIQUES

Make a ten or use part-part-whole diagrams to help you subtract.

Do You Remember?

Try It!

Find the sum or difference. Tell what hints you used.

1. 11 − 3
2. 16 − 9
3. 15 − 4
4. 12 − 8
5. 9 + 6
6. 9 + 9
7. 8 + 6
8. 5 + 7

Write + or – to complete each sentence.

9. 15 ● 7 = 8
10. 5 ● 8 = 13
11. 17 ● 9 = 8
12. 7 ● 7 = 14
13. 11 ● 5 = 6
14. 12 ● 7 = 5

Think About It

15. Complete this sentence as many ways as you can: ■ + ▲ = 12. How do your sentences show the Commutative Property? Explain in writing.

Do You Remember?

Cumulative Review

Amazing Facts

Did you ever look at something and imagine it much bigger? Read these surprising facts from *The Guinness Book of Records*. Use them to answer the questions.

The tallest sunflower was more than 25 ft tall.

Sunflowers

1. Which is taller, you or the sunflower? About how much taller?

The longest human hair ever recorded was 146 in.

Hair

2. Suppose another person's hair is 5 in. shorter than the longest hair. What is its length?

One of the most famous clocks in the world is Big Ben in London.

Big Ben

3. What time will the clock show in 4 hours?
4. What time was it 4 hours ago?

The longest daisy chain was about 6,980 ft long. It was made in 7 hours.

The biggest . . .
- candle is 80 ft high
- vase is about 6 yd high
- needle is 6 ft long

The tallest sand castle was about 20 ft high.

Daisy Chains

5 If the chain makers started at 2 o'clock, what time did they finish?

6 Is the daisy chain length closer to 6,000 or 7,000 feet?

The Biggest . . .

7 Which is taller, the candle or the vase? Explain.

8 Is the needle longer than 84 in.? How can you tell?

9 Name an object on this page that is taller than the sand castle. How much taller is it?

Check Your Math Power

10 Here are the lengths of four daisy chains.

7 ft 2 ft 5 ft 8 ft

Suppose you connect two or three of these chains. List all the different lengths you can make.

LESSON 6 Light Weights

100¢
125¢

What You'll Need
- *ounce weights*
- *1-oz lumps of clay*
- *small classroom objects*

The pygmy shrew is one of the world's lightest animals. Twenty of them equal one **ounce (oz).** The lump of clay on this page weighs 1 oz.

ACTIVITY 1 Which Is Heavier?

With Your Partner You can compare the weights of two things. Just hold one object in each hand.

1. Choose two small objects. Use > and < to write which you think weighs more. Try again with two other items.

   Weight of glue stick > **Weight of roll of tape**

2. Now compare an object to a 1-oz weight. Record your findings in a chart like this.

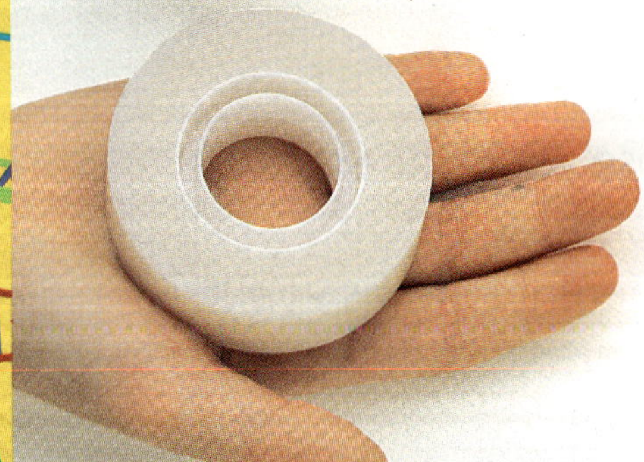

ACTIVITY 2

How Heavy Is It?

With Your Partner Can you think of a better way to weigh things? Here's one way.

1. Choose a classroom object. Place it on one side of a balance.
2. Add 1-oz weights to the other side until it balances. How much does your object weigh?
3. Weigh three or four other objects. Which one weighs the most? Share your results.

What You'll Need

- *1-oz weights*
- *balance scale*
- *classroom objects*

Do You Remember?

Try It!

Tell if the object weighs more or less than 1 oz.

1. duck
2. baseball
3. leaf
4. fly
5. pencil
6. frog

Use the three numbers to write two number sentences.

7. 20, 90, 70
8. 80, 50, 30
9. 40, 110, 70
10. 90, 30, 120

Think About It

11. How did you find the answers for Exercises 1 through 6?

DRAWING TO LEARN

Think of three objects with different weights. Draw pictures of them in order by weight.

LESSON 7

Balancing Act

The biggest tomato on record weighed about seven **pounds (lb).** It was as big as your head! Do you think a pound is more than an ounce?

ACTIVITY 1 Sum of a Pound

On Your Own

1. Find an object that weighs a pound, such as a box of corn starch. Put it on one side of the balance. Add ounce weights to the other side until it balances.

2. Write a number sentence showing how many ounces are in a pound.

■ oz = 1 lb

3. Which classroom objects would you measure in ounces? Which would you measure in pounds?

What You'll Need

- *1-oz weights*
- *1-lb weight*
- *balance scale*
- *objects weighing one pound*

ACTIVITY OPTION

Compare weights *Find some classroom objects. Use a balance to weigh each object.*

- *Write number sentences with > and < to show how the weights compare to a pound.*

ACTIVITY 2 How Many More?

With Your Group Long ago, the Egyptians used a scale to find weight. You can use one to find missing addends.

1. How many ounces would you need to balance the scale below? Think of a missing addend.

2. Use the fruits shown. Suppose you put one piece of fruit on each side of the scale. How many ounces would you need to make it balance? Write a number sentence to show your answer. Repeat with two other fruits.

The Egyptians used scales more than 5,000 years ago.

REASONING AND PROBLEM SOLVING

Write these number sentences:
$8 + 2 = 10$ $10 = 8 + 2$
Do they have the same meaning? Explain.

✔ **Self-Check** *Use a calculator to find the weight of the following: 100 apples, 52 plums, 17 oranges. What would be the total weight of 5 plums, 12 strawberries, and 4 apples?*

Activity 3 Fruit Salad

On Your Own Use the pictures below to help you make a pound of fruit salad.

1. How many of each fruit make up about 1 lb?
2. Now mix up the fruits. How can you make a total of 1 lb?
3. Write number sentences to show your answers. Share them with the class.

Plum 2 oz	Strawberry 1 oz	Apple 10 oz	Orange 6 oz

Do You Remember?

Try It!

Find the missing addend. What pattern do you see?

1. 3 + ■ = 15 **2.** 4 + ■ = 15 **3.** 5 + ■ = 15
4. 6 + ■ = 15 **5.** 7 + ■ = 15 **6.** 8 + ■ = 15

Use the clock to find the time.

7. 5 minutes earlier **8.** 15 minutes later
9. 1 hour earlier **10.** 3 hours later

Think About It

11. How is subtracting like finding missing addends? Draw or write your answer.

Big Eaters

LESSON 8

Sometimes an animal eats as much as it weighs. The chart below describes some animals that eat a lot.

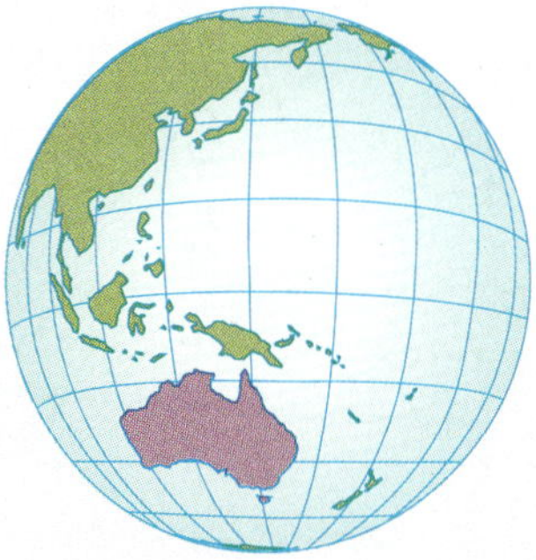

ACTIVITY 1 Balance the Diets

With Your Partner

	Weight	Length	Food Each Day
Platypus	4 lb	2 ft	4 lb
Dolphin	160 lb	7 ft	20 lb
Sea lion	600 lb	8 ft	25 lb

The platypus, shown above, is from Australia and Tasmania. It has a tail like a beaver, feet and a bill like a duck, and fur. It is truly a strange animal!

1. Which animal weighs the most? How can you tell from the chart?
2. Which animal eats the most?
3. Compare each animal's weight with the amount of food it eats each day. What do you notice?
4. Which animals eat less than their weight in food each day?

CONNECT AND COMMUNICATE

Does an animal's size always tell you how much it eats? Explain.

Pick a Pet

Dogs, cats, birds, horses, and even spiders can be pets. This chart has information you might find at a pet store. Use it to answer the questions.

Pet Information

	Length or Height	Weight	Amount of Food a Day
Petey (bird)	2 in. long	1 oz	Less than an ounce
Silver (pony)	4 ft tall	350 lb	38 lb
Sparky (dog)	3 ft tall	60 lb	20 oz
Spike (spider)	2 in. long	3 oz	Less than an ounce
Muffin (cat)	8 in. long	6 lb	8 oz

1. List the animals from lightest to heaviest.
2. Which pet weighs the most?
3. Which weighs the least?

4. Which pet eats the most food?

5. How much taller than Sparky is Silver?

6. Which pets weigh more than you do?

7. How much more food does Sparky eat than Muffin?

8. Write a number sentence to compare the lengths of two animals in the chart.

9. Pick one of the Exercises 6 through 9. Sketch your answer.

10. Use the information in the chart. Write a problem of your own. Trade with a partner and solve.

Petey

1200

LESSON 9 Hold It!

Lake Victoria is the world's second largest fresh water lake. It lies in central Africa.

A large public swimming pool holds as much water as 1,100 bathtubs. Is the pool big? You would need millions of swimming pools to fill Lake Victoria in Africa. Do you still think the pool is big?

What You'll Need

- *containers of different shapes and sizes, including 1-cup container*
- *beans*

ACTIVITY 1 Which Holds More?

With Your Group Choose four containers and compare how much they hold.

1. Which container do you think holds the most, the second most, the third most, and the least? Record your guesses.

2. Check your guesses. Use a smaller container to scoop beans into the other four. How many scoops can each container hold? Record the actual order.

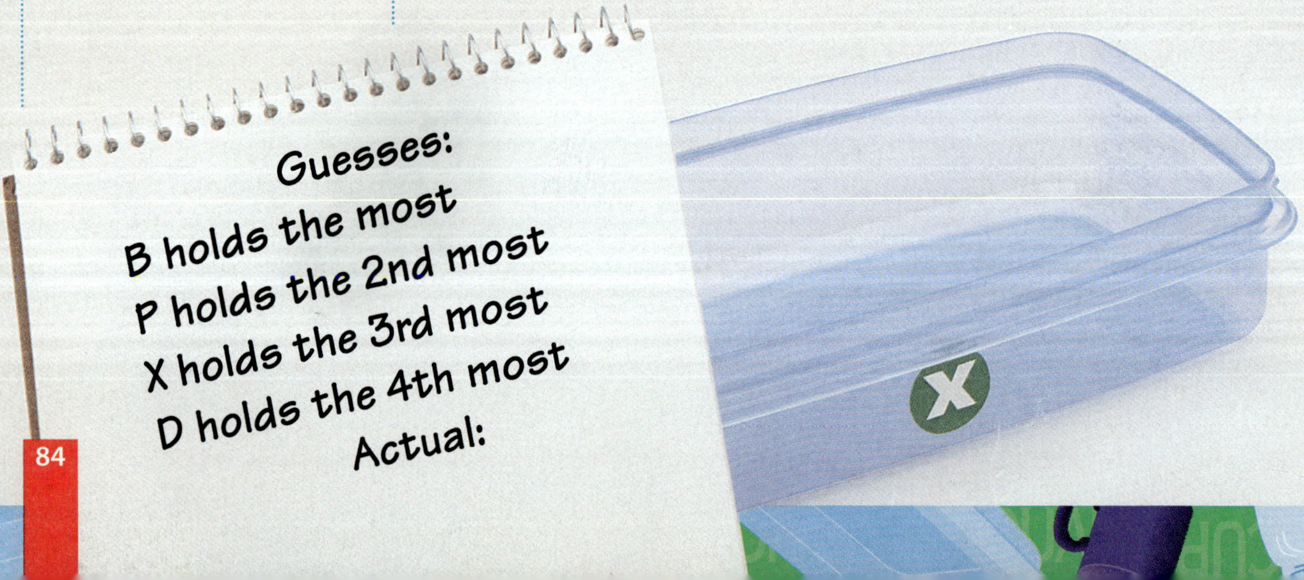

With Your Class A serving of milk is about one **cup (c).** How many cups do your containers hold?

3. Fill a one-cup container with beans. Guess whether each container holds more or less than a cup.
4. Check your guesses by pouring a cup of beans into the containers.
5. Did some containers hold less than you expected? Which ones? Discuss.

Can your hand hold more or less than 1 c? Use beans to find out. What other things besides beans could you use?

What You'll Need

- *containers of different shapes and sizes, including 1-qt container*
- *beans*
- *marker*
- *tape*

Self-Check *Draw a chart showing cups and quarts. Make it answer these questions: How many cups are in 2, 3, 4, or 5 quarts?*

ACTIVITY 2 More Measures

With Your Group The pitcher below can hold about a **quart (qt).**

1. Do you know how many cups are in a quart? How can the picture help you estimate?
2. Choose one of your containers and put tape on the side. Guess how many cups it holds. Check by pouring one cup of beans at a time into the container. Mark the container.

1 quart = ■ cups

3 This paint can shows two other units of measure, **pints (pt)** and **gallons (gal).** What numbers belong in the spaces below?

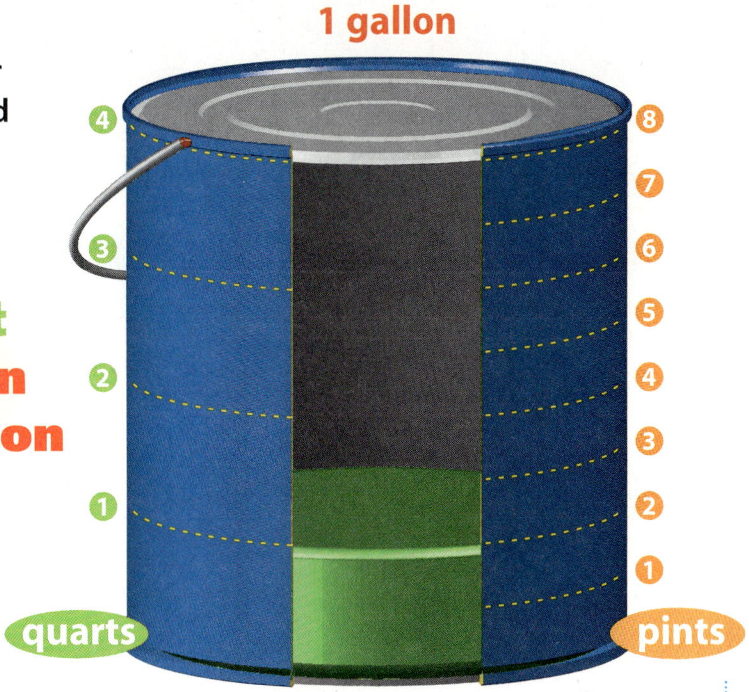

? **pints in a quart**
? **pints in a gallon**
? **quarts in a gallon**

4 Look at the containers you measured before. Which hold about a pint? Which hold about a quart? Do any hold a gallon?

Do You Remember?

Try It!

Subtract. Include the units in your answers.

1. 7 c − 3 c
2. 8 pt − 3 pt
3. 9 qt − 3 qt
4. 10 gal − 3 gal

Tell how many:

5. cups in a quart
6. quarts in two gallons

Mentally subtract 100 from the number.

7. 154
8. 4,201
9. 256
10. 780

Think About It

11. Think of a bathtub, a wading pool, a glass of juice, and a medicine bottle. Would you measure them in cups or gallons?

REASONING AND PROBLEM SOLVING

A gallon of water weighs about 8 lb. How much do you think a quart weighs? How did you get your answer?

LESSON 10

Growth Patterns

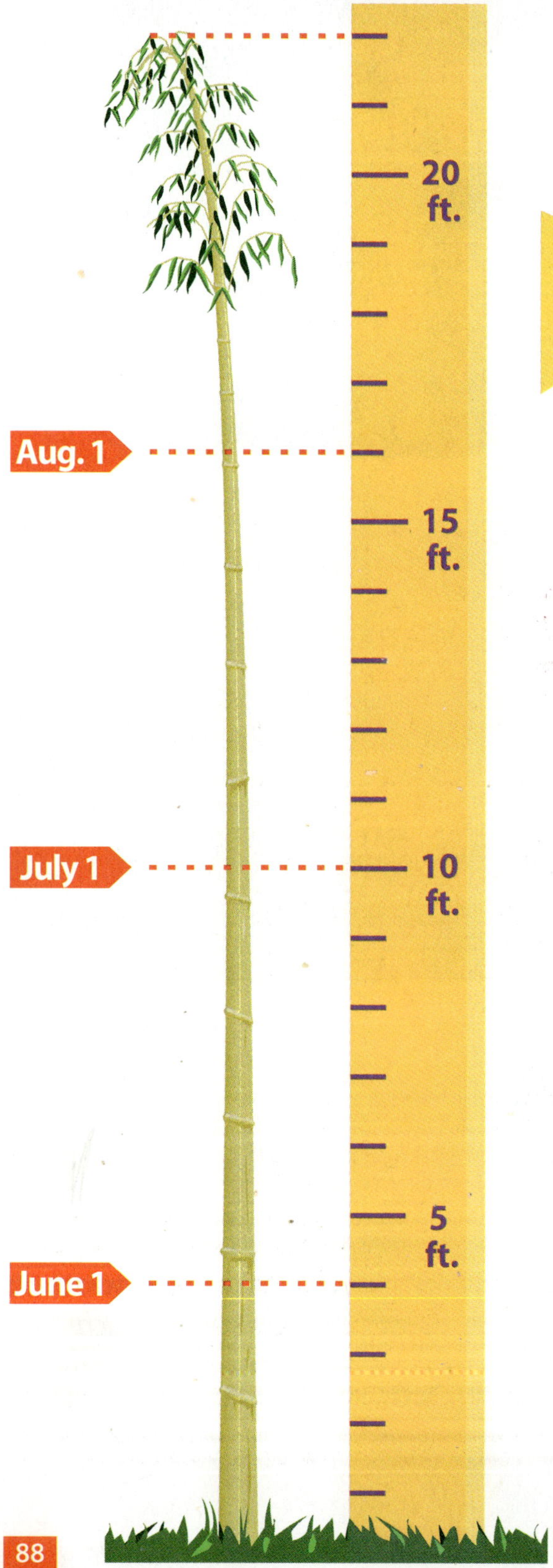

Did you know that you grow about 2 to 3 in. a year? Bamboo is a type of grass that grows even faster.

ACTIVITY 1 Growing Up

With Your Group The picture shows one bamboo's height on different dates.

1. How much did the bamboo grow between June 1 and July 1? How much did it grow between July 1 and August 1? Plants don't always grow the same amount every month. But number patterns can help you make good guesses.

2. Look at this pattern:

   4, 10, 16, __, __

   How tall do you think the bamboo will be on September 1 and October 1? Are you sure?

3. Find the next three numbers in each pattern. Use a calculator if you need to.

   a. 2, 7, 12

   b. 8, 32, 56

   c. 41, 72, 103

4. Create your own pattern.

ACTIVITY 2 What's Left?

With Your Partner It takes almost 30 hours to fill a large swimming pool. You can use the chart below to find out how long it takes to empty it.

1. How much water is draining each hour?
2. What numbers are missing from the chart?
3. Continue the pattern. When will the pool be empty?
4. Make your own addition or subtraction pattern. Use at least five numbers.

Hours	Gallons
1	14 hundred
2	12 hundred
3	10 hundred
4	? hundred
5	? hundred
6	? hundred

CONNECT AND COMMUNICATE

Some pools hold about 16,000 gal of water. After 2 hours of filling, there are 8,000 gal in a pool. How full would it be after 3 hours? How full would it be after 4 hours? Describe the pattern.

DRAWING TO LEARN

Draw a number line from 0 to 12. Draw dots at 1, 4, and 7. What number comes next in the pattern?

Activity 3 Secret Rules

With Your Group Try to find the secret rule for a number pattern.

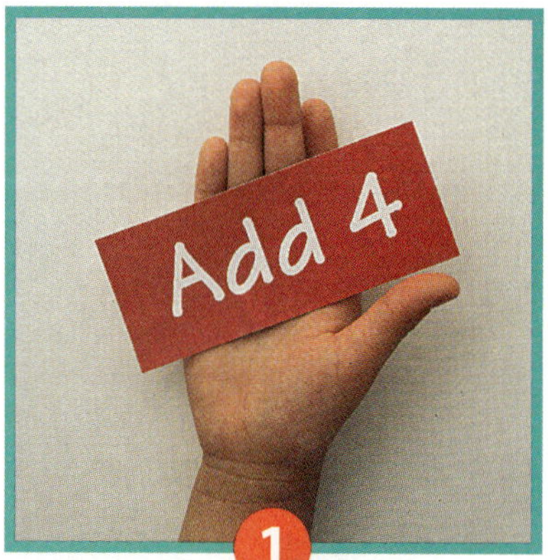

1 Let one person write a secret rule on a card. It might be "add 4." Turn the card over.

2 Each other group member says a number. The person with the secret rule writes it on a chart like this.

3 The secret keeper writes new numbers beside the old ones using the secret rule.

4 **Group members look at the chart. They take turns trying to guess the secret rule.**

5 **Whoever guesses the rule is the new secret keeper. Make a new chart and start again.**

ACTIVITY OPTION

Exchange your game chart with another team. Can your group guess the secret rule?

"What do I do to 3 to get 7?"

3 + ■ = 7

Do You Remember?

Try It!

Find the missing number. Then rewrite as subtraction sentences.

1. 4 + 3 = ■
2. 2 + ■ = 6
3. ■ + 3 = 8
4. 4 + ■ = 6
5. 6 + 6 = ■
6. 9 = ■ + 5

Write the numbers in order from least to greatest.

7. 43 34 304
8. 378 786 83
9. 690 609 90
10. 687 678 768
11. 89 809 98
12. 54 450 49

Think About It

13. Write the number sentence from Exercise 6 at least two other ways.

Do You Remember?

Cumulative Review

Looking Back

Choose the right answer. Write *a, b, c,* or *d* for each exercise.

1. Which sum is less than 8 + 7?
   a. 7 + 5 + 5 b. 9 + 6
   c. 7 + 3 + 2 d. 8 + 8

2. Which sum is greater than 9 + 4?
   a. 1 + 1 + 9 b. 6 + 8
   c. 2 + 6 + 4 d. 7 + 2

3. Which difference is equal to 5?
   a. 25 – 5 b. 11 – 8
   c. 14 – 7 d. 7 – 2

4. Find the missing addend.
   10 + ■ = 50
   a. 5 b. 60 c. 40
   d. none of these

5. Find the missing addend.
   7 + ■ + 8 = 15
   a. 1 b. 0 c. 15
   d. none of these

6. Which has the same sum as 9 + 4 + 6 + 6?
   a. 9 + 1 + 5 + 2 b. 8 + 5 + 2
   c. 7 + 3 + 7 + 8 d. 6 + 2 + 8 + 4

7. Which sum or difference equals 1 ft?
   a. 6 in. + 7 in. b. 5 in. – 4 in.
   c. 9 in. + 3 in. d. 8 in. – 2 in.

8. Which sum equals one pound?
   a. 8 oz + 4 oz b. 7 oz + 9 oz
   c. 3 oz + 5 oz d. 6 oz + 4 oz

Use the chart below to answer Exercises 9 and 10.

Item	Weight	Length
calculator	5 oz	6 in.
magazine	9 oz	11 in.
scissors	1 oz	5 in.
book	15 oz	9 in.

9. Which is heavier than a pound?
   a. 2 magazines
   b. a book and scissors
   c. 3 calculators
   d. a magazine and a calculator

10. List the items from shortest to longest. Which order is correct?
   - a. magazine, book, calculator, scissors
   - b. scissors, calculator, book, magazine
   - c. scissors, book, calculator, magazine
   - d. calculator, book, scissors, magazine

11. Which is true?
   - a. 2 pt < 1 qt
   - b. 4 qt = 1 gal
   - c. 2 pt = 1 gal
   - d. 4 qt < 1 pt

12. Which is true?
   - a. 3 ft > 1 yd
   - b. 2 yd = 8 ft
   - c. 12 in. < 2 ft
   - d. 1 yd > 40 in.

13. Which is false?
   - a. 9 in. + 3 in. = 1 ft
   - b. 1 ft + 8 ft = 3 yd
   - c. 6 yd – 5 yd = 3 ft
   - d. 7 ft – 6 ft = 10 in.

14. Which is false?
   - a. 4 pt – 3 pt = 2 c
   - b. 4 qt + 1 qt = 1 gal
   - c. 2 pt + 2 pt = 2 qt
   - d. 3 c + 1 c = 1 qt

Use this pattern to answer Exercises 15 and 16.

4, 9, 14, 19, ...

15. What is the rule for the pattern?
   - a. add 6
   - b. subtract 3
   - c. subtract 2
   - d. add 5

16. What are the next two numbers in the pattern?
   - a. 23, 27
   - b. 24, 31
   - c. 24, 29
   - d. none of these

Check Your Math Power

17. The five tallest trees in the United States are shown below. Choose three of them. List them in order by height.

18. Write at least two subtraction sentences to compare heights of trees. Explain what each difference means.

Tall Trees	
Douglas fir Coos County, Oregon	329 ft
Sugar pine Yosemite National Monument, California	270 ft
Giant sequoia Sequoia National Park, California	275 ft
Redwood Humboldt Redwoods State Park, California	363 ft
Noble fir Mount Saint Helens National Monument	272 ft

Module 2 Investigations

Measure Hunt

You can learn some surprising things if you do a little research. Try it with one of these investigations.

Investigation A Top of the Charts

1. **Choose** a topic. You might pick kinds of dogs or things in your book bag. List four animals or objects for your topic.

2. **Find** the weight, height, and other measurements of your objects. Measure them or look in books. Make a chart for your data.

Topic: Birds

	Height or Length	Weight	Number of Eggs	Time Until Eggs Hatch
Ostrich	8 ft tall	300 lb	10	6 weeks
King penguin	3 ft tall	100 lb	1	8 weeks
Flamingo	4 ft tall	6 lb	1	4 weeks
Bald eagle	3 ft long	10 lb	2	12 weeks

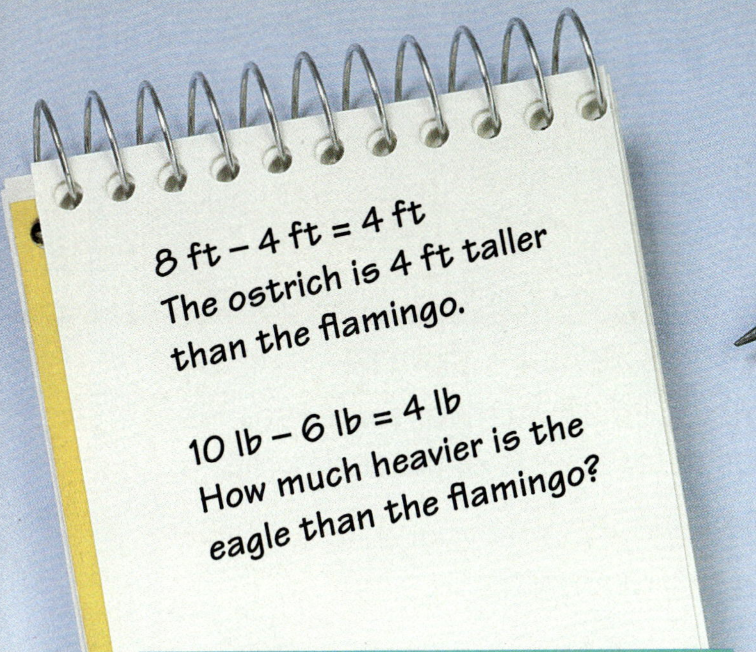

3. **Write** a report with your data. Tell which objects were biggest and smallest. Describe any patterns you found.

4. **Share** your report with other students. Have them help you write number sentences for your data.

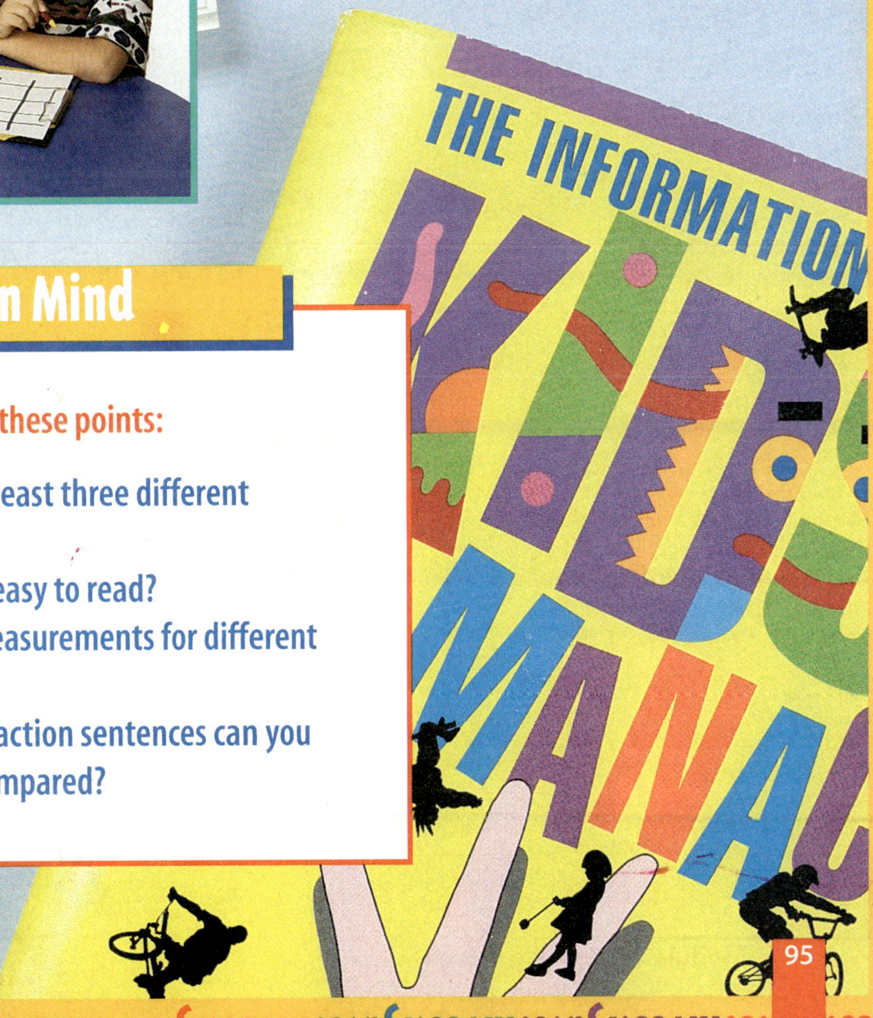

Keep in Mind

Your work will be judged on these points:

- ☐ Does your chart show at least three different measurements?
- ☐ Is the data in your chart easy to read?
- ☐ How did you compare measurements for different objects?
- ☐ What addition and subtraction sentences can you write for the data you compared?

Investigation B

Big Baby

Were you a big baby or a small baby? Find out!

1. Find out your birth weight and length. If you can't, find the information for someone else. Do the same for at least 20 other classmates.
2. Make a chart and look at your data. Do longer babies weigh the most?
3. Write number sentences to explain what patterns you find.
4. Share what you found with the class.

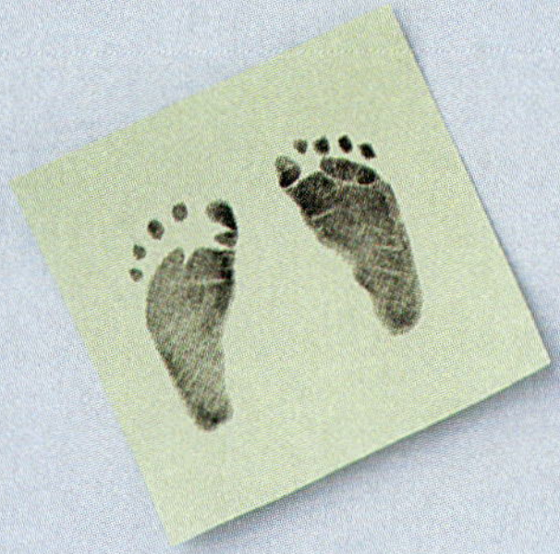

Ongoing Investigation

"How Do We Grow?" Revisited

It's time to measure your height and reach again. How much has your class grown so far? Use the addition strategies you learned to help you find the class totals. Then look for growth patterns. Is each student growing the same amount? Are boys or girls growing faster? Write a report about what you discover. Be sure to explain

- how you used addition strategies
- what patterns you found in the heights

MODULE 3

Have a Party

People all over the world celebrate special events. They have parties on birthdays and name days. They celebrate freedom days and give thanks for a good harvest. What do you like to celebrate?

Imagine that you want to have a party. Could you use math to help you plan it?

SECTION A
Exploring Addition

SECTION B
Exploring Subtraction

SECTION C
Metrics

SECTION D
Using Thousands

Party Count

When you plan a party, you will need to count. How many people will you invite? Sometimes you may estimate. Would you need to know how many bags of confetti to buy?

1 Piñata

Estimate the number of treats that will fit in the piñata. If someone took away 10 treats, would you change your estimate? What if everyone in the class took away 10 treats?

2 Apple Bob

You have 20 apples in a tub of water. Now try taking out 10. Put them back. Now try adding 10. Does 10 make a bigger difference in the piñata or the apple tub? Explain.

3 Balloons and Prizes

Plan an imaginary party. Estimate how many of the following you would need for your party.

a. balloons b. guests
c. punch bowl d. prizes

Word Bank

- centimeter
- degrees Celsius
- kilogram
- liter

Which would you count? Which would you estimate?

Would it make a difference if you added 10 to your estimates? 250? 1,000?

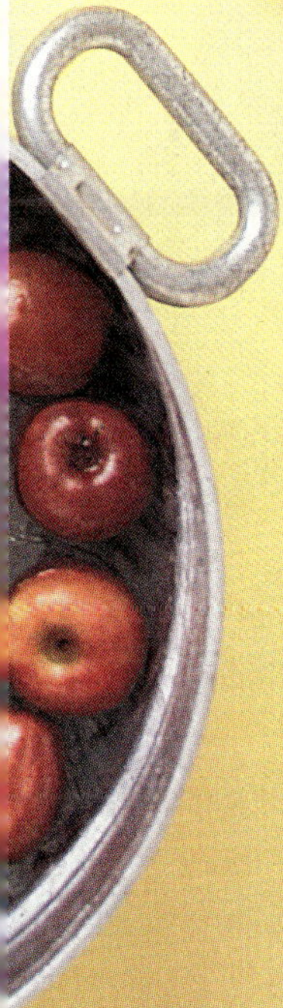

Investigations Preview

Learn about addition, subtraction, and metric measurement. These tools can help you count and measure things in the world around you.

WOW (pages 120 – 121)
What is a palindrome? Use your addition skills to find out.

Showing 10,000 (pages 142 – 144)
Can you picture 10,000? Practice thinking about and describing large numbers.

SECTION A **Exploring Addition**

LESSON 1

Add 'em Up

What You'll Need
- *base ten blocks*

ACTIVITY 1 Party Adding

With Your Group You are having a party. Invite other classes from your school. How can you add up a large number of guests?

1. Use your base ten blocks to add. How many students are in the first two classes on the party list on page 101?

You can trade ten cubes for a rod of ten. How does that help you add up your total? What's the total?

TOOLS AND TECHNIQUES

In these problems, one cube equals one student. How many students does a rod stand for? a flat?

2 Now add more classes to your party total.

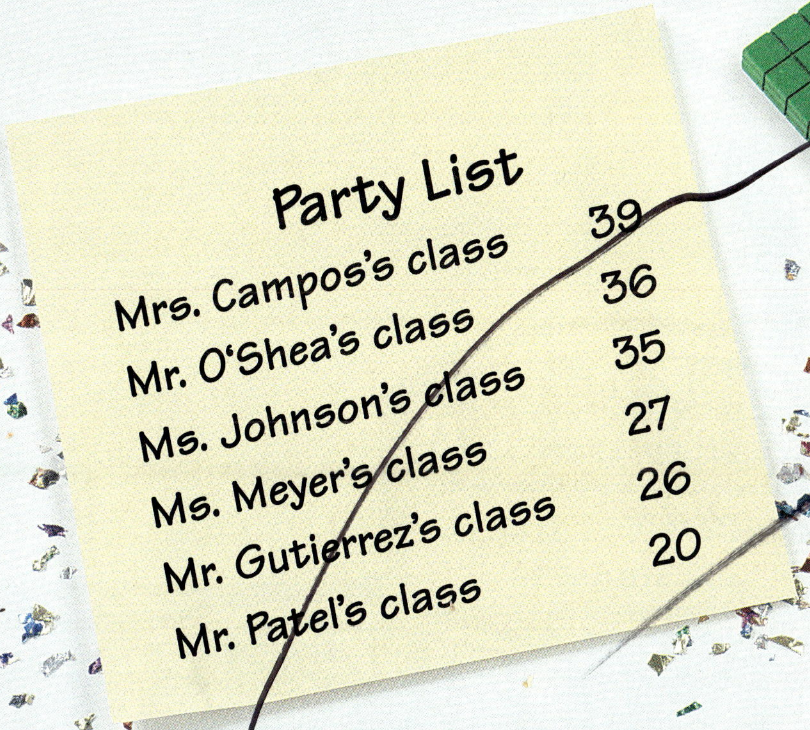

3 Answer these questions.

a. What is the total for all the classes?

b. How did the hundreds' flat help?

What You'll Need

- *base ten blocks*

ACTIVITY 2 A Really Big Party

With Your Group What if you could invite hundreds of people to your party? You can still use base ten blocks to add up your totals.

1. How many students go to Cabrera School? How many go to Elm School? The base ten blocks below each school tell you.

2 Elm School and Cabrera School are having a party together. All the students from both schools are invited. How many people will that be? Use your base ten blocks.

3 Tell how you got your answer. What trades did you make?

DRAWING TO LEARN

If you do not have base ten blocks, you can make drawings. What would you draw to stand for 10? 100?

4 Plan three giant parties. Match pairs of schools listed on the six buses. Each pair can have no more than 525 people.

5 Discuss your answer with another group. Did they match the same schools?

What You'll Need
- *spinner*
- *base ten blocks*

Activity 3 Spin 999

With Your Partner Try this party game.

1. Make a spinner with these numbers— 200, 90, 70, 40, 30, 8, 6, 5.

2. **Take turns spinning. Add totals with base ten blocks. Try using mental math.**

3. **Write your new total after each spin. The first player to reach 999 or more wins.**

Do You Remember?

Try It!

Write two addends that have the given sum. Use base ten blocks to help.

1. 372	2. 198	3. 570
4. 245	5. 519	6. 117

Round to the nearest hundred.

7. 364	8. 248	9. 472
10. 786	11. 802	12. 905

Think About It

13. Explain in writing how to add three-digit numbers with base ten blocks.

ACTIVITY OPTION

Use your calculator to add 99 and 99. Add 99 over and over. What pattern do you see? Tell how you can do the additions with mental math.

Numbers, Please

LESSON 2

Base ten blocks help you add up your party lists. You will not always want to use blocks, though.

ACTIVITY 1 Blocks to Numbers

With Your Group Add these totals using base ten blocks. As you add, keep a record. Use numbers to record each step you take. Explain your way of recording.

What You'll Need

- *base ten blocks*

CONNECT AND COMMUNICATE

In Your Journal *Write instructions telling how your recording method works. Show two or three examples. Use different numbers.*

ACTIVITY 2 How They Did It

With Your Group Three students recorded their addition. See if you can tell how each method works.

1 Did this student start with ones or hundreds? How do you know?

2 Why did this student cross out the 5?

3 Why is there a 1 above the 6? Why is there another 1 above the 3?

4 Which way is most like your own? Which seems easiest? Tell why you think so.

ACTIVITY 3

The Sum Game

With Your Group Try this game. As you play, arrange number cards to show different addends. Your group will earn points.

1 Draw a sheet like this. Make cards using the numbers 2, 3, 4, 5, 6, and 7.

2 Move the cards around. Find addends to make a sum with only one zero. Each example is one point. Record on a separate sheet.

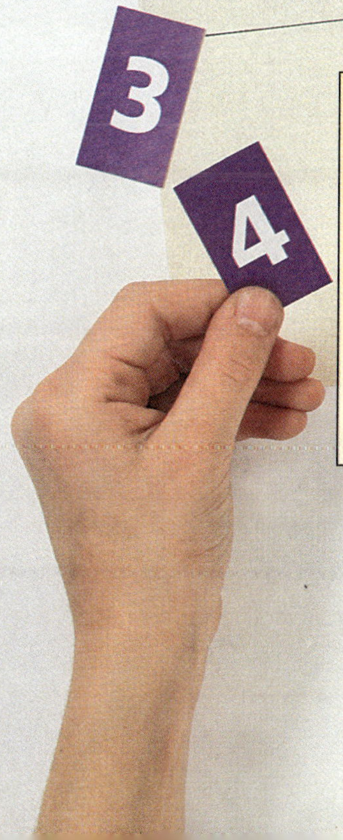

3 How many different additions can you find for the sums below?

a. sums with two zeros
b. additions with one trade
c. additions with two trades

The team with the most points in 3 minutes wins.

What You'll Need

- scissors
- ruler

REASONING AND PROBLEM SOLVING

Which pairs of cards add up to ten? Which pairs add up to more than ten? How will this help you play the Sum Game?

What You'll Need
- play money

ACTIVITY 4 Party Planners

With Your Group Help buy party prizes. Then join the decoration team.

1 **Prize Team** You are on the prize team. You have $9.00 to spend on prizes.

Estimate the total cost of the glasses and bubbles in dollars. Is it more than $3? Use play money to find the sum. Record.

$2.75
+ $1.50
?

Now decide what other prizes on this page you can buy. Add to find out.

2 Decoration Team You have $9.00. Which supplies will you buy?

TOOLS AND TECHNIQUES

Try making lists to help with this activity. List all the things your team will buy. Then add up the cost. If you spend too much, change your list.

Do You Remember?

Try It!

Guess which sums are greater than 500. Then add.

1. 316 + 275
2. 146 + 410
3. 249 + 236
4. 418 + 112
5. 316 + 182
6. 584 + 337

Name some coins and bills that make this amount.

7. $1.50
8. $2.63
9. $9.41
10. $7.72
11. $8.25
12. $3.37

Think About It

13. Explain the trades you made for any exercise from 1 to 6.

SECTION B Exploring Subtraction

LESSON 3 It's a Party!

What You'll Need
- *base ten blocks*

ACTIVITY 1 Everybody's Coming

With Your Group Your class made party invitations of different colors. There were 243 blue invitations. You sent 155 of them to King School.

1. Show 243 with base ten blocks.
   - Estimate how many blue invitations are left after you send 155.
   - Will the answer be more than 100? How do you know?

2. Now use base ten blocks to find an exact answer. Remove 155 blocks from 243. Do you have to make any trades?

3. How many invitations are left? Record the number sentence. How close was your estimate?

4. Send invitations to the first school on the list. Match the school with a color. Use base ten blocks or mental math to find the number of invitations you will have left in that color. Write a number sentence.

5. Match the other schools with colors. Then write number sentences to show how many invitations of each color will be left.

REASONING AND PROBLEM SOLVING

How could your group help another group with Step 2? What would you show them?

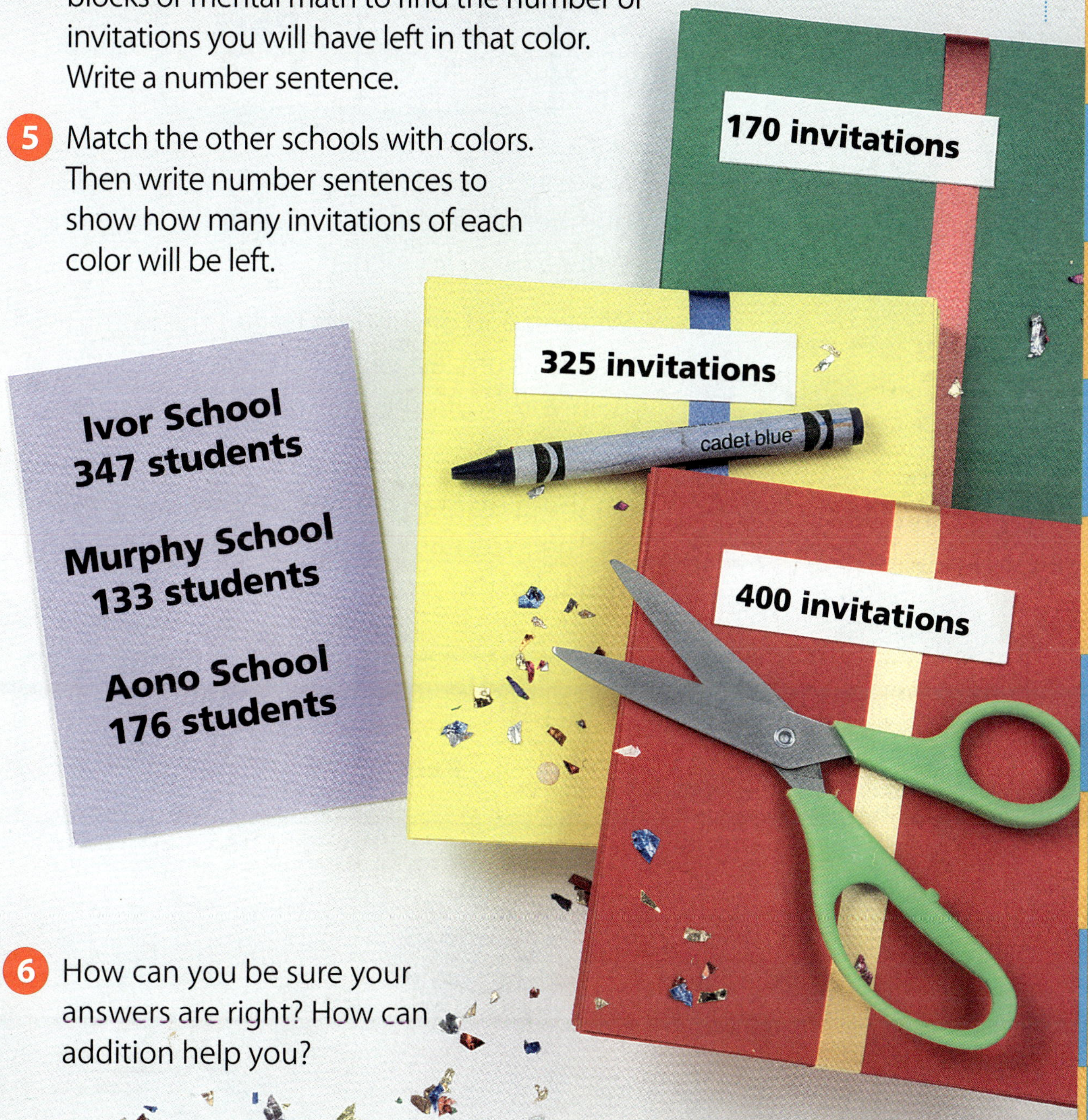

6. How can you be sure your answers are right? How can addition help you?

What You'll Need

- *ruler*
- *base ten blocks*

Self-Check

Remember that you can add to find the whole when you know the two parts.

ACTIVITY 2 The Winner Is . . .

With Your Partner The prize team has 579 stickers to give away. This amount includes one roll of 450 stickers and some stickers from last year.

Whole ?	
Part ?	Part 450

1. Make a chart like this one. Is 579 the whole number of stickers you have or part of them? Write 579 on your chart.

2. Will you add or subtract to find the number of stickers from last year? Use base ten blocks to help you. Write the number on your chart.

3. Write two story problems using the numbers on these diagrams. Trade problems with your partner. You can use base ten blocks to help you solve the problems.

Whole 316	
Part 152	Part ?

Whole 129	
Part ?	Part 37

3 Spin to Zero

With Your Partner You played a game like this one on page 104. Use the same spinner. Take turns. The game ends when one player reaches zero.

What You'll Need
- *spinner*
- *base ten blocks*

1. Use base ten blocks to show 500. Then write 500 at the top of a sheet of paper.
2. Spin to get a number.
3. Use your base ten blocks. Subtract the number you spin from 500. Write your answer.
4. Every time you have a turn, subtract the number from your last answer.

Do You Remember?

Try It!

Subtract. Use base ten blocks or mental math.

1. 232 − 5
2. 98 − 20
3. 367 − 48
4. 283 − 30
5. 152 − 46
6. 222 − 19

Write the date.

7. last Sunday
8. next Saturday
9. yesterday
10. tomorrow
11. the last day of the year

Think About It

12. Explain in writing how you could use mental math to find the answer to Exercise 1 or 2.

LESSON 4 Party Games

What You'll Need
- *base ten blocks*

ACTIVITY 1 Take It Away

With Your Partner The games teams need game pieces for the party. Help them keep track of these.

1. A box contains 205 game pieces. For one game, each group needs 20 game pieces. How can you use mental math to subtract 20 at a time? Continue the pattern.

   205, 185, 165, ?, ?, ?

2. Was it easy to subtract 20 mentally? If you use base ten blocks to take 2 tens from 205, will you need to make trades? Explain.

	H	T	O
	2	0	5
−		2	0

3 One team began with 108 game pieces. They used 46. Use base ten blocks to find out how many pieces were left.

	H	T	O
	1	0	8
−		4	6

- Copy the numbers from the notebook onto your paper.
- Decide whether you need to make any trades.
- Use numbers to keep track of everything you do.
- Be ready to explain your work.

4 Suppose a team began with 958 game pieces and used 194. Find out how many game pieces would be left. Record all of your steps.

ACTIVITY OPTION

You might want to show someone at home how to use base ten blocks to subtract large numbers. You can use play money marked $100, $10, and $1 in place of the blocks.

CONNECT AND COMMUNICATE

In Your Journal *List times when you use subtraction or see someone else using subtraction. Ask a person in your family who shops for groceries to help you with your list.*

ACTIVITY 2

Which Way Works?

With Your Class Look at another example. These two students recorded trades. Perhaps you recorded your trades a different way. Think about which way might work best for you. Tell why.

1 Explain the trades the two students made.

a. Why was the 8 changed to a 7?

b. Where did the 15 come from?

c. Why did the student cross out the 9 and 5?

2 How could estimation help you decide whether your answer makes sense?

Activity 3 Make a Choice

On Your Own Think about the best way to solve these problems. You can use a calculator, paper and pencil, mental math, or blocks. Find the answers.

What You'll Need
- *base ten blocks*

TOOLS AND TECHNIQUES

You can think of dollars as hundreds, dimes as tens, and pennies as ones. Remember to show a dollar sign and decimal point in the sum.

1. The host for your talent show wants to dress up like the person in the picture. What would you buy for your host if you could spend $5.00? How much change would you have?

2. If you had $8.00 to spend, could you buy everything the talent show host wants? List as many items as you can that have a sum of $8.00 or less.

3. The host will give kazoos to 200 students in the talent show. How many kazoos are in the boxes? Will you need more or will you have some left over?

4. Talk with your partner about how you solved the problems.

Party Time

The day of your party is here! Is everything ready? Check your supplies.

Party Hats

1 Some third graders made funny hats. They made 16 hats from red paper and 32 from blue paper. What is the total number of hats?

2 How many more blue hats are there than red hats?

3 A friend gave you 22 yellow hats and 16 striped hats. How many hats do you have if you add these to the red and blue hats?

4 There are 79 third graders. How many hats will be left if each third grader gets 1 hat?

Decorations

5 There were 220 balloons in one package. You used 126 red balloons to decorate the tables. How many balloons were not used for tables?

6 You want to put the rest of the balloons on the windows and the door. The room has 10 windows. If you put 2 balloons in each window, will you have enough to put 10 around the door?

Party Dishes

7 The school cafeteria sent you 167 spoons. You need 345. How many spoons do you still need?

8 There are two boxes of plates in the storeroom. Each box holds 250 plates. Are there enough plates for 345 guests? Will you have extra plates? How many?

Party Games

9 You have 48 party pencils, 127 high-bounce balls, and 98 funny glasses. How many favors do you have?

10 How many favors will be left after the party if guests take 230 favors home?

Investigation

WOW

You can play a party game with palindromes. The numbers 55 and 303 are palindromes. The title of this investigation is also a palindrome. Have you figured out what a palindrome is yet? It is a number or a word that reads the same forward and in reverse.

Palindrome Club Use addition to make palindromes. Join the club!

1. Write down a two-digit number. Under your number, write the digits in reverse order. Then add.

$$\begin{array}{r} 72 \\ +27 \\ \hline 99 \end{array}$$

Here is another one:

$$\begin{array}{r} 23 \\ +32 \\ \hline 55 \end{array}$$

2. Is the sum a palindrome? If not, repeat Step 1 using the sum as your new number. Do this until you get a palindrome. Each sum counts as one step.

$$\begin{array}{r} 85 \\ +58 \\ \hline 143 \\ +341 \\ \hline 484 \end{array}$$

3 How many steps does it take if you start with a two-digit number? Use a hundred chart to record the number of steps for each number you try. Use a different color for each number of steps.

a. Why are the numbers 23 and 72 shaded in the same color?

b. Why is 58 shaded in a different color ?

4 Look at the colors on your chart. Do the colors make any patterns? Tell why some numbers take more steps than others.

Ask Yourself

- ☐ How can I use addition to make palindromes?
- ☐ Which two-digit numbers are already palindromes?
- ☐ How will I keep track of the numbers I try?
- ☐ Do the colors make a pattern? Should I try some numbers again?
- ☐ How will I explain why some numbers take more steps?

Do You Remember? Cumulative Review

Party Pro

Addie is a professional clown. She knows parties better than anyone! Think of how addition and subtraction help her with her work.

Animal Balloons

1. **Addie loves to make giraffes and poodles. Last year she made 940 of them. If she made 512 giraffes, how many poodles did she make?**

2. **Addie bought a bag of 800 balloons. She has used 460. How many balloons does she have left?**

3. **Last week at the hospital, Addie visited 126 children. If she gave two balloons to each child, how many balloons did she use?**

Clowning Calendar

4. **Look at Addie's schedule. How many children will she see this week?**

5. **Look at the calendar. How many weeks are there from October 13 until Addie's Clown College Reunion on October 27?**

Addie's Schedule

Mon. 8
Louis school 120 kids

Wed. 10
Pip Daycare 120 kids

Fri. 12
Nikks party 16 kids

Sat. 13
block party 52 kids

OCTOBER

	1	2	3	4	5	6
7	8	9	10	11	12	13
14	15	16	17	18	19	20
21	22	23	24	25	26	27
28	29	30	31			

Clown Gear

6 It takes Addie $1\frac{1}{2}$ hours to put on her make-up. She has to leave for a party at 1:15 P.M. At what time should she start putting on make-up?

7 Addie's shoes are 1 ft 3 in. long. Her feet are only 9 in. long. How much longer are her shoes than her feet?

8 Is the length of one shoe closer to 1 ft or 2 ft?

Check Your Math Power

9 For her birthday, Addie received a $10.00 gift certificate to the Clown Store. Name four sets of these items that she could buy.

10 Suppose you buy the goofy teeth. Give three combinations of coins you could use to buy them. Remember to use exact change.

LESSON 5 Party-Metrics

What You'll Need

- *centimeter ruler*

REASONING AND PROBLEM SOLVING

Measure something familiar, such as a pencil. Then use it to help you estimate how long other things are.

ACTIVITY 1 Centimeter Search

With Your Group Try this centimeter search. Use the centimeter ruler to help.

Centimeter Search

1 to 10 cm	11 to 20 cm	21 to 30 cm
peanut, 3 cm	pencil, 12 cm	the side of an English book, 26 cm

1. **Write a score sheet like this one. Players have already started to fill out this sheet.**
2. **Find objects around the room for each column on the sheet. Estimate first, then measure. List at least 3 objects in each column.**

3. **Search until the teacher says stop. The group with the most objects wins.**

ACTIVITY 2 Cookie Cutters

What You'll Need

- *centimeter ruler*
- *construction paper*
- *scissors*

With Your Group **Perimeter** is the distance around a shape. Use perimeter to make some cookie cutters.

1 **What is the perimeter of the triangle cookie? How does addition help?**

2 **Measure the sides of the other cookies. What length strip of tin would you use to make a cookie cutter for each cookie?**

3 **Make a paper model of a cookie cutter. Use a strip of paper 20 cm long. Then draw your cookie shape.**

DRAWING TO LEARN

Plan your own party space. Make a drawing like the one on page 127. Use centimeter grid paper. Then answer the questions in Steps 1 and 2 for your space.

ACTIVITY 3

The Party Meter

On Your Own Some things are too big to measure with centimeters. Instead you can use **meters (m).**

100 cm = 1 m

1. Study the party room drawing. What is the perimeter of each of the following?
   a. the room
   b. an eating table
   c. a ticket table
   d. the game space

2. Help plan the party.
   a. One student used 1 roll of streamers to decorate a 10-m wall. How many rolls will she use for the whole party room? Explain.
   b. She also wants to rope off the game space. She will leave an opening of 2 m. How much rope will she need? Explain.

Do You Remember?

Try It!

Estimate the length in centimeters or meters. Then list all six objects in order from shortest to longest.

1. calculator
2. bus
3. paperback book
4. paper clip
5. classroom
6. playground

Do the same with these objects but use inches and feet.

7. chalkboard
8. marker
9. this book
10. dollar bill
11. giraffe's neck
12. teacher's desk

Think About It

13. Tell in writing how you estimated the shortest and longest objects on the lists.

LESSON 6 Spills and Chills

Self-Check *Add up the liters in your recipe. Be sure your total is 8 L or less.*

ACTIVITY 1 Party Punch

On Your Own The boy is pouring apple juice from a pitcher that holds a **liter (L).** How many glasses do you think he can fill from one pitcher?

1. **Look at the other juice jugs. Estimate. Tell which ones can hold the following amounts.**
   a. **about 1 L**
   b. **more than 1 L**
   c. **less than 1 L**

2. **Write a recipe for fruit punch to fill the bowl. The bowl holds 8 L.**

ACTIVITY 2

A Table of Treats

With Your Partner How heavy is a liter of milk? You can give the answer in **kilograms (kg).** A liter of milk weighs about 1 kg.

1 **Match each of these kilogram labels with treat a, b, or c on the table.**

2 kg

8 kg

3 kg

2 **Play Mystery Grab Bag. Choose three of the four treats with Kg labels. Tell your partner the total kilograms. Your partner names treats one by one to guess what is in the bag.**

ACTIVITY OPTION

Play Mystery Grab Bag with objects from your classroom that weigh 1 kg or more. Estimate how many kilograms each object is. Label each. Play with three, four, or five objects in a grab bag.

TOOLS AND TECHNIQUES

How can you compare the weight of two objects without a scale? For an estimate, try the "hands test." Hold one object in each hand. Which seems heavier? How much heavier does it seem?

3 How heavy are two raisins or two blueberries? You can measure lighter things in **grams (g).**

is about 1 g

1,000 g = 1 kg

Would you measure each of these in grams or kilograms? Arrange from lightest to heaviest.

a. five cherries
b. cracker
c. apple
d. party table
e. punch bowl
f. large jar of jam

ACTIVITY 3 A Cool Party

With Your Group You can use **degrees Celsius** to measure temperatures. What temperatures do the pointers show?

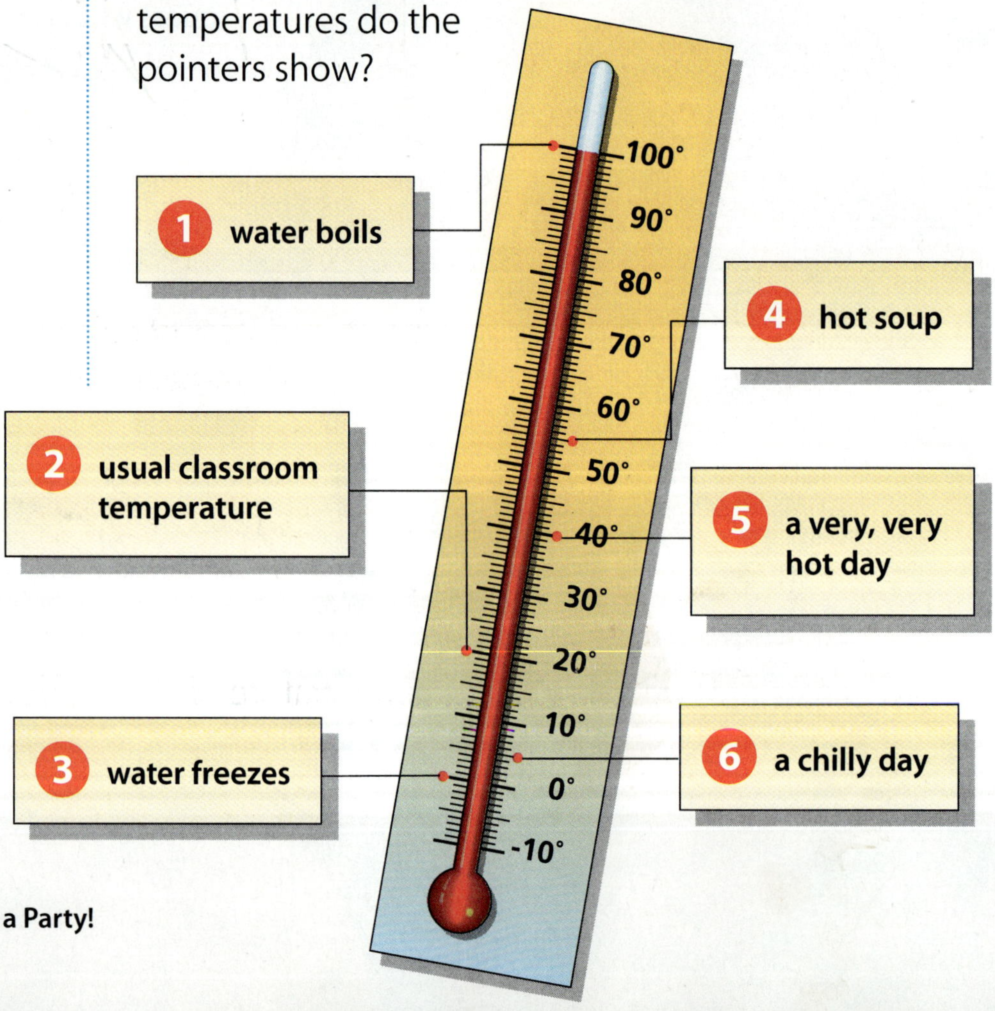

ACTIVITY 4

A Chilling Story

With Your Group Spin a "chilling" story.

1 **Make a spinner like this. Each person spins to get a temperature. Each person then adds to a story using that temperature.**

2 **Record the story like this and tell it to the class.**

What You'll Need

- *spinner*

CONNECT AND COMMUNICATE

In Your Journal *Try this activity on your own. Spin for a temperature. Start your story at that temperature. Spin again and again to continue the story. Write the story in your journal.*

Do You Remember?

Try It!

Estimate grams or kilograms and Celsius temperature.

1. snowball	**2.** hot cocoa	**3.** 2 liters of cold milk
4. ice cube	**5.** banana	**6.** fresh-baked pie

Write < or >.

7. 9 ● 7	**8.** 1 cm ● 1 m	**9.** 1 ft ● 9 in.
10. 1 kg ● 8 g	**11.** 3 pt ● 1 qt	**12.** 9 c ● 1 gal

Think About It

13. How did you estimate the temperature of a snowball? hot cocoa?

LESSON 7 Elephant Party

LITERATURE

In this section you will read about a zoo that gave a big party for an elephant's birthday. But first, read the poem by Louis Phillips. He has another idea about elephants and birthdays. It's a very unusual idea!

The Elephant

Of all the facts about mammals
This is most relevant:
It takes a lot of paper
To gift-wrap an elephant.

Louis Phillips

ACTIVITY 1 Happy Birthday!

With Your Group In 1991 an elephant in a zoo had a birthday. The zoo had a party for her. Many people came. You can show the number of people at the party in two ways. You can use words—eleven thousand people came. You can also use numerals—11,000.

1. Suppose you have blocks like the ones shown here. Think about showing 11,000 with blocks.

2. You can use the blocks to help you think of names for one thousand.
   a. Trade one thousand for hundreds. How many hundreds do you have?
   b. How many tens make a thousand?
   c. How many ones?

What You'll Need

- base ten blocks

DRAWING TO LEARN

What do you think a ten-thousands' block would look like? a hundred-thousands' block? With your group, draw these blocks. Share your drawings with the class.

Elephant
5,170 kg

Rhinoceros
3,400 kg

Activity 2 Reading Thousands

With Your Partner Many facts about a zoo have large numbers. Use the chart to help you learn to read large numbers.

Thousands			Ones		
Hundreds	Tens	Ones	Hundreds	Tens	Ones
	2	1,	4	3	0

Read the number in front of the comma—twenty-one thousand.

Read the other part of the number—four hundred thirty.

1. Look at the pictures. Which animal is five thousand one hundred seventy kilograms?
2. Use numerals to write this number. A blue whale is two hundred thousand kilograms.

Do You Remember?

Try It!

Write the number.

1. one thousand one hundred
2. fourteen thousand
3. sixteen hundred
4. twenty-five tens
5. fifty-two thousand one hundred twenty-three

Estimate. Then find the sum or difference.

6. 200 + 190
7. 391 + 102
8. 999 − 111
9. 482 − 112
10. 197 − 19
11. 799 − 101

Think About It

12. Use words to write Exercises 3 and 4 in another way.

3. If you roll +, then add the number you land on to your 15,000 points. If you roll −, then subtract the number you land on from your 15,000 points.

4. You have three choices at the loop. You can stay on the main trail. Or, take the addition loop to get a higher score. Or, take the subtraction loop to lower your score. While on the loop, roll only the 1, 2, 3 cube.

5. When all players reach the Party Place, compare scores. Talk about the choices you made to get a score close to 15,000 points.

CONNECT AND COMMUNICATE

When you subtract, how do you decide whether to use mental math or paper and pencil? Explain.

If you land on a party picture, you can choose to add or subtract. Remember, you want to have 15,000 points at the end of the game.

If you land on a calculator picture, use your calculator to do the math.

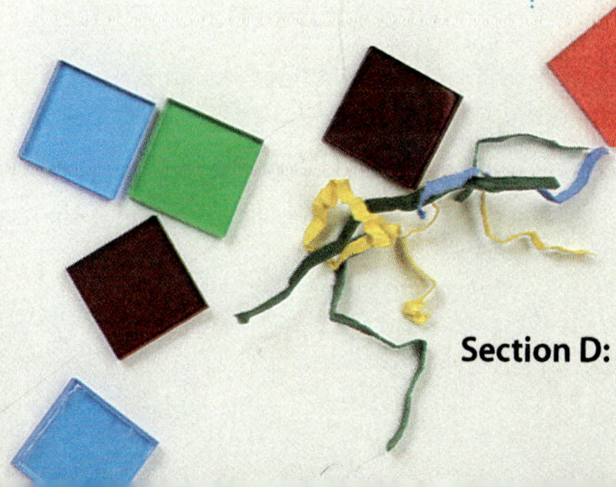

Self-Check *How can you be sure your answer makes sense? Think about how estimation will help you.*

Activity 3 Onion Cake?

With Your Group The big birthday cake for the elephant was made of hay, vegetables, and fruit. Use the zoo's grocery order to find out what other things zoo animals eat.

Weekly Zoo Grocery Order

2,000	Apples
1,350	Heads of lettuce
1,575	Bananas
10	Papayas
400	Onions
60,000	Carrots
65	Sweet potatoes
1,680	Potatoes
12,000	Worms
9,000	Crickets

1. The animals eat apples, bananas, and papayas. How many pieces of these fruits did the zoo order?
2. The zoo ordered carrots, lettuce, and onions. How many of these vegetables did they order?

3. Some of the animals get crickets and worms for treats. Which do they eat more of? How many more?

4. Did the zoo order more pieces of fruit or more vegetables, including both kinds of potatoes? How many more?

5. Some elephants weigh more than 6,600 kg. The elephant who had the party will probably weigh about 3,500 kg when she is grown. How much more would larger elephants weigh?

6. Write a question of your own about the zoo's grocery order or about what the animals weigh.

REASONING AND PROBLEM SOLVING

There are many ways to show one thousand. Write three ways. Which way do you think will work best when you want to add or subtract?

Do You Remember?

Try It!

Write the number you would subtract to change the digit shown in green to a zero without changing other numbers.

1. 12,970	2. 98,765	3. 32,607
4. 13,012	5. 30,452	6. 24,000

Write a number to make the sentence true.

7. A month is about __?__ days.
8. A week is __?__ days.
9. February usually has __?__ days.
10. A year is __?__ months.
11. Sometimes February has __?__ days.
12. Fall lasts __?__ months.

Think About It

13. Which two numbers in Exercises 1 through 6 would you add to get a sum close to 60,000? Explain your answer.

Do You Remember?

Cumulative Review

Looking Back

Choose the best answers. Write a, b, c, or d.

Add, Subtract, and Measure

1. What is another way to show 305?

   a. 3 tens, 5 ones
   b. 30 tens, 50 ones
   c. 29 tens, 50 ones
   d. 29 tens, 15 ones

2. What number is ten less than 3,000?

   a. 3,010
   b. 2,999
   c. 2,990
   d. 2,900

3. What is the sum of 6 thousands and 40 ones?

   a. 6,040
   b. 6,041
   c. 46
   d. none of these

4. In two days Roya read 236 pages. She read 119 pages the first day. How many pages did she read the second day?

   a. 127
   b. 117
   c. 355
   d. none of these

5. Find the missing addend.
   426 + __?__ + 0 = 547

   a. 937
   b. 4,807
   c. 1,210
   d. none of these

6. What is the next number in this pattern?
   370, 395, 420, __?__

   a. 445
   b. 425
   c. 815
   d. none of these

7. What is the next number in this pattern?
240, 210, 180, ___?___

a. 30
b. 630
c. 150
d. 135

8. What is another way to show the sum of two thousand and 43 thousand?

a. 43,200
b. 63,000
c. 43,002
d. 45,000

9. What is the perimeter of this shape?

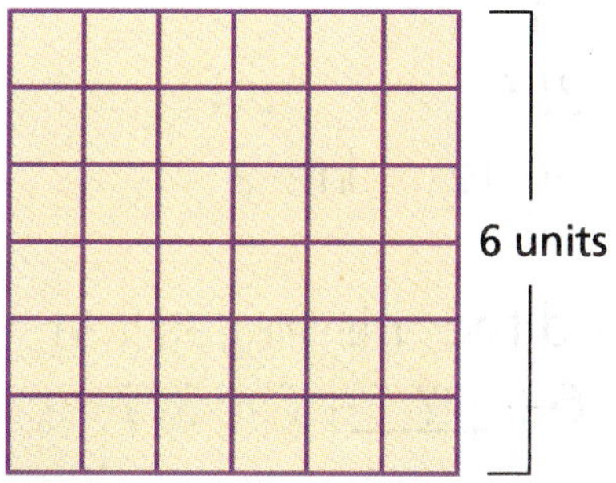

[redacted]
b. 12 units
c. 24 units
d. 36 units

10. About how heavy is one large bag of groceries?

a. 5 kg
b. 500 g
c. 500 kg
d. 5 g

11. About how long is a broom handle?

a. 2 cm
b. 20 cm
c. 1 m
d. 10 m

12. About how much water does a dishpan hold?

a. 2 L
b. 20 L
c. 200 L
d. 2,000 L

Check Your Math Power

13. Write a postcard about an imaginary trip. Include four of these measures or four metric measures of your own. Start with the postcard below or make up a postcard of your own.

a. 100°C
b. 0°C
c. 650 m
d. 25 L
e. 35 cm
f. 6 g
g. 82 kg
h. 33°C

MODULE 3 **Investigations**

Showing 10,000

How big is 10,000? Try to help your classmates see 10,000. Make a display and give a short report that shows 10,000.

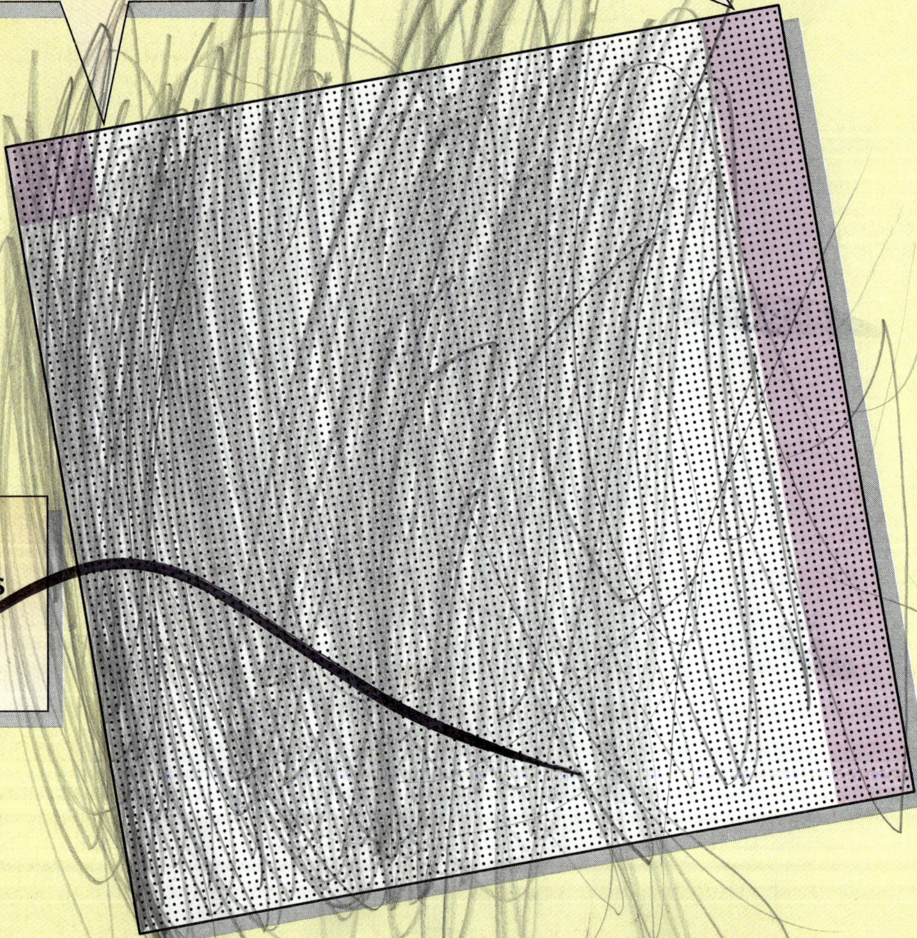

Investigation A

10,000 Paper Links?

How can you show 10,000? Try to think what 10,000 paper links would look like.

Do the dots on page 142 help you understand 10,000? Why or why not? Think of your own way to show 10,000. How much space would 10,000 peanuts take? Use your imagination! Show 10,000 in a way your classmates will remember.

Hint: You can just show 100 or 1,000. Then you can tell what 10,000 will look like.

Keep in Mind

Your report will be judged by how well you do the following things.

- ☐ How clearly you describe the objects and their size
- ☐ How well you explain your idea of 10,000
- ☐ How you show that you understand how 10,000 is related to 10 or 100

Investigation B — Can You Imagine?

Think of a way to show 100,000. For example, how many times would a chain of 100,000 paper clips go around your classroom? How many dictionaries would you need to make 100,000 pages? Use your imagination. See who can think of the most interesting way to show 100,000.

Investigation C — Right Before Your Eyes

Try drawing 1,000 shapes! Can you do it on just one piece of paper?

- First draw 1 shape. Just how small should it be?
- What is the easiest way to make 100 shapes on the page?
- Will 100 fit on the page? 1,000? You may have to change the size of your shapes.

Computer Option Use a drawing program to see whether you can fit 1,000 shapes on one page.

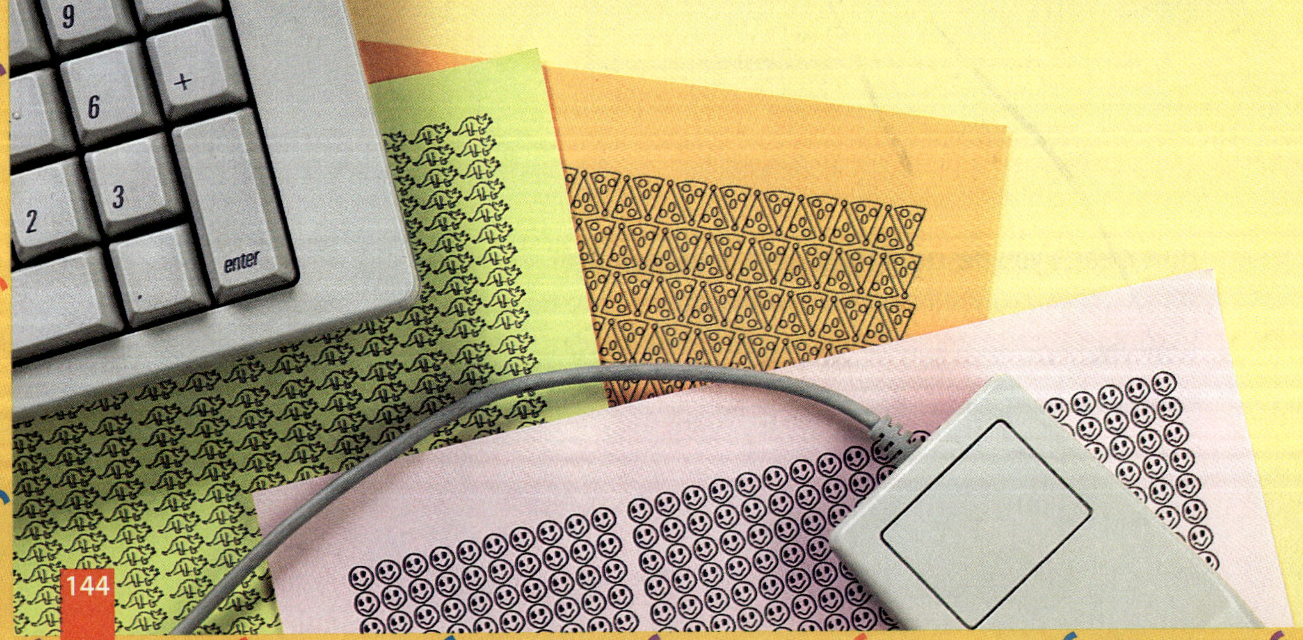

MODULE 4

Multiply!

Check out all these apples!
Can you figure out how many apples are shown here without counting each one? Once you learn how to multiply, you'll be able to tell how many without counting one apple!

SECTION A
Exploring Groups and Arrays

SECTION B
Connecting Arrays to Multiplication

SECTION C
Multiplication Strategies

SECTION D
Choosing Multiplication Strategies

MODULE 4 Multiply!

Count Up a Row

Now look at these bins.

- How can you use the word *rows* to describe the number of bins?
- How can you use rows to help you estimate the total number of apples?

1 Look Around You

Where can you find rows around your school or neighborhood? Look up at the ceiling. Look down at the floor. List the places where you see rows.

2 Go Out and Draw

Use your list to help you start looking for rows. Make a drawing of each group of rows you find.

Word Bank

- array
- combination
- factor
- multiplication
- product

3 Share with Your Class

Share your drawings with your class. Did any of your classmates draw the same rows you did?

Investigations Preview

Learn about rows, arrays, and multiplication. They can help you plan and make everything from a better egg carton to a great playground.

Yolks for 24 Folks (pages 156–157)

How would you make an egg carton for 24 eggs? Knowing what an array is will help you.

Plan a Perfect Playground

(pages 190–192)

How would you plan a playground? You will use multiplication to help you plan one.

SECTION A

Exploring Groups and Arrays

LESSON 1

Sizing Up Groups!

Lots of things come in groups. Chopsticks come in groups of 2. Checkers come in groups of 24. Make a list of all the groups you can find on these pages.

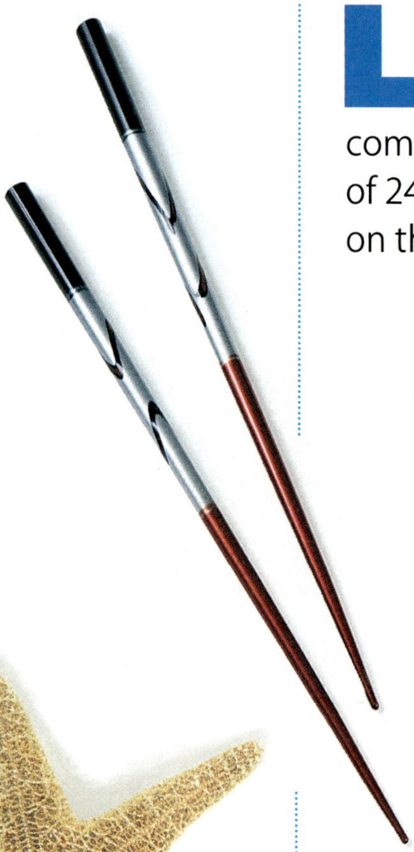

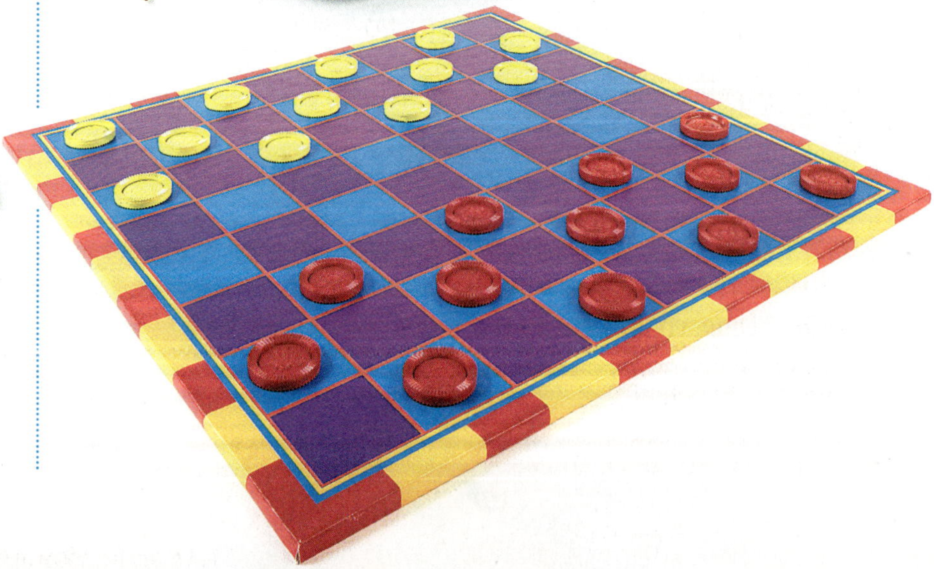

ACTIVITY 1 Go Group Hunting!

With Your Group Go group hunting in your classroom. You can find groups in desks, under chairs, even on people! Pick one person in your group to be the recorder. Share your list with the class.

1. What is the biggest group anyone found?
2. What size group did your class find most often?
3. Why do you think that size of group was found most often?

TOOLS AND TECHNIQUES

You could use a chart like the one above to write down what you find. How else could you record the groups you find?

ACTIVITY 2 How Many in All?

On Your Own All spiders have eight legs. How many legs do three spiders have in all? Drawing a picture can help you solve problems.

DRAWING TO LEARN

Draw a picture of the question you write. Your classmate can use it to help answer the question

1 Draw pictures to answer any two of these questions.

a. How many wheels are on 5 cars?
b. How many legs are on 6 frogs?
c. How many cans are in 4 six-packs?

2 Write a question of your own. Have a classmate solve it.

3 Drawing a chart is another way to solve a problem. Draw a chart like the one below. Find the total number of objects in more than one group.

4 Compare the patterns you find with those a classmate found.

REASONING AND PROBLEM SOLVING

Ask yourself, "Can I find any patterns in the chart?"

Do You Remember?

Try It!

Tell how many. Then tell which has the greatest number.

1. cans in 3 six-packs
2. days in 3 weeks
3. legs on 3 frogs
4. tennis balls in 4 cans
5. legs on 6 frogs
6. legs on 4 spiders

Use number sense. Find only the sums greater than 2,400 + 1,600.

7. 2,435 + 1,611
8. 2,394 + 1,587
9. 1,907 + 2,000
10. 3,912 + 5,126

Think About It

11. Describe in writing a pattern you find in your chart.

LESSON 2

What's an Array?

ACTIVITY 1 Groups and Rows

With Your Class Some groups of objects can be arranged in a pattern called an **array.** You can use counters to make arrays.

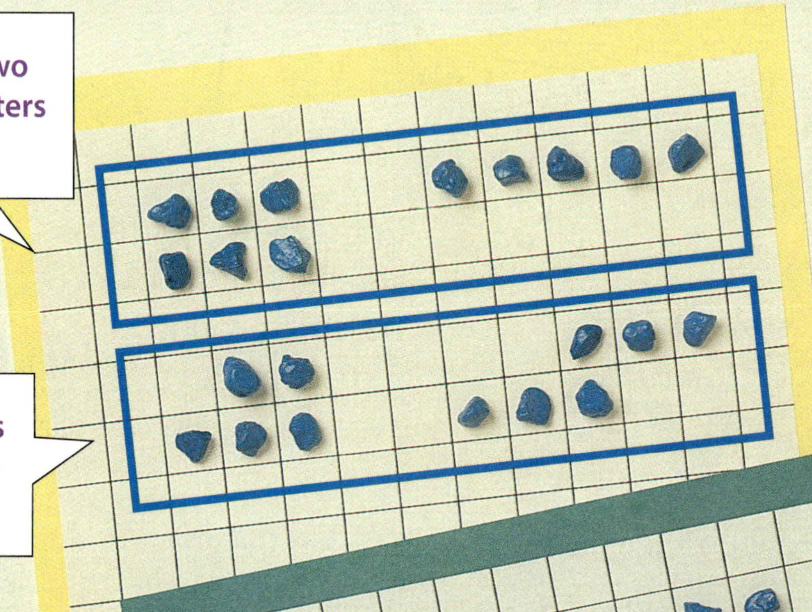

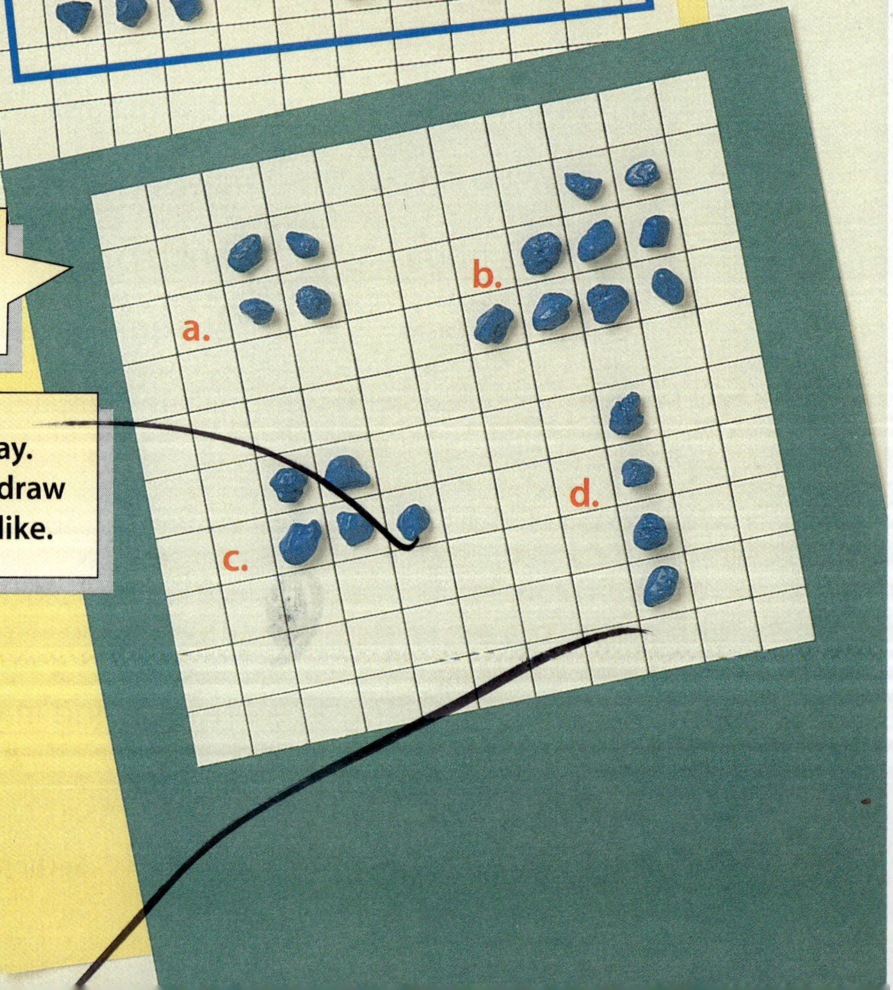

1. Which of the four groups are arrays?

2. Describe an array. Use words and draw pictures, if you like.

Self-Check *Look for patterns around you that show an array.*

Activity 2 Tables of Arrays

On Your Own Show an array. Then make a table that describes your array. Use drawings or counters.

What You'll Need

- *12 counters*

This pattern is a 2-by-3 array. The table describes the array.

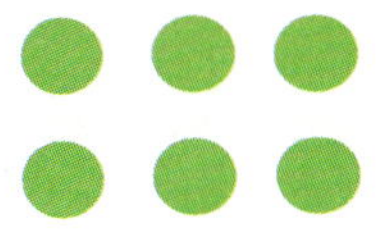

Rows repeated	Number in row
2 times	3

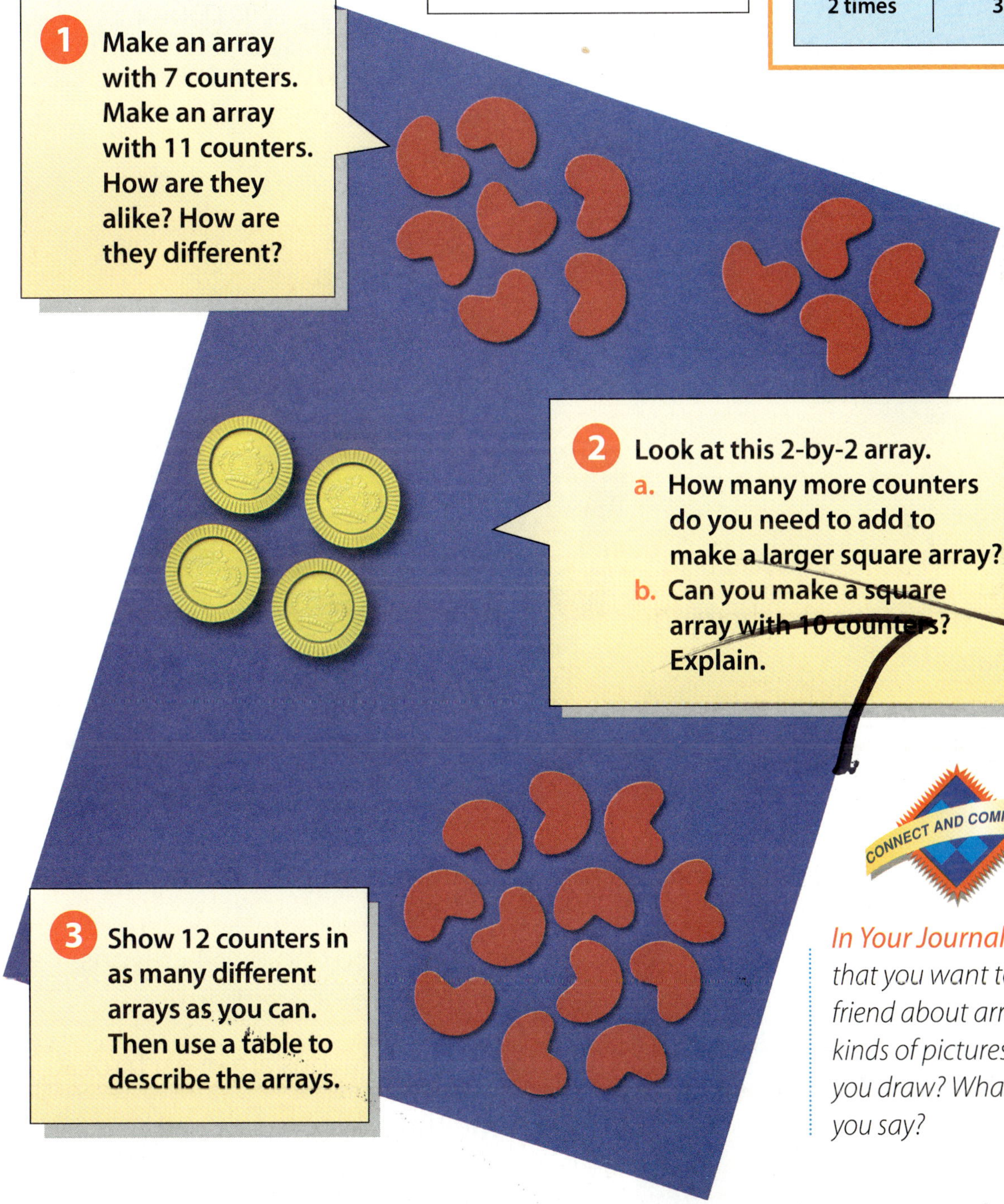

1 Make an array with 7 counters. Make an array with 11 counters. How are they alike? How are they different?

2 Look at this 2-by-2 array.

a. How many more counters do you need to add to make a larger square array?

b. Can you make a square array with 10 counters? Explain.

3 Show 12 counters in as many different arrays as you can. Then use a table to describe the arrays.

CONNECT AND COMMUNICATE

In Your Journal *Suppose that you want to tell a friend about arrays. What kinds of pictures would you draw? What would you say?*

Exercises and Problems

Arrays Around You

Take a look at these arrays. Write your answers on your own sheet of paper.

Muffin Pans

1. How many rows does this pan have?
2. Can you count the rows in the pan in more than one way? Explain your answer.

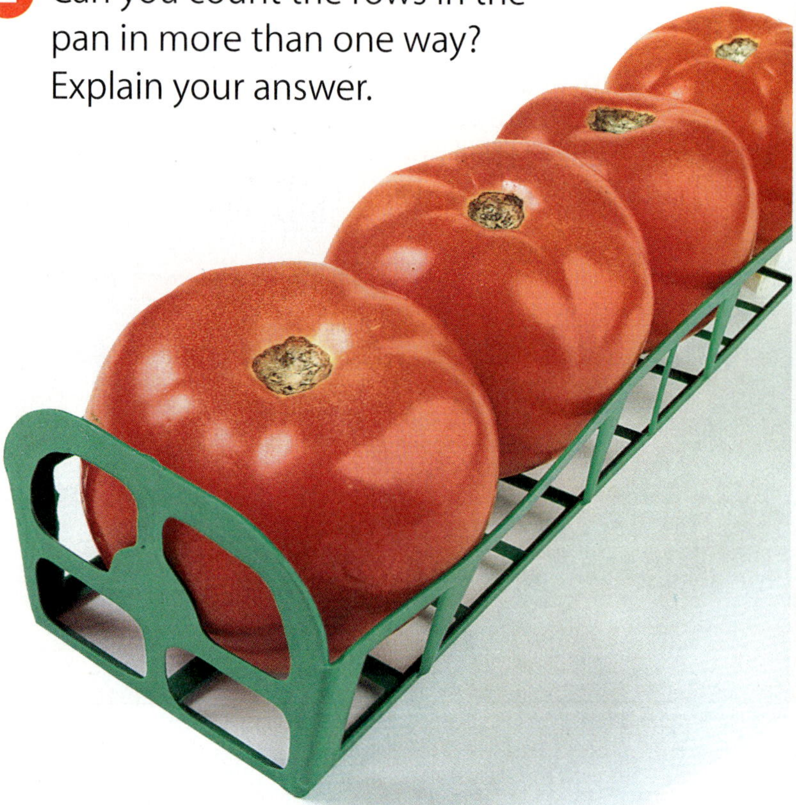

Tomato Pack

3. Draw a different array showing 4 tomatoes.
4. How many different arrays can you make with 5 tomatoes?

Crayons

5. This crayon box holds 64 crayons. How many rows are there?
6. How many crayons are in each row?
7. Name the crayon array.

Watercolors

8 Draw an array showing how many paints are in this paint set. Name the array in two different ways.

9 Make a drawing showing one more row in the array. Name the new array.

Telephone

10 Draw an array showing the phone buttons. Name the array in two different ways.

11 Make a drawing showing how you would add 3 new buttons to the phone array. Name the new array.

Drink Tray

12 The 4 cups below make a square array. Draw two other square arrays.

13 Find two arrays on these pages with the same number of rows. How are the arrays alike? How are they different?

14 Draw two arrays that hold an odd number of objects. Do you think arrays with an odd number of objects always have an odd number of rows? Write a sentence to explain.

Investigation

Yolks for 24 Folks

Imagine you own a company that sells eggs. You want to sell eggs in cartons of 24. Other egg companies sell eggs in cartons of 12! What you need to do is design a carton to hold 24 eggs. Good luck!

What would it be like to carry one row of 24 eggs home from the store?

Work with your group. Here are your goals.

1. **Think** of different ways to make a carton for 24 eggs. Use what you know about arrays.
2. **Choose** a design you think works well.

Now work on your own.

3. **Suppose** all your classmates buy eggs from your company. Explain in writing why your carton for 24 eggs is a good idea.
4. **Think** about making an egg carton for 23 eggs. Explain how your plan would change.

This egg package comes from Japan. It is made of rice straw.

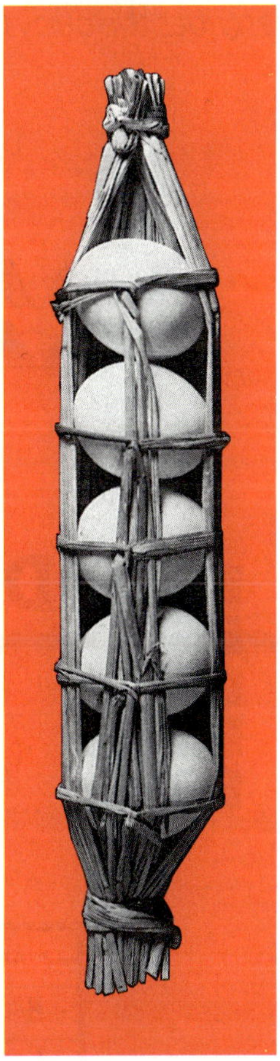

Ask Yourself

- ☐ What do I need to know about eggs before I begin?
- ☐ How can I use drawings and arrays to help me plan my carton?
- ☐ Will my plan work?
- ☐ Will my carton make it safe and easy to carry 24 eggs?
- ☐ What can I say about my carton so that others will think it is a good idea?

SECTION B

Connecting Arrays to Multiplication

LESSON 3

Factors and Times

TOOLS AND TECHNIQUES

You can draw arrays on a computer. You can also use the computer to make a table that describes the arrays.

You can write a number sentence to tell how many objects are in an array.

ACTIVITY 1 Arrays and Factors

With Your Class

1. Complete a table like this for the arrays below.

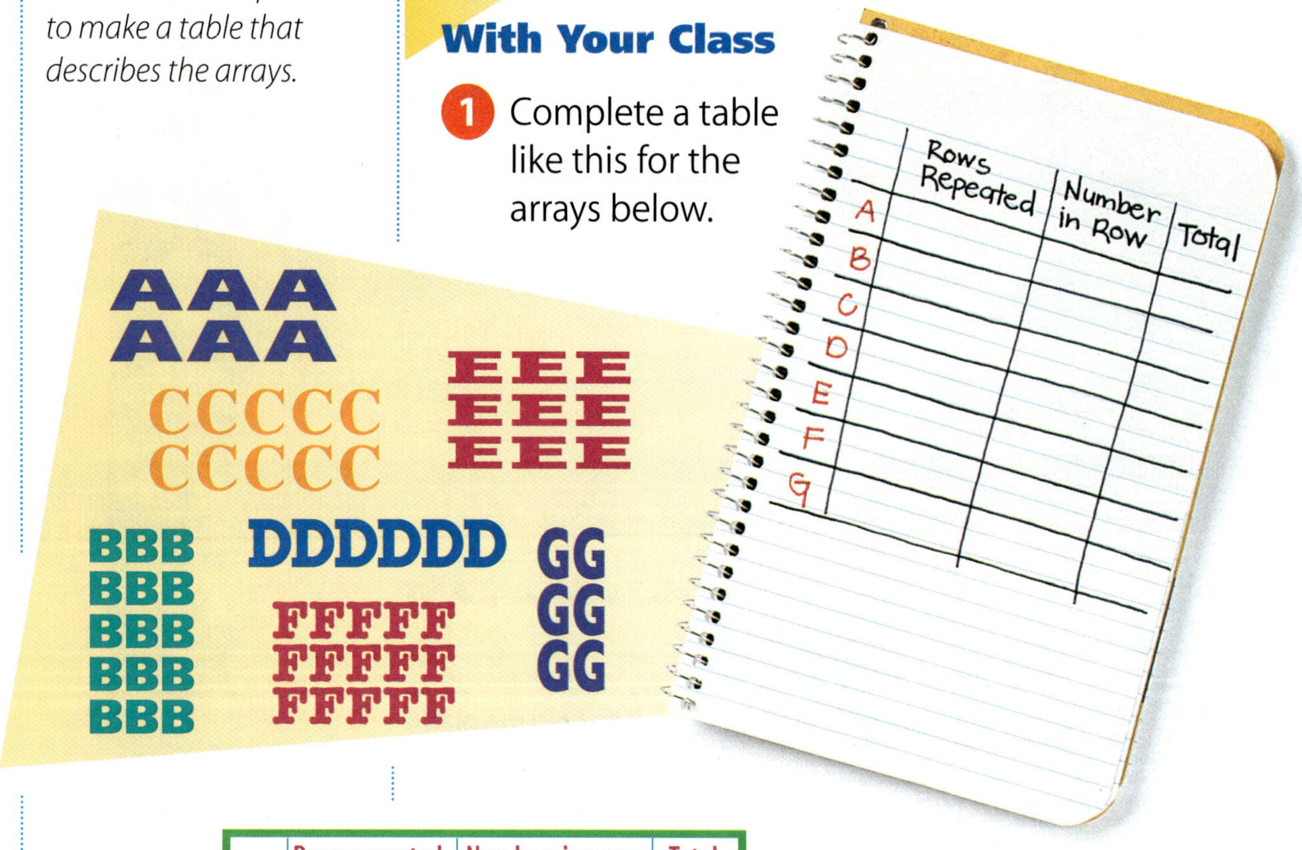

	Rows repeated	Numbers in a row	Total
H	5 times	2	
I	2 times	5	
J	4 times	6	
K	3 times	4	

2. Draw each array described in this table. Then complete the table.

Activity 2 Arrays and Sentences

With Your Class A table is one way to describe an array. You can also write a **multiplication** sentence.

Row Repeated		Number in Row		Total
5	×	2	=	10
factor		factor		product

Five times two equals ten.

Write a multiplication sentence for each array that you drew in Activity 1.

Do You Remember?

Try It!

Which have the product 12? Draw arrays.

1. 4 × 3 2. 3 × 3 3. 2 × 6 4. 3 × 5

Is 3 a factor? Write yes or no.

5. ■ × ▲ = 20
6. ■ × ▲ = 12
7. ■ × ▲ = 8
8. ■ × ▲ = 18

Use mental math. Find the sums greater than 30.

9. 24 + 7 10. 12 + 13 11. 26 + 8
12. 19 + 22 13. 15 + 12 14. 23 + 13

Think About It

15. How can you use arrays to find out if 4 is a factor of 20? Write to explain.

Self-Check *How can you use addition to check your product? How else can you check your product?*

LESSON 4

THE GREAT ARRAY GAME

What You'll Need

- *gameboard*
- *2 number cubes*
- *grid paper*
- *scissors*
- *marker or crayon*

ACTIVITY 1 Rules of the Game

With Your Partner The object is to cover more squares with arrays than your partner does.

1. **Roll** number cubes. Think of the numbers you roll as a pair of factors.

2. **Choose** a color. Use the same color for the whole game.

3. **Color** an array for the numbers you rolled. Write a multiplication sentence.

4. **Cut** out the array.

5 **Cover up.** Take turns. Cover an empty part of the gameboard with your array. Do not overlap arrays. If your array is too large to fit, you lose your next turn. If each player loses three turns in a row, the game is over.

6 **Add** the products for each player's arrays. The player with the greatest sum wins.

DRAWING TO LEARN

Draw one of your arrays twice. Make the number of rows in the second drawing equal the number in a row of the first. Repeat for two other arrays. What do you notice?

What You'll Need

- *gameboard*
- *2 number cubes*
- *arrays from Activity 1*

ACTIVITY 2 Game Twists!

Pick one or two new ways to play the game.

1. **Product Play** Roll the number cubes. Find two arrays with the same product, and place both of them on the gameboard.
2. **Two-Square Touch** Place the first array. Each new array must touch two squares of another array.
3. **Roll Again** If an array is too big, roll one number cube again. Make an array with the one new factor and the old factor. If the array is still too big, you lose your next turn.

Do You Remember?

Try It!

Find a pair of factors for each product. Draw arrays for help.

1. 30
2. 24
3. 18
4. 15
5. 36
6. 12
7. 20
8. 4

Write the numbers in order from least to greatest.

9. 763; 209; 454
10. 1,327; 1,806; 928
11. 555; 333; 777
12. 6,259; 4,783; 6,315

Think About It

13. Compare the pairs of factors for Exercises 1 and 4. What do you notice? Do the same for Exercises 2 and 6 and Exercises 3 and 5. Describe any patterns you see.

Gathering the Facts

LESSON 5

Use what you know about arrays with factors 1 through 6.

Activity 1 Make a Table

On Your Own Make a blank multiplication table like the one in the picture.

1. Cover squares on the table with two pieces of paper. The numbers shown in blue are the factors. The picture shows a 6-by-6 array.

2. The product of 6 × 6 is 36. The product is written on the bottom right corner. Write the product of 6 × 6 in your own table.

3. Now move your two pieces of paper. Show a 5-by-5 array. Write the product of 5 × 5 in your table.

4. How many squares will be in a 3-by-4 array? Find out by using your pieces of paper. Write the product 3 × 4 in your table.

5. Cover different parts of the table. Write the product of the two factors in each square.

CONNECT AND COMMUNICATE

What can you say about the numbers across from the factor 6 and the numbers down from factor 6?

What You'll Need

- *grid paper*
- *ruler*
- *scissors*

What You'll Need

- *arrays from Great Array Game*

ACTIVITY 2

Arrays in Your Table

With Your Group Use some of the arrays from the Great Array Game. Place a dot in the upper left corner of each array. Place a dot on the table.

1 **Take one of your arrays. Place its array dot on top of the table dot.**

2 **Lift the lower right corner of the array. What number do you see? How does that number compare with the product written on the array? Explain.**

3 **Take turns with other arrays, too.**

ACTIVITY OPTION

Pick a number between 1 and 36 that is not in your table. Explain in writing why it doesn't appear in the table.

ACTIVITY 3 Patterns, Patterns

With Your Group Go back to using two pieces of paper, as you did on page 163.

1. Each group member should place the two papers to show the product 20. What are the factors?

2. Draw an array matching the factors in Step 1. Do all group members have the same array? Explain your answer.

3. Write a multiplication sentence for the array you drew in Step 2. How is your sentence different from the sentences of other members of your group?

Do You Remember? Try It!

Draw one array for each product. Write a multiplication sentence. Use your multiplication table for help.

1. 12 **2.** 24 **3.** 16 **4.** 25 **5.** 15 **6.** 3

Estimate. Find exact answers for estimates greater than 20.

7. 77 − 56 **8.** 38 + 51 **9.** 127 − 109

10. 250 − 51 **11.** 19 + 17 **12.** 227 − 200

Think About It

13. Compare the products in Exercises 1 through 6. Do all odd products have two odd factors? Explain.

Do You Remember?

Cumulative Review

Stamps

Check out the stamps! Stamps are used to pay for the cost of mailing letters and packages. When you buy stamps at the post office, you pay the number of cents printed on each stamp.

Answer these questions. Choose mental math, paper and pencil, or a calculator.

Price Check!

1. What is the price of the Indian Art stamp?

2. What is the difference between the price of the Giraffe stamp and the Box Turtle stamp?

3. How much do two Love stamps cost?

4. What is the total price of the stamps in the 1-by-5 array?

Check the Facts.

5. The Beaver and the Blue Jay stamps came out in 1987. How many years ago is that?

Find the Stamps.

6. Suppose you need 50¢ in stamps to mail a letter to Brazil. Find at least two ways to choose the stamps.

7. Choose the stamp you like best. If you buy one of these stamps with $1, how much change do you get back?

8. Imagine that your new collection includes 5 Giant Panda stamps and 13 Blue Jay stamps. Trade 8 Blue Jay stamps for 6 Giant Panda stamps. How many of each stamp will you have?

9. How many 29¢ stamps can you buy with the money shown below? How much will be left over?

Check Your Math Power

10. Suppose that you can still buy all of these stamps at the post office. Which stamps would you buy to spend exactly $2? Show at least three ways.

LESSON 6 Multiplying with [redacted] Two-Two

LITERATURE

Read this story to find out how Jacob got his strange name. You'll also learn a little about multiplication.

When he was six years old, a mere [redacted], he was known as Jacob Two-Two. He was given the name because he was two plus two plus two years old. He had two ears and two eyes and two feet and two shoes. He also had two older brothers, [redacted] and [redacted], and two older sisters, [redacted] and [redacted]. But most of all, he was given the name because, as Jacob Two-Two himself once admitted, "I am the littlest in our family. Nobody hears what I say the first time. They only pay attention if I say things two times." But now that he was eight years old he felt that he was too grown up to go by such a childish name. All the same, it stuck to him. After all, he still had two older brothers and two older sisters. And, as they were quick to point out, if he had once been two plus two plus two years old, he was now—come to think of it—only two times two times two years old. Not much of a difference, they said, but they really didn't understand.

From *[redacted] Two-Two and the Dinosaur*
by Mordecai Richler

ACTIVITY 1

Double Once

With Your Class Jacob uses addition and multiplication to think about his age. Try thinking like Jacob!

1. Write an addition sentence for "two plus two plus two years old."
2. You can think of "Two-Two" as 4. Write an addition sentence.
3. Write a multiplication sentence for two twos. You may want to draw a 2-by-2 array for help.

When you multiply by 2, think of the addition double. This method is called doubling.

$$2 \times 9 = 18$$

Think

$$9 + 9 = 18$$

REASONING AND PROBLEM SOLVING

How is a multiplication sentence like an addition sentence? How is it different?

Do You Remember?

Try It!

Write a multiplication sentence for each.

1. 7 + 7
2. 8 + 8
3. 5 + 5

Find the products greater than 5 + 5.

4. 2 × 3
5. 2 × 5
6. 9 × 2
7. 4 × 2
8. 2 × 7
9. 6 × 2
10. 2 × 9
11. 2 × 6
12. 3 × 2

Find the missing number.

13. 2 ft = ■ in.
14. 2 lb = ■ oz
15. 2 gal = ■ qt

Think About It

16. Is it faster to double a number by adding, or by multiplying? Write your answer.

CONNECT AND COMMUNICATE

In Your Journal *Write a note to a friend about doubling. Explain how addition can help you think about multiplying by two.*

What You'll Need

- *24 counters*

Activity 2 Double Twice

With Your Group What happens when you double a number twice? Use arrays to find out.

1 Make an array with one row.

2 Double the array. Doubling is like multiplying by two.

$2 \times 3 = 6$

Think

$3 + 3 = 6$

3 Double the array again. Doubling two times is like multiplying by four.

$$\begin{array}{r} 3 \\ \times\ 4 \\ \hline 12 \end{array}$$

You can show multiplication this way too.

Think

$2 \times 3 = 6$

and

$2 \times 6 = 12$

Reasoning and Problem Solving

Is there more than one way to double an array? Explain in writing some ways.

4 Find the product. Double a double or draw arrays to help.

a. 4×5 **b.** 4×6 **c.** 5×4 **d.** 7×4

ACTIVITY 3 What's Your Order?

With Your Class Work with counters or draw pictures to show arrays.

1. This array shows 6 groups of 4. What is the product of 6 and 4?

2. Make an array to show 4 groups of 6. What is the product of 4 and 6?

3. How do 4 × 6 and 6 × 4 compare?

4. Draw arrays to show 4 × 3 and 3 × 4. How do the products of 4 × 3 and 3 × 4 compare? Draw a picture to show your answer.

> **When we multiply, the order of the factors does not matter. We call this the**
>
> **Commutative Property of Multiplication.**
>
> **4 × 3 = 3 × 4**

5. Explain how the Commutative Properties of Multiplication and Addition are alike.

What You'll Need

- *24 counters*

ACTIVITY OPTION

Write some doubling doubles problems of your own. Trade problems with a partner.

DRAWING TO LEARN

Draw arrays to show

- *how old you will be when you are two times three times two years old.*
- *double the number of pencils on your desk. Double again.*

What You'll Need

- *mutiplication table*

Activity 4 Table the Facts

On Your Own Use the multiplication table. Record all the products of the twos and fours.

×	1	2	3	4	5	6	7	8	9
1									
2							14		
3									
4									
5									
6									
7									
8									
9									

1. The table shows $2 \times 7 = 14$. Where else did you show that the product of 2 and 7 is 14?

2. a. How many different twos facts are there?
   b. How many different fours facts are there?

3. Explain how you can use the Commutative Property to make learning the facts easier.

Do You Remember?

Try It!

Use your multiplication table. Write two number sentences for the product.

1. 8 **2.** 2 **3.** 32 **4.** 20 **5.** 14

6. 10 **7.** 28 **8.** 18 **9.** 16 **10.** 24

Use mental math to solve.

11. $7 + 6$ **12.** $14 - 8$ **13.** $8 + 4$ **14.** $16 - 9$

Think About It

15. How could you use doubling to fill in the eights on your multiplication table?

Five, Ten, Fifteen . . .

LESSON 7

What would you buy with a bunch of nickels? Spend away!

ACTIVITY 1 Nickel Counts

With Your Class

1. How many nickels do you see? How many cents do these nickels make?
2. Spend 7 nickels. Write a multiplication sentence to show how much you spent.
3. Explain how you can use nickels to find the product in this multiplication sentence.

$$6 \times 5 = ?$$

4. Suppose you don't have any nickels to count. Explain one way you can multiply by five.

ACTIVITY 2 Skip by Fives

On Your Own Do you like to skip count?

What You'll Need
- *multiplication table*

1. Find these products.

a. 4 × 5	b. 8 × 5	c. 5 × 5
d. 5 × 6	e. 5 × 3	f. 9 × 5

2. Now fill in the fives facts on your multiplication table.

Count Your Change

Go shopping with nickels. Write multiplication sentences to record your answers.

Marbles

1 a. How many marbles can you buy with 9 nickels?
b. How many marbles can you buy with 25 nickels?

Bubbles

2 How many nickels do you need to buy the bubbles? Write how you found out.

Shells

3 a. How many nickels do you need to buy 1 shell?
b. How many nickels do you need to buy 6 shells?

Balloons

4. How much do 8 balloons cost?
5. Explain how you can use doubling to figure out the price of balloons.

Cactus

6. How can you skip count to find how many nickels you need to buy this cactus? Write to explain.

Stickers

7. How many nickels are needed to buy the stickers?
8. Which costs more, one marble or one sticker? Explain how you know.

Chalk

9. How much does it cost to buy 3 pieces of chalk?
10. Can you buy 6 pieces of chalk with 4 nickels?

LESSON 8 Keeping Count

What You'll Need
- *1 large sheet of paper*
- *markers*
- *4 craft sticks (colored on one side) or 4 coins*

People of all cultures like to play games. Here is a game that uses four sticks and a game circle. It is much like a game that is played by some Apache people. The Apache are Native Americans.

ACTIVITY 1 Play the Game!

With Your Partner Draw a game circle. Toss the sticks to move. Try to be the first to move a marker three times around the game circle.

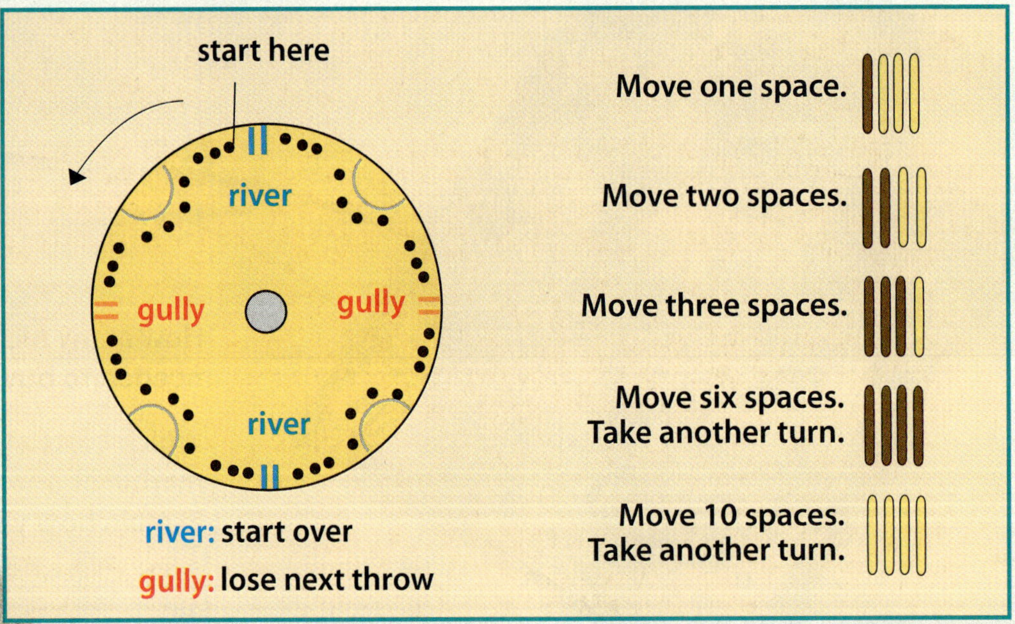

When you toss a stick, are you more likely to get (dark stick) than (light stick)? Why or why not?

ACTIVITY 2 Counting Pictures

With Your Group Pictographs help you compare numbers of objects or people.

1. How can skip counting help you read this graph?
2. How many thousand Apache people live in Arizona? Explain how you got your answer.
3. How can the graph tell you how many times more Apache people live in New Mexico than in Texas?

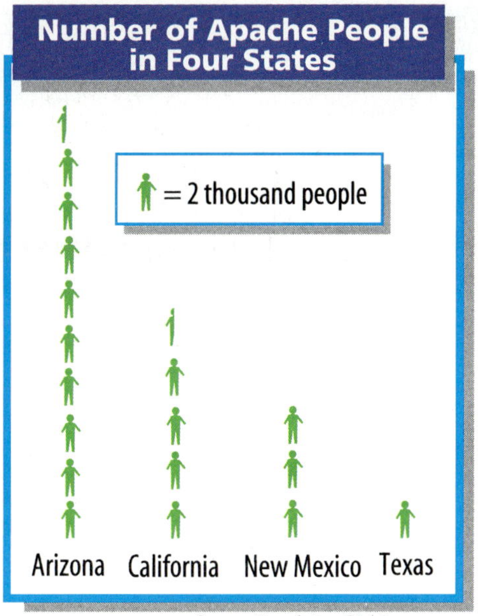

Source: Population Division, Bureau of the Census, 1992

Do You Remember? Try It!

 stands for 5 books. Write a multiplication sentence.

1.  2. 

3. 

Draw a picture to stand for 4 trees. Use the picture to show the following.

4. 8 trees 5. 12 trees 6. 24 trees

Estimate.

7. 76 + 12 8. 94 + 9 9. 80 − 14
10. 58 + 18 11. 92 − 23 12. 105 + 25

Think About It

13. How could you use doubling in Exercise 1 to show 30 books?

TOOLS AND TECHNIQUES

How to Read a Pictograph

1. *Look at the key to find out how many each picture stands for.*
2. *Count the pictures in the column.*
3. *Multiply the number of pictures in the column by how many each picture stands for.*

LESSON 9 Multiply Your Way

TOOLS AND TECHNIQUES

The multiplication table below shows all the facts you learned in Section C. How can you use these facts to help you multiply by three?

×	1	2	3	4	5	6	7	8	9
1		2		4	5				
2	2	4	6	8	10	12	14	16	18
3		6		12	15				
4	4	8	12	16	20	24	28	32	36
5	5	10	15	20	25	30	35	40	45
6		12		24	30				
7		14		28	35				
8		16		32	40				
9		18		36	45				

ACTIVITY 1 Times Three

With Your Group You know different ways to multiply. You've made arrays to multiply. You've used doubling to multiply by two and four. You've skip counted to multiply by five. Now use all you know to find your own way to multiply by three.

1. Start by using the ways you know.
   a. Try skip counting to find 3 × 8.
   b. You know 2 × 7. Use this fact to complete the sentence below.

   3 × 7 = ?

   c. You know 4 × 6. How can you find 3 × 6?

   3 × 6 = ?

2. Now use the strategy you like best to multiply.

   a. $\begin{array}{r} 9 \\ \times 3 \\ \hline \end{array}$ b. $\begin{array}{r} 5 \\ \times 3 \\ \hline \end{array}$ c. $\begin{array}{r} 3 \\ \times 4 \\ \hline \end{array}$ d. $\begin{array}{r} 3 \\ \times 3 \\ \hline \end{array}$

3. Take turns teaching each other your ways for multiplying by three. Try with one of the multiplications below.

3 × 7 or **8 × 3**

4. Now fill in the threes facts on your multiplication table.

Which way do you like best?

DRAWING TO LEARN

Draw a picture to help explain your multiplication method.

Do You Remember?

Try It!

Which products are odd? Which are even? Guess before you multiply.

1. 7 × 3
2. 3 × 8
3. 3 × 6
4. 9 × 3
5. 3 × 7
6. 3 × 9
7. 5 × 3
8. 3 × 4
9. 6 × 3

Use mental math.

10. 29 + 8
11. 16 + 7
12. 15 + 8
13. 23 + 8
14. 36 + 6
15. 48 + 9

Think About It

16. Write true or false. Explain.
    odd × even = odd   odd × odd = even

CONNECT AND COMMUNICATE

Discuss the different ways of multiplying by three that your class found. How are the ways different from one another? What do they all have in common?

REASONING AND PROBLEM SOLVING

Use your calculator to multiply some of the data by 1,000. Look for a pattern. Do you think you will always need a calculator to multiply by 1,000?

ACTIVITY 2 Multiplying Data

One piece of data tells a fact. A group of data tells a story. What stories do the data below tell?

With Your Group The tables show how much grain was produced in five states in one year.

Each number shows how many millions of bushels were produced. One million is a big number: 1,000,000!

Millions of Bushels Produced

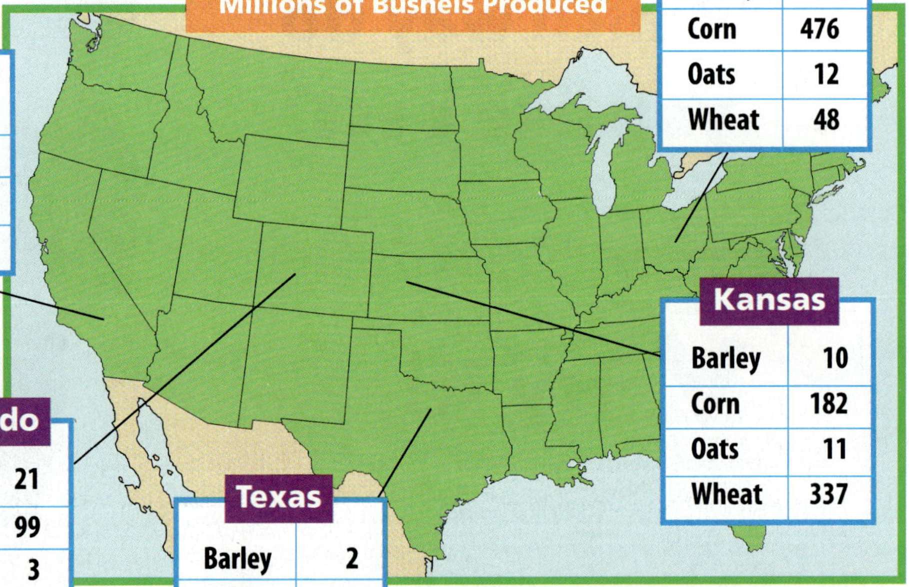

California

Barley	24
Corn	38
Oats	3
Wheat	52

Colorado

Barley	21
Corn	99
Oats	3
Wheat	96

Texas

Barley	2
Corn	149
Oats	8
Wheat	120

Ohio

Barley	<1
Corn	476
Oats	12
Wheat	48

Kansas

Barley	10
Corn	182
Oats	11
Wheat	337

Source: *Agriculture Statistics, 1987* 1988 edition. USDA

1. You know $8 \times 3 = 24$. How can you use this fact to tell about barley and oat production in California?

2. How can you use $3 \times 4 = 12$ to compare oat production in California and Ohio?

3. Compare one of the following.
   a. oat and barley production in Colorado
   b. oat and barley production in Texas

ACTIVITY 3 Making Oatmeal

On Your Own Use the recipe on the lid. Answer these questions.

1. How much water do you need to make oatmeal for 6 people?
2. Pick a group of people. List what you need to make oatmeal for them.

Now make up your own problems.

3. Write two problems you can answer using the chart. Then find the answers.
4. Now write two problems you cannot answer using the chart. List the data you need to answer these problems.

Quick Oats

Servings	1	3	6
Water*	2/3 cup	2 cups	4 cups
Oats	1/3 cup	1 cup	2 cups
Salt (optional)	dash	1/8 tsp.	1/4 tsp.

*For thicker oatmeal use less water. For thinner oatmeal use more water.

Do You Remember? Try It!

Make the number sentence true.

1. $4 \times 3 = ■$
2. $3 \times ■ = 27$
3. $3 \times ■ = 18$
4. $■ + 8 = 12$
5. $12 + ■ = 18$
6. $5 \times ■ = 15$
7. $■ \times 3 = 9$
8. $6 + ■ = 15$
9. $16 - ■ = 12$
10. $8 \times 3 = ■$

Think About It

11. Write $■ \times ■ = 24$ in four different ways.

ACTIVITY OPTION

Write down a fact you found in any of your school books. Use the fact to write a problem for someone to solve.

LESSON 10 Combination Lunch

CONNECT AND COMMUNICATE

Be sure you understand a problem before you start to solve it. You may want to try explaining the problem to a friend.

Here are 4 breads and 3 fillings. How many different kinds of sandwiches can you make?

bagel	cheese
naan	turkey
pita	tomato
tortilla	

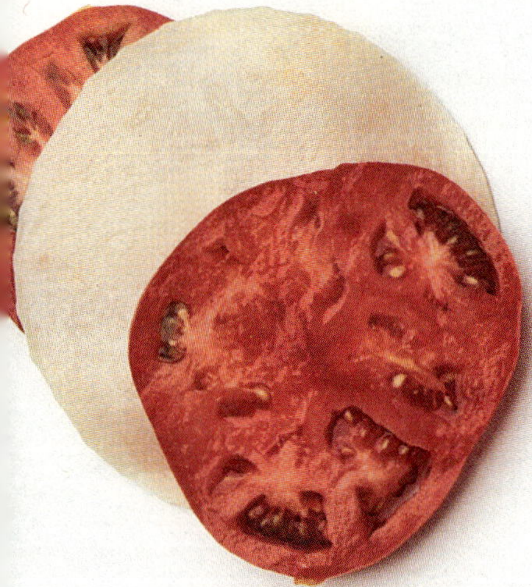

ACTIVITY 1 What's for Lunch?

With Your Group Use 1 bread and 1 filling for each sandwich.

1. Name some of the kinds of sandwiches.

2 Choose a way to find all the combinations. Making a chart is one. Making a list is another. Name another way. Then pick one way.

3 Use your way to find all the combinations.

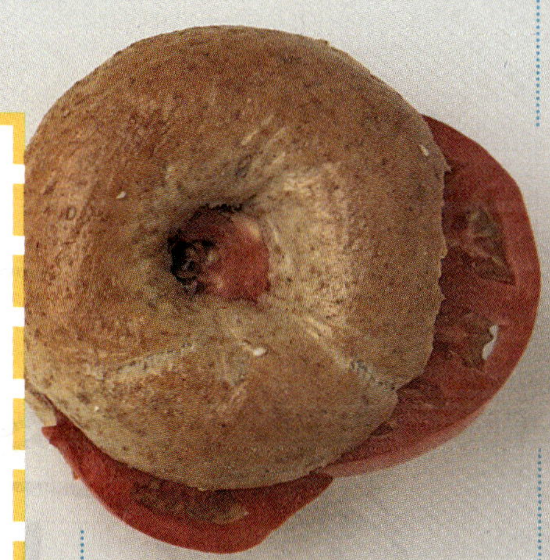

Do You Remember?

Try It!

Find the number of combinations for each.

1. 3 breads, 4 fillings
2. 2 breads, 3 fillings
3. 5 breads, 6 fillings
4. 3 breads, 1 filling
5. 4 breads, 4 fillings
6. 4 breads, 5 fillings

Solve those with answers less than 1,000.

7. 356 + 78
8. 411 − 94
9. 906 + 755
10. 788 + 222

Think About It

11. What way do you like best to find combinations of breads and fillings? Explain in writing.

Self-Check *Check your work by trying another strategy. Did you find the same number of combinations?*

LESSON 11

On a Roll!

You know how to add two numbers. How is addition different from multiplication? Roll some number cubes to find out.

What You'll Need

- *2 number cubes*

ACTIVITY 1 Compare Some Pairs

With Your Partner For each turn follow these steps. Keep track of your work in a chart.

1. **Roll** the number cubes. Write the two numbers under *Numbers* on your chart.

2. **Write** the sum of the two numbers under *Sum*. Then write the product of the two numbers under *Product*.
3. **Take** turns until each partner has rolled ten times.
4. **Fill in** the *Symbol* column on your chart.

- If the sum is less than the product, write <.
- If the sum is the same as the product, write =.
- If the sum is greater than the product, write >.

5. Use your chart. Answer these questions.
   a. Does any pair of numbers have a sum equal to its product? If so, which pair?
   b. How many of your pairs have a sum less than the product?
   c. Which pairs of numbers have a sum greater than the product?

6. Look at the products with 1 as a factor. Write a sentence to explain what happens when you multiply by 1. Fill in the facts for 1 in your multiplication table.

Self-Check *The multiplication table can help you check your facts. Do you see patterns? If not, a product may be wrong.*

Do You Remember?

Try It!

Use the following number sentence.

■ × ▲ + ● = ?

Arrange the numbers in each exercise to get the greatest total. Use a calculator if you need it.

1. 2, 4, 5 **2.** 1, 4, 6 **3.** 4, 5, 6 **4.** 3, 5, 6 **5.** 2, 3, 5

Write the numbers in order from least to greatest.

6. 3,427; 3,724; 3,274 **7.** 21,857; 28,751; 25,817

8. 9,498; 9,849; 9,489 **9.** 8,702; 8,207; 8,072

10. 67,512; 65,721; 67,251 **11.** 10,429; 14,209; 14,902

Think About It

12. Think about Exercises 1 through 5. How would you arrange three numbers to get the least total? Explain.

5 Ways to Multiply

How do you multiply? Look at five different ways. Choose three of the five ways. Write sentences to explain your thinking.

Arrays

1. Write a multiplication sentence to describe the number of boxes shown on the right. Explain it.

2. How can multiplying help you find the number of items in an array?

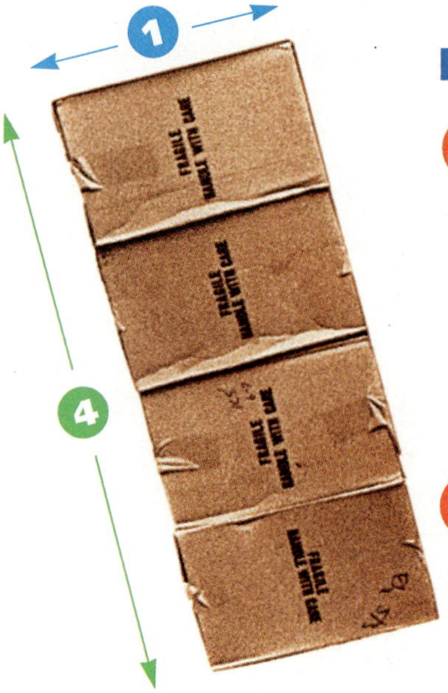

Doubling

3. Double the array on the left. Then double the new array. Write a multiplication sentence for each array.

4. How could you use doubling to teach yourself how to multiply with 8?

Skip Counting

5. When do you use skip counting outside of math class?

6. How is skip counting like adding?

7. How is skip counting like multiplying?

"Five, ten,

Each of the boxes in the picture holds foam plastic hats. Each box weighs five pounds.

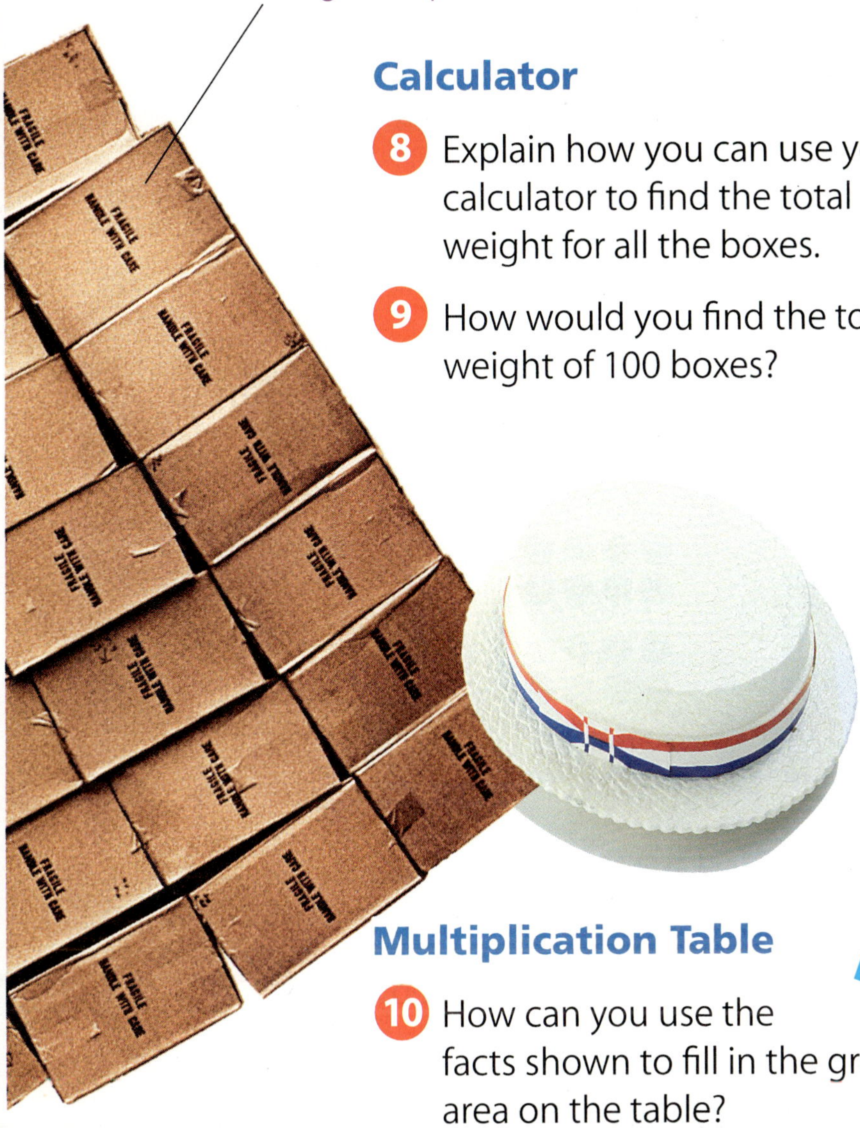

Calculator

8 Explain how you can use your calculator to find the total weight for all the boxes.

9 How would you find the total weight of 100 boxes?

Multiplication Table

x	1	2	3	4	5	6	7	8	9
1	1	2	3	4	5				
2	2	4	6	8	10				
3	3	6	9	12	15				
4	4	8	12	16	20				
5	5	10	15	20	25				
6	6	12	18	24	30				
7	7	14	21	28	35				
8	8	16	24	32	40				
9	9	18	27	36	45				

10 How can you use the facts shown to fill in the green area on the table?

11 How many facts do you have left to learn? Explain how you got your answer.

12 Did you count 7 × 6 and 6 × 7 as one fact or two facts? Explain.

CONNECT AND COMMUNICATE

In Your Journal Look at the different ways to multiply on these pages. Which way is the easiest for you? Which way is the hardest for you? Explain your answers.

fifteen, twenty..."

Do You Remember? Cumulative Review

Looking Back

Choose the best answer. Write *a, b, c,* or *d*.

1. Which is a double 2-by-5 array?

a. 

b. 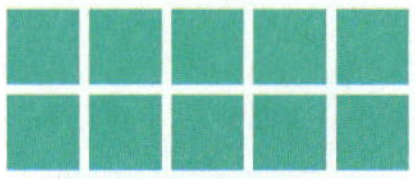

c. 

d. none of these

2. Which strategy will find the product of 4 × 3?
   a. adding 3 + 3 + 3
   b. finding 2 × 3 and doubling
   c. adding 4 + 3 and doubling
   d. none of these

3. How many circles are shown?

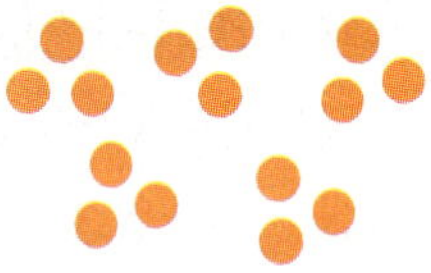

   a. 3 + 3 + 3 b. 3 × 4
   c. 5 × 3 d. 3 × 3

4. Which pairs have the same product?
   a. 4 × 2 and 5 × 3
   b. 9 × 4 and 5 × 8
   c. 3 × 8 and 6 × 4
   d. 2 × 6 and 4 × 5

Use the pictures shown below to do Exercises 5 through 7.

a. 

b. 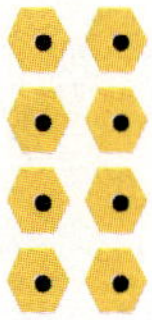

c. 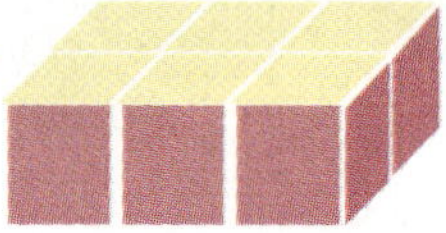

d. 

5. What picture above shows 16 objects?

6. What picture is 2 × 2 doubled?

7. Which picture shows a double of another?

8. Which product is greater than 20?
   a. 4 × 6 b. 2 × 8

9. Which product is the same as 2 × 6?
   a. 3 × 5 b. 3 × 4

Use the graph for Exercises 10 and 11.

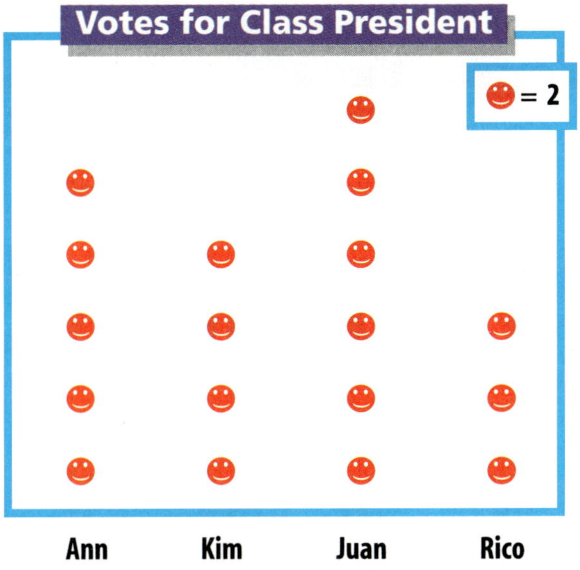

10. What does the graph tell you?
    a. Ann got 12 votes.
    b. Kim got 4 × 2 votes.
    c. Rico got 3 votes.
    d. There were 18 votes in all.

11. Which of the following is true?
    a. Juan got twice Ann's votes.
    b. Ann got 1 more than Kim.
    c. Kim and Rico together have more votes than Juan.
    d. none of the above

12. How many sides are on 5 squares?
    a. 9 × 5 b. 5 × 8
    c. 5 × 5 d. 4 × 5

13. Which one is 6 yd *not* equal to?
    a. 18 ft b. 216 in.
    c. 3 ft d. 4 yd 6 ft

14. How many minutes are there from  to  ?
    a. 2 hours b. 30 minutes
    c. 90 minutes d. 60 minutes

Check Your Math Power

Find at least 4 ways to spend exactly 15¢ to buy stamps. You can use a stamp more than once.

15. a. Show your work with number sentences. Be sure to include multiplication.
    b. Explain in writing how you found your answer.
    c. Explain in writing why some of your combinations used addition.

Module 4 Investigations

Plan a Perfect Playground

People who build playgrounds know that they should be fun, but safe too. Choose one of these three investigations.

Investigation A: Be a Playground Designer

Suppose that your town is getting a new playground. The town wants you to design it. Choose the equipment you want from the chart on the next page.

1. **Think** about which pieces of equipment will fit into the space. You have only 240 squares to work with.

Equipment List

Piece	How big is it?	How many kids can play?
Slide	6 squares	5
Jungle gym	36 squares	5
Swing set	18 squares	3
Sandbox	16 squares	4
Seesaw	5 squares	2
Basketball court	60 squares	20

2 **Design** the playground to have enough equipment for at least 35 children. Be sure to have different kinds of equipment, too.

3 **Prepare** a report. Show two plans you like. Compare the plans. Tell why you think one may work better than the other.

Keep in Mind

Be sure to do the following things in your report.

- ☐ Explain how each plan used multiplication.
- ☐ Describe what you like about each plan. Make a list or use drawings to compare the plans.
- ☐ Describe what problems each plan might have.
- ☐ Tell which plan you think will work better. Give reasons for your choice.

Investigation B

Costing It Out

Your school wants to build a new playground. It has a budget of $3,000 for equipment. People in your neighborhood will do the work, so that it is free. Look at the price tags. Make a plan.

1. **Find** the cost for two plans you like. Show how you found the costs.
2. **Decide** which plan gives the most playground for the $3,000.
3. **Write** a report telling which plan you think is best. Give reasons for your choice. Tell why some plans may be too expensive.

Ongoing Investigation

Measuring Up

It's time to measure your height and reach again. Add your results to the class totals. How much has the class grown so far? Do you want to change the predictions you made at the beginning of the investigation?

MODULE 5

Facts on Parade

Come See the Parade!

What do you get when you mix marching bands, floats, and crowds of people together? You get a parade! You have a front-row seat at this parade. Multiplication will help you along the way. Come on! The facts parade is about to begin.

SECTION A — Multiplication Facts and Strategies

SECTION B — Parts of a Whole

SECTION C — Setting Up Division

SECTION D — Dividing Shapes

Parade Count

In many parades people march in rows. The children in this picture are marching in the Juneteenth parade in Austin, Texas. This parade is in honor of June 19, 1865. On that day African Americans in Texas learned they were freed from slavery.

Word Bank

- area
- cone
- cube
- cubic unit
- cylinder
- face
- pyramid
- remainder
- sphere
- volume

1 Use What You Know

What's the quickest way to find out how many children are in the picture?

2 Look Down the Row

Suppose you know the total number of people and the number of people in each row. How could you find the number of rows?

Investigations Preview

Follow the parade of multiplication and division facts. Along the way you will explore number patterns and plan your own parade.

Number Design (pages 206–207)
What patterns can numbers make? You can use multiplication facts to help you look for patterns.

March to Your Own Beat (pages 238–240)
How would you organize marchers in a parade of your own? What you know about multiplication and division can help you find out.

SECTION A Multiplication Facts and Strategies

LESSON 1

Facts to Know

x	1	2	3	4	5	6	7	8	9
1									
2									
3									
4									
5									
6									
7									
8									
9									

Look at the shaded portion of the table. You know all these facts. Now review them.

ACTIVITY 1 Use a Strategy

With Your Class Discuss the different strategies you can use to help remember the facts.

1 How many people are in this picture?

2 Multiply 4 times the number of marchers in a row.

3 Fill in the table as you continue to review the facts.

ACTIVITY 2 Pick a Fact

With Your Group Play a game to review the multiplication facts for 1 through 5. Make a number sheet with the numbers 1 through 9. Use any strategy to help you remember the facts.

What You'll Need

- *spinner labeled 1–5*
- *different colored crayon or marker for each player*
- *a 9-by-9 grid with the numbers 1–9 written in any order*
- *multiplication table*

1. **Spin and Multiply** Take turns spinning the spinner. Use your spinner number as a factor. Find another factor on the sheet. If you know the product of the two numbers, circle the factors on the sheet.
2. **List the Facts** Keep filling in facts on your multiplication table as you review them.
3. **Plan to Move** You can claim numbers across, up, down, or diagonally. The first player to claim five numbers in a row wins.

REASONING AND PROBLEM SOLVING

How can you use a multiplication fact you know to help you learn a new fact?

Activity 3 Fill the Table

On Your Own Complete the table with as many facts as you know. What facts do you still need to fill in on your multiplication table? Choose whether to use the Commutative Property or another strategy to help you fill in more facts.

1 The Commutative Property means that you can multiply numbers in any order and get the same product. How can this help you know some of the facts with 7, 8, and 9?

TOOLS AND TECHNIQUES

Drawing arrays can help you understand the Commutative Property. Draw a dot array for 5 × 7. Then draw one for 7 × 5. You should have the same number of dots for both.

3 × 7 = 21
7 × 3 = 21

Fill in the commutative facts you know.

2. Look at the numbers in this table. What rule was used to get from the factor to the product?

Factor	1	6	4	7	5	2	9	8
Product	4	24	16					

3. Explain how you can find the missing products.

4. Make a table for another set of facts. Describe your table. What's the rule? Write these facts on your multiplication table.

5. You've reviewed most of the facts. Now you're ready to move on to new facts.

REASONING AND PROBLEM SOLVING

On your calculator, press 0 [+] 8 [=]. Keep pressing [=]. How can you describe what is shown on the display in terms of multiplication?

Do You Remember?

Try It!

Write the product. Order products from least to greatest.

1. $3 \times 7 = ■$
2. $4 \times 8 = ■$
3. $4 \times 6 = ■$
4. $1 \times 6 = ■$
5. $2 \times 8 = ■$
6. $2 \times 7 = ■$
7. $5 \times 6 = ■$
8. $5 \times 3 = ■$
9. $5 \times 7 = ■$

Compare. Write >, <, or =.

10. 13 + 45 ● 58
11. 99 ● 189 − 93
12. 200 + 47 ● 312 − 53
13. 14 + 6 + 4 ● 50
14. 75 − 18 ● 387 − 355
15. 60 + 112 ● 155

Think About It

16. What strategies helped you find each product?

LESSON 2 The Final Ten

x	1	2	3	4	5	6	7	8	9
1	1	2	3	4	5	6	7	8	9
2	2	4	6	8	10	12	14	16	18
3	3	6	9	12	15	18	21	24	27
4	4	8	12	16	20	24	28	32	36
5	5	10	15	20	25	30	35	40	45
6	6	12	18	24	30				
7	7	14	21	28	35				
8	8	16	24	32	40				
9	9	18	27	36	45				

These are facts that you have left to learn. (purple)

You can use the Commutative Property to know these facts. (yellow)

Your multiplication table should be almost all filled in now. You're ready for the last ten facts in the parade.

ACTIVITY 1 Know the Nines

With Your Class You already know some of the nines facts. Here is one way to think about them.

1 What patterns do you see in the products?

2 How can those patterns help you know the new facts?

With Your Partner Suppose a marching band has 9 rows of marchers. If each row has 6 people, how many marchers are there? Use any of these strategies to figure out the product of 9 × 6.

3 **Use ten.** How can you use a tens fact to figure out the product of 9 × 6?

$$10 \times 6 = 60$$
$$9 \times 6 = ?$$

4 **Use a fact you know.** If you know that 9 × 5 = 45, how can you figure out the product of 9 × 6?

5 **Use your own strategies** to find the products of 9 × 7, 9 × 8, and 9 × 9. List these new facts on your multiplication table. Now there are only six facts left.

Self-Check *How can you check your answers for Step 5 to see whether you multiplied correctly?*

What You'll Need

- *grid paper*
- *crayons or markers*

x	1	2	3	4	5	6	7	8	9
1	1	2	3	4	5	6	7	8	9
2	2	4	6	8	10	12	14	16	18
3	3	6	9	12	15	18	21	24	27
4	4	8	12	16	20	24	28	32	36
5	5	10	15	20	25	30	35	40	45
6	6	12	18	24	30				54
7	7	14	21	28	35				63
8	8	16	24	32	40				72
9	9	18	27	36	45	54	63	72	81

REASONING AND PROBLEM SOLVING

How can an array help you know whether a product will be even or odd?

ACTIVITY 2 Facts in a Square

With Your Class Marching bands sometimes make square patterns. A 6 × 6 array has a square pattern too. Choose one of the following strategies to figure out the product of 6 × 6.

1 Cut an array into two parts. How can you use the two smaller parts to find the product of 6 × 6?

3 × 6

3 × 6

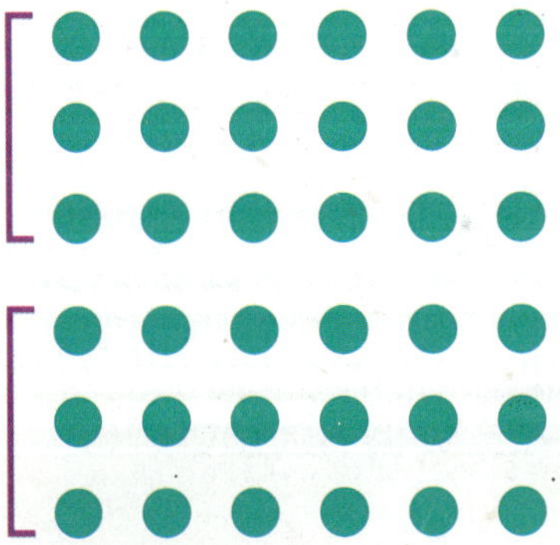

2 **Use a fact you know.** How can you use the product of 6 × 5 to figure out 6 × 6?

3 Now try some other facts. What strategy would you use to figure out 7 × 7? 8 × 8? Write these facts on your multiplication table. Only three facts to go!

DRAWING TO LEARN

On grid paper, draw arrays to show 7 × 7, 8 × 8, and 9 × 9. If you were to cut each array in two parts, would you get the same amount in both parts? Explain.

On Your Own Arrays can help you find **area,** the amount of space an object covers. You can find the area of a square by counting the small squares.

4 Color a 6 × 6 square on grid paper. What is the area? How do you know?

5 Draw three different squares on grid paper. Count the squares inside to find the area.

6 Trade drawings with someone else. See if you can find the area of each other's squares.

7 How can you find the area without counting all of the small squares?

ACTIVITY 3 Meet the Last Facts

With Your Group You have only three facts left to learn. Use strategies to help you.

7 × 6

x	1	2	3	4	5	6	7	8	9
1	1	2	3	4	5	6	7	8	9
2	2	4	6	8	10	12	14	16	18
3	3	6	9	12	15	18	21	24	27
4	4	8	12	16	20	24	28	32	36
5	5	10	15	20	25	30	35	40	45
6	6	12	18	24	30	36			54
7	7	14	21	28	35		49		63
8	8	16	24	32	40			64	72
9	9	18	27	36	45	54	63	72	81

8 × 6

How can you use the Commutative Property to find these products?

8 × 7

ACTIVITY OPTION

Play the multiplication review game from page 197. Use a spinner with the numbers 1 through 9.

1. What strategy would you use for 7 × 6? Discuss your strategies.
2. Now use strategies to figure out 8 × 6 and 8 × 7. You've learned all the facts!

Activity 4 Multiply with Zero

With Your Partner The facts parade is almost over. Explore one more set of facts.

1. Show 3 groups of 2. Then show 3 groups of 1. Write these facts.
2. How can you show 3 groups of 0? What fact would you write?
3. Try multiplying other numbers by 0. What did you find out?

4 × 0 = ?

What You'll Need
- *counters or tiles*

REASONING AND PROBLEM SOLVING

How can you use mental math to figure out 2 × 3 × 0?

Do You Remember? Try It!

Find the product. Which products are greater than 50? Which are less than 50?

1. 6 × 7 = ■
2. 7 × 8 = ■
3. 0 × 9 = ■
4. 8 × 9 = ■
5. 8 × 6 = ■
6. 6 × 0 = ■

Write +, −, or × to make the sentence true.

7. 3 ● 17 = 20
8. 44 ● 11 = 33
9. 4 ● 25 = 100
10. 2 ● 18 ● 0 = 20
11. 700 ● 300 ● 50 = 950
12. 35 ● 17 = 18

Think About It

13. How can you use what you know to figure out the products you don't know? Explain in writing.

Investigation

Number Design

You've probably seen gameboards that have designs and patterns in them. Do you think you can make designs and patterns with numbers? Use the information on these pages and some number tables to find out. You can use multiplication tables and hundred charts. Or, you may want to create your own chart or table.

1. **Shade In Products** Choose a number from 0 through 9. On a table shade in the products with that number as a factor. Is there a pattern or design?

2. **Predict Patterns** Use two different numbers. What patterns do you think all their products will make? Why do you think so?

3 **Choose Colors** Decide which colors you want to use on each table. How can you use different colors to show the designs?

4 **Share Your Findings** Write a report telling what you discovered. Did your products make designs? Which do you like best? Why? Include your drawings with your report.

Ask Yourself

- ☐ What is a factor? What is a product?
- ☐ What factors will you use?
- ☐ Did you shade in the correct products for each factor?
- ☐ Are all of your designs the same or different?
- ☐ How could you explain how to make your design to another person?

LESSON 3 Multiplication Parade

ACTIVITY 1 Add or Multiply?

With Your Partner Many towns have pet parades. How can you use addition and multiplication to answer pet parade questions?

Children get ready to march in a parade with their costumed pets.

1. Suppose there are 7 dogs, 6 cats, and 5 birds in the parade. This model shows the numbers of these pets.

?			} Whole
7	6	5	} Parts

Would you add or multiply to find the total? Why?

2 What's the whole? Write a number sentence that shows the answer.

3 Now suppose there are the same number of dogs, cats, and birds in the parade. What is the fastest way to find the total number of these pets? Why?

4 What's the whole? Write two different number sentences that show the answer.

On Your Own

5 Suppose 5 birds lead the parade and 3 birds are at the parade's end. How many birds are there altogether? Copy the model below. Fill in the parts and the whole.

6 Could you use addition to find the whole? Explain. Could you use multiplication? Explain. Discuss your answers with a classmate.

ACTIVITY OPTION

Write two addition and two multiplication questions. Trade with your partner. Answer the questions you get. Draw models to show how you answered them.

Self-Check *Did you use the simplest and fastest way to solve Exercise 4?*

Your Pet Parade

Use multiplication, addition, or subtraction to answer these questions. Write whether you used mental math, calculator, or pencil and paper.

Furry Friends

Use the graph on this page to answer Exercises 1 through 5.

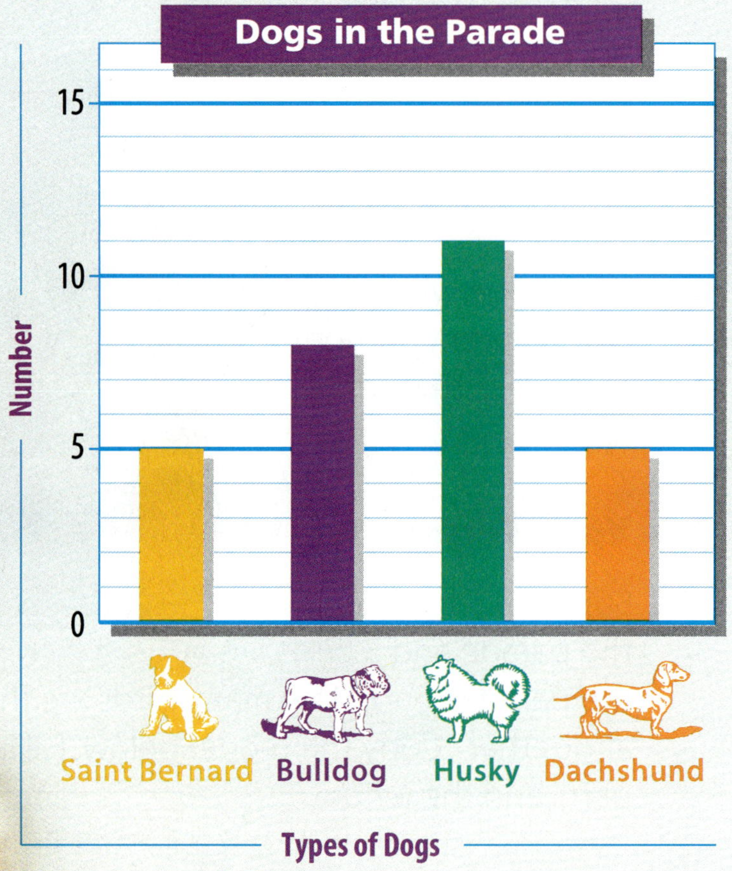

1. What is the total number of dogs in the parade?
2. Suppose twice as many bulldogs as shown take part. How many dogs would then be in the parade?
3. Suppose only 4 of each type of dog are in the parade. How many dogs would there be in all?

4. Draw a model to show 5 times as many bulldogs as shown. Write a number sentence to find the whole.
5. Draw a model showing the number of bulldogs, huskies, and Saint Bernards. Write a number sentence that shows the whole.

Perfect Pets

Use the graph on this page to answer Exercises 6 through 8.

6 Two of each kind of pet shown in the chart will lead the parade. How many pets will follow behind?

7 Suppose there are 5 times as many birds as shown. How many birds, rabbits, and cats are there altogether?

8 The number of birds is equal to the total number of turtles and cats. How many birds, turtles, and cats are there altogether?

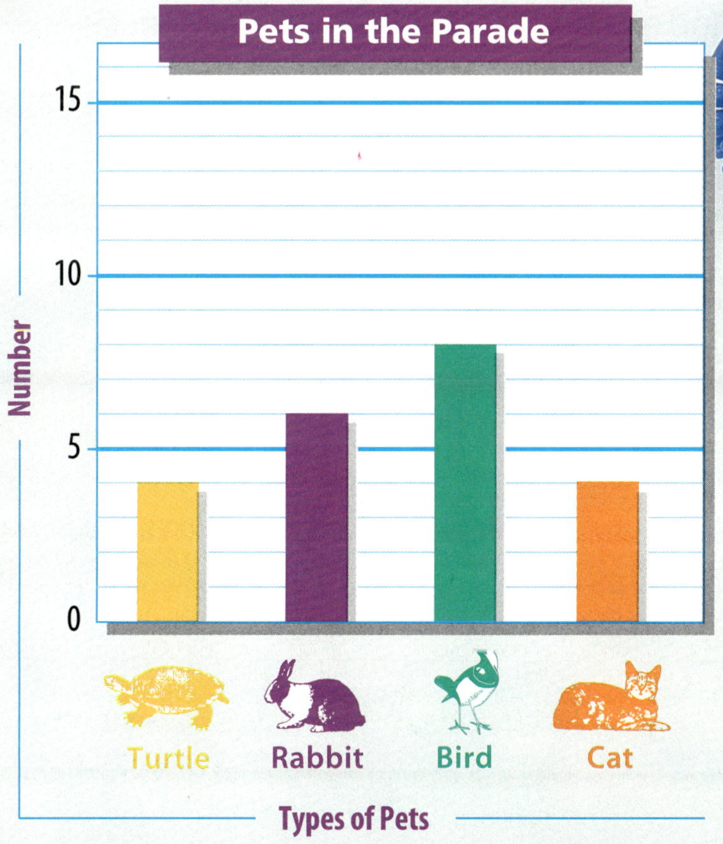

9 Suppose your class wants to have a pet parade. Find out what kinds of pets your classmates have. Then separate the pets into groups. How many pets are there in all?

10 Draw a graph to show the information you gathered. Share it with the class.

LESSON 4 Shaping Multiplication

What You'll Need

- *small empty food box*

ACTIVITY 1 Comparing Boxes

With Your Group Volunteers at the pet parade are handing out boxes of dog snacks. How does the shape of the boxes compare with other shapes?

1. The shape on the left is a **rectangular prism.** Describe the shape.
2. Find an empty food box. Is it a rectangular prism? Why?
3. Each side of a shape is called a **face.** Outline all of the faces of your box on paper. What is the shape of each face?

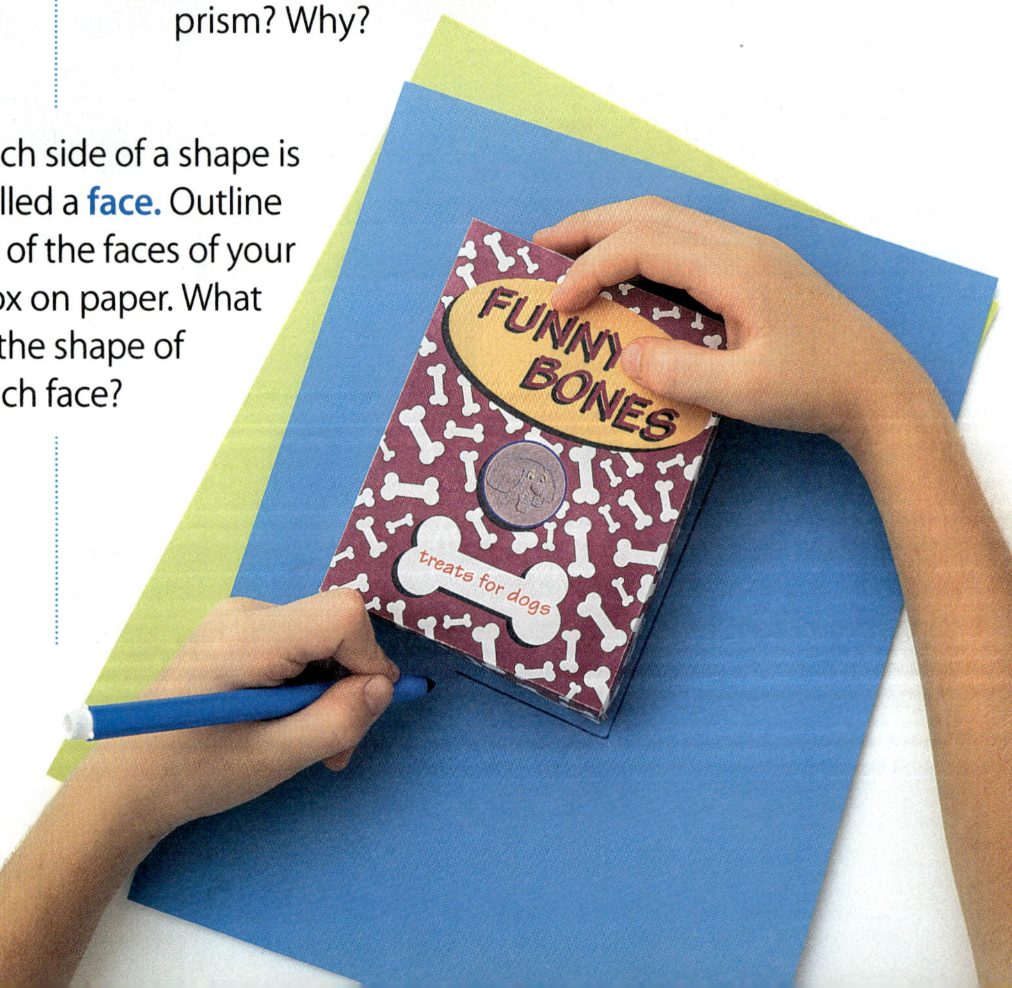

4. This shape is called a **cube.** Describe the shape and its faces.

5. How are cubes and rectangular prisms alike? How are they different?

DRAWING TO LEARN

Use your Geometry Tool to draw the faces of a cube and a rectangular prism.

ACTIVITY 2 Taking Up Space

With Your Partner You can use cubes to measure the space inside a shape. Find the number of **cubic units.**

What You'll Need

- *small empty food box*
- *ones' cubes*

1. Make a model of your empty food box out of cubes. Build it as close to the box's size and shape as possible. About how many cubes could be fit into the box? How do you know?

2. Trade models with your partner. Count the cubes. How much space does the model take up in cubic units? The **volume** of a shape is how much space it takes up.

3. Suppose you cover the bottom of a box with one layer of cubes. How can you use this number of cubic units to estimate the volume of the box?

What You'll Need

- *ones' cubes*

ACTIVITY 3 Changing Prisms

On Your Own Choose which activity you'll do first, 3 or 4. Does changing the shape of a rectangular prism change its volume?

1. Make as many different rectangular prisms as you can out of 24 cubes. How many did you make? Find out whether your classmates made the same number.

2. What is the volume of each prism in cubic units? Did the volume change as you changed the prism's shape? Why?

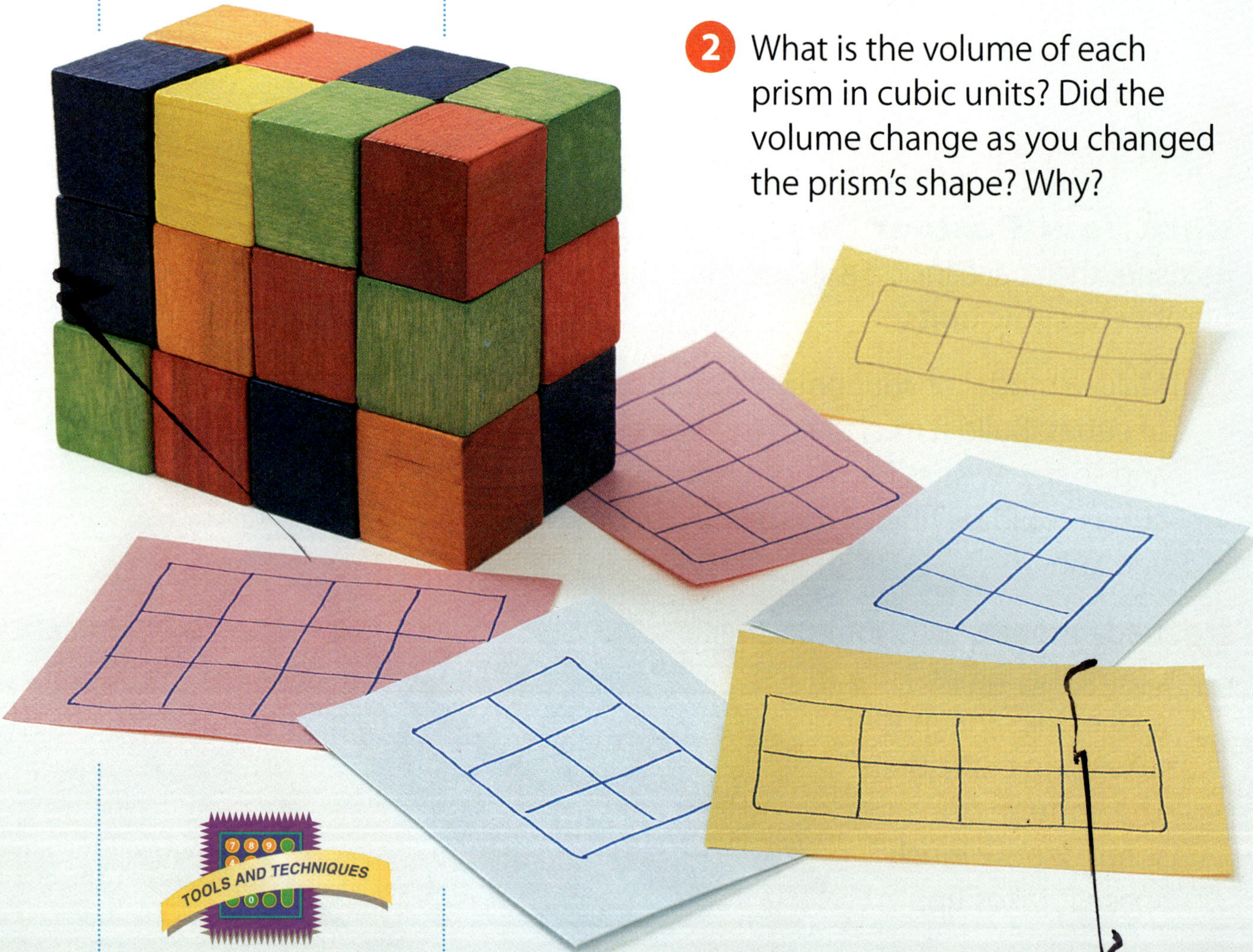

TOOLS AND TECHNIQUES

Draw the six faces of each prism you make. This record will help you keep track of how many prisms you've made.

3. Divide the last prism shape you made into two smaller prisms. What is the volume of each prism? How do you know?

Activity 4 Missing Cubes

With Your Partner What happens to the volume of a shape when cubes are taken away?

1. What is the volume of this shape? How many cubic units would be needed to make the shape into a rectangular prism? What would the volume of the prism be?
2. Make your own prism. Take out a few cubes from one corner. What is the volume of the new shape?
3. Trade shapes with your partner. How many cubic units are needed to make the shape into a prism? What would its volume be?

What You'll Need
- *ones' cubes*

Do You Remember? Try It!

Write *rectangular prism, cube, both,* or *neither* for each clue.

1. All of its faces are squares.
2. It has 6 faces.
3. All of its faces can be traced.
4. It has only 4 faces.
5. Some of its faces are bigger than others.

Write the value of the underlined digit. Then write the values in order from greatest to least.

6. 42
7. 107
8. 305
9. 55
10. 16

Think About It

11. How would you divide a shape with a volume of 6 cubic units into a rectangular prism and a cube?

Do You Remember?

Cumulative Review

Freedom Festival

September 16 is Independence Day for Mexico. Answer these questions about Mexican Independence Day celebrations in Los Angeles and Santa Ana, California.

Mexico

Freedom Count

1. Spain ruled Mexico from 1521 to 1821. Is that more or less than 250 years?

2. In 1810 Mexico began fighting Spain for freedom. Mexico won 11 years later. What year was that?

Costa Rica, El Salvador, Guatemala, Honduras, and Nicaragua also celebrate their independence from Spain.

Costa Rica

El Salvador

Celebration Amounts

3. The parade route in Los Angeles is 4 miles long. If there are 1,760 yards in a mile, about how many yards long is the route?

4. If 6 people rode on each of 9 floats in the parade, how many people were on floats?

5. About 500 thousand people went to Santa Ana's celebration. Suppose 650,000 people went the next year. What's the difference?

6. A salsa musician played for 90 minutes, starting at 3:00. You got there at 3:30 and stayed until the end. For how long did you hear the music?

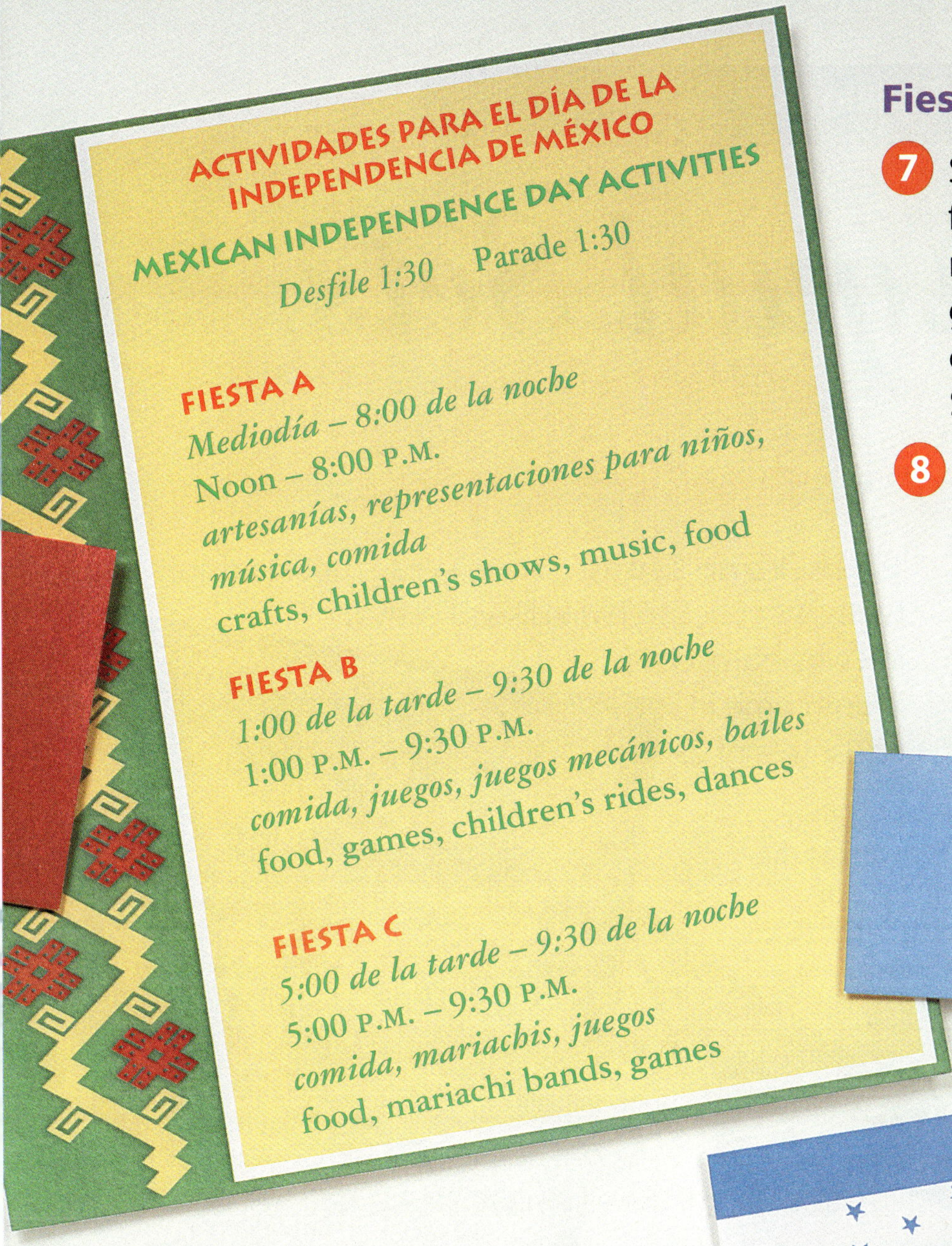

Fiesta Dollars

7. Suppose you bought food for 9 people. Each meal cost $4. If you gave the cashier $40, could you get back a $5 bill? Explain.

8. At the crafts fair 8 people spent $7 each. Another group of 6 people spent $9 each. Which group spent more money?

Guatemala

Honduras

Check Your Math Power

9. Suppose you can stay at the festival from noon until 6:00 P.M. Make a schedule of events you would attend.

10. At which times do all three fiestas overlap? Draw a diagram to help you find out.

Nicaragua

SECTION C Setting Up Division

LESSON 5 Equal Sets

ACTIVITY 1 Two of a Kind

Twins from all over the country enjoy the festival's parade and games.

With Your Class Once a year, thousands of twins meet at the Twins Days Festival in Twinsburg, Ohio. Twins come in equal sets of 2.

1. **Suppose you are taking pictures of 10 twins at the festival. If you take one picture of each set of twins, how many pictures will you take?**

CONNECT AND COMMUNICATE

In Your Journal Explain why a class with an odd number of people in it can't be divided into two equal sets.

2 **Divide your class into 2 equal sets. How many people are in the whole class? in each set?**

3 **Have your whole class pair up like twins. Then count all the sets. How many are there?**

ACTIVITY 2 Parade Sets

With Your Partner The Twins Days Festival begins with a parade. You will use counters to solve division problems about the parade. Then you will make arrays to see how multiplication and division are related. Record your answers.

What You'll Need

- counters or tiles

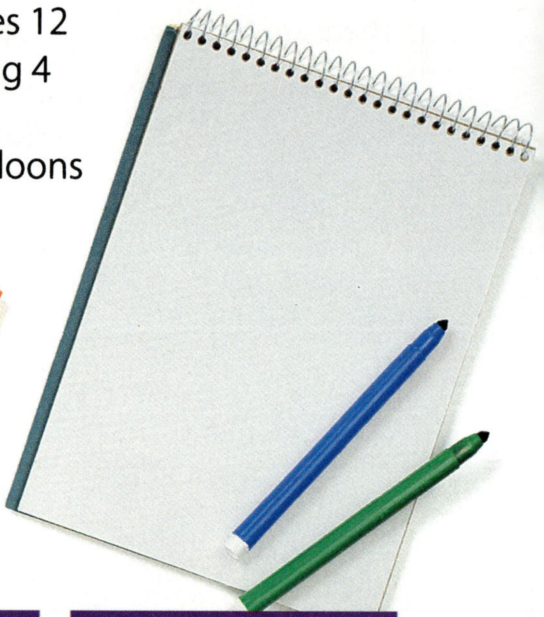

Show how you used the counters to divide. Then show the array you could make from the division.

1 Suppose a clown shares 12 balloons equally among 4 children watching the parade. How many balloons does each child get?

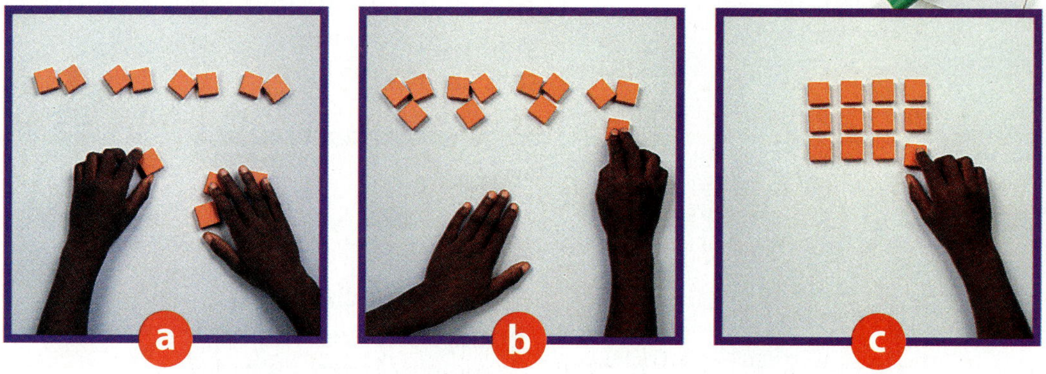

a **Use 12 counters. Make 4 equal groups.**

b **The 4 equal groups have 3 counters each.**

c **Move the groups into an array. What multiplication fact does it show?**

Answer two of the following questions. Act out the problem with counters.

2 Each float has 6 people. If 24 people ride on floats, what is the total number of floats?

3 One band has 56 members. If there are 8 equal rows, how many marchers are in each row?

4 There are 9 marching bands carrying a total of 36 flags. Each band has the same number of flags. How many does each have?

Do you need to find the number of groups or the number in each group?

ACTIVITY 3 Set Symbols

On Your Own How can you divide things into sets without using counters? Here's one way.

What You'll Need

- *counters*

1. How many twins are in 1 row if you put 6 twins in 2 equal rows?

a. This array stands for the 6 people.

b. You can divide the 6 people into 2 sets.

2

c. How many people are in each set? Write the answer above the array.

3

2

d. Write the division using a number in place of the array. How did you do it?

Use counters to find the answers to the following problems. Then show your answer with

- an array and $\overline{)\quad}$
- numbers and $\overline{)\quad}$

2 There are 9 people to play on 3 teams. Each team has the same number. How many are on each team?

3 Divide 12 game prizes equally among 3 people. How many prizes will each person get?

4 Divide 30 name tags into sets of 5 for game teams. How many teams will you have?

ACTIVITY 4 Division Patterns

On Your Own You can also show division with a ÷ sign. The answer is called the **quotient.**

$6 \div 2 = 3$ is the same as $2\overline{)6}$ with quotient 3

1 What is the quotient when you divide 25 by 5? Show two ways to write the division.

CONNECT AND COMMUNICATE

In Your Journal *Which way do you like to show the division? Why?*

2 Copy the table. What rule was used to go from the number divided to the quotient? How can you find the missing quotients?

Number divided	8	12	16	20	32	28	40
Quotient	2	3					

$8 \div ? = 2$

3 Tell how multiplication could help you find the missing answers.

ACTIVITY OPTION

Draw a division table of your own. Write five sets of top and bottom numbers. Share your table with the class.

Do You Remember?

Try It!

Solve. Write a related multiplication fact.

1. $63 \div 9 = ■$
2. $35 \div 7 = ■$
3. $48 \div 6 = ■$
4. $8\overline{)64}$
5. $3\overline{)24}$
6. $6\overline{)54}$
7. $42 \div 7 = ■$
8. $81 \div 9 = ■$
9. $27 \div 3 = ■$

Estimate. If the answer is greater than 100, find the exact answer.

10. $43 + 27 = ■$
11. $37 + 66 = ■$
12. $185 - 52 = ■$
13. $75 + 16 = ■$
14. $113 - 11 = ■$
15. $163 - 58 = ■$

Think About It

16. What factors do the answers for Exercises 3 and 4 share?

LESSON 6 Division Stories

ACTIVITY 1 Divide 'em, Cowboy

With Your Partner Read about Justin's visit to a parade. Then write your own division problems.

Nat Love was a famous cowboy of the Old West. He worked in cattle drives from 1869 to 1889.

LITERATURE

Justin has heard many stories about famous African American cowboys. He sees some of these cowboys for the first time in a parade.

Finally the horses came. Justin cheered and whistled with the crowd. Cowboys from the rodeo in boots and spurs rode tall in their saddles, doffing their cowboy hats. Some did lasso tricks. One cowboy's horse did special dance steps and bowed when the audience applauded.

From *Justin and the Best Biscuits in the World*
by Mildred Pitts Walter

1. Suppose there are 24 cowboys riding in a parade. How many equal groups can the cowboys make? First, list the multiplication facts that have 24 as a product.

2. Draw an array for each multiplication fact. Write each fact beside each array. How do the arrays help you see the multiplication as division?

3. Use each multiplication fact to write a division problem. One student used $4 \times 6 = 24$. The division problem reads, "The 24 cowboys rode in 4 rows. How many were in each row?"

4. Draw the groups and rows to show the division.

REASONING AND PROBLEM SOLVING

How did you find all the factors of 24?

Activity 2 Parade Stories

With Your Partner Practice division as you add words to silly stories about a circus parade. Then you'll have a chance to write your own story.

1. Copy the division story below. Ask your partner for the type of word listed beneath each blank.

Beautiful old circus wagons are part of the Great Circus Parade in Milwaukee, Wisconsin.

The 6 animal trainers ________ (verb) on the circus wagon. Some are at the back, feeding the ________ (adjective) giraffe. Some trainers are at the front, taking care of the ________ (plural noun). If there is an equal number of trainers at the front and the back of the wagon, how many trainers are at each place?

2. Write your partner's words in the blanks. Then read the story aloud with its new words.

TOOLS AND TECHNIQUES

Use counters or drawings to solve the problem.

3. Decide together what the division problem is. Solve the problem. Think about these questions:
   - How many things are there in all?
   - How many groups are there?
   - How many things are in each group?

4. Choose a or b. Fill in the blanks and solve the problem as you did for the first story. If you want, draw pictures.
   - **a.** Copy the two silly stories shown.
   - **b.** Make up your own silly story with a division problem in it.

There are 18 elephants ________ (verb) down the street wearing purple and gold ________ (plural noun). Dancing and waving their ________ (adjective) hats, 9 clowns watch over the elephants. The clowns are divided equally among the elephants. How many elephants does each clown watch over?

Maria pushes a cart through the crowd selling ________ (plural noun). She sings while she ________ (verb). Her cart is painted bright colors and has a big ________ (noun) on top. Some kids buy a bag of 56 peanuts from Maria. If 7 kids will share the peanuts equally, how many will each child get?

With Your Class

5 Collect the stories written by your classmates. Read each one aloud.

6 Solve each story problem. Choose one of these ways to show your work.

a. groups of counters
b. numbers and $\overline{)\quad}$
c. numbers and ÷

Self-Check How can you be sure your problems show the correct division?

Do You Remember?

Try It!

Make the number sentence true.

1. 16 ÷ 2 = ■
2. 18 ÷ ■ = 6
3. 20 ÷ ■ = 5
4. 9 ÷ 1 = ■
5. 21 ÷ 7 = ■
6. 12 ÷ ■ = 2
7. 24 ÷ ■ = 6
8. 72 ÷ 8 = ■

Use mental math. Find the sums that are less than 40.

9. 32 + 11
10. 23 + 18
11. 15 + 21
12. 35 + 7
13. 12 + 27
14. 24 + 24

Think About It

15. Explain in writing how multiplication can help you solve Exercises 2 and 7.

LESSON 7 Spare Parts

The carnival's in town! How can you use division as you work your way through the carnival?

ACTIVITY 1 Close to the Facts

What You'll Need
- *counters or tiles*

With Your Group Not everything divides evenly. Sometimes there are leftovers. Use counters and multiplication facts to help you solve each division problem. Write the division.

1. There are 4 people to share 13 carnival prizes. How many prizes would each person get?

a

How many are in each group? Think: What number times 4 comes closest to 13?

b

There is one left over. That number is the remainder.

You can write your work two ways.

TOOLS AND TECHNIQUES

The letter R *stands for the word* remainder.

2 A fishing game costs 5 cents a turn. You have 32 cents. Can you take 7 turns? Why or why not?

3 The bean bag toss has 35 bean bags. If 9 people play, how many bean bags will each person get?

4 There are only 29 tickets left for the Ferris wheel. If 8 people want to buy 4 tickets each, how many people can buy tickets?

5 Everyone gets 2 rings to throw at the ring toss game. If there are 19 rings, how many sets of rings can be handed out?

Self-Check *Why don't you get a remainder when you divide 24 by 8?*

ACTIVITY 2 Remainder Maze

What You'll Need
- *gameboard*
- *cube labeled 1–6*
- *game pieces or counters*

With Your Group Find your way through the Amazing Remainder Maze. The person with the fewest remainder points wins.

1. **Roll to Move** Each player places a counter on a different Start space. Take turns rolling the number cube to move. If you land on a Move Ahead space, roll again. Then choose which arrow to follow.
2. **Choose a Fact** If you land on a number, think of a multiplication fact. The product should be close to the number without going over.
3. **List the Remainders** Subtract the product from the number on the space. What is the remainder? Keep a list of your remainders throughout the game.

4 **Win the Game** The game ends when the last person reaches Finish. Add the remainders on your list. The player with the fewest points wins.

What can I multiply to get a product that is close to this number?

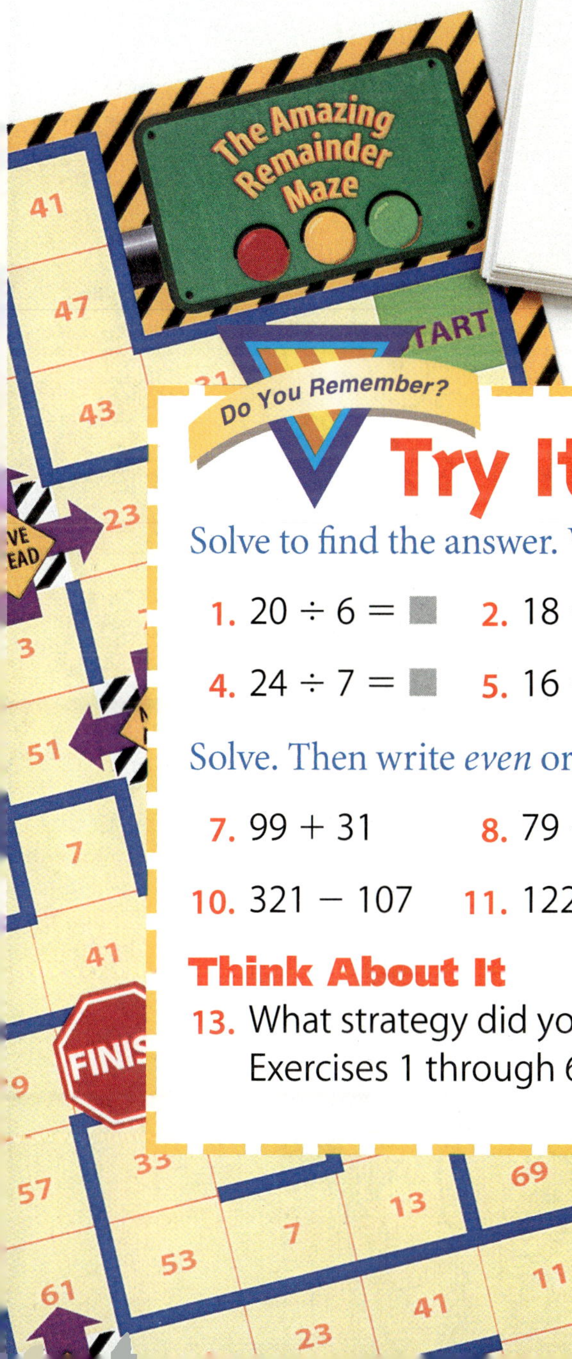

CONNECT AND COMMUNICATE

In Your Journal *Explain how you can use multiplication to check that 37 ÷ 5 = 7 R2.*

Do You Remember?

Try It!

Solve to find the answer. What is the remainder?

1. 20 ÷ 6 = ■   2. 18 ÷ 4 = ■   3. 36 ÷ 5 = ■

4. 24 ÷ 7 = ■   5. 16 ÷ 3 = ■   6. 30 ÷ 4 = ■

Solve. Then write *even* or *odd* for each answer.

7. 99 + 31   8. 79 + 65   9. 200 − 70

10. 321 − 107   11. 122 + 37   12. 49 + 51

Think About It

13. What strategy did you use to remember the facts for Exercises 1 through 6? Write your answer.

LESSON 8

Shape Faces

What You'll Need

- models of a cone, cylinder, pyramid, and sphere

ACTIVITY 1

Parade of Shapes

With Your Group Answer the questions on the next page. Choose one person to write your answers.

DRAWING TO LEARN

Try to trace the faces of one of the shapes. Can you trace all the faces?

cone cylinder pyramid sphere

1. Find as many of the above shapes as you can in the picture.
2. Describe each shape. How many flat faces are there? What shapes are the faces?
3. Compare the shapes. How are they different? How are they alike?
4. Discuss your answers with other groups.

Activity 2 Shapes That Roll

What You'll Need

- *models of a cone, cylinder, pyramid, and sphere*

With Your Group Pick up each shape. Look at it carefully. See what you can find out about the shapes as you discuss these questions.

1. Test each shape. Which shapes roll? Do they all roll in the same way?
2. Think about uses for each shape. Could you bowl with any of these shapes? Which shapes might hold something? Explain.

3. Organize your results. What did you [illegible] cover? How will you report what you lear[illegible]
4. Compare with other groups. Did t[illegible]d out the same things?

Reasoning and Problem Solving

Would a rectangular prism roll? Why or why not?

ACTIVITY 3 Shapes to Make

With Your Partner - You're in charge of making decorations for a carnival. The decorations will use shapes of cubes, pyramids, and rectangular prisms. Choose two of the following questions to answer. Show the division.

REASONING AND PROBLEM SOLVING

What information do you need to find the answers?

1. How many cubes could you make from 14 squares?
2. How many cubes could you make from 24 squares?
3. How many rectangular prisms can you make from 37 rectangles?
4. How many pyramids could you make from 10 triangles and 3 squares?

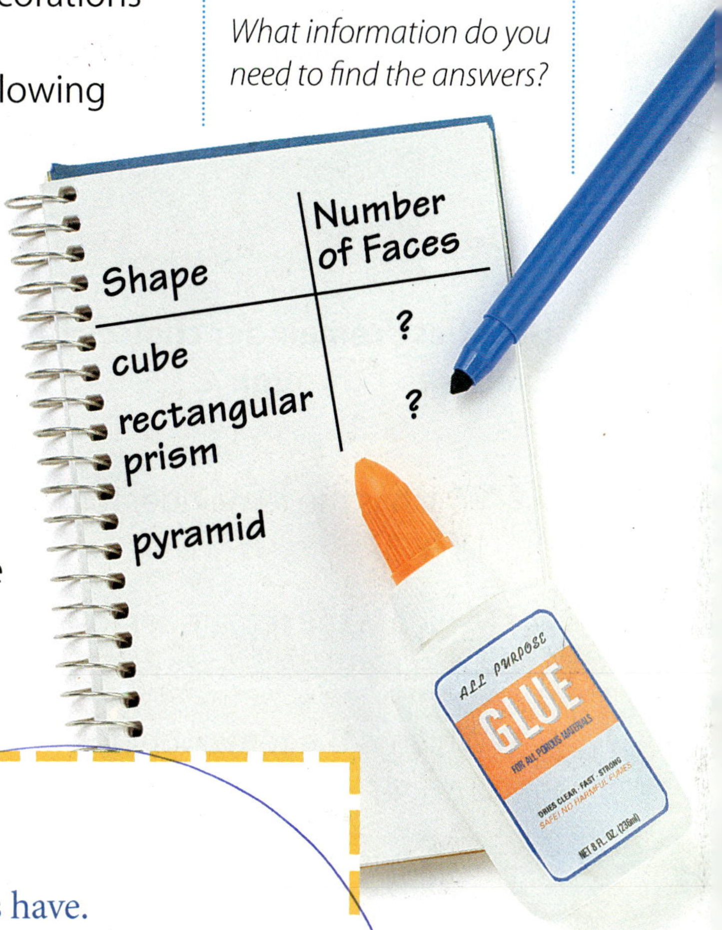

Do You Remember? Try It!

Identify the shapes the following objects have.

1. beach ball
2. soup can
3. clown hat
4. tent
5. globe
6. shoe box

Arrange the numbers in order from least to greatest.

7. 55 million
8. 37,267,000
9. 8,999,000
10. 74,332
11. 8 million
12. 76 thousand

Think About It

13. If all of the above objects had a pyramid shape, would they still be useful? Why or why not?

Do You Remember?

Cumulative Review

Looking Back

Choose the best answer. Write *a, b, c,* or *d* for each question.

Use these remainder choices for Exercises 1 through 4.

a. 2 **b.** 3 **c.** 1 **d.** 0

1. Which is the remainder for $13 \div 3$?

2. Which is the remainder for $44 \div 6$?

3. Which is the remainder for $27 \div 4$?

4. Which is the remainder for $64 \div 8$?

5. Which array stands for a number multiplied by itself?

a. 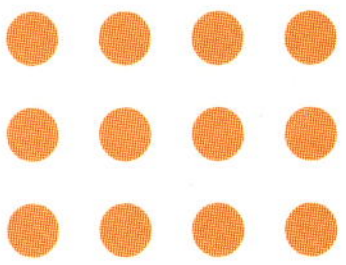

b. 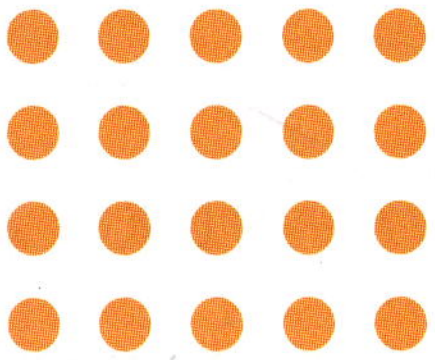

c. 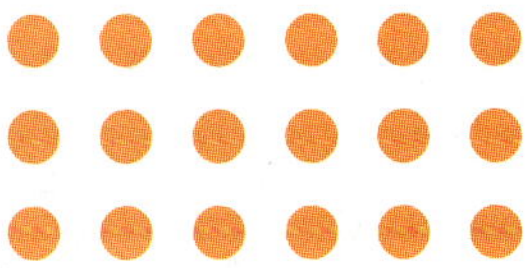

d. 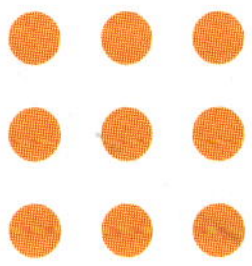

6. Which statement is true about the money shown?

   a. The total amount of money is less than three dollars.
   b. The coins total 30 cents.
   c. The total amount of money is more than two dollars.
   d. None of these.

Use this table to answer Exercises 7 through 8.

Factor	3	9		8
Product	21	63	35	

7. If the factor is 8, which of these is the product?

a. 50 + 6 b. 56 ÷ 8
c. 7 + 8 d. 5 × 7

8. If the product is 35, which of these is the factor?

a. 30 ÷ 5 b. 35 − 5
c. 5 × 6 d. 5 × 1

9. Which shows pairs that have the same answer?

a. 18 ÷ 4 and 3 × 6
b. 4 × 2 and 48 ÷ 6
c. 15 ÷ 3 and 4 × 1
d. 4 × 3 and 12 ÷ 3

10. Choose the best estimate for 763 + 915.

a. 1,700 b. 1,600
c. 200 d. 1,800

11. Erin gave each of her 3 friends 3 cookies. How many did she give in all? Which model shows the problem's parts and whole?

a.

b.

c.

d.

Use these shapes to answer Exercises 12 through 15.

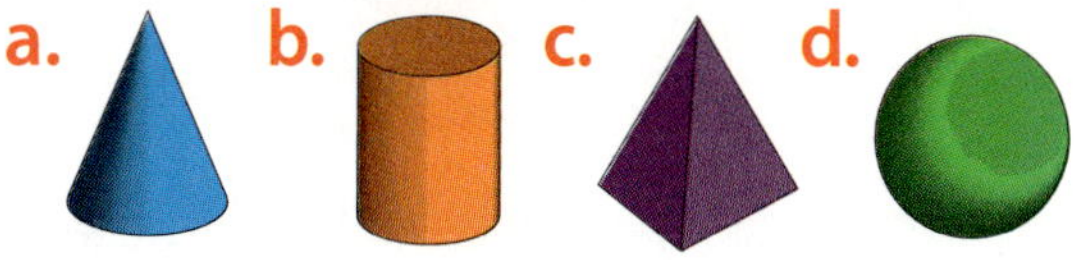

12. Which shape has the greatest number of flat faces?

13. Which shape has a face shaped like a triangle?

14. Which shape has more than one face shaped like a circle?

15. Which shape has exactly two faces that are the same?

Check Your Math Power

16. Write the multiplication fact for this array. Explain how you can change the array to model other multiplication facts. List the facts.

17. The length of one face of this shape is 8. Can you tell what the length of all the shape's other faces are? Why?

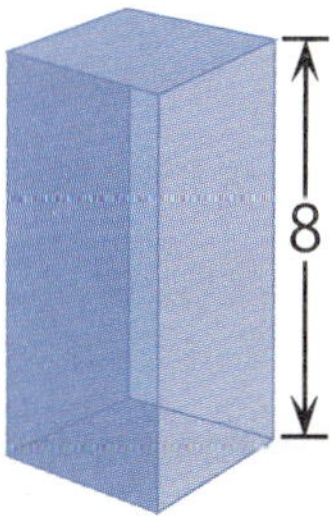

MODULE 5 **Investigations**

March to Your Own Beat

How would you plan a parade? How many people would you have in your parade? What theme would it have? What do you need to think about when you plan a parade?

Investigation A Plan a Parade

Make a plan to organize people for your parade.

1. **Decide the size for your parade. Will you include everyone In your grade? in your school? What's your plan for finding out the total number of students?**

2 **Organize** the groups of people. If the whole school marches, will each grade march in a separate group? If only third graders march, will each class be in a separate group?

3 **Make** a marching pattern. How many students are in each row? How can multiplication and division help you work with any remainders?

4 **Think** about how you will present your plan. Will you write a report? Will you make a speech to explain your ideas? Include any drawings you made of your plan.

Keep in Mind

Your report will be judged on these points:

- ☐ How did you explain the pattern you chose?
- ☐ What did you do if the number of marchers was greater than the multiplication facts you know?
- ☐ Did you show more than one way to arrange the groups? Which way do you think is better?
- ☐ Did you explain how you used multiplication and division?

Investigation B — Color a Parade

Make a color pattern for a parade with the students in your class. Decide how many different colors of shirts you'd want each row of students to have. Would 3 colors work? Would 4 or more colors work better? Write a report that

- describes or shows the color pattern
- explains why you chose the number of colors you did
- tells why some numbers are easier to work with than others

Computer Option You can use a computer drawing program to design a color pattern.

Investigation C — Shape a Float

Use what you know about shapes to plan a float. Suppose you have 15 squares, 15 triangles, 15 rectangles, and 15 circles. What combinations of these shapes will you use? Are some shapes easy to combine with others? What will you do with remainders? Write a report about the shapes you will use for your float.

MODULE 6

Crafty Fractions

You have probably done many different kinds of crafts. In this module you will do craft projects like paper stars and paper houses. You will even make your own books! While you are doing your craft projects, you will learn all about special numbers that describe parts of a whole. Have fun!

SECTION A
Discovering Fractions

SECTION B
Comparing Fractions

SECTION C
Adding and Subtracting Fractions

SECTION D
Fractions in Sets and Probability

MODULE 6 Crafty Fractions

Art in Parts

When you divide a piece of paper evenly, you make equal parts. Equal parts are the same size.

1 Find Parts

Which papers on this page have equal parts? How many equal parts make up each whole? How many of these parts can you find in the craft projects on page 243?

2 Make Parts

Divide one piece of paper into equal parts. Divide another paper into parts that aren't equal. Trade papers with a partner. Which papers have equal parts? How do you know?

Word Bank

- denominator
- equivalent fraction
- fraction
- mixed number
- numerator
- prediction

3 Craft Parts

Share equal parts with your partner. Make a picture like the ones on this page. Use all or just some of your parts. Color, fold, cut, or paste them together. Tell what you did with the parts to make the picture.

Investigations Preview

Learn all about the special numbers that describe parts. Use them to plan and make craft projects.

Weaving Fun (pages 274–275)
Weave with paper. Adding and subtracting equal parts will help you cut the paper and plan a pattern.

Facts and Fiction (pages 286–288)
Make a book using pictures and crafts to share what you have learned. Your book can help others learn about comparing, ordering, adding, and subtracting parts.

Section A Discovering Fractions

Lesson 1 Every Part Counts

How many ways can you divide your geoboard in half? Try it and see!

A shape can be divided into equal parts. Each part is a **fraction** of the whole shape.

Activity 1 Equal Parts

With Your Class Look at the shapes below. They are divided into equal parts.

1. One part of shape A is one half. Write the name for one part of shape B.
2. Write the name for one part of shape C.

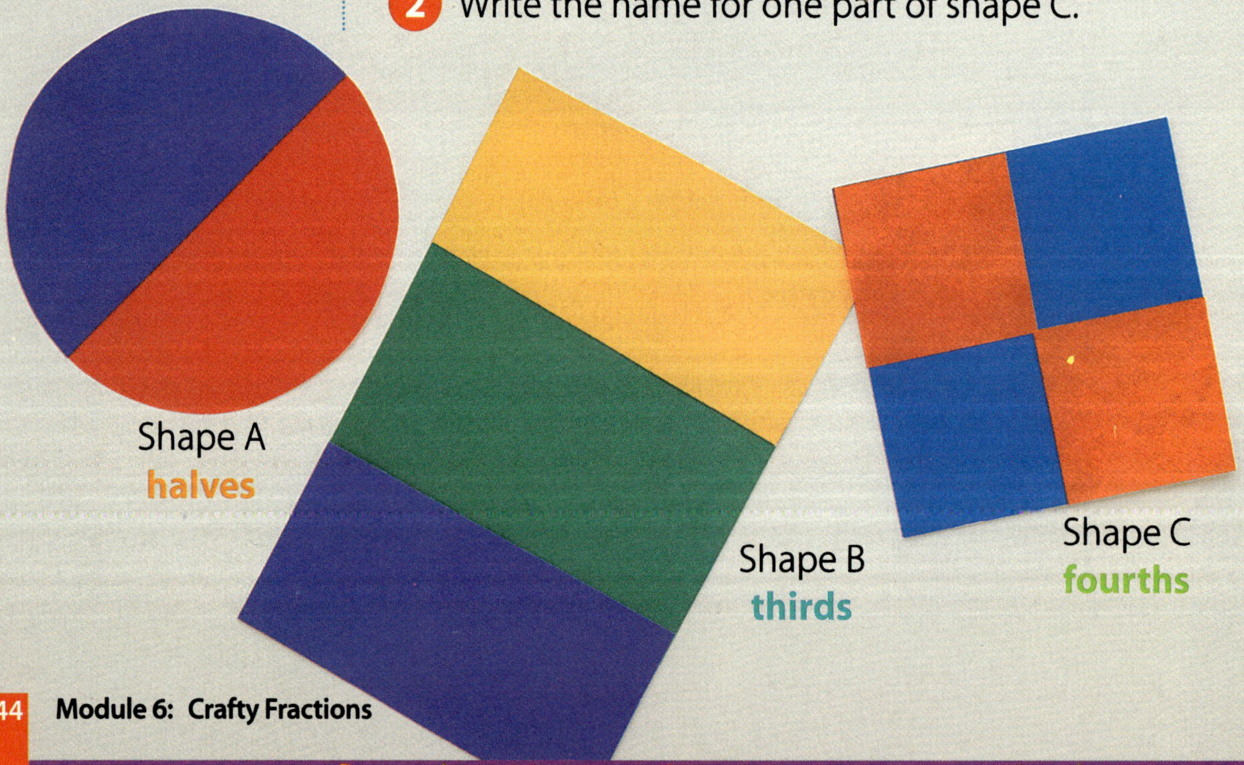

ACTIVITY 2 Folding Fractions

With Your Group Folding paper can help you make equal parts.

1 **Match the corners of a sheet of paper. Then fold it down the middle. Unfold the paper. How many parts does it show?**

2 **Fold two more sheets of paper into halves. Unfold them. Place all three sheets of paper in a row.**

3. Count the halves for two sheets of paper. How many halves did you count?
4. Count the halves for all three sheets of paper. How many halves did you count?
5. Fold three sheets of paper. Choose between folding the paper into thirds or into fourths. Count the parts.

ACTIVITY OPTION

Do you think you can divide circles into equal parts? Try this activity again. Fold fractions using paper circles.

What You'll Need

- *grid paper*
- *crayons or markers*
- *scissors*

CONNECT AND COMMUNICATE

In Your Journal *One fourth is also called one quarter. Write how you have heard each term used.*

Activity 3 Fitting Fourths

On Your Own Create your own fraction puzzle with equal parts. Each piece should be the same size, but it doesn't have to be the same shape.

1 **Use an 8-by-8 square of grid paper.**

2 **Divide the square into fourths.**

3 **Choose four crayons. Color the fourths. What fraction of the whole square is each color?**

4 Cut out each fourth. Now you have made a puzzle!

5 Can you put your puzzle squares back together? Give it a try!

6 Repeat the steps to make another puzzle. Trade puzzles with a classmate.

Do You Remember?

Try It!

Write a name for the shaded part of the shape.

1. 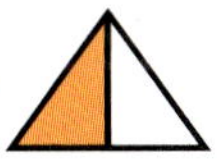
2. 
3. 
4. 
5. 
6. 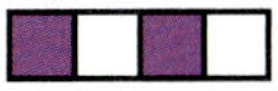

Find the missing numbers.

7. 24 ÷ ■ = 4
8. ■ ÷ 4 = 4
9. ■ ÷ 4 = 7
10. 81 ÷ ■ = 9
11. ■ ÷ 8 = 7
12. 40 ÷ 5 = ■

Think About It

13. How does the number of parts in a whole help you write a fraction name?

LESSON 2 Number the Parts

You know how to write fractions in word form. Now see how you can write fractions with numbers.

ACTIVITY 1 Writing Fractions

With Your Partner Look at the square below. How many equal parts does it have?

1. The square is one half green. You can write one half as $\frac{1}{2}$.
   a. What do you think the 2 in $\frac{1}{2}$ means?
   b. What do you think the 1 in $\frac{1}{2}$ means?
   c. What fraction of the square is white?

1 → **number of green parts**
2 → **total number of parts**

1 is called the numerator.
2 is called the denominator.

2 Look at the circles below. What fractions do you think of when you look at each circle?

a. Which circle shows thirds? How many parts can you count on that circle?

b. Write a fraction for each third. Label the numerator and the denominator.

c. Why can you write the same fraction for each part?

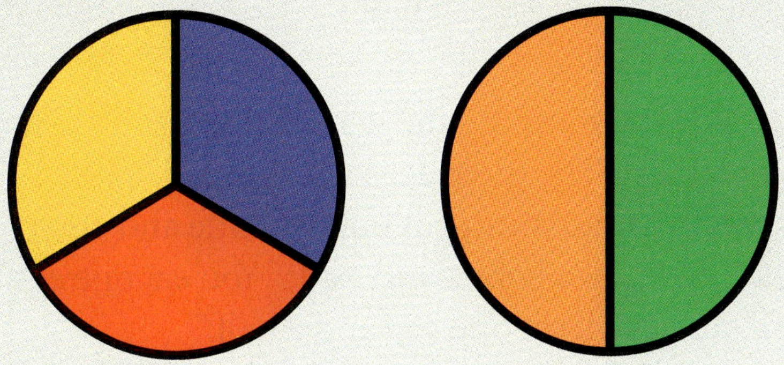

3 Look at the rectangle the student is shading.

a. What fraction tells about the shaded part?

b. What fraction tells about the part not shaded ?

DRAWING TO LEARN

Draw a rectangle. Divide it in thirds. Share your drawing with your partner. How are the drawings alike? How are they different?

What You'll Need

- *Tracing Tool or tracing paper*
- *construction paper*

Activity 2 Friendly Fractions

With Your Class In the story, Selim hopes to find a friend. He will know he has found a friend when he finds someone who shares.

LITERATURE

In this story from Egypt, a young sultan searches for a true friend.

The following morning the woodcutter's son came to breakfast. The three eggs were served. Selim held his breath as the youth got out his knife and cut one of the eggs in two halves and said, "You eat one egg and a half, and I will eat one egg and a half."

Selim laughed for joy, and later when he told his mother the story she said, "This is the friend who seeks you for yourself. Cherish and honor this friendship."

"A Mother's Advice"
told by Ahmed and Zane Zagloul
from *The Black Prince and Other Egyptian Folk Tales*

With Your Partner Selim and his friend each ate one egg and half an egg. One and a half is called a **mixed number.**

$1\frac{1}{2}$ **A mixed number is a whole number and a fraction.**

If Selim had served only one egg, how much of the egg do you think each boy would have eaten?

1. **Look** at the shapes shown below. Each one is part of a whole. Choose one of the parts. Use your Tracing Tool to follow the steps below.

2. **Trace** a part. Trace it again, connecting it to the first drawing. Trace the part four times in all. Did the four parts make a whole? Did the four parts make more than a whole?
3. **Write** the fraction, whole number, or mixed number that describes your drawing.
4. **Choose** another part and try again.
5. **Sketch** your drawings in your journal.

What You'll Need

- *construction paper or newspaper*
- *scissors*

ACTIVITY 3

Fraction Figures

With Your Partner When you count parts, you might have enough parts to make a whole.

1 **Look at the chain of stars. Which fractions make wholes?**

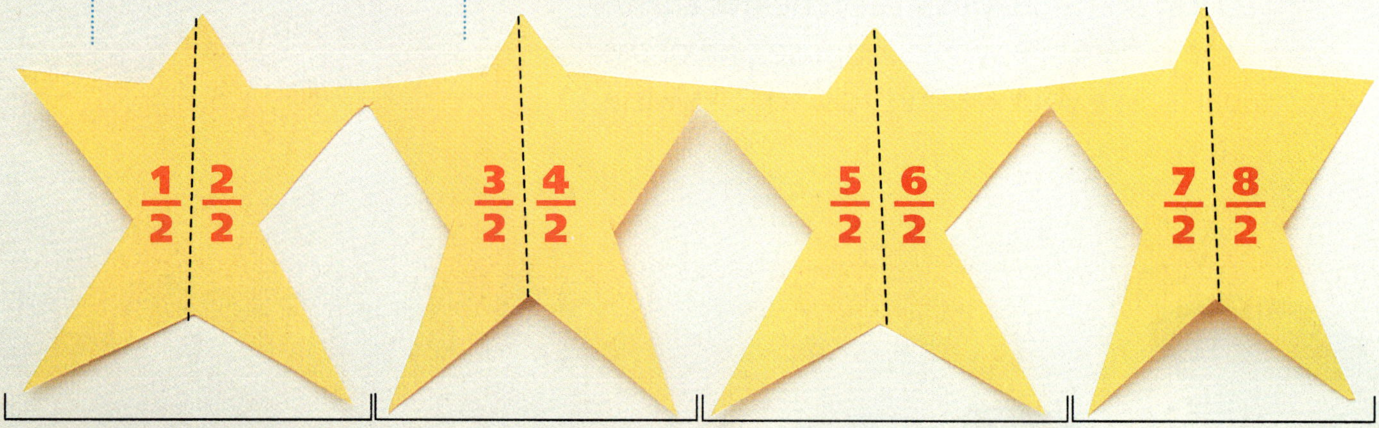

1 whole **2 wholes** **3 wholes** **?**

2 **Now make your own chain. Each person should fold a sheet of paper into fourths or sixths.**

3 **Draw a shape along the middle fold. Have your partner copy the shape. Cut around the shapes as shown. Leave part of your shape uncut on each side so the chain will stay together.**

✔ **Self-Check** *Your denominator should not change as you count fractions across whole shapes.*

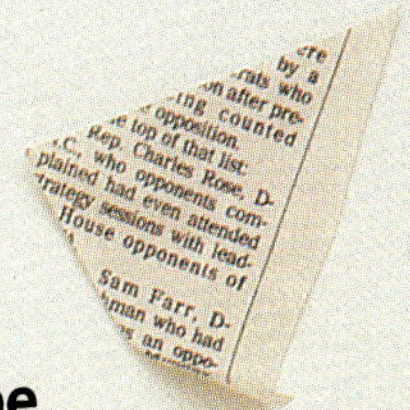

4 **Unfold the paper. Tape your chain to your partner's chain. Count all the parts. Write fractions or whole numbers on the parts.**

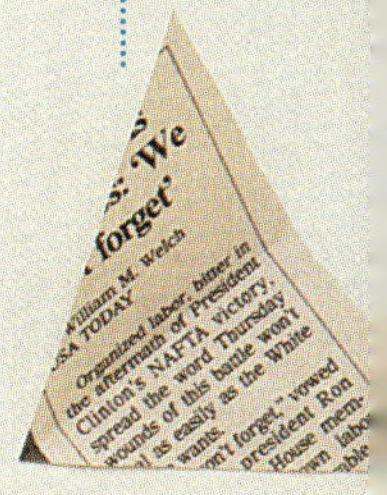

Do You Remember?

Try It!

Write the fraction for the shaded part of the shapes. Then write the mixed number.

1. 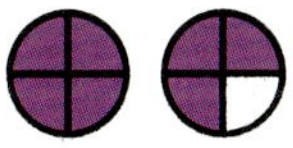
2. 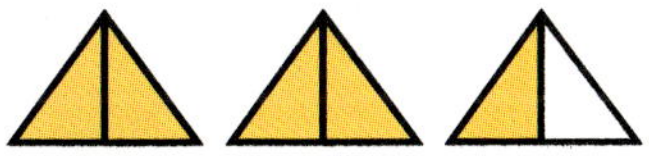
3. 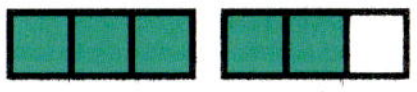
4. 
5. 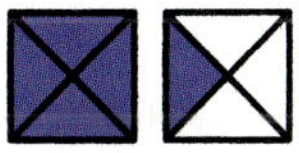
6. 

Round both numbers to the nearest ten. Estimate the sum.

7. 42+ 32
8. 67 + 13
9. 58 + 9
10. 83 + 29
11. 10 + 22
12. 55 + 54

Think About It

13. How do the numerator and denominator help you know whether a fraction is equal to a whole number?

Section B Comparing Fractions

Lesson 3 Size Them Up

You have one third of a circle. Your friend has one fourth. Which piece is bigger? Are both pieces the same? A craft project can help you find the answer.

What You'll Need

- *Fraction Tool or circle shape and ruler*
- *construction paper*
- *scissors*

Activity 1 Fraction Creatures

With Your Class Draw two circles with your Fraction Tool. Cut them into fourths. Make the creatures below. Arrange the parts on your paper.

1. Write the parts as fractions of the circle.
   a. the fish's tail $\frac{?}{4}$
   b. one butterfly wing $\frac{?}{4}$
   c. the whole butterfly $\frac{?}{4}$
   d. the butterfly and the fish's tail $\frac{?}{4}$

2 Now draw another circle. Cut it in thirds to make a cat.

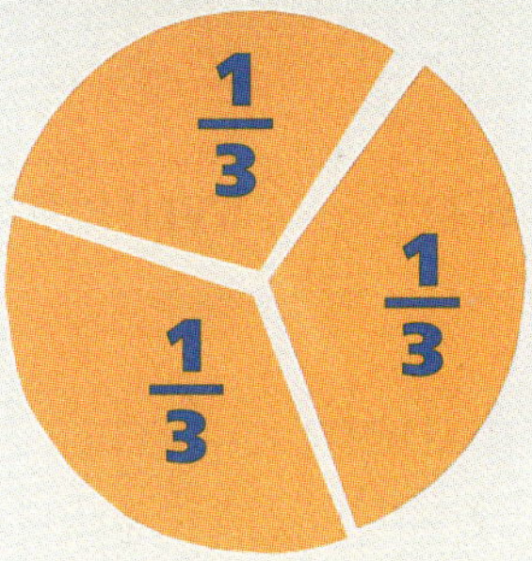

3 Compare creature parts. Write a number sentence for each pair below. Use <, >, or =.

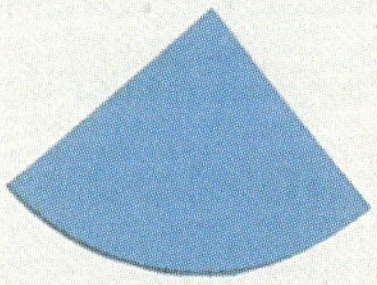

$\frac{1}{4} < \frac{3}{4}$

a. the fish's head and body ● one butterfly wing
b. the fish ● the butterfly and the fish's tail
c. the cat's neck ● the cat's head
d. the whole cat ● the cat's neck

4 Compare more parts. Write a number sentence for each pair. Use <, >, or =. Write a rule for comparing fractions.
a. one butterfly wing ● the cat's head
b. the fish's tail ● the cat's neck
c. the fish's head and body ● the whole cat

$\frac{1}{3} > \frac{1}{4}$

REASONING AND PROBLEM SOLVING

Explain how you compared fractions that have the same denominator. Is it different from comparing fractions that have the same numerator? How?

DRAWING TO LEARN

When you compare parts of circles, why is it important to draw all of the circles the same size?

What You'll Need

- *Fraction Tool or circle shape and ruler*
- *scissors*
- *construction paper*

Self-Check *Are all of your fractions or mixed numbers written correctly? To check, put the parts of each creature back into its original circle.*

ACTIVITY 2

Great and Small

With Your Partner Comparing fractions can help you put them in order. Draw and divide three circles that are the same size. Make fourths, sixths, and eighths.

1 What fraction of a circle is each part? Write the fraction on the back of the part.

2 Look at the pieces below. Put them in order from least to greatest. How would comparing two fractions at a time help you order them?

$\frac{2}{6}$  $\frac{1}{8}$  $\frac{1}{4}$ 

3 Each set below has three fractions or mixed numbers. Use the fraction pieces you made to order the numbers from least to greatest.

a. $\frac{1}{6}, \frac{1}{8}, \frac{1}{4}$ **b.** $\frac{2}{4}, \frac{2}{6}, \frac{2}{8}$

c. $\frac{5}{6}, \frac{3}{8}, \frac{2}{4}$ **d.** $2\frac{1}{6}, 1\frac{3}{8}, 1\frac{1}{6}$

4 Explain how you decided the order for the mixed numbers in d.

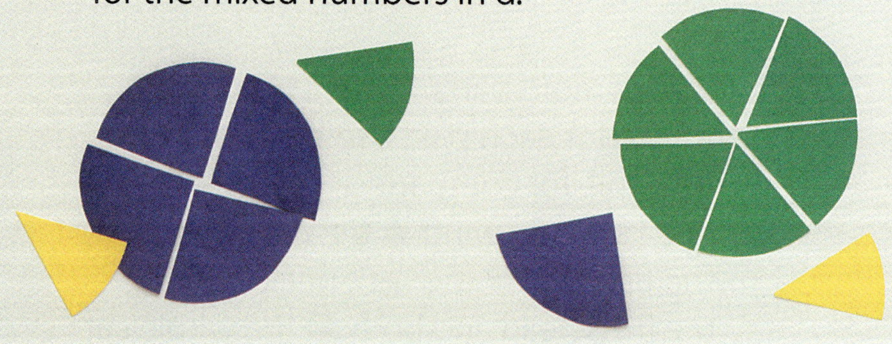

5 Make up four more different sets of three fractions to order. Trade with a partner.

ACTIVITY 3 Same but Different

With Your Class Sometimes fractions that look different are really the same. How can that be? Follow the steps below and find out.

What You'll Need
- *drawing paper*
- *string*
- *scissors*
- *crayons or markers*

1. Make four strips of paper. Fold a piece of paper lengthwise. Then cut along the folds.

2 **Fold each strip in half. Unfold each strip and color half of it.**

3 **Fold one strip into fourths. Fold another into eighths. Fold the third strip into more equal parts. Draw dark lines along the folds.**

4 **On each strip, count the total number of parts. Count the shaded parts. Write a fraction for the shaded parts.**

5. Are all the fractions you wrote equal to $\frac{1}{2}$? How do you know? Fractions that are equal are called **equivalent fractions.**

6. Use your paper strips to make a craft creature. Choose the one shown here or think of one of your own.

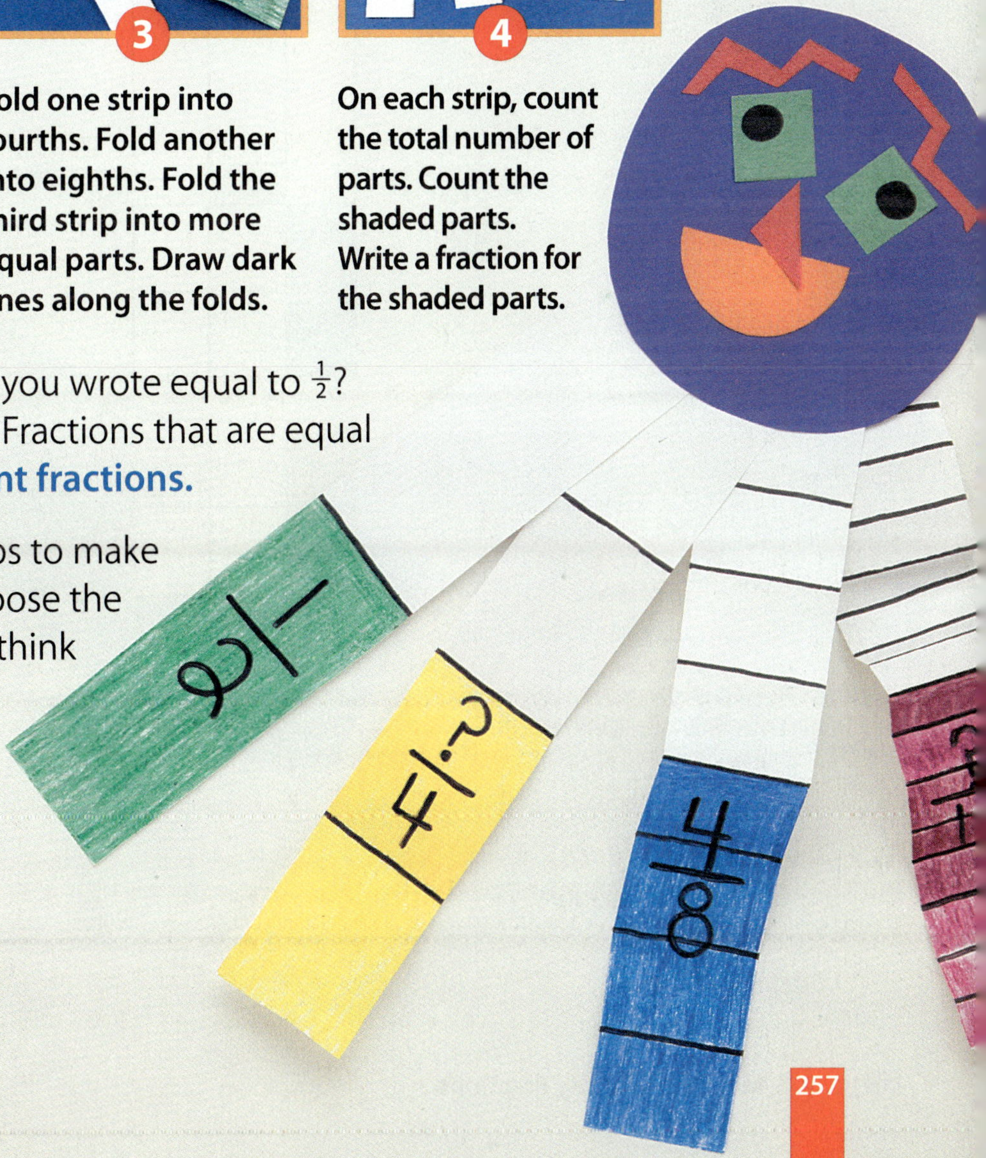

What You'll Need

- *drawing paper*
- *crayons or markers*
- *scissors*
- *paste or tape*

ACTIVITY 4 Fraction Flags

With Your Partner How can you find equivalent fractions for $\frac{1}{3}$? Make a fraction flag and see!

1. Fold three sheets of paper into thirds. Unfold them. Shade one third of each sheet a different color.
2. Fold one of the sheets into sixths. Fold another into even more equal parts.
3. Unfold your sheets. Write a fraction for the shaded part of each sheet.

DRAWING TO LEARN

Draw rectangles on grid paper. Make one side of each rectangle 3 squares long. Shade $\frac{1}{3}$ of each rectangle. Count squares to help you name fractions equal to $\frac{1}{3}$.

4. Are all the fractions equal to $\frac{1}{3}$? How do you know? How could you find other fractions equal to $\frac{1}{3}$?

5. Put aside the sheet divided into thirds. Cut out the shaded parts on the other two sheets. You can cut these parts into smaller equal pieces.

6. Make a flag. Paste the pieces you cut on the sheet divided into thirds. Does each color cover $\frac{1}{3}$ of the flag? How do you know?

REASONING AND PROBLEM SOLVING

Look at the fractions you found equal to $\frac{1}{3}$. Do you see a pattern in numerators and denominators? Use the pattern to guess other fractions equal to $\frac{1}{3}$.

Do You Remember?

Try It!

Write an equivalent fraction. Fold and shade a sheet of paper to help you.

1. $\frac{1}{4}$ 2. $\frac{3}{4}$ 3. $\frac{2}{3}$ 4. $\frac{1}{6}$ 5. $\frac{2}{6}$ 6. $\frac{2}{2}$

Choose the best way to measure. Write *kg*, *L*, or *km*.

7. a long walk 8. a bag of fruit 9. fruit juice
10. cereal 11. a trip to the moon 12. tub of water

Think About It

13. Do you think someone could list all the fractions equal to $\frac{1}{2}$? Why or why not?

Lesson 4 In Between

You see numbers on a number line. In between are other numbers you do not see. Find out more about them.

What You'll Need

- *Fraction Tool or circle shape and ruler*
- *construction paper*
- *string*
- *paper clips*
- *crayons or markers*
- *paste, glue, or tape*

Activity 1 Fraction Hang-ups

With Your Group Estimate where fraction creatures belong on a number line.

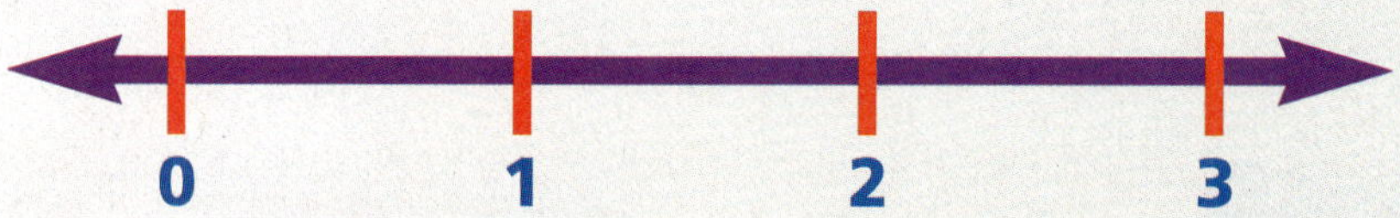

1. How many halves of a circle are in each creature? Write a fraction or a mixed number. Where would you place each number on the number line? How did you decide?

2. Now make your own fraction creatures. Each person should make a creature with a different number of fourths. Draw the circles you need. Cut them into fourths.

3. Glue your creature to a slip of paper. Write its fraction or mixed number on the back.

ACTIVITY OPTION

Make another mobile with creatures made from thirds and sixths of a circle.

4. Work together to make a mobile. Fold three different color sheets of paper the long way. Fold the long way again. Cut on the middle fold.

5. Tape your strips to each other lengthwise. Keep the fold on top. Run a string under the fold. Mark 0, 1, 2, and 3 on your number line.

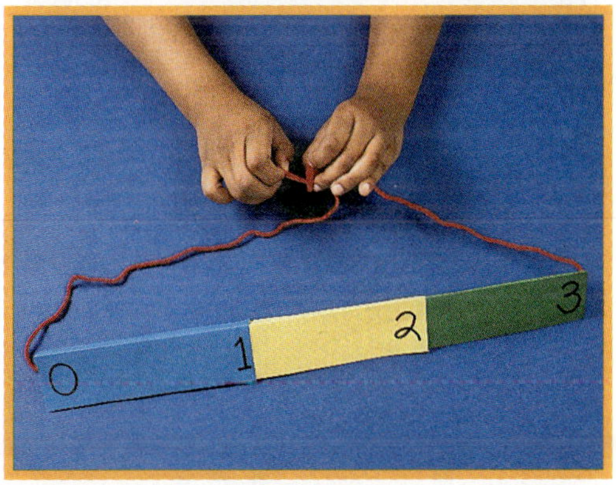

6. Tape or tie a string to each creature. Tie the string to a paper clip. Discuss where to hang your creatures on the number line. See whether other groups agree.

What You'll Need
- *ruler*
- *scissors*

TOOLS AND TECHNIQUES

With a drawing program you could draw and compare figures on the computer screen.

ACTIVITY 2

House of Fractions

With Your Partner How is your ruler like a number line? You know the ruler numbers show inches. What do the marks in between them show?

1 **Find the mark that divides one inch (1 in.) in half. This mark shows $\frac{1}{2}$ in. Find the mark that shows $1\frac{1}{2}$ in.**

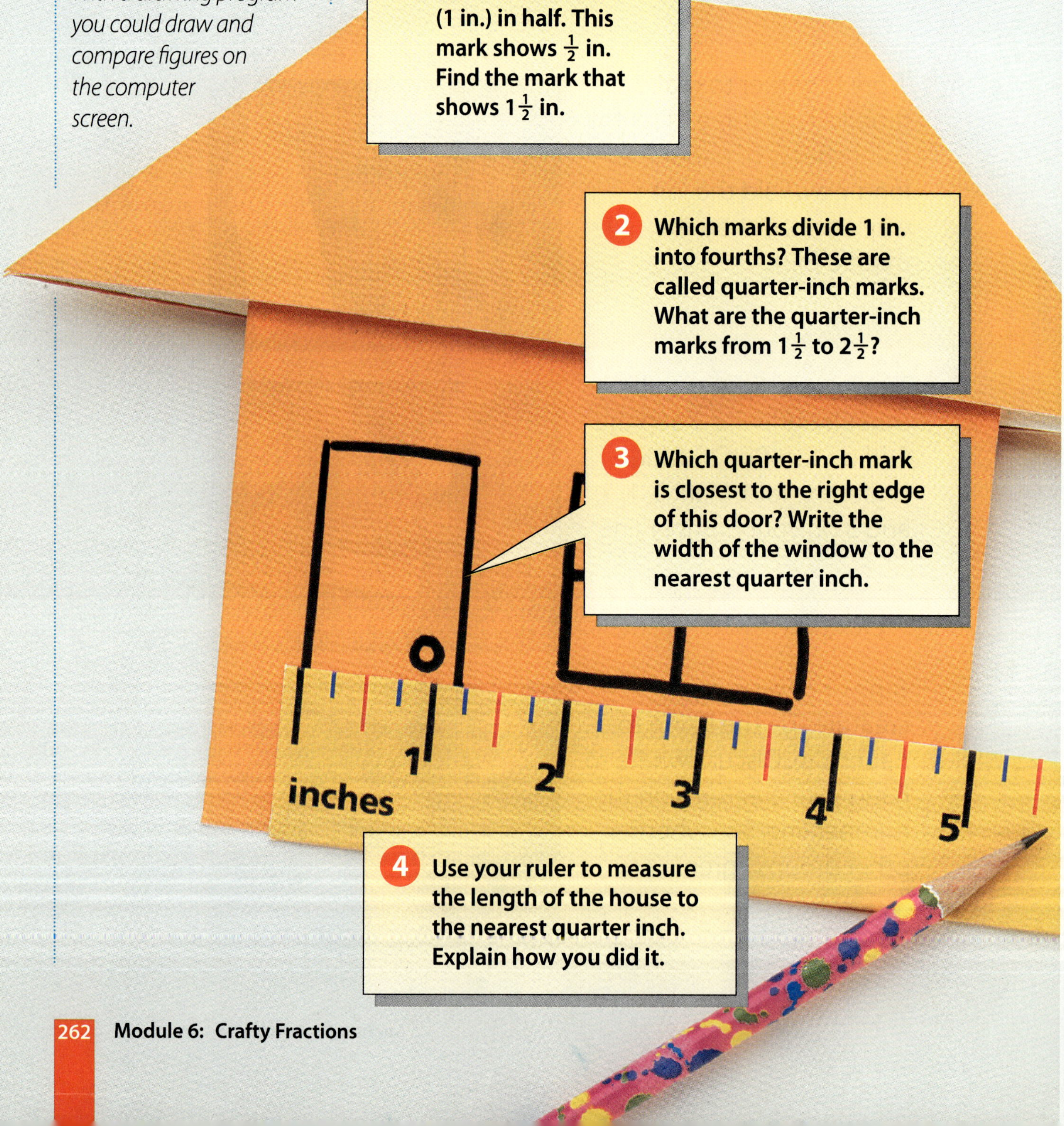

2 **Which marks divide 1 in. into fourths? These are called quarter-inch marks. What are the quarter-inch marks from $1\frac{1}{2}$ to $2\frac{1}{2}$?**

3 **Which quarter-inch mark is closest to the right edge of this door? Write the width of the window to the nearest quarter inch.**

4 **Use your ruler to measure the length of the house to the nearest quarter inch. Explain how you did it.**

5

Make a paper house to measure. Fold and cut a sheet of paper in half.

6

Fold one of the pieces in half like a book. Draw a window and a door. Fold the other piece in half the long way. Fold the corners down to make a roof.

7

Measure parts of your house to the nearest quarter inch. Record the measurements. Give your house to a partner to measure. Compare your measurements.

Do You Remember?

Try It!

Look at the shapes in this box. Measure the distance between the points to the nearest quarter inch.

1. A to B
2. B to C
3. C to D
4. A to D
5. D to B
6. A to C

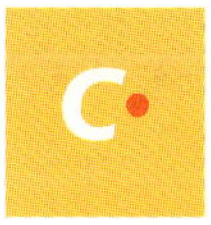

Find the missing factor.

7. $2 \times \blacksquare = 18$
8. $3 \times \blacksquare = 21$
9. $\blacksquare \times 4 = 16$
10. $9 \times \blacksquare = 45$
11. $\blacksquare \times 3 = 36$

Think About It

12. You can measure to the nearest quarter inch or the nearest half inch. Which is more exact? Why?

Craft Corner

It's craft time! Help the students in this class plan projects and share craft supplies.

1. You hand out 17 pairs of scissors to 5 groups. Each group gets the same number of scissors. How many pairs are left over?

2. Help 3 students share their craft sticks. One student has 56 sticks. One has 13 sticks. One has 21 sticks. How many groups of 10 sticks should each student get?

3. A student needs 3 blue, 4 pink, 5 green, and 6 red tiles for a project. Show how many are needed for 2, 3, 4, and 5 students. Make a chart.

4. Students are covering box lids with square tiles. The first lid is 7 tiles long by 4 wide. The second is 7 by 7. The third is 9 by 5. Which lid needs the most tiles?

5 Look at the craft table. Which objects are spheres? shaped like cylinders? like rectangular prisms?

6 Name three objects on the craft table that have flat faces.

7 How can you divide 4 sheets of paper equally among 16 students?

8 A student covered a box with green and yellow paper. The box is a cube. If 2 faces of the box are yellow, how many faces are green?

9 One side of a cube is 8 cm wide. To wrap yarn 2 times around the middle of the cube, how much yarn do you need?

Check Your Math Power

10 Students cut some felt into pieces. Each piece was 2 square units. Each student took $\frac{1}{5}$ of the felt. What shape might the felt have been before they cut it?

a. Draw three possible shapes on grid paper.

b. Shade $\frac{1}{5}$ of each shape.

LESSON 5 Paper Chain

What You'll Need
- *construction paper*
- *scissors*
- *tape, paste, or glue*

ACTIVITY 1 Linking Fractions

On Your Own Fold your paper in half three times. Fold the same way each time. Unfold the paper. What fraction is each part? Write an addition or subtraction for each question below.

1. Cut apart the eighths. Trade some with another student. How many eighths are left?

2. Put the new eighths with the eighths you had left. How many do you have?

3. Make two chains with different numbers of eighths. How many eighths are in both?

ACTIVITY 2 Chain Exchange

With Your Partner Fold two pieces of paper into sixths. Cut off two sixths. Start a chain.

1. Cut off more sixths. How many sixths are left on that sheet? Write a subtraction sentence.
2. Connect the sixths you cut to the sixths on the chain. Write an addition sentence.
3. Repeat until you have no more sixths. Cut off a different number of sixths each time.

What You'll Need

- *2 sheets of construction paper*
- *scissors*
- *tape, paste, or glue*

Do You Remember? Try It!

Name two fractions that give each sum below. Write the number sentence.

1. 4 thirds
2. 10 fifths
3. 2 fourths
4. 8 tenths
5. 6 halves
6. 12 ninths

What is the remainder?

7. $5\overline{)28}$ 8. $9\overline{)87}$ 9. $7\overline{)52}$ 10. $8\overline{)65}$ 11. $9\overline{)72}$

Think About It

12. Explain how you found the two fractions to add in Exercises 1 through 6.

CONNECT AND COMMUNICATE

How are fractions like whole numbers when you add and subtract them?

LESSON 6 Fractions in Action

What You'll Need
- *inch grid paper*
- *scissors*
- *crayons or markers, 2 colors*

Get in on the action. Add and subtract with fractions.

ACTIVITY 1 Pick a Pattern

With Your Partner Make fraction patterns with shapes and numbers.

1 **Plan how to cut your grid into five different pieces. Each piece should have from three to eight squares.**

2 **For each piece, shade some parts yellow, some parts green, and leave some parts plain.**

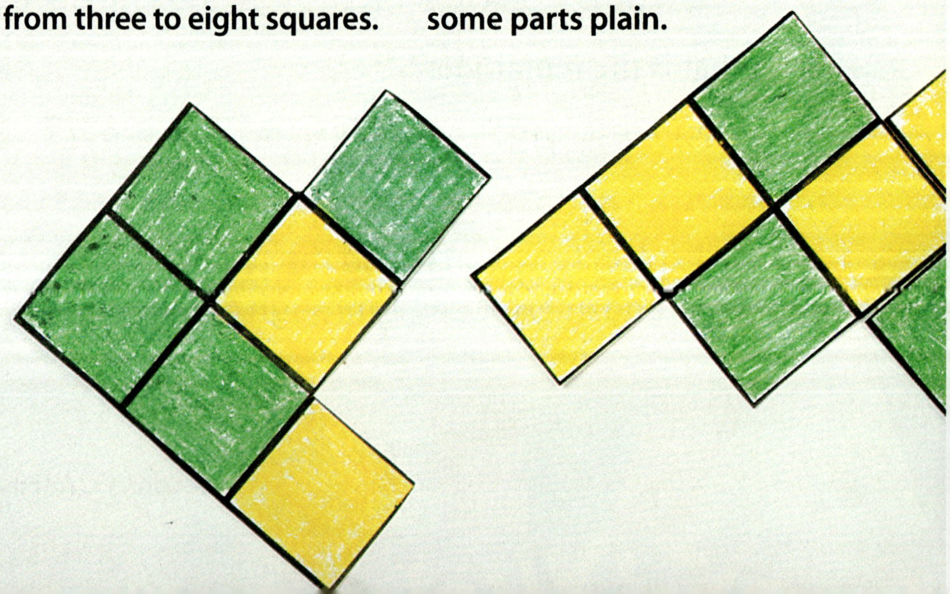

REASONING AND PROBLEM SOLVING

Look at the additions and subtractions you wrote. How did you get the numerator in each answer? How did you get the denominator?

3 Write an addition sentence like the one above or below for each grid piece. Tell what your sentence means.

$$\frac{1}{6} + \frac{2}{6} = \frac{3}{6}$$

4 Write a subtraction sentence like the one above or below for each grid piece. Tell what your sentence means.

$$\frac{6}{6} - \frac{3}{6} = \frac{3}{6}$$

DRAWING TO LEARN

Make a grid piece for each row on the chart. How does the grid piece help you add or subtract fractions?

5 **Suppose you shaded all the squares in some grid pieces. Copy and complete the chart below to find the missing fractions.**

FRACTION SQUARES

What You'll Need
- *gameboard*
- *color tiles*
- *cube labeled 2, 4, and 8*
- *cube labeled + and −*
- *game pieces*

ACTIVITY OPTION

Play a variation of this game. A player must finish covering a quilt square before starting another.

Activity 2 Quilt a Fraction

With Your Group In this game, you will get a chance to use what you have learned about fractions. Play the game in a group of four. Try to be the first one in your group to cover your whole quilt!

Getting Ready to Play the Game

1. Make a 2, 4, 8 number cube and a +/− cube. Then make a spinner labeled 1 through 5.
2. Choose a quilt and trace it. Cut out the small triangles to use as game pieces.
3. Roll the number cube. Use the number as the denominator for two fractions. Then spin the spinner two times to get the numerators.
4. Roll the +/− cube. Add or subtract the fractions to get your score.

How to Put Tiles on Your Quilt

5. Use your score to cover part of a quilt square with game pieces. Each square is outlined in black. Try to be first to cover your six squares.
6. Place tiles on a square when it is completely covered.
7. Check other players after each turn. Is their score correct? Are their tiles placed correctly?
8. The first player to complete a quilt wins.

Self-Check *Equal fractions can help you cover your quilt. Which equal fractions let you place one tile? two tiles?*

Star Crafts

Look at the stars on this page. They are made from squares of paper that have been folded and cut. Add and subtract fractions to solve the problems.

1 Cut and Fold

The square on the right is divided in half. How many squares must be cut to have $\frac{5}{2}$?

2 Cut-and-Paste Star

a. What part of the big star is yellow? Write the fraction.

b. What part of the star is blue? Write the fraction.

3 Six-Point Stars

Describe how you would use squares of paper to make one of the stars at the right. Use fractions to show what you would do.

4 Four-Point Star

a. What fraction of the star is colored blue and red?

b. What is the sum of the blue parts and the yellow parts?

5 Open Star

a. What fraction of the star is the darker part?

b. What fraction of the star is the lighter part?

6 Eight-Point Star

a. What two equal fractions describe half of the star?

b. What is the sum of the shaded parts?

c. What fraction of the star is yellow?

Investigation

Weaving Fun

The Ashanti people of Africa weave kente (KEN-tay) cloth from strips of silk. You can do the same thing with paper. Use fractions to plan a pattern and tell what you did.

1 Use different colored paper for each weaving. Pick colors you like. Cut the sheets into 12-in.-by-1-in. strips.

2 Fold a large sheet of paper. Fold it in half the short way. From the fold, cut slits 1 in. apart. Stop 1 in. from the top. Unfold.

3 Weave color strips through the slits. One strip goes over, under, over, under. The next strip goes under, over, under, over.

4 Make two weavings. Plan each pattern. What fraction of the strips will be in each color? In what order will you weave the color strips?

5 Write a report about your weavings. Use fractions to tell what you did. Add and subtract fractions to compare your patterns.

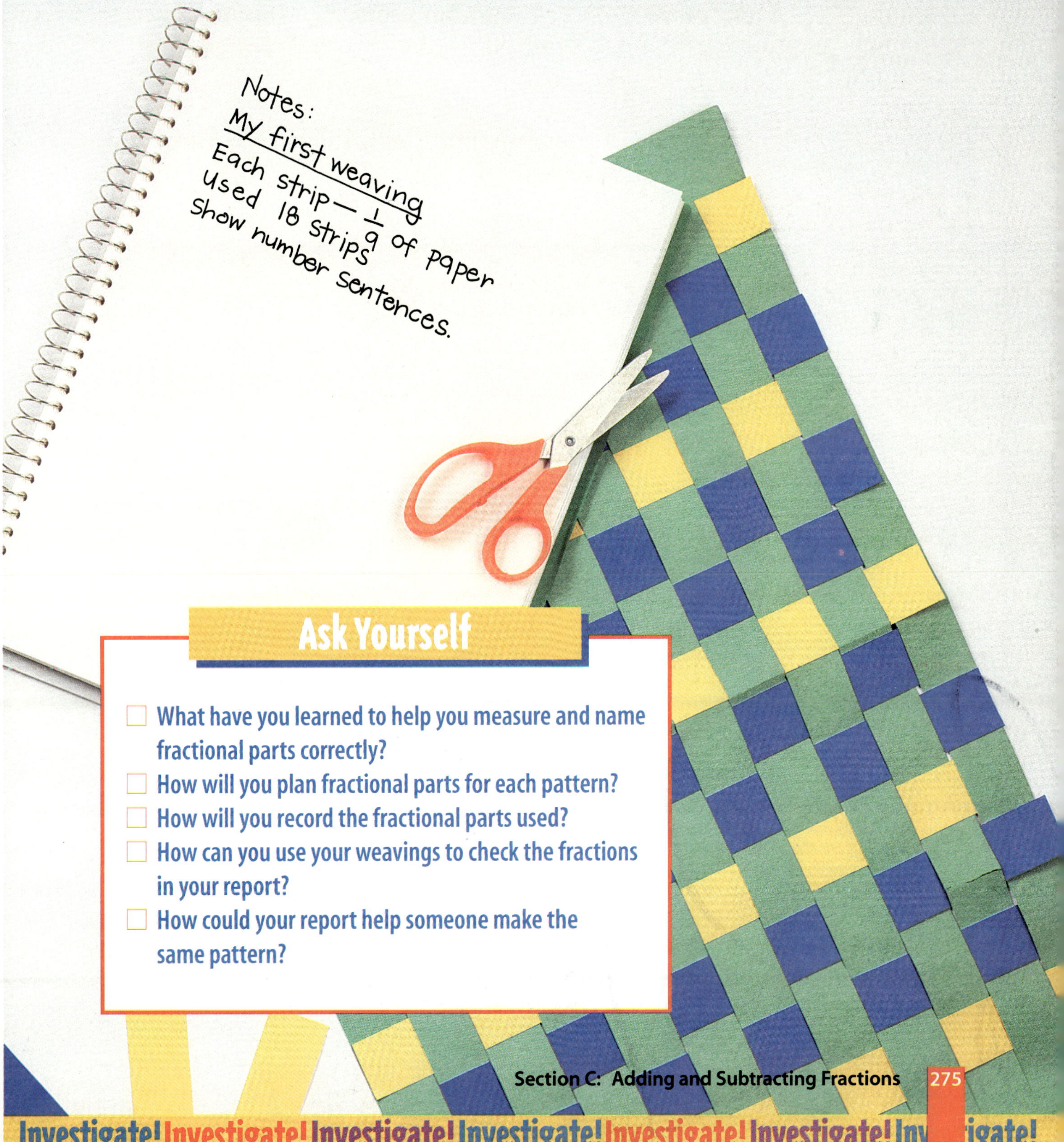

Ask Yourself

- ☐ What have you learned to help you measure and name fractional parts correctly?
- ☐ How will you plan fractional parts for each pattern?
- ☐ How will you record the fractional parts used?
- ☐ How can you use your weavings to check the fractions in your report?
- ☐ How could your report help someone make the same pattern?

Section D Fractions in Sets and Probability

Lesson 7 Fair Share

How can a group fairly share a box full of craft supplies?

Activity 1 Some for Everyone

With Your Class You can find a fraction of a whole. You can also find a fraction of a set.

1. The set of crayons below is divided into two equal parts. What fraction of the set is each part? How many crayons are in each half?

2. Show another way to divide the set in half. Make a sketch.
3. Draw another set of 12. Make three equal parts. How many are in each third?

CONNECT AND COMMUNICATE

Talk about how arrays help you find fractions of a set.

With Your Group Look at the set of 12 craft items shown below.

4. Why can you say that the crayons are $\frac{4}{12}$ of the set?

5. Answer these questions in any order.
   a. What fraction of the set are the scissors?
   b. What fraction of the set are not sheets of paper?

6. Describe how you would change the items in the set so that each fourth could have the exact same items.

What You'll Need
- *Geometry Tool or shapes to trace*
- *construction paper in various colors*
- *scissors*
- *tape, paste, or glue*
- *index cards*

ACTIVITY 2 Picture the Parts

On Your Own Mosaic patterns are sets of small pieces of color. Make your own mosaic.

1. What fraction of the set above are circles?
2. What fraction of the set above are squares?
3. What fraction of the set below are triangles?

4. Use your Geometry Tool to make and cut out different shapes. Make as many as you need to create your own mosaic pattern.
5. What fraction of your mosaic is each shape? What fraction is each color?

With Your Partner Cut out more paper shapes. Paste them on index cards.

6. What fraction of the set is each shape? Write fractions on the back of the card.

7. Trade cards. Look at the shapes. What fractions do you see? Write fractions in your notebook. Compare your fractions to those on the back of the card.

DRAWING TO LEARN

Make a sharing bulletin board. Draw an item you have shared. Pin the drawing onto the board.

Do You Remember?

Try It!

Write the fraction for the part of the set that is not shaded.

1. 

2. 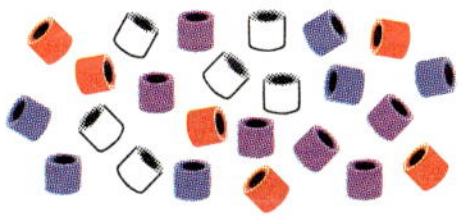

3. 

4. 

5. 

6. 

Find the product.

7. 7×7 8. 6×9 9. 7×6 10. 9×8 11. 6×5

Think About It

12. How will your answers for Exercises 1 through 6 change if you add one more red shape?

LESSON 8

Chances and Choices

Think about flipping a coin. Do you think you are more likely to flip heads or tails? Which do you have a greater chance of flipping? Why?

What You'll Need

- *crayons or markers*
- *tape*
- *scissors*
- *small paper bag*

ACTIVITY 1 Chance Crown

With Your Class Make a crown!

1. Draw and cut 4 strips of 8 rectangles each.
2. Put a red, a blue, and a yellow crayon in a bag. Do you have an equal chance of picking a red, a blue, or a yellow? Explain your answer.
3. Pull a crayon from the bag without looking. Color one rectangle.

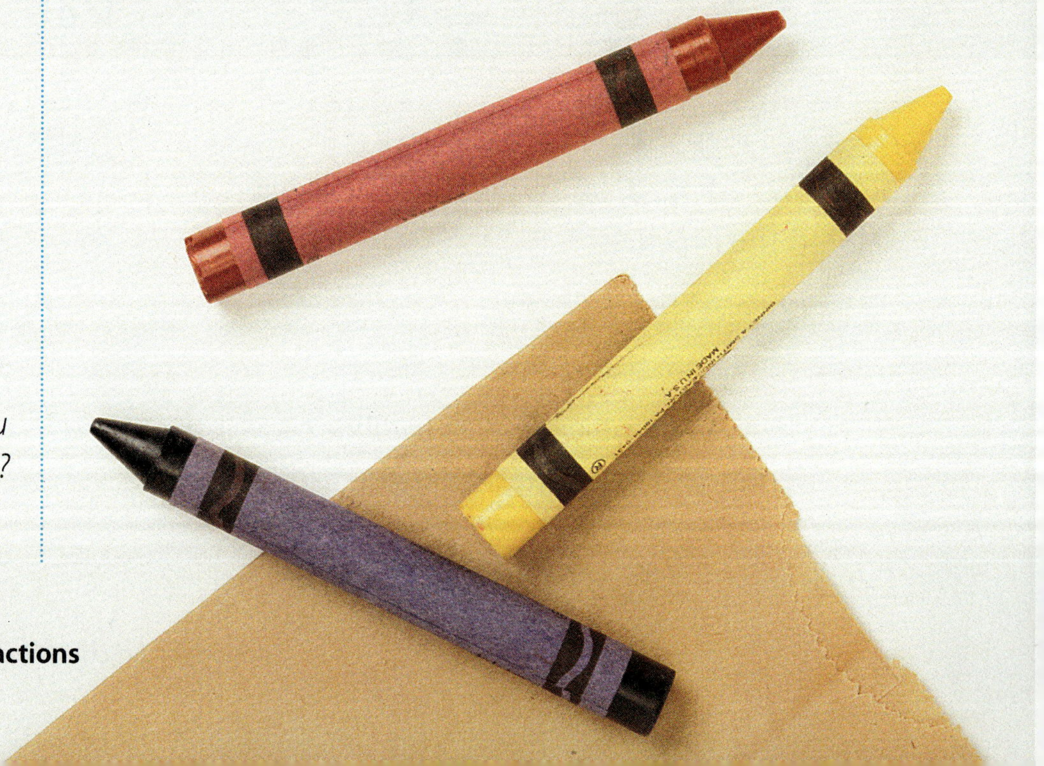

Self-Check *Do you have four strips of paper? Does each strip have eight rectangles?*

4. Follow these steps. Pull out a crayon. Color a rectangle. Return the crayon to the bag. Repeat until you have colored all the rectangles on two strips. How many rectangles of each color do you have?

5. Empty the bag. Put one red and two blue crayons in the bag. Do you have the same chance of picking either color? Explain.

6. Pull crayons from the bag. Follow Steps 3 and 4. Describe your strips.

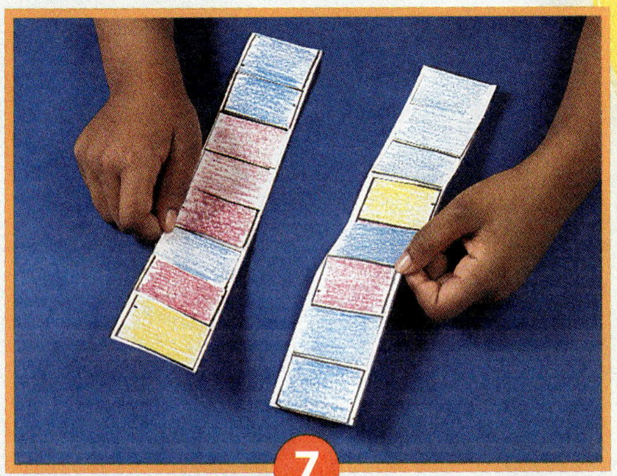

7. **Compare two strips of paper. Why do they look different?**

8. **Choose two strips. Tape the ends together to make a chance crown.**

CONNECT AND COMMUNICATE

In Your Journal *Write about a game you have played that uses a spinner. How does a spinner depend on chance? Why does a spinner keep a game fair?*

What You'll Need

- *grid paper*
- *crayons or markers*
- *spinners*

TOOLS AND TECHNIQUES

How can you use your Fraction Tool to help you make spinners with three equal parts?

Activity 2 Color Your Chances

With Your Partner You can make **predictions** to tell what you think will happen.

1. Choose to make spinner A or B. Then complete the activity.
   a. Make three equal parts. Color two parts yellow and one part green.
   b. Make three equal parts. Color one yellow, one blue, and one green.

Spinner A

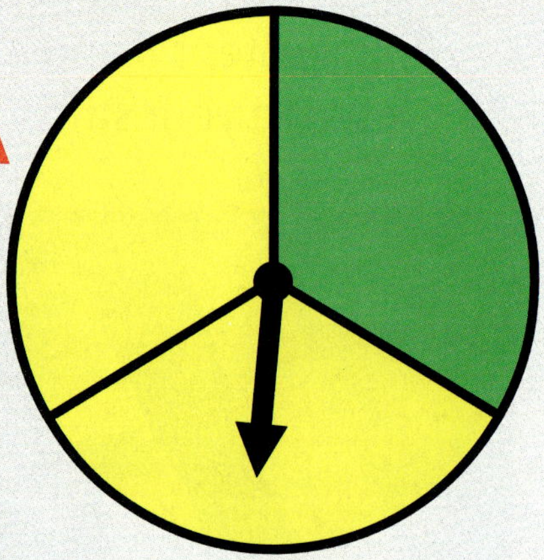

Spinner B

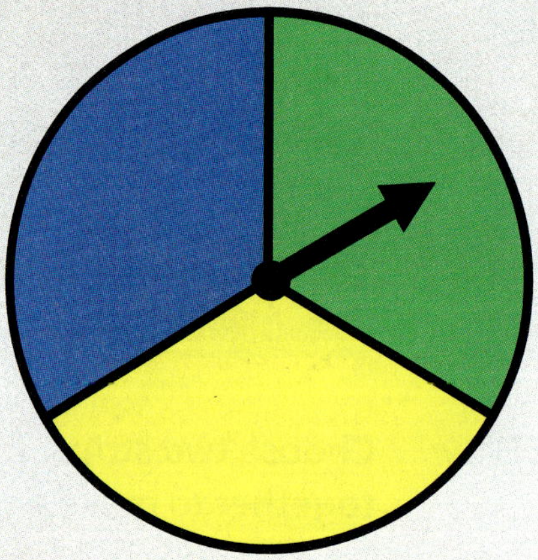

2. Predict which color you are likely to spin most often. Why did you make that prediction?

3. Test your prediction. Do 20 spins. For each spin, color a square on a sheet of grid paper.

4. Look at your grid paper. Did you spin one color more often than another? Why do you think that happened?

5. Compare the results to your prediction.

6. Design and make another spinner. Predict what will happen. Test your predictions.

REASONING AND PROBLEM SOLVING

Think of another tool you could use to test chance. How could you use that tool to complete this activity?

Do You Remember?

Try It!

Tell whether or not you have an equal chance of spinning red.

1. 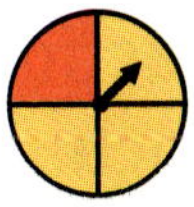 2. 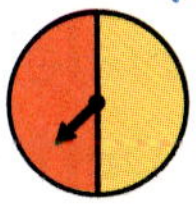 3.  4. 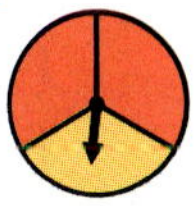 5. 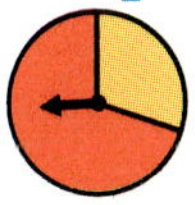 6. 

What is the volume?

7.  8. 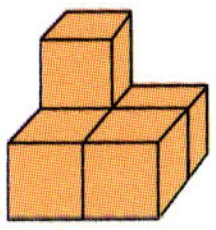 9. 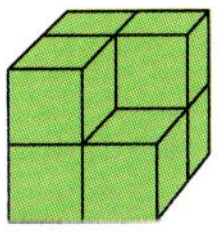 10. 

Think About It

11. On which two spinners in Exercises 1 through 6 do you have twice the chance of spinning red as spinning yellow? Explain.

Do You Remember?

Cumulative Review

Looking Back

Choose the right answer. Write *a, b, c,* or *d* for each question.

Match each sentence with the square or squares it describes. Use the squares for Exercises 1 through 3.

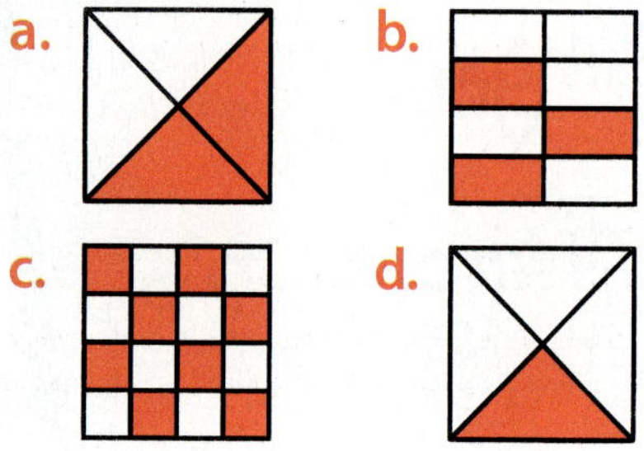

1. $\frac{1}{4}$ of the square is red.
2. $\frac{3}{8}$ of the square is red.
3. $\frac{1}{2}$ of the square is red.

Choose the best place on the number line for the fraction or mixed number. Use the number line for Exercises 4 through 7.

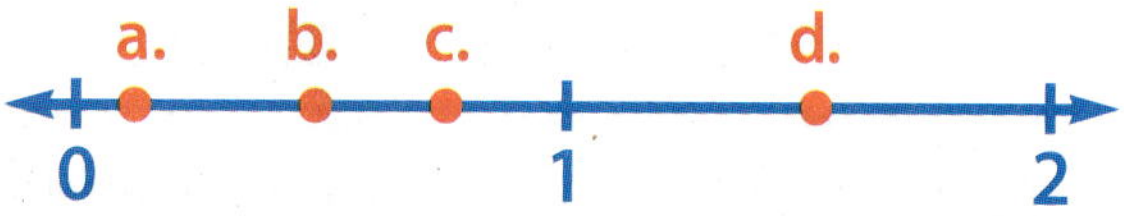

4. $1\frac{1}{2}$
5. $\frac{1}{8}$
6. $\frac{3}{4}$
7. $\frac{3}{2}$

Measure each line in Exercises 8 through 11 to the nearest quarter inch. Match the line with its measurement below.

a. $1\frac{2}{4}$ in. b. 1 in.

c. $\frac{3}{4}$ in. d. $2\frac{1}{4}$ in.

8.
9.
10.
11.

Name two equivalent fractions for the shaded part in each picture below.

12.

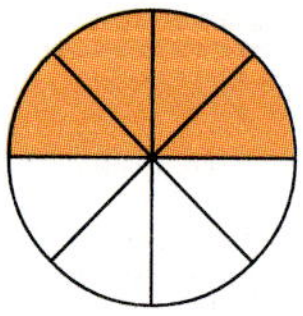

a. $\frac{2}{4}, \frac{2}{8}$ b. $\frac{1}{2}, \frac{4}{8}$ c. $\frac{8}{12}, \frac{4}{6}$ d. $\frac{4}{12}, \frac{1}{3}$

13.

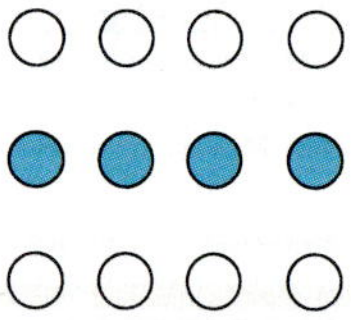

a. $\frac{2}{4}, \frac{2}{8}$ b. $\frac{1}{2}, \frac{4}{8}$ c. $\frac{8}{12}, \frac{4}{6}$ d. $\frac{4}{12}, \frac{1}{3}$

Use the spinners below for Exercises 14 through 16.

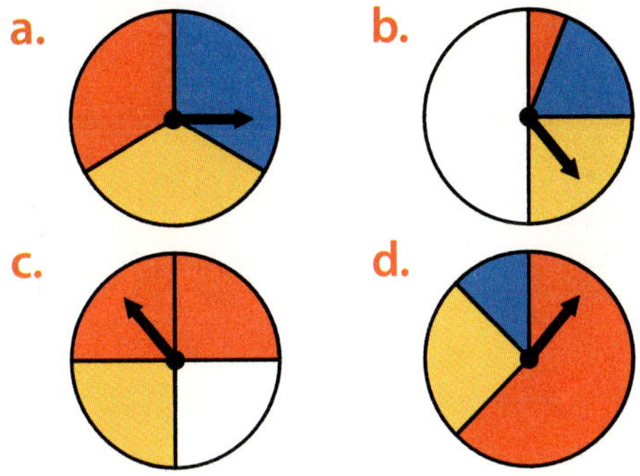

14. With which spinner do you have the greatest chance to spin red?

15. With which spinner do you have the least chance to spin red?

16. With which spinner do you have an equal chance to spin each color?

Add or subtract parts of these circles. Use the answers below for Exercises 17 through 20.

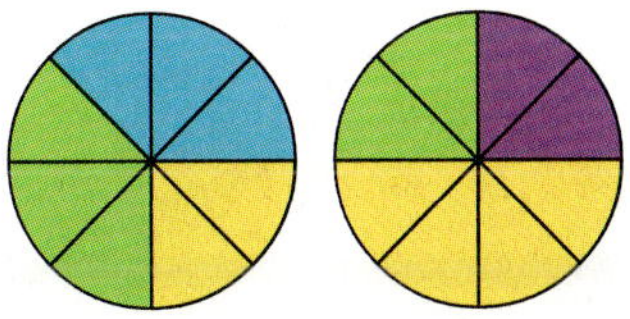

a. $\frac{5}{8}$ b. $1\frac{6}{8}$

c. $\frac{6}{8}$ d. $1\frac{3}{8}$

17. blue parts + purple parts

18. yellow parts + green parts

19. 2 circles − purple parts

20. 1 circle − blue parts

A box had 12 stars. Asha took $\frac{1}{4}$ of the stars. Juan took $\frac{1}{3}$. Chris took $\frac{1}{6}$. Barb took 3. Use this information for Exercises 21 through 23 .

21. Who took the same number of stars as Barb?

    a. Asha b. Chris
    c. Juan d. nobody

22. Chris and Juan put their stars together. Count them. What fraction of the stars do they have?

    a. $\frac{1}{2}$ b. $\frac{2}{6}$
    c. $\frac{2}{3}$ d. $\frac{1}{6}$

23. How many more stars does Barb need to have $\frac{2}{3}$ of the stars?

    a. 8 b. 2
    c. 3 d. 5

Check Your Math Power

24. Write three different number sentences to add any shaded parts of these squares.

25. Three pieces of string add up to 2 inches in length. How long might the pieces be? Give two possibilities.

MODULE 6 **Investigations**

Facts and Fiction

Making a book about fractions is a good way to share what you learned with other people. A book can teach new ideas. It can also tell a story.

Investigation A Read All About It

How would you make a book to teach a second grader about fractions? Use the information on the next page to make your book.

1. In your book, you will need to tell what a fraction is. Choose at least one more thing to teach about fractions.
2. Decide how many pages your book needs. Make a plan to show what will be on each page.
3. Write one or two sentences on each page. Use pictures and craft constructions to help explain your ideas. Be creative! You can use fraction creatures. You can make a pop-up book.
4. Find a way to put your pages together with a cover. How will they stay together?
5. Help a second grader read your book. Is there anything the student doesn't understand? Change any words or pictures or add new pages if you have to.

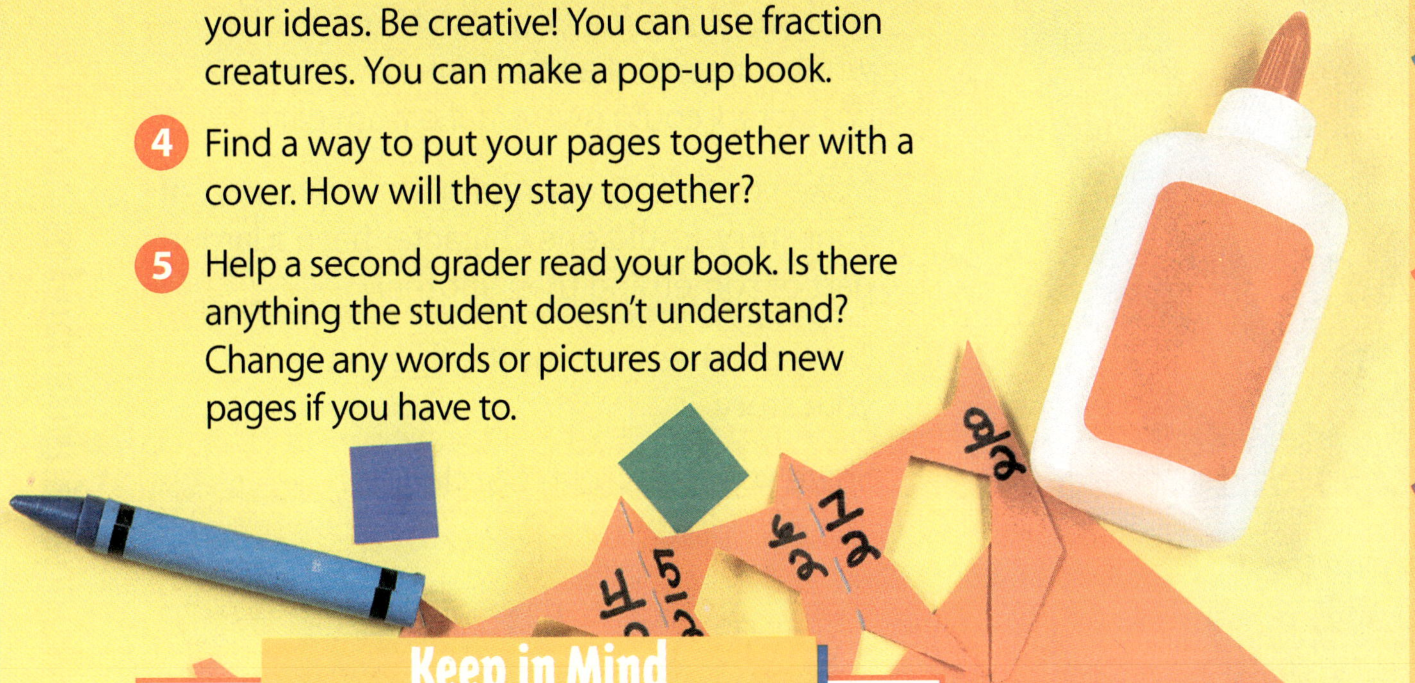

Keep in Mind

Your work will be evaluated on the following points:

- ☐ Would your book help a younger student understand what a fraction is?
- ☐ Do you share more than one thing about fractions?
- ☐ Do you use pictures or crafts to explain your ideas?
- ☐ Can some one follow your plan to make a book of their own?
- ☐ Are your sentences and words easy for a second grader to read?

Investigation B

Fraction Tales

1. Write a storybook using fractions. Try to put a fraction in almost every sentence. You can fold sheets of paper in half to make a book.
2. Make adding or subtracting fractions part of your story. The fractions can be parts of a whole or parts of a set. Think about what characters could give or take from each other.
3. Make comparing or ordering fractions part of your story. Could one character have a larger part of something than another?
4. Draw pictures to show the fractions in your story.
5. Share your story with the class.

Ongoing Investigation

How Do We Grow?

Are students in your class growing at different rates? Measure your height and reach again. Find the total number of inches your class has grown in height and in reach. Then find the totals for all the girls in your class and all the boys. Which group has grown more? How can you use fractions to show what part of the total growth is the girls' growth? the boys' growth?

MODULE 7

Food for Your Life

Everyone needs good food. There are so many fun kinds from which to pick! How do you decide what to eat? How much do you eat? Do you ever buy food? Math can help you learn new things about food!

SECTION A
Multiplication Count

SECTION B
Understanding Multiplication

SECTION C
Exploring Decimals

SECTION D
Using Money

Ready for the Market

It is a good idea to eat foods from each of these groups every day. They will help you stay healthy! How would you pick foods to buy at a market?

Word Bank

- decimal
- decimal point
- hundredth
- tenth

1 Add or Multiply

You decide to buy a muffin, lettuce, a bag of nuts, and cheese. Each of these has a different price. Would you use addition or multiplication to find the total price? Why?

2 Make Change

You found the total price. How can math help you find out what change you should get back?

3 Total It

You still have some money left. You decide to buy 6 apples for 25¢ each. Would it be best to use addition or multiplication to find out how much they will cost? Why?

Investigations Preview

Learn more about multiplication. It can help you make discoveries about factors and products. You can be sure to have all the food you need for a picnic.

Multiply Three Ways (pages 300–301)

What happens to products when you multiply three factors? Multiply, multiply, multiply to find out!

Pack a Picnic (pages 334–336)

How can you use multiplication to help plan a picnic? Pick the foods you want and multiply by the people you will invite.

SECTION A Multiplication Count

LESSON 1 How Many Tens?

What You'll Need

- *beans*
- *paper cups*

CONNECT AND COMMUNICATE

How do the cups help you multiply?

ACTIVITY 1 Bean Count

With Your Group Protein helps your body grow and fix itself. Meat, poultry, fish, dry beans, eggs, and nuts have a lot of protein. How can multiplication help you count protein foods?

1. In one class, 20 students eat the cafeteria's lunches. Each lunch has 1 protein food. How many groups of 10 are there?
2. How many protein foods do these students get in 3 lunches? Find out by counting beans as shown.

a **Count out 20 beans to stand for protein foods eaten in 1 day. Use 1 cup to hold each group of 10 beans.**

b **Count out the beans to stand for protein foods eaten in 3 days.**

3. Protein foods are underlined on the menu below. On what dates does lunch include chicken?

4. Suppose 50 students eat chicken when it is on the menu. For the 2 weeks shown, how many chicken lunches are eaten?

5. For each day fish is on the menu, 80 servings are baked. How many servings are baked in the 2 weeks shown?

Self-Check *Using the calendar below, how many school days are there from April 19 to April 29?*

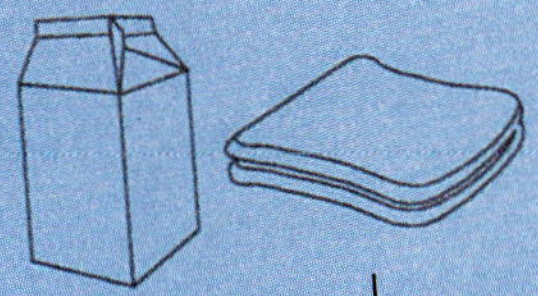

End-of-April Menu

Monday	Tuesday	Wednesday	Thursday	Friday	Saturday Sunday
17 Beef tacos Spanish rice Tossed salad Fresh fruit Milk or juice	18 Baked fish Potatoes Peas Fruit salad Milk or juice	19 Glazed turkey Pasta salad Corn Fresh fruit Milk or juice	20 Hot dog Potato cakes Baked beans Fruit salad Milk or juice	21 Chicken Fried rice Green beans Fruit gelatin Milk or juice	22–23 No School!
24 Sausage pizza Tossed salad Fresh fruit Milk or juice	25 Turkey and stuffing Peas Fruit salad Milk or juice	26 Hamburger Potato cakes 3-bean salad Fresh fruit Milk or juice	27 Chicken pie Rice Spinach Fruit salad Milk or juice	28 Baked fish Rolls Tomato soup Fruit gelatin Milk or juice	29–30 No School!

DRAWING TO LEARN

You can draw marks to stand for sandwiches. Circle the marks to group them into tens.

ACTIVITY 2 Calculator Count

With Your Class One week a class ate 40 peanut butter sandwiches. Suppose they eat about the same number of peanut butter sandwiches each week.

1. How can a calculator help you find the number eaten in 2 weeks? One way is to press these keys.

   2 [×] 40 [=]

   What is the total? What other ways could you use a calculator to find it?

2. How can you use a calculator to find the total for 3, 4, 5, or 6 weeks? Complete this multiplication sentence several ways.

   $\blacksquare \times 40 = \blacktriangle$

3. Think of 40 as 4 tens. How can you multiply 7×40 without a calculator or counters? Explain why you think your method works.

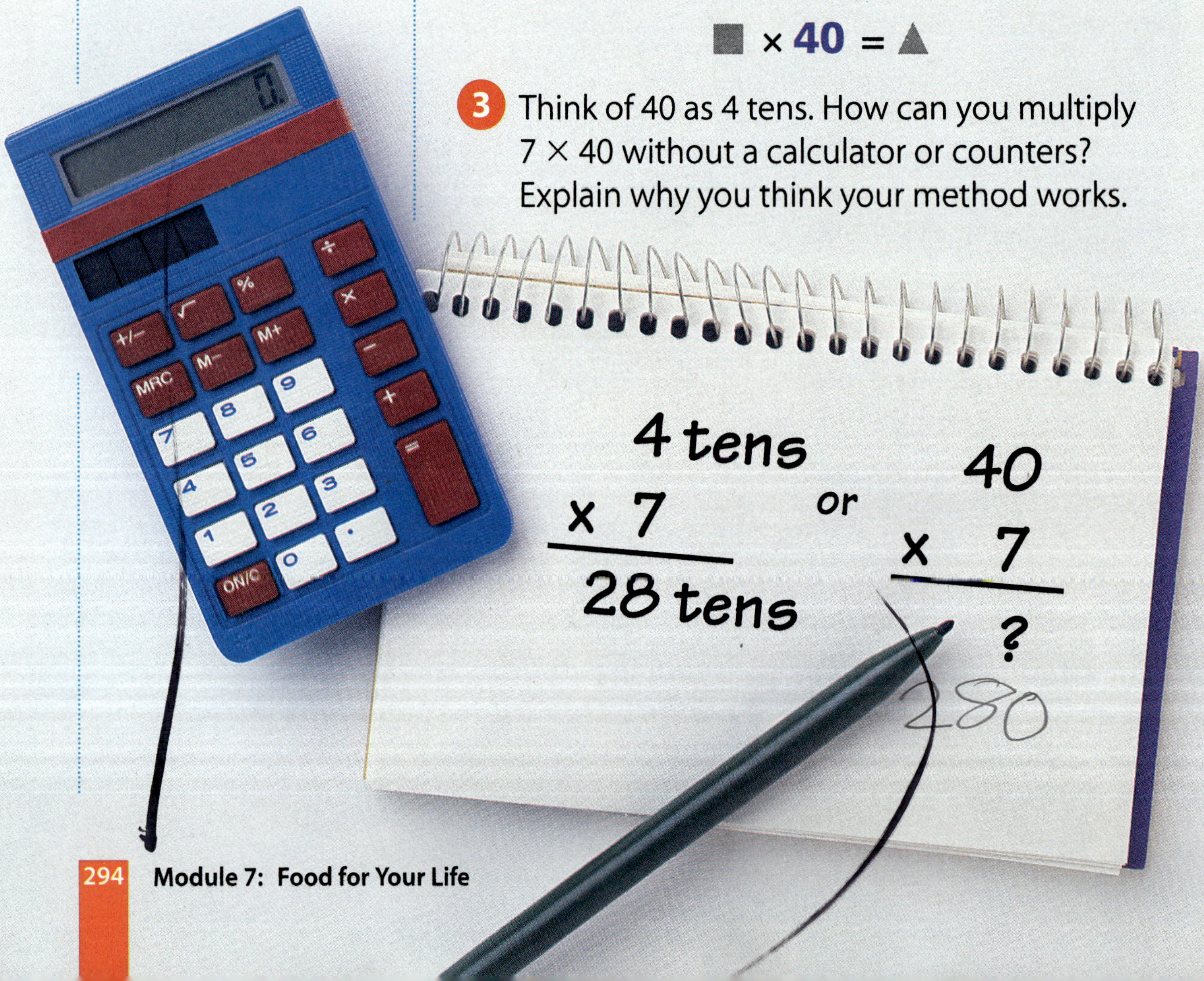

With Your Partner Don't use your calculator for this activity. Choose Exercise 4 or 5 and copy it. Write a one-digit number in place of the question mark. Write the answer. Then answer the same question using other numbers.

4. There are 50 taco shells in a box. How many taco shells are in __?__ boxes?

5. The school cafeteria uses 60 eggs to make a batch of egg salad. How many eggs would be needed to make __?__ batches of egg salad?

REASONING AND PROBLEM SOLVING

What is a rule for multiplying a two-digit whole number ending in zero by a one-digit number? Why does it work?

Do You Remember?

Try It!

Complete each number sentence.

1. $5 \times 40 = ■$
2. $3 \times 30 = ■$
3. $■ \times 50 = 100$
4. $40 \times ■ = 160$
5. $7 \times 60 = ■$
6. $5 \times ■ = 50$

Use the calendar to find each date.

7. second Tuesday
8. fourth Monday
9. first Friday
10. one week after May 15
11. five days after May 8
12. two weeks before May 30

MAY

S	M	T	W	Th	F	Sa
			1	2	3	4
5	6	7	8	9	10	11
12	13	14	15	16	17	18
19	20	21	22	23	24	25
26	27	28	29	30	31	

Think About It

13. How can multiplication facts help you find the answers for Exercises 1 through 6?

LESSON 2

Graphing to Estimate

What You'll Need

- *grid paper*

ACTIVITY 1

Serve It Up

With Your Class The chart below shows protein foods. Did you eat any of them yesterday? Collect data on the number of servings of protein foods your class ate.

1. List all of the foods from the protein group that you ate yesterday.
2. Count up the data for the whole class using a tally chart on the board. Students can take turns going to the board to mark tallies for what they ate.

On Your Own

3. Use the tally chart. Count the tally marks for each kind of food.
4. Draw a bar graph for your data on grid paper.
5. Which kind of protein food was eaten most often? Which kind was eaten least often?

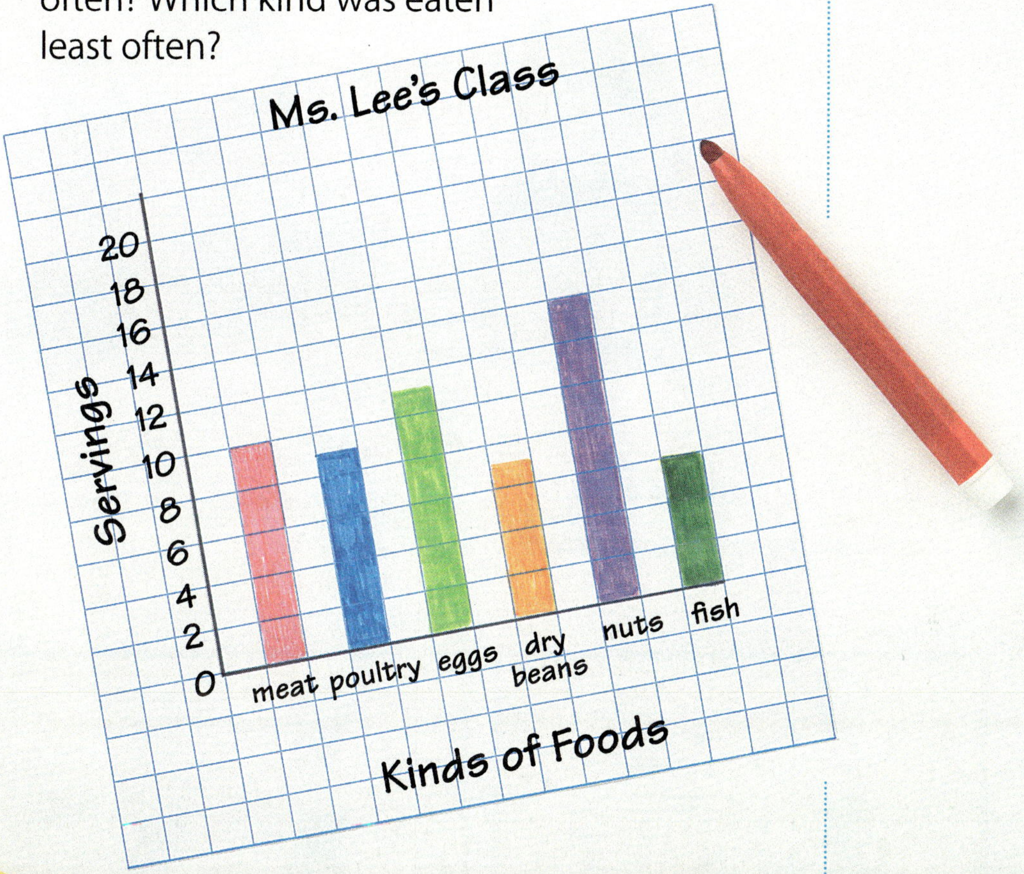

TOOLS AND TECHNIQUES

You can use a computer graphing program to draw a bar graph of your class data.

ACTIVITY 2 Trade and Multiply

With Your Partner Estimates are very important. Even when you need an exact answer, it is a good idea to estimate first.

1. Suppose the class ate 18 servings of chicken in 1 day. Estimate how many servings the class would eat in 3 days. Explain how you estimated.

What You'll Need
- *beans*
- *paper cups*

ACTIVITY OPTION

Gather data from your family on how often they eat foods from each food group in a day. What do they eat in a week? a month?

2 Now find 3 × 18 exactly. One way is shown.

$$3 \times 18 = ?$$

a **Show 3 groups of 18.**

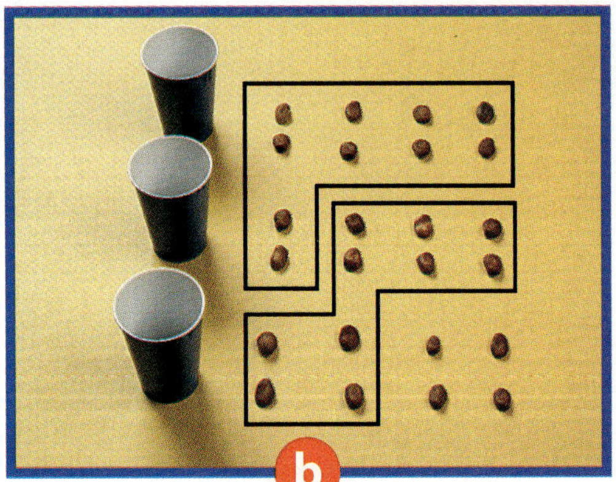

b

Trade the 20 ones for 2 tens.

c

What is the total?

3 The cafeteria made 120 servings of chicken. Is this enough for 4 classes of 24 students? Estimate 4 × 24 to find out. Explain how you estimated.

4 Suppose the cafeteria has 95 servings of chicken. Is that enough for every student in 4 classes of 24? Explain how you know.

5 Use data from Activity 1. Complete a chart like this one. Multiply the number of servings by the number of days. Use counters if you want.

6 Suppose you collect this type of data for 5 days. Do you think the results would match the chart exactly? Explain.

Do You Remember?

Try It!

Estimate whether the product will be greater or less than 100. Then find the product. Use counters to help you.

1. $5 \times 11 = ■$ 2. $2 \times 38 = ■$ 3. $4 \times 22 = ■$

4. $3 \times 41 = ■$ 5. $2 \times 53 = ■$ 6. $3 \times 16 = ■$

7. $7 \times 13 = ■$ 8. $6 \times 27 = ■$ 9. $9 \times 12 = ■$

Say each time using fractions of an hour.

10. 4:15   11. 11:45   12. 5:30

13. 8:45   14. 2:30   15. 10:15

Think About It

16. Explain in writing how you estimated for Exercises 1 through 8.

Investigation

Multiply Three Ways

In the stack of cans shown below, there are two equal layers. How many cans are in each layer? How could you multiply to find the total number of cans? In this investigation you will use one-digit numbers as factors. What can you learn about products of three factors?

1. **Choose Factors** Choose three numbers from 0 to 9 to use as factors. Then multiply. Do this at least 20 times. You may want to make a chart like the one on the next page.

2 Explore Choose some of these questions. Try other factors if you need to.

- What happens to the product when one factor is 0? 1?
- What happens when you change the order of the factors?
- Did you get more odd or even products? Why?
- What do you notice about different factors that give the same product?

3 Report Explain what you discovered. How might this help you arrange cans?

Ask Yourself

- ☐ What do the factors stand for?
- ☐ How will I organize my work?
- ☐ How will I find the products?
- ☐ How can I test my ideas about factors?
- ☐ How will I share my discoveries?

LESSON 3 Trading Tens

How many fruits and vegetables do you buy? How many do you eat? You can use multiplication to find out.

What You'll Need
- *base ten blocks*

ACTIVITY 1 Multiply Your Way

With Your Class Suppose your class went strawberry picking. If 4 students picked 23 strawberries each, how many strawberries did they pick altogether? How can you find the product of 4×23? Use base ten blocks to find out.

Copy this on your paper.

	Tens	Ones
	2	3
×		4

1. How would you show 1 group of 23 using base ten blocks? How would you show 4 groups?

2 How many tens are in 4 groups of 23? How many ones? How would you record your way of multiplying?

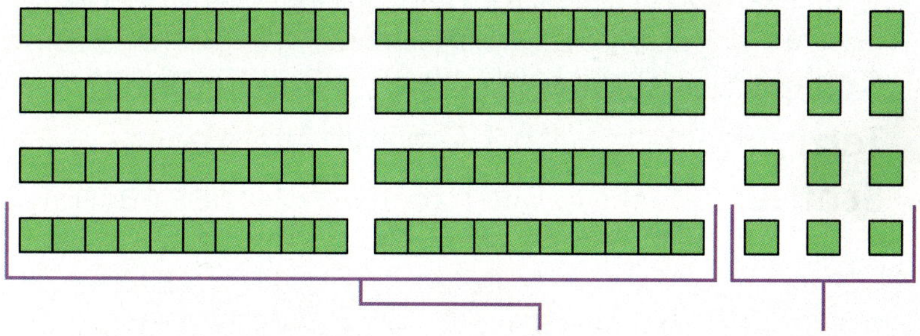

You might think of the multiplication this way.

$$\begin{array}{r} 20 \\ \times\ 4 \\ \hline ? \end{array} \qquad \begin{array}{r} 3 \\ \times\ 4 \\ \hline ? \end{array}$$

3 You can trade 10 ones for 1 ten. How many ones do you have now? How many tens?

4 These notebooks show two ways of recording the result. Is either one like your way?

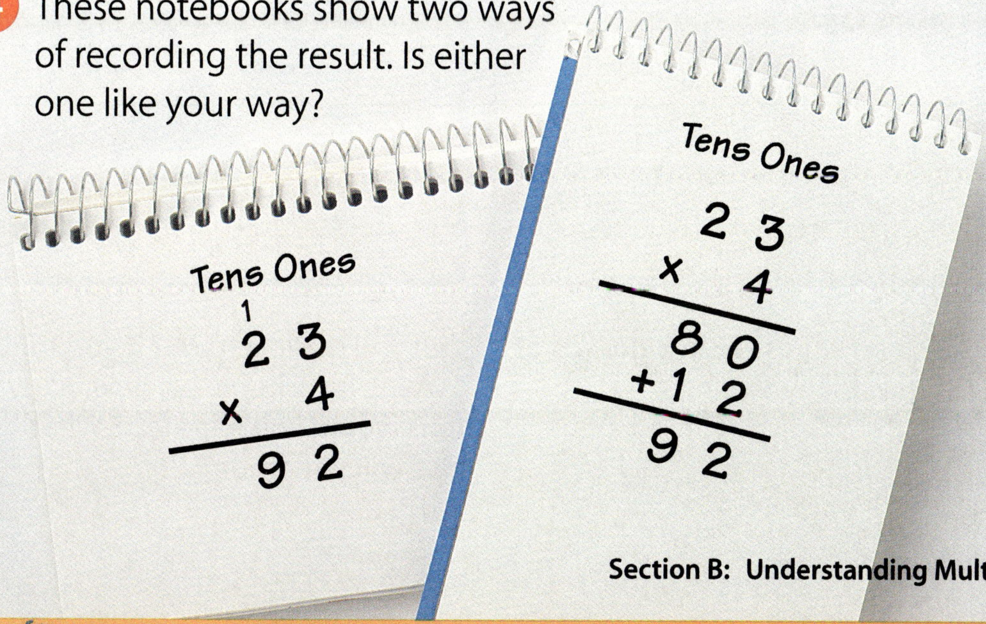

Self-Check *Add 23 + 23 + 23 + 23 to check your answer.*

REASONING AND PROBLEM SOLVING

Suppose you need to find these sums: 36 + 36 + 36 = ? 28 + 43 + 43 = ? Should you multiply or add? Explain.

What You'll Need

- *base ten blocks*

On Your Own Three students picked strawberries. Multiply to find out how many each person picked. Who picked the most? Use base ten blocks. Record your work by using paper and pencil.

Rosita: 5 baskets with 19 strawberries each
Terri: 7 baskets with 13 strawberries each
Scottie: 3 baskets with 26 strawberries each

ACTIVITY 2 Trade Your Way

With Your Group Suppose you need 45 cherries for one pie. How many cherries would you need to make 3 pies for the class? Find the product by following the steps below. Record your work at each step.

1

How many ones are in 3 groups of 45? How many tens?

2

Can you make a trade? If you trade 10 tens for 1 hundred, how many tens would you have left? What else will you trade?

3. How many cherries are needed altogether?
4. Does either notebook show how you recorded your answer? Explain.

TOOLS AND TECHNIQUES

A place-value chart with hundreds, tens, and ones can help you keep track of the multiplication.

With Your Class Choose three fruits. Have your classmates vote on their favorites. How many votes did each fruit get? What if 5 classes voted? How can multiplication help you guess the total votes for each fruit? Discuss your results.

ACTIVITY 3 Going Bananas!

What You'll Need

- *cube labeled 3–8*
- *cube labeled 21, 25, 27, 28, 30, 31*
- *counters (different color for each player)*
- *game sheet*

With Your Group Play this game to practice multiplication or go on to the Try It!

1. **Get Ready to Play** Write the numbers 3 through 8 on one cube. On the other cube, write the numbers 21, 25, 27, 28, 30, and 31.

2. **Roll and Multiply** Roll both cubes. Multiply the two-digit number by the one-digit number. Look for that product on the game sheet. When you find a product, cover it with a counter.

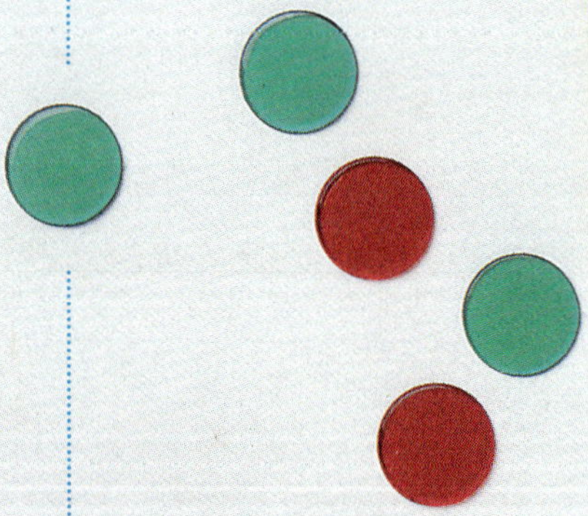

3 **Match Three Fruits** Take turns rolling the cubes and finding the products. The winner is the first person to claim three fruits that are the same.

ACTIVITY OPTION

If you don't have the game sheet, you can still play the game. Roll the cubes and multiply. The person who has the biggest product wins.

Do You Remember?

Try It!

Complete each number sentence. Use these factors: 2, 44, 5, 23, 51, 7.

1. $\blacktriangle \times \blacksquare = 255$
2. $\blacktriangle \times \blacksquare = 115$
3. $\blacktriangle \times \blacksquare = 88$
4. $\blacktriangle \times \blacksquare = 102$
5. $\blacktriangle \times \blacksquare = 357$
6. $\blacktriangle \times \blacksquare = 220$

Draw a model for the fraction.

7. $\frac{1}{4}$
8. $\frac{1}{8}$
9. $\frac{3}{4}$
10. $\frac{1}{3}$
11. $\frac{5}{8}$

Think About It

12. What other products can you make from the factors above?

LESSON 4 Trading Hundreds

What You'll Need
• *base ten blocks*

ACTIVITY 1 Tony's Tomato Total

With Your Group Tony has 5 boxes of tomatoes in his vegetable market. If there are 132 tomatoes in each box, how many tomatoes are there altogether? Work together to find the product. How will you record your work?

1. Start with an estimate. What multiplication fact can help you estimate?
2. Show 1 group of 132 with your base ten blocks. Now show 5 groups.

3. Multiply the hundreds, tens, and ones. What trades can you make? How many ones do you have after you make trades? How many tens? How many hundreds?

4. How close was your estimate to the exact answer? How did you record each step? Is either method shown close to your way?

CONNECT AND COMMUNICATE

In Your Journal *Tell what trades you made. What did you multiply first? Did you get more tens, ones, or hundreds?*

On Your Own The chart below shows vegetables Tony has to sell. Use the chart to write two story problems about Tony's vegetable market. Trade problems with your partner to solve. Record your work for each story.

	Number of Boxes	Number in Box	Total
lettuce	**6**	**135**	**?**
cucumbers	**7**	**124**	**?**
onions	**3**	**135**	**?**
tomatoes	**2**	**251**	**?**

DRAWING TO LEARN

How can drawing an array help you see whether you multiplied correctly?

What You'll Need

- *index cards*

ACTIVITY OPTION

What is the least product you can make using four digits?

REASONING AND PROBLEM SOLVING

Does multiplying by the greatest one-digit number always give you the greatest product? Why or why not?

ACTIVITY 2

The Greatest Product

With Your Group Write the digits 0 through 9 on separate cards. Shuffle the cards. Pick four. Now put your multiplication power to work.

1. Arrange the digits to show a one-digit number times a three-digit number. Write the product.

2. Put the four digits in a different order. Try this several times. What is the greatest product you can make? Use a calculator to test your result.

3. Put the four digits back. Choose four new digits and multiply. Try different locations for the digits. Which of the four sets of digits gave you the greatest product? Discuss your answers with another group.

ACTIVITY 3 Lattice Products

On Your Own If you lived in England 400 years ago, you might have multiplied 3×247 this way.

What You'll Need

- *base ten blocks*

1. **Write the digits of the factors beside the squares like the one below.**

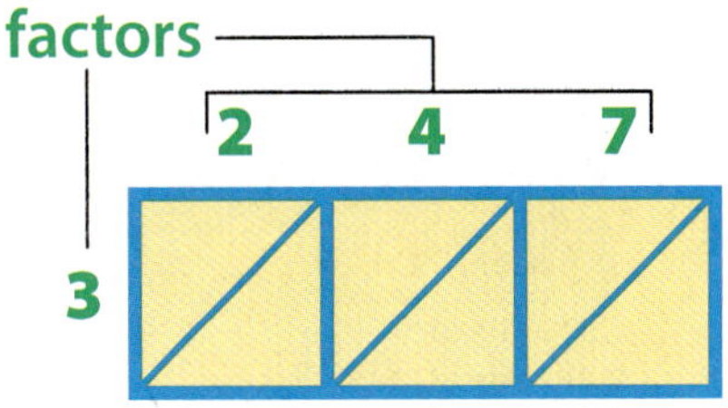

2. **Use basic facts to fill all the squares. Then add in the direction of the arrows.**

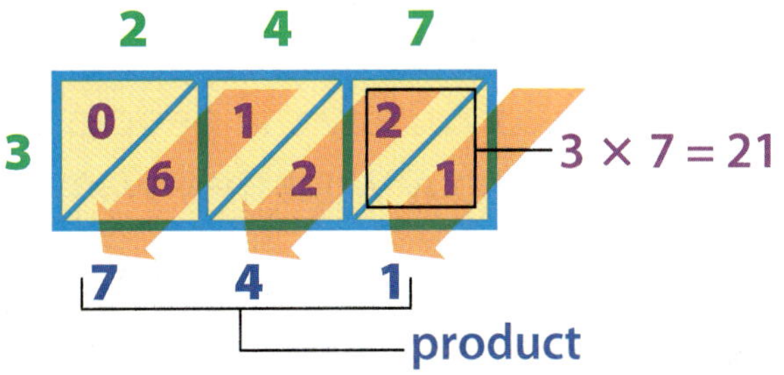

3. Now you try. Multiply 3×326. Check your answer by using base ten blocks.

Do You Remember? Try It!

Estimate which product will be the greatest. Then multiply.

1. 105×4
2. 318×5
3. 300×3
4. 207×3
5. 126×4

Decide whether to use mental math, paper and pencil, or a calculator. Then find the answer.

6. $4 \times ■ = 32$
7. $30 \div 6 = ■$
8. $8 \times 278 = ■$
9. $8 \times 40 = ■$
10. $5{,}000 - 20 = ■$
11. $0 \times 94{,}383 = ■$

Think About It

12. How did you estimate the greatest product in Exercises 1 through 5? Explain in writing.

Do You Remember?

Cumulative Review

Floating Markets

People in Thailand can buy food at markets on boats. These markets are on waterways called *klongs*. How can people use math to help them buy what they want?

1. How much would 3 pounds of peppers cost? You pay with \$5.00. How much change should you get?

2. Monkeys are taught to pick coconuts. One monkey picks about 500 coconuts in one day. How many can she pick in 3 days?

3. You buy 2 bags of 12 oranges. Sketch two ways to show arrays of the oranges you bought. How many oranges did you buy?

4. You live 2 hours from the market. If you left home at 10:00 A.M., what time would you arrive at the market?

5. Look at the 2 coconuts. A basket can hold 5 times as many. How many coconuts does it hold? How much would they all cost?

6 The markets are very busy at half past five in the morning. Write this time using numbers.

7 A basket is $\frac{1}{8}$ full of fruit. What fraction of the basket is empty?

8 Which costs more, 2 pineapples or 2 mangoes?

9 You buy some juice at the floating markets. Would a jug hold 4 L or 400 L? Why?

Check Your Math Power

10 Choose a number between 8 and 16. Suppose you are buying that many mangoes. Look at the prices. Which market would you buy from? How much will you spend? Explain your answer.

LESSON 5 What's a Tenth?

ACTIVITY 1 Bits and Pieces

With Your Class All of our numbers are based on 10. Try these on your calculator.

1,000 ÷ 10 = ?
100 ÷ 10 = ?
10 ÷ 10 = ?
1 ÷ 10 = ?

What pattern do you see? Each of these pictures shows one whole divided into 10 parts, or **tenths.**

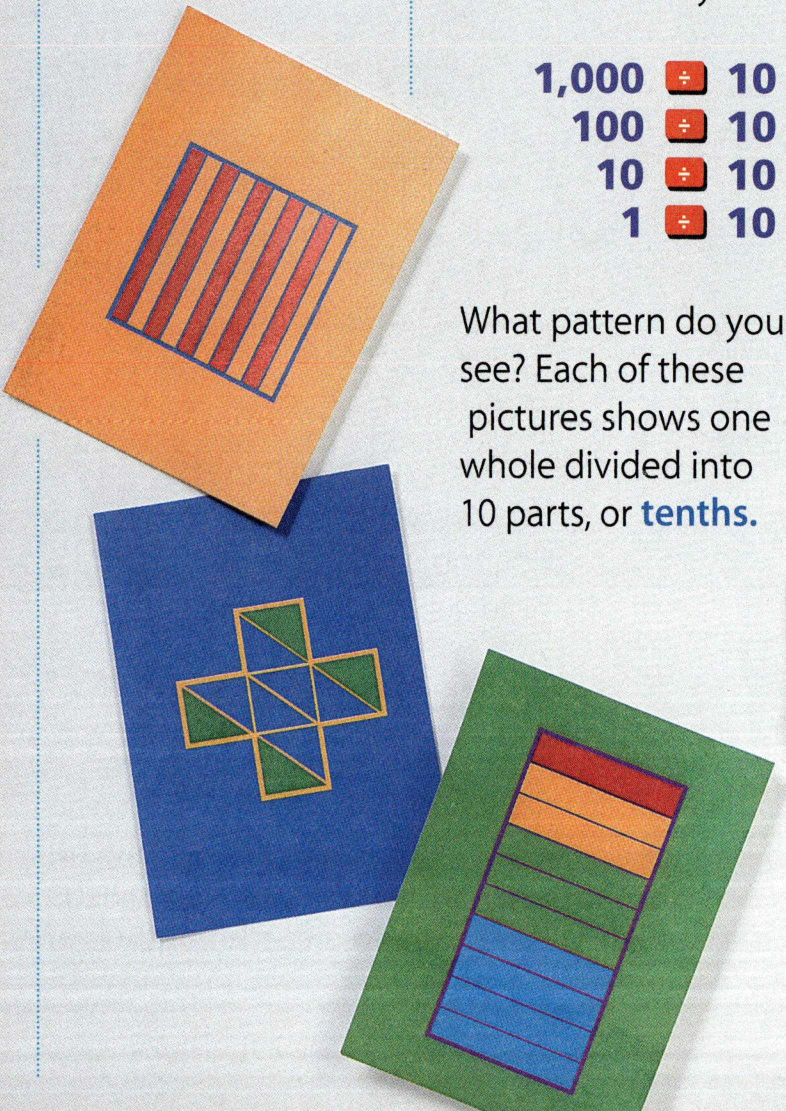

1. Tortillas are a kind of flat bread. They are used to make this Mexican food called a *quesadilla*. How many pieces are shown in all?

2. How much of the quesadilla is being taken away?

3. How many parts is this bar divided into? Write a fraction for the shaded part.

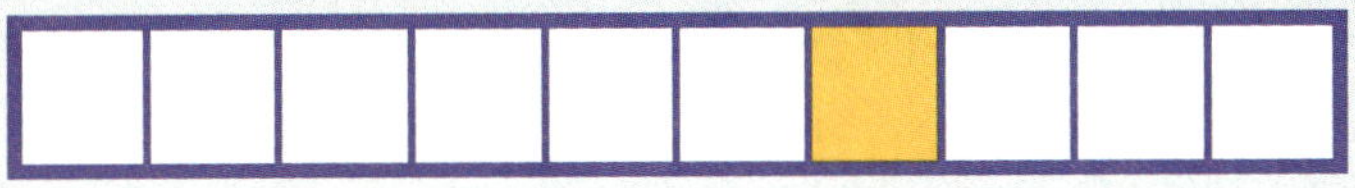

4. You can also write one tenth as a **decimal,** 0.1. Why is there a 0 in the ones' place?

Tens	Ones		Tenths
	0	.	1

↑ decimal point

5. Draw and shade a picture for each of these fractions. Then write them as decimals.

a. $\frac{2}{10}$ **b.** $\frac{5}{10}$

c. $\frac{9}{10}$ **d.** $\frac{3}{10}$

CONNECT AND COMMUNICATE

How many tenths would be shaded to equal 1? What is the fraction?

Self-Check *Did you divide your tenth pictures into 10 parts that are equal? How did you do it?*

What You'll Need
- *index cards*

ACTIVITY 2 Decimal Challenge

With Your Group Make your own cards to play this decimal game for 2 to 4 players.

1. Write 0.1 on a card. On a second card, write the decimal in words. On a third card, write the fraction. Draw a tenths picture for one tenth on another card.
2. Repeat Step 1 to make a set of cards for each of these decimals: 0.2, 0.3, 0.4, 0.5, 0.6, 0.7, 0.8, 0.9.

3. Mix up the cards. Each player gets 6 cards. Put the rest of them in a pile face down.
4. Match any cards in your hand that are part of the same set. If you have all 4 cards for any number, put them on the table.

5. Decide which cards to collect to get sets of 4. Ask a player for one of the needed cards. If that player has it, it is given to you. If not, pick a card from the top of the pile.
6. Take turns asking for cards. The first player who matches all the cards held wins.

Activity 3 Plus or Minus Tenths

With Your Class How can you add and subtract decimals?

1. There are 10 servings in a container of cereal. Your family eats 2 servings one day and 3 servings the next. How many servings were eaten?

Day One Day Two

2. Each cereal serving is a tenth of the jar. What is the sum of 2 tenths and 3 tenths? How can you write it using decimals?
3. How many servings are left in the jar? How can you write the part left as a decimal?

Draw some tenth picture cards using new shapes of your own. Use them in the game.

REASONING AND PROBLEM SOLVING

Would it be easy to use a triangle shape for a tenths picture? Explain.

On Your Own

4 Copy and fill in this addition sentence for the picture. Rewrite using fractions.

0.5 + 0.2 = ■

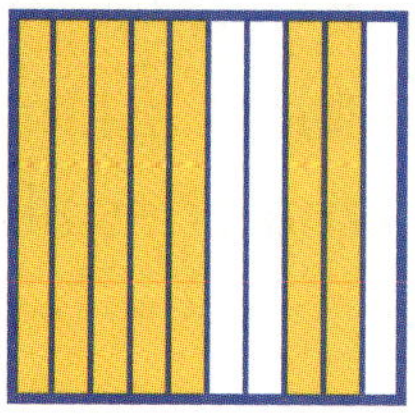

5 Copy and fill in this subtraction sentence for the picture. Rewrite using fractions.

0.6 − 0.2 = ■

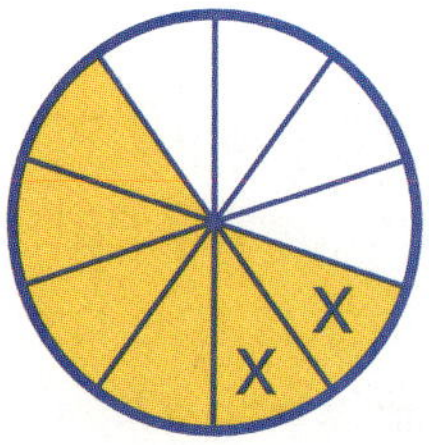

Do You Remember?

Try It!

Find the answers by drawing and shading in your own pictures.

1. 0.2 − 0.1	2. 0.4 + 0.3	3. 5 tenths + 1 tenth
4. 0.1 + 0.8	5. 0.8 − 0.2	6. 9 tenths − 4 tenths

Use the numbers to write two or more number sentences.

7. 6, 15, 9	8. 18, 6, 3	9. 6, 36, 6
10. 8, 16, 8	11. 3, 8, 11	12. 6, 48, 8

Think About It

13. Which answer for Exercises 1 through 6 is less than one half? Explain in writing how you know.

ACTIVITY 4

Mixing Decimals

With Your Class Now look at decimals for amounts 1 or greater. The shaded circles show two and three tenths.

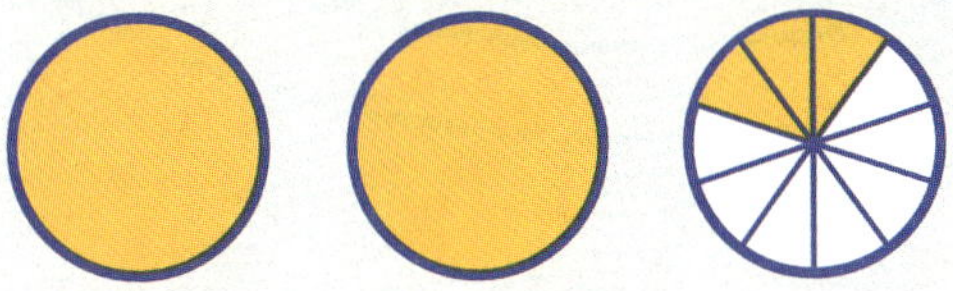

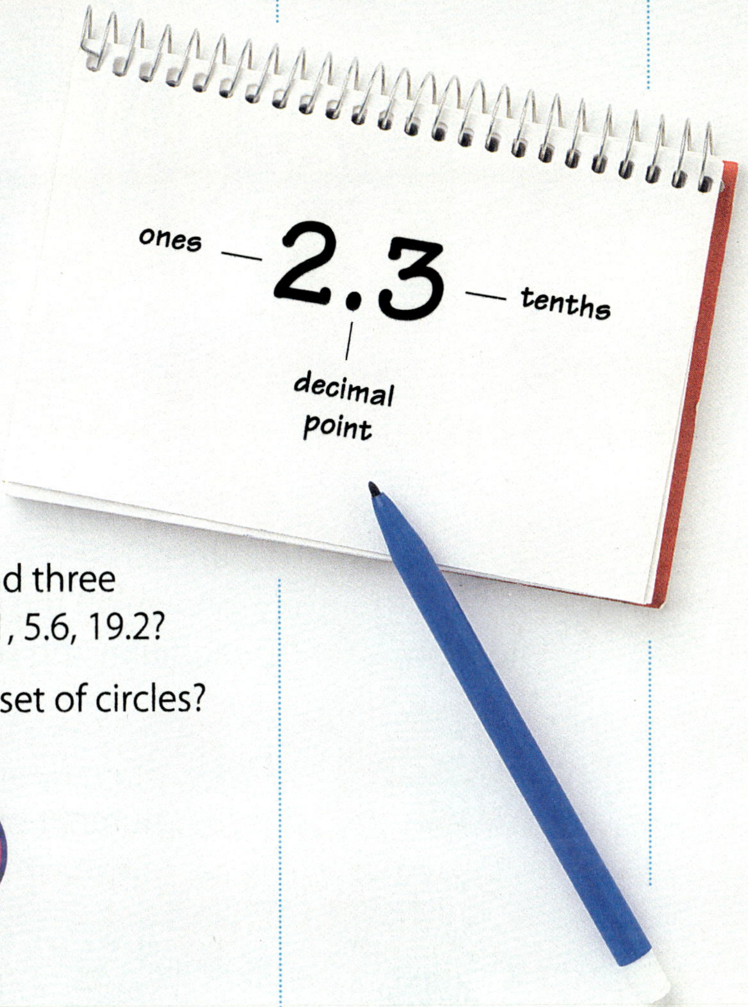

1. To read the decimal, say "two and three tenths." How would you read 4.1, 5.6, 19.2?

2. What decimal is shown by each set of circles?

   a. 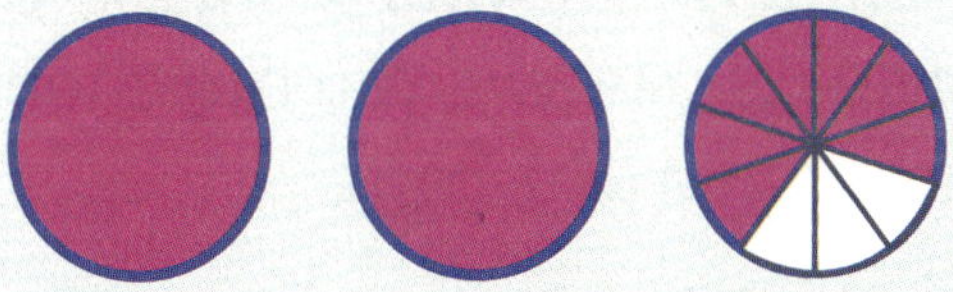

   b. 

3. What is the total of the purple and the green parts? Write a number sentence to show the sum of all the whole circles. Write another number sentence sentence to show all the tenths. How would you write the sum?

4. Draw circles for any two of these sentences. Find the answers.

   a. 2.2 + 1.4   b. 8.8 − 5.0

   c. 3.5 − 0.8   d. 6.4 + 3.6

You can trace the circles on this page when drawing your answers for Step 4.

DECIMAL DINNER

What You'll Need

- *spinner*
- *gameboard*
- *game pieces*

TOOLS AND TECHNIQUES

Use a calculator to check your answers.

ACTIVITY 5 Adding Up to Nine

With Your Group Now that you're warmed up, play this game. Make a spinner like the one shown on the next page. Keep track of your addition and subtraction on paper.

1. **Get a Start** Begin at the space marked 1.0. Spin the spinner. Move your marker the number of spaces shown. You can choose to move either way on the path.

2. **Add or Subtract** If you land on a light space, add the number to 1.0. If you land on a dark space, subtract the number from 1.0. On your next turn, you will add or subtract from this new number.

3 **Spin and Move** Take turns spinning and moving in either direction. The first player to reach 9 or more wins.

Do You Remember?

Try It!

Write each missing number as a decimal.

1. 2 + 0.5 = ■
2. 3 + ■ = 3.5
3. 1.5 + 0.3 = ■
4. 0.7 + 3.3 = ■
5. 2 + 4.6 = ■
6. 4.9 + ■ = 5

Measure the length to the nearest quarter inch.

7.
8.
9.
10.
11.

Think About It

12. To find the answer to Exercise 4, did you need to trade tenths for ones? Explain.

LESSON 6 The Next Place

What You'll Need
- *mixed pasta*
- *glue*
- *construction paper*
- *ruler*

ACTIVITY 1 Pasta Parts

With Your Group If you divide something into 100 parts, you get **hundredths.** The decimal in the chart is fifteen hundredths or $\frac{15}{100}$.

Ones	.	Tenths	Hundredths
0	.	1	5

1 This part of the design is $\frac{4}{100}$ or four hundredths. You can write this as 0.04.

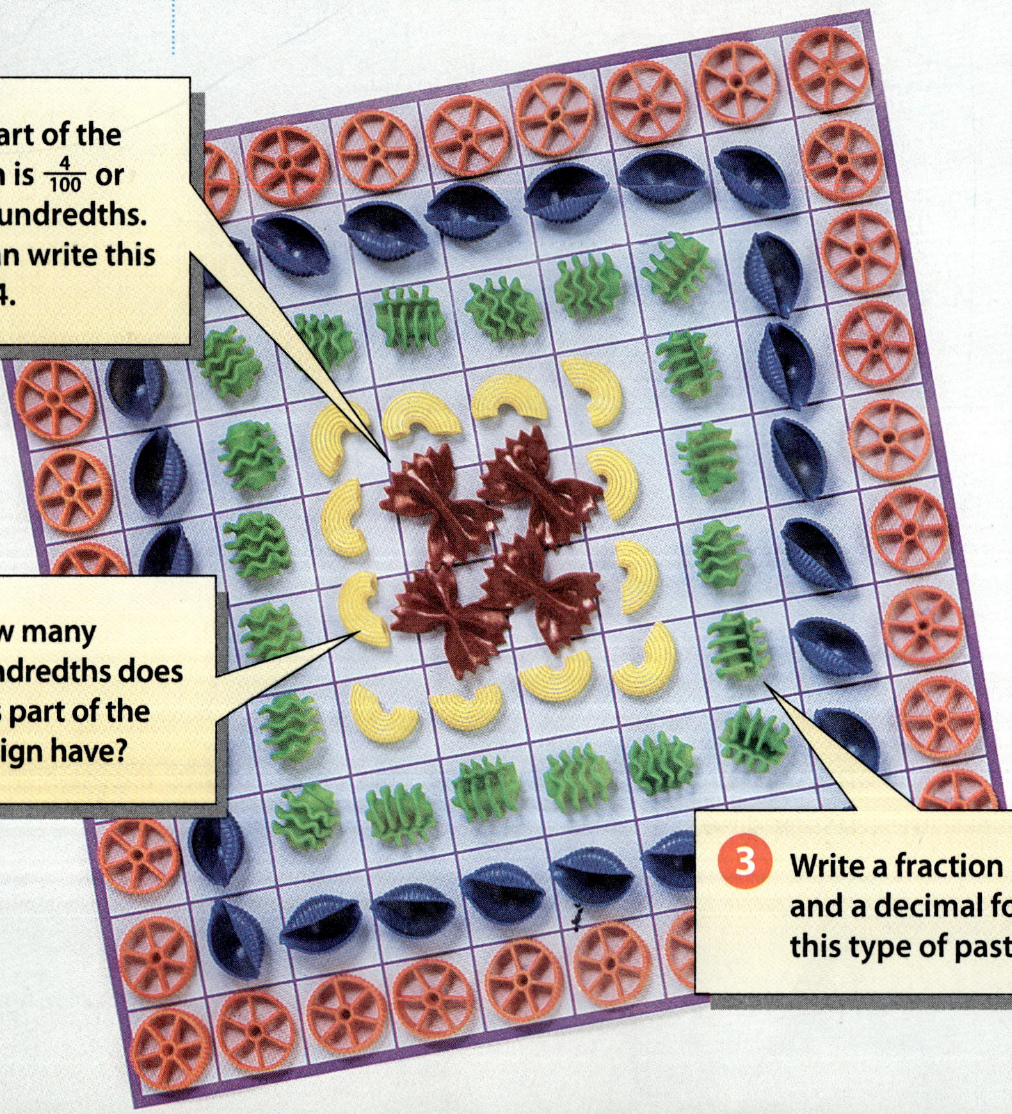

2 How many hundredths does this part of the design have?

3 Write a fraction and a decimal for this type of pasta.

With Your Partner Use a square divided into a hundred parts to make your own pasta designs. How many kinds of pasta will you use? Write each portion of your design as a decimal and a fraction.

4. How many kinds of pasta take up more than 0.10 of your design?

5. Are there any groups of pasta that take up more than 0.25?

ACTIVITY OPTION

Use the hundredths square to make a letter. How many hundredths would you have to color to make your initial? Write a decimal to represent the shaded squares.

Do You Remember?

Try It!

Write each fraction as a decimal.

1. $\frac{52}{100}$ 2. $\frac{93}{100}$ 3. $\frac{7}{100}$ 4. $\frac{3}{100}$

Write each decimal as a fraction.

5. 0.6 6. 0.06 7. 0.12 8. 0.2

Draw a picture to show each fraction or decimal.

9. $\frac{1}{4}$ 10. 0.3 11. $\frac{1}{8}$ 12. 0.5

Think About It

13. Which two fractions in Exercises 1 through 4 have a sum of 1? Explain your answer in writing.

CONNECT AND COMMUNICATE

In Your Journal *One box of macaroni and cheese has 7.25 ounces of macaroni. What do the digits 7, 2, and 5 represent?*

LESSON 7 More Money

LITERATURE

Jenny Archer and her classmates don't like the school lunches. Read about Jenny's lunch plans.

"Stop!" said Wilson suddenly. He turned to Jenny and held up his hand like a crossing guard. "I have a great idea! I'll give you my lunch money if you'll make my lunch every day."

Jenny did some arithmetic in her head. The school lunch cost \$1.50. \$1.50 times 5 days a week = \$7.50 a week.

Seven dollars and fifty cents a week! Just for making one extra lunch!

"Wilson, you're a genius!" said Beth.

From *What's Cooking, Jenny Archer?*
by Ellen Conford

ACTIVITY 1 Money Matters

What You'll Need
- *play money*

With Your Group Imagine you are Jenny's partner. How can you figure out how much she will make? Use play money to figure out her earnings.

1. Suppose you sell 3 lunches at \$1.50 each. What is the total cost?

This grouping of money shows 3 × $1.50. Use play money to make trades. How can you show the fewest number of coins?

How would you multiply 3 × $1.50? Suppose you don't use coins and bills to solve the problem. Why might it be helpful to think of $1.50 as 150¢?

2. Jenny earned $6.00 a day making lunches. How much could she earn in 4 days?

3. Suppose 6 people each paid Jenny $1.50 for lunch. How much would she make?

On Your Own Suppose you started your own lunch business. How can multiplication help you figure out how much you will earn?

4. How much would you charge to make each lunch? How much would you earn in 4 days?

5. Suppose 6 students paid you $1.25 each for their lunches. How much would you earn in 5 days?

CONNECT AND COMMUNICATE

In Your Journal *Explain how multiplying money is the same or different from two-digit or three-digit multiplication.*

Exercises and Problems

Milk Money

Shop for milk, yogurt, cheese, and butter. As you write each answer, tell whether you used addition, subtraction, or multiplication.

How Much Milk?

1. How much milk can you buy with 7 quarters?
2. How much would 3 pints of chocolate milk cost?
3. If you have $1.25, can you buy 2 pints of chocolate milk? Why or why not?

Milk

half pint	33¢
chocolate milk (pint)	69¢
quart	99¢

Yogurt

cherry (1 cup)	$.76
plain (1 cup)	4 for $2.00

You Need Yogurt

4. Can 15 dimes buy you 2 cups of cherry yogurt? Explain.
5. Which costs more, 4 cups of cherry yogurt or 4 cups of plain yogurt?

Butter and Margarine

butter	**$1.69 (per package)**
margarine	**$.69 (per package)**

Butter Bargains

6 How much butter could you buy with 8 quarters?

7 How much margarine could you buy with 9 quarters and 30 pennies?

8 Think of your own family. How much margarine would you buy? Find the cost.

Cheese

American	**$1.79 (per package)**
Swiss	**$3.03 (per package)**
Cheddar	**$1.50 (per package)**

Cheese Choices

9 Which two packages of cheese could you get for about $5.00?

10 Suppose you had a 10¢ coupon to use for each package of cheese. How much would you need to pay for each package?

LESSON 8 Making Change

What You'll Need
- *play money*

ACTIVITY 1 Count Your Change

With Your Partner Suppose you want to make purchases. If you give the clerk more than the exact amount, you will get change back.

1. You pay 4 dimes for a half pint of milk. The milk costs 34¢. What coins could you get as change? Use coins to count up from 34 to 40.

2. Pretend you are the clerk. Someone pays $1 for milk. What numbers would you say as you count out the change?

3. Use $1.00 to buy each item on the page. How much change will you get back?

TOOLS AND TECHNIQUES

Subtract the price of the item from $1.00 to see whether you have the correct change.

ACTIVITY 2 The Change Game

With Your Group Play a game to practice making change from $1.00. Whoever has the most change at the end of the game wins.

1. **Label the Cubes** Write 5¢, 6¢, 7¢, 8¢, 9¢, and 0¢ on one cube. Label the other cube 20¢, 30¢, 40¢, 50¢, 60¢, 70¢.
2. **Find the Sum** Roll both cubes. Find the sum of the two numbers. This is the cost of one item. Count out the coins needed to make change from $1.00. Players should make change from the play money pile.
3. **End the Game** Take turns rolling the cubes and making change. The game ends when a player cannot make change. The person with the most change wins.

What You'll Need

- *play money (30 pennies, 10 nickels, 15 dimes, 20 quarters)*
- *2 number cubes*

Self-Check *How can you be sure you counted the correct amounts of change?*

What You'll Need

- *play money*

Activity 3 Dollars and Cents

With Your Partner Now you are ready to make change using bills and coins. Take turns being the cashier and the customer. What coins and bills should you give back?

1. Buy: a pint of frozen yogurt
   Pay: $5.00
2. Buy: a half gallon of frozen yogurt
   Pay: $10.00
3. Buy: a pint and a half gallon of frozen yogurt
   Pay: $10.00
4. Buy: two half gallons of frozen yogurt
   Pay: $10.00

frozen yogurt (half gallon) $4.39
frozen yogurt (pint) $2.89

Complete Exercise 5 or 6.

5. You bought a half gallon of frozen yogurt. You got exactly eleven cents change. How much did you pay?

6. You bought two pints of frozen yogurt. You got two cents change. How much did you pay?

DRAWING TO LEARN

In Your Journal Draw coins and bills to show the amounts of change given.

Do You Remember?

Try It!

Make change from $5.00. List the coins or bills you need.

1. $1.35
2. 69¢
3. $1.65
4. $.89
5. $2.80
6. $[illegible]27

Write the missing number.

7. 3 × ■ = 21
8. 4 × ■ = 36
9. 7 × ■ = 63
10. 8 × ■ = 56
11. 8 × 4 = ■
12. 9 × ■ = 81

Think About It

13. How did add[illegible] you to [illegible] change?

Do You Remember?

Cumulative Review

Looking Back

Choose the best answer. Write *a, b, c,* or *d* for each exercise.

This graph shows the number of apples picked by students in a minute. Use the graph to answer Exercises 1 through 3.

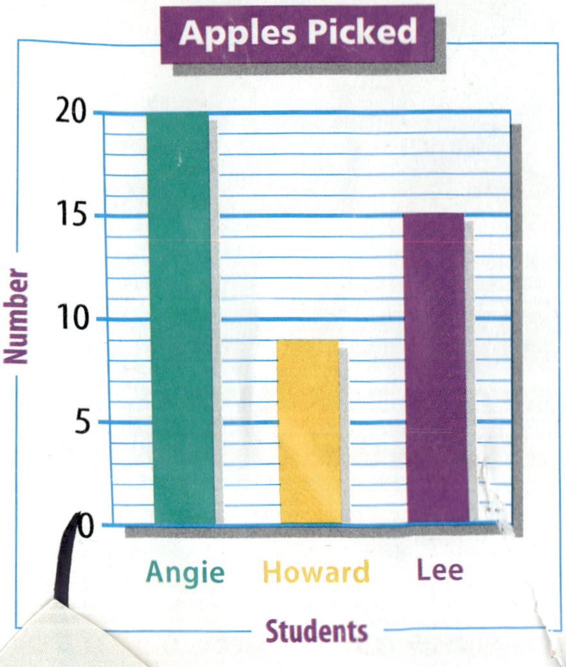

many apples could
pick in one hour? What
uld you multiply to

1 ×

2. How many apples could Angie pick in 3 minutes?

a. 60 apples b. 23 apples
c. 40 apples d. 80 apples

3. Suppose Lee sold the apples she picked for 10¢ each. How much money would she get?

a. $150
b. 25¢
c. $1.50
d. none of these

4. What is another way to show the same number as 4 × 35?

a. 40 × 5
b. 35 + 4
c. 4 × 53
d. none of these

duct is equal to five

b. 5 × 10¢
d. 50 × $1

6. You pay 3 quarters for a pear that costs 60¢. Which coins could you get as change?

a. two dimes
b. 35 pennies
c. a dime and a nickel
d. three dimes

7. Suppose you pay $5 for an item that costs $2.88. What change should you get?

a. a dime and two pennies
b. three dollars, 2 dimes, and 2 pennies
c. two dollars, 1 dime, and 2 pennies
d. none of these

Use this circle to answer Exercises 8 through 10.

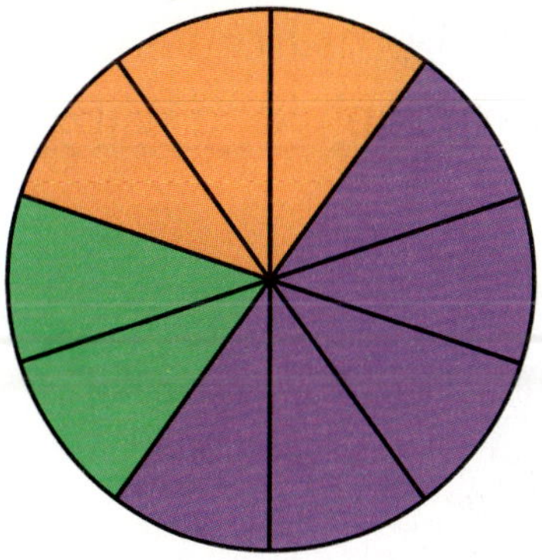

8. What part of the circle is not orange?

a. 0.3
b. 0.5
c. 0.7
d. none of these

9. Which is not a way to show the amount shaded purple?

a. 0.5
b. 0.2
c. $\frac{2}{10} + \frac{3}{10}$
d. $\frac{5}{10}$

10. How much more is shaded purple than green?

a. 7 tenths
b. $5 - 0.2$
c. none of these
d. 0.3

Check Your Math Power

11. Suppose you spend between $3 and $4 for some of these foods. Tell two combinations of foods you could buy. For each answer, draw a group of coins that you could get as change from $4.00.

12. Write at least three pairs of factors that have a product of 200.

MODULE 7 Investigations

Pack a Picnic

What foods do you like to eat at a picnic? In this investigation you will plan a picnic. Imagine that someone else will pay for the food and supplies. You need to make the plan and explain the costs.

Investigation A Plan a Picnic

Create a plan for a picnic.

1 **Choose** a menu. Pick items from each of the five food groups. How much food will each person get?

2. **Decide** how many people will be coming. How much food will you need? What other supplies will you need?

3. **Make** a shopping list. Show how you would use multiplication to decide how much to buy. If hot dogs come in packages of 8, how will you decide how many packages to buy?

4. **Plan** how you will present your information. Will you write a report or make a presentation to your class? Include the menu you made for your picnic.

Keep in Mind

Think about the following questions as you make a report about your picnic.

- [ ] Is your meal balanced?
- [ ] How did multiplication help you decide how much food you will need?
- [ ] Is there a fair way to divide the food into servings?
- [ ] How can you organize a shopping list?
- [ ] Will everyone get the same amount of food?

Investigation B: Plan Meals

Plan three meals for your family using the five food groups. How many people would you serve? Suppose you had only $10.00 to spend for each meal. Could you buy everything you need? Compare food prices at two different stores. Use addition or subtraction to find out how much you would have to spend for the same items at both stores.

Write a report.

- Explain how much each item costs.
- Describe which store has the better bargains.
- Tell how much you would spend on each meal.

Investigation C: Plan a Garden

Plan a vegetable garden shaped like a square or rectangle. Draw ten equal parts. Decide how many tenths each vegetable will take up. Use addition or subtraction of decimals to describe your garden. Describe which vegetables you chose. Explain how you arranged them.

Computer Option You can use a computer drawing program to construct a pattern for your garden.

MODULE 8

Puzzles, Shapes, and Games

You play games and work puzzles all the time. In this module you are going to explore shapes by playing games. You will work with puzzles, too. You will even learn how to divide up game pieces and equipment so that you can play a game. Start by looking at the gameboards below. What shapes do you see?

SECTION A
Points, Lines, and Angles

SECTION B
Figure It Out

SECTION C
Division Is Sharing

SECTION D
Congruence and Symmetry

Shapes and Sharing

1 Fair Shares

Sometimes you have to share game pieces or equipment. How would you share the equipment below among the players?

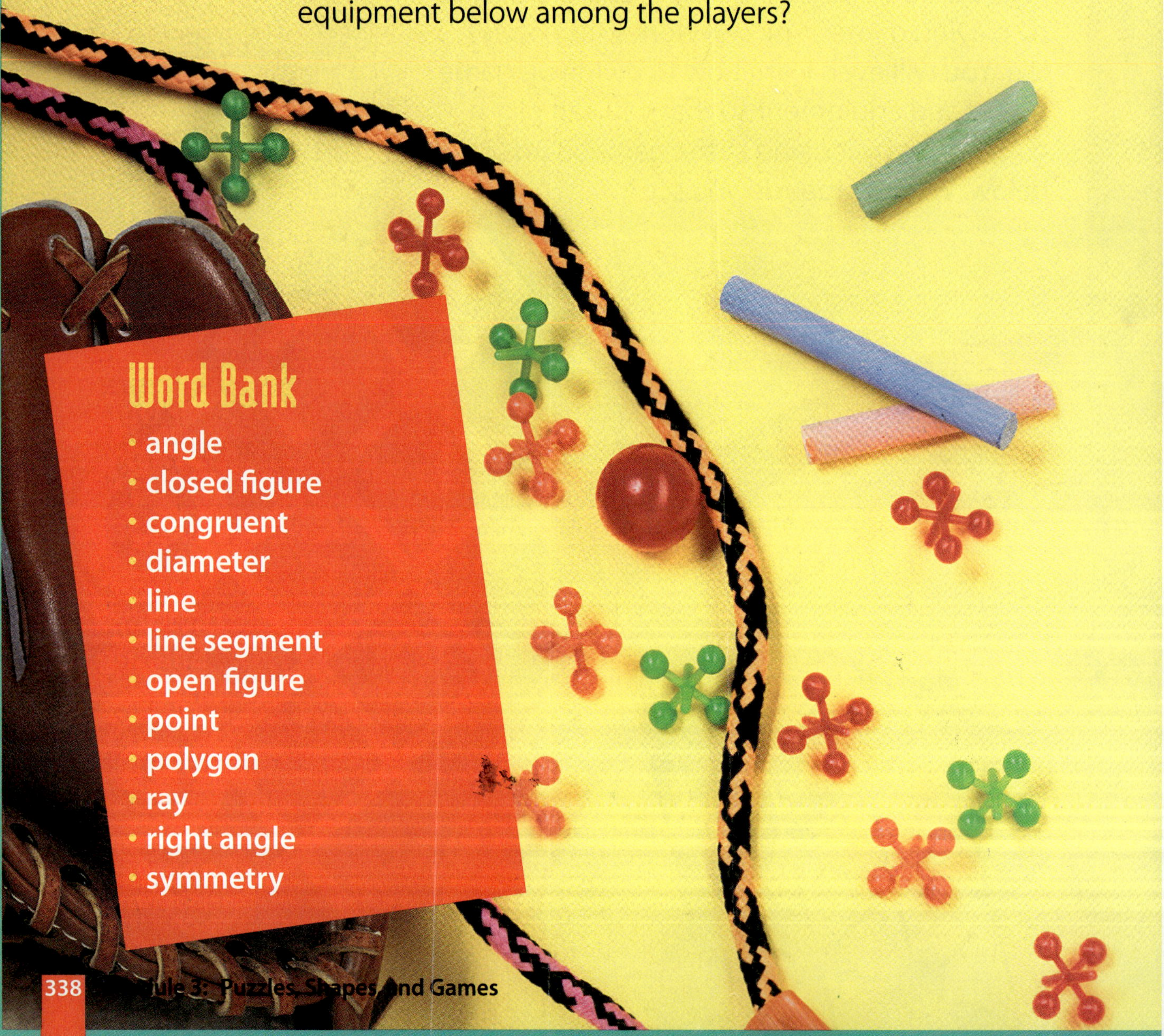

Word Bank

- angle
- closed figure
- congruent
- diameter
- line
- line segment
- open figure
- point
- polygon
- ray
- right angle
- symmetry

2 Around Your Class

Now talk about games and puzzles you play. What shapes can you find in them? How do you share equipment or game pieces in the games you play?

Investigations Preview

Learn about geometry and division. You will work with a puzzle called a tangram and learn more about your process for dividing.

Tangram Tryout (page 355)
Make shapes and polygons using an ancient Chinese puzzle.

The Lost Key (page 369)
How can you divide on a calculator with a broken division key?

Puzzle Pictures (page 382)
Design your own puzzle and trade with a friend.

LESSON 1 What's Your Line?

What You'll Need
- *4 playing pieces, 2 each of 2 colors*

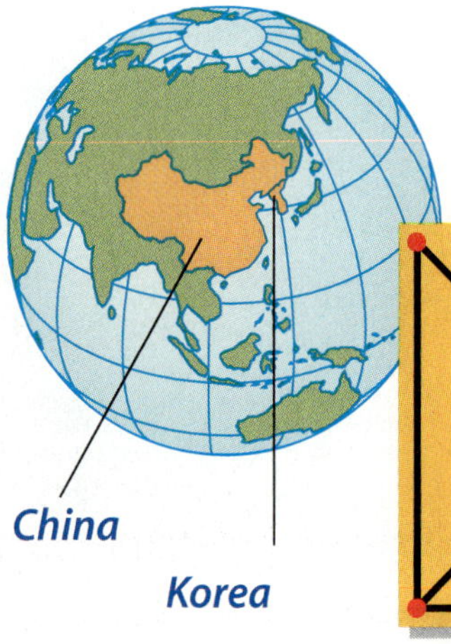

ACTIVITY 1 Block Your Partner

With Your Partner Play this game or square tick-tack-toe. Either one can be first. *Pong hau k'i* is a game played in China and in Korea, where it is called *ou-moul-ko-no.* The gameboard is shown below. Try to block your partner's pieces!

1. Copy the gameboard shown. Each player gets two playing pieces. Take turns placing one piece on a dot until all four pieces are on the board. Never place more than one piece on a dot.

2. Take turns sliding your pieces along the paths between the dots. The board below shows how two players started. The player who blocks both of the other player's pieces wins.

Look for a strategy to block your partner's pieces.

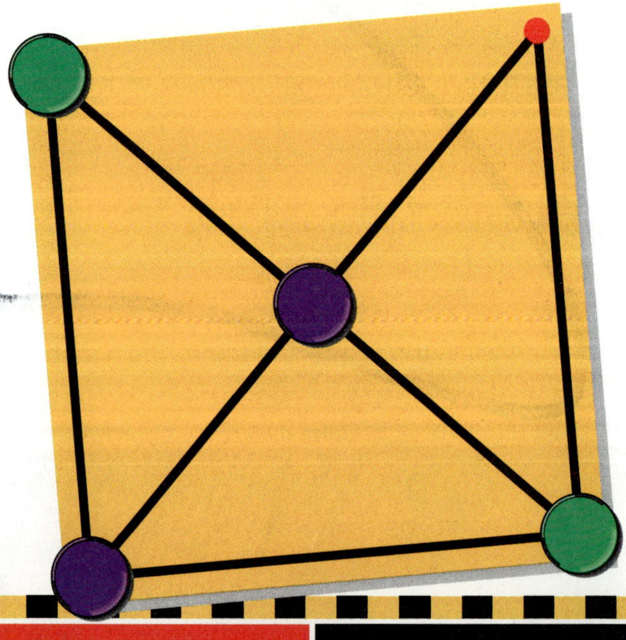

ACTIVITY 2

Square Tick-Tack-Toe

With Your Partner Get three game pieces in a row and win the game!

1. Draw the gameboard shown. Each player gets five game pieces.
2. Take turns placing pieces on dots where lines meet.
3. The first player to place three game pieces in a row wins the game. Rows can be in any direction.

What You'll Need

- *10 playing pieces, 5 each of 2 colors*

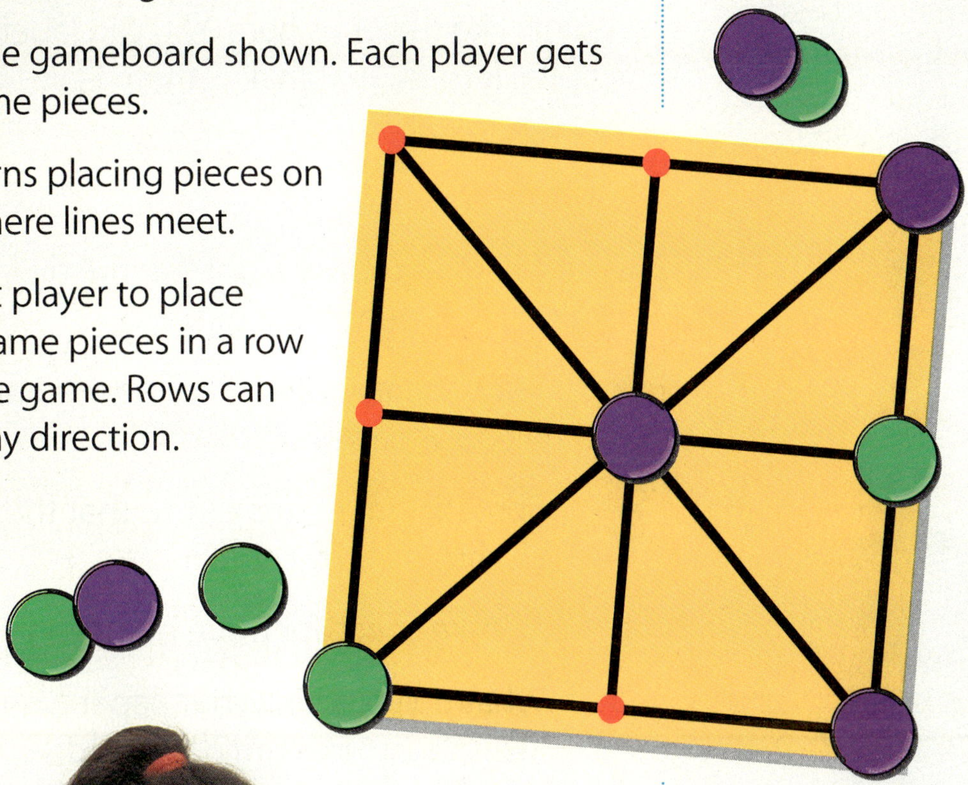

Where must green move next to block purple?

TOOLS AND TECHNIQUES

You can call the labeled points in the diagram point A *and* point B.

ACTIVITY 3 Making Points

With Your Class The dots on the gameboards are also called **points.** Make some points like the ones here. You can label points with capital letters. That makes them easy to talk about.

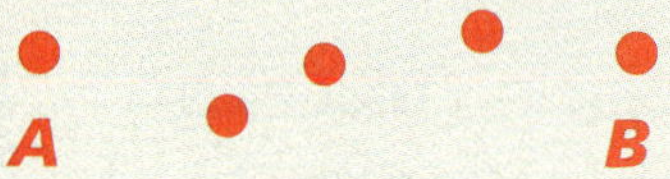

A **point** is a dot like the tip of a pencil or a pin.

1. Take twenty seconds to draw points on a piece of paper.
2. Spread your points out so that they aren't all clumped in the center.
3. Is there space for more points on your paper?
4. What do you think your paper would look like if you took 30 minutes to draw points?

ACTIVITY 4

Connect the Points

With Your Partner Make drawings by connecting points.

1. Use a ruler to connect points. Connect points to draw any shapes you can think of!

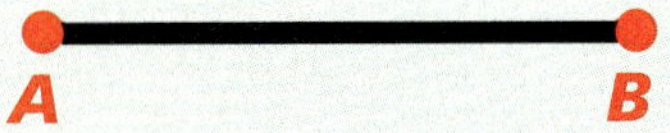

A straight path between two points is a **line segment.** Line segment *AB* is shown above.

2. How many line segments did you draw to make your drawing?

3. Describe how you drew your figure. How might labeling points help make your description clearer?

What You'll Need

- *ruler*

DRAWING TO LEARN

When you draw a picture like a stick figure, you are using line segments. What other pictures can you draw using only line segments?

With Your Class Look for line segments on the gameboards you have used. Look for line segments in your classroom, too. Make a list of the line segments you find.

CONNECT AND COMMUNICATE

You can show a line with arrows on either end. Those show that the line goes on and on. The diagram shows line AB.

ACTIVITY 5

Line Up

With Your Class Now you know about points and line segments. What if you connected points forever in a straight path?

A **line** is a straight path that goes on forever.

1. Look at the picture of the students playing tug-of-war. If the rope went straight in both directions forever, it would be like a line.

2. Discuss things that remind you of a line. Why is a street a better model of a line than a pencil? Why are neither exact models of a line?

ACTIVITY 6

Model a Line

With Your Partner Show your class what points, line segments, and lines look like.

1. Make models of points and line segments. Use string, beads, and crayons or markers. Try making a model of a line.
2. Present your models to your class.

What You'll Need

- *string*
- *beads*
- *crayons or markers*

Self-Check *Ask yourself, "Can I describe points, line segments, and lines?"*

Do You Remember?

Try It!

Draw and describe each of these.

1. a point **2.** a line segment **3.** a line

Which of these has a curved surface? a flat surface? both?

4.  **5.**  **6.**  **7.** 

Use the labels in the diagram to name an example of each.

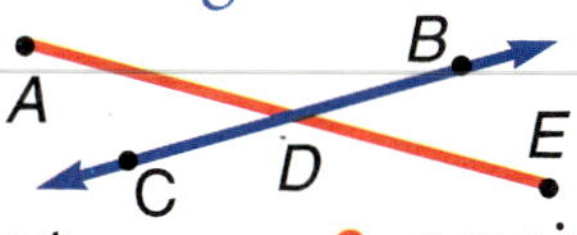

8. a line segment **9.** a point **10.** a line

Think About It

11. What makes a line different from a line segment?

LESSON 2 Angles Everywhere

What You'll Need
- *Tracing Tool or ruler*

ACTIVITY OPTION

Look at the labeled angles on the gameboards below. Put them in order from smallest to largest. Which two are the same size?

ACTIVITY 1 Angles, Right?

On Your Own Use your Tracing Tool. Trace the ray below. Turn the Tracing Tool to form angles.

A **ray** has one end point and goes on and on.

Two rays form an **angle.**

1. The size of an angle means how far apart its rays are. How long the rays are doesn't matter. If you move one ray closer to the other, does the angle get smaller?
2. A square corner is called a **right angle.** Use the square corner of a piece of paper. Find out whether other angles are right angles.
3. Compare the marked angles on these gameboards. Use your square corner of paper. Which angles are right angles? Which angles are less than right angles? greater?

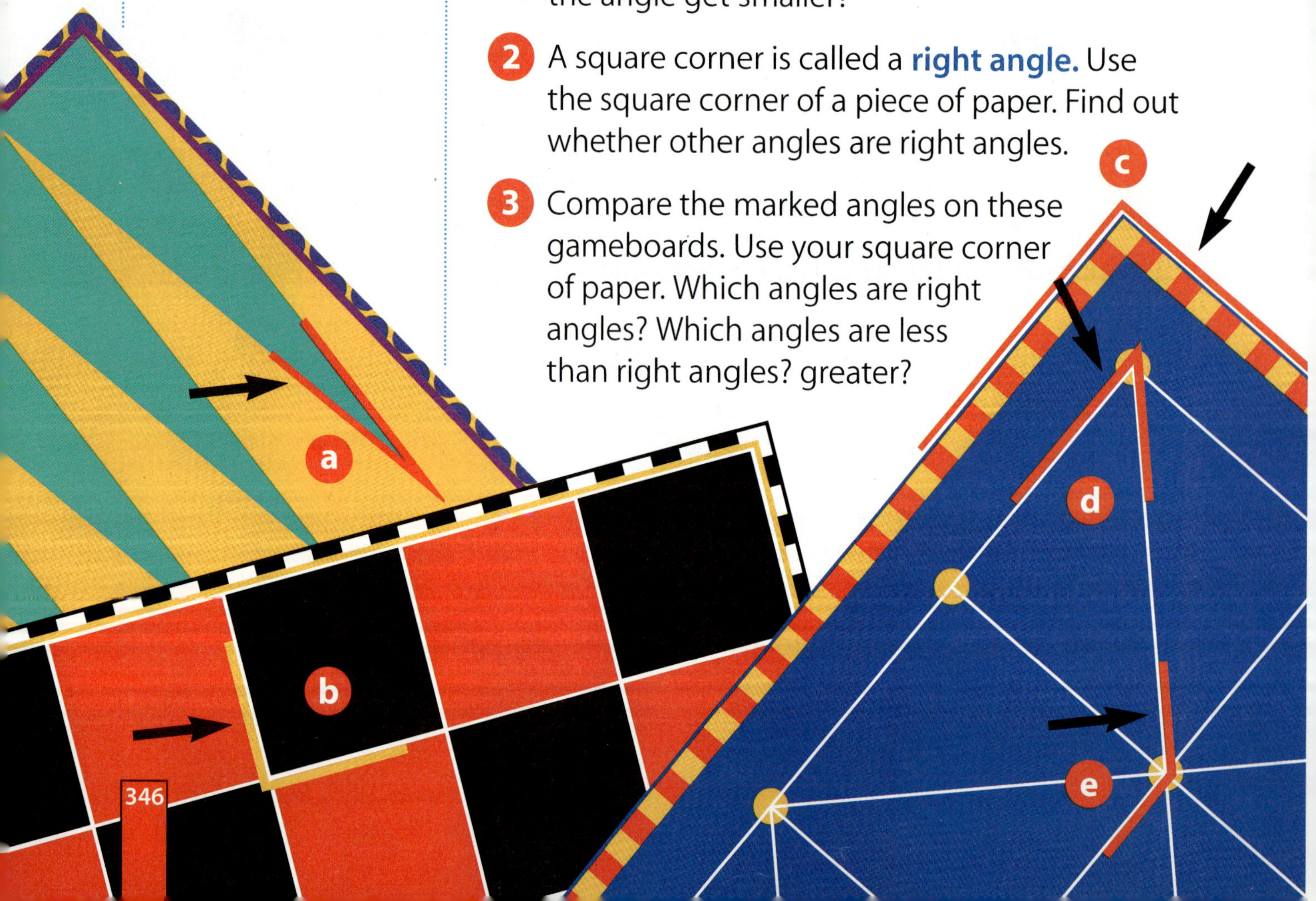

ACTIVITY 2

Drawing Angles

On Your Own Draw some angles. Compare them with your square corner.

1 Use a ruler to draw four angles of any size. Remember, larger angles have rays that are more open.

2 Beside each angle write whether it is less than, equal to, or greater than a right angle.

3 Did you draw a right angle? Use your square corner to help you draw some right angles.

Do You Remember?

Try It!

Draw each figure.

1. a right angle
2. an angle less than a right angle
3. an angle greater than a right angle
4. a rectangle divided into two equal parts
5. a rectangle divided into two unequal parts
6. a circle divided into four equal parts
7. a circle divided into four unequal parts
8. a circle divided in half

Think About It

9. Does the face of a cube have right angles? Write your answer.

LESSON 3 Open or Closed

ACTIVITY 1 Close the Figure

With Your Partner Have you played this game? Use line segments to close the most squares. Make a board six dots high by six dots wide.

1. **Take turns. Draw a line segment to connect two points. You can draw your line segment anywhere on the sheet. Line segments must be straight across or up and down.**

2. **Close a square by drawing the last line segment. Put your initial inside the square to claim it. When you close a square, draw another line segment.**

3. What did you do to keep your partner from closing a square?

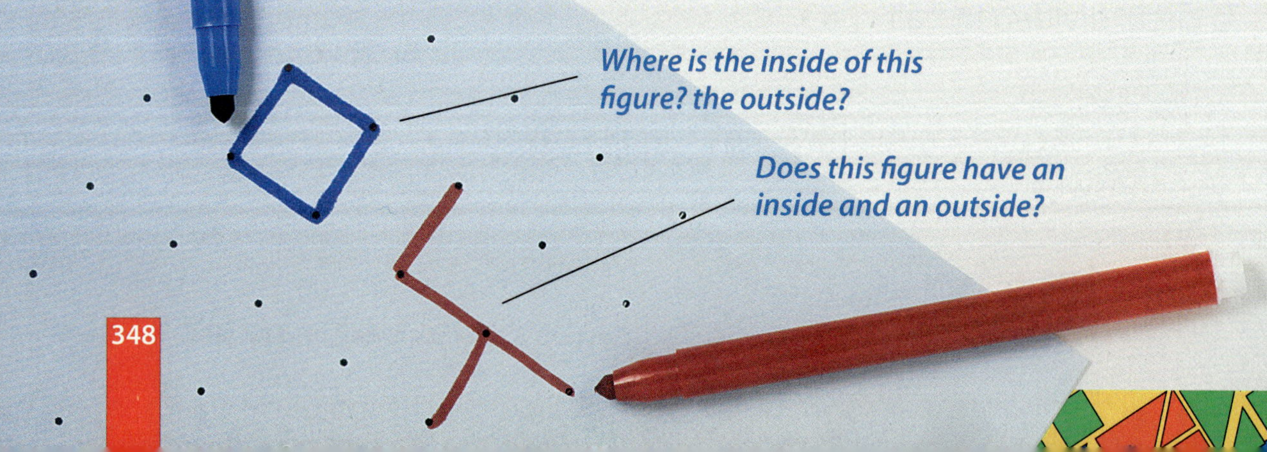

Activity 2 What's Different?

With Your Group Explore other figures.

1. How are the orange figures on this page alike?
2. How are the green figures alike?
3. The green figures are **open figures.** The orange figures are **closed figures.** What makes a figure open or closed? Explain.

Self-Check *Are the blue figures more like the orange figures or the green figures?*

Do You Remember?

Try It!

Make an open figure with this number of line segments.

1. 4
2. 3
3. 7
4. 6

Make a closed figure that has these parts.

5. two right angles
6. six line segments
7. five angles

Solve. Write the answers in order from least to greatest.

8. 4.9 − 3.9 = ■
9. 0.5 + 1.8 = ■
10. 3.4 − 1.7 = ■
11. 6.2 − 5.6 = ■
12. 4.2 + 2.6 = ■
13. 0.2 + 0.5 = ■

Think About It

14. Look at the figure you drew for Exercise 3. How can you make it a closed figure? Explain in writing.

LESSON 4

How Many Sides?

What You'll Need
- geoboard
- rubber bands
- grid paper
- scissors
- ruler

ACTIVITY 1 Polygons

With Your Group Use a geoboard and a rubber band to explore figures made from line segments. Compare with other students in your group as you work.

1. Make a closed figure on your geoboard.
2. Trade with a partner. Cut some sheets of grid paper into fourths. Draw your partner's figure on a piece of grid paper.

a How many sides does the figure have?

b What is the least number of sides you need to make a closed figure?

3. Make and draw more figures. Make them with different numbers of sides.

4. Look at the figures your group made. Which ones are made of line segments that do not cross each other? Those are **polygons.**

ACTIVITY 2 Alike and Different

With Your Group Each group member should make four or five polygons. Then decide how to sort the polygons into different kinds.

1. Will you sort them by size? by number of sides? by size of angles?
2. Compare polygons with the same number of sides. How are they alike or different?
3. Use the grid your polygons are drawn on to estimate the area of one or two of them. Explain how you estimate area.

What You'll Need

- *grid paper*
- *ruler*

CONNECT AND COMMUNICATE

The word polygon *comes from a Greek word that means "having many angles."*

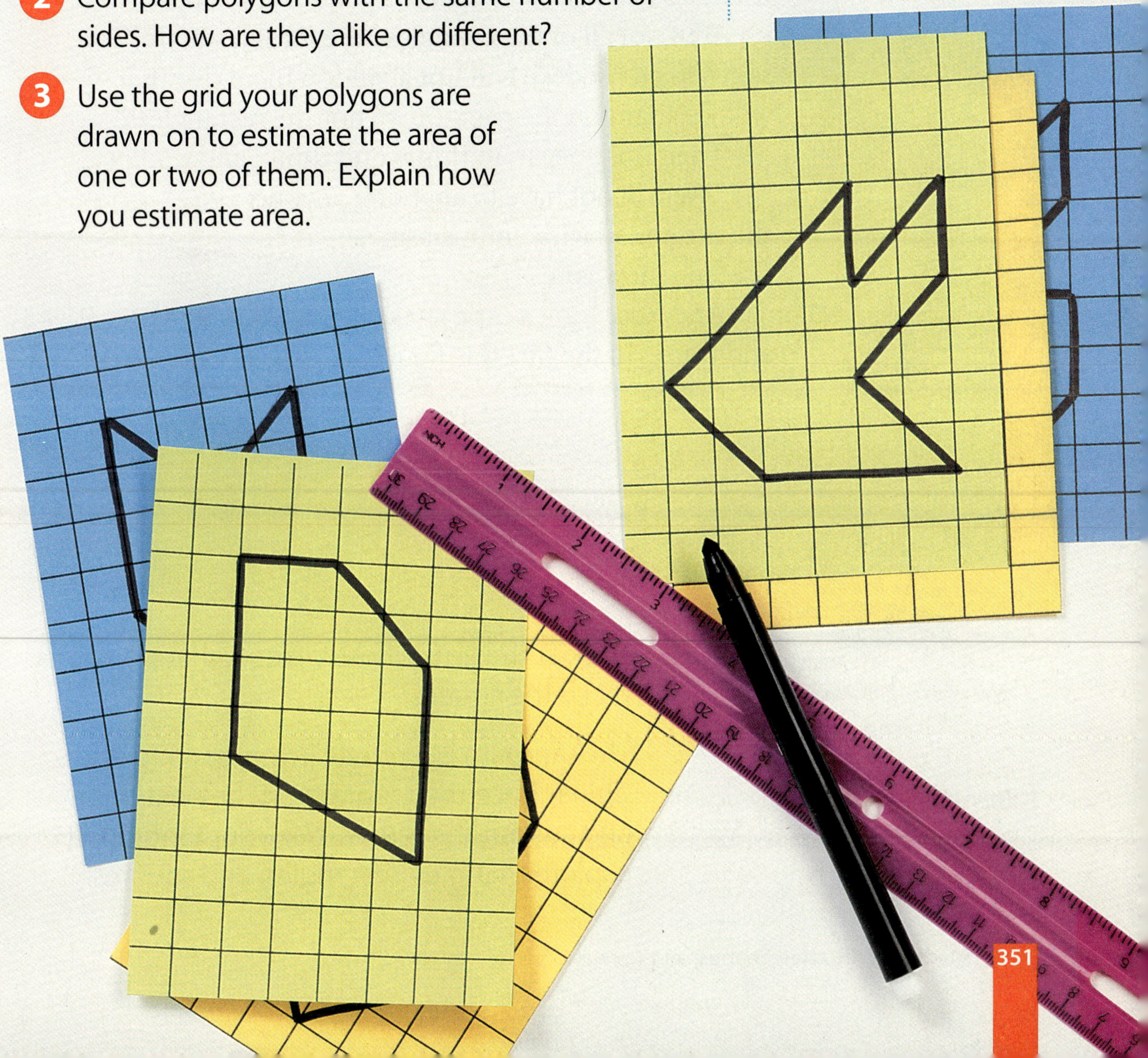

What You'll Need

- *tracing paper*
- *ruler*
- *scissors*
- *grid paper*

ACTIVITY 3 Special Polygons

With Your Group You already know some polygons—triangles, squares, and rectangles.

LITERATURE

King Square VII thought squares were the perfect shape. He ordered all other shapes to live within a walled square of land.

"I have an idea that might help you and your brothers and sisters escape," Rose told Violet. "Look, if two triangles like you join together, you form a square."

"But not all of the triangles here form a square," said Violet, "and we will not abandon them. Neither will we abandon the rhombuses nor the rectangles!"

Then Rose began to think, and think, and think . . .

"We will not have to abandon anyone," she exclaimed with enthusiasm. "Let me show you!"

And Rose took a little stick and traced in the dirt this figure:

From *The Kingdom of Geometry* by Alma Flor Ada

ACTIVITY OPTION

How can other shapes join to disguise themselves as squares? Draw a square. Then draw rectangles, squares, and triangles to fill the square.

1. Look at the figure Rose made. What polygons make the square?
2. The tangram is a puzzle invented long ago in China. Trace the tangram on the next page and cut out the pieces. Use your tangram to explore triangles, rectangles, and squares.

3. In Activity 1 did you make a polygon with three sides? Three-sided polygons are called triangles.

4. How many triangles are in your tangram? How many of them have a right angle?

5. Draw several triangles on grid paper. How would you group them into different kinds?

6. Find the square in your tangram. How would you describe its angles and sides?

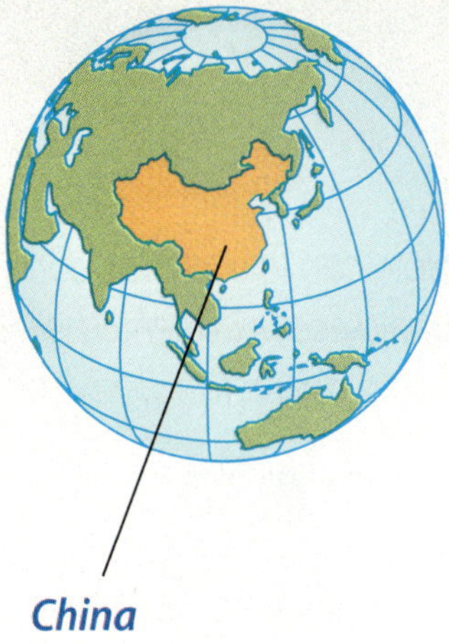

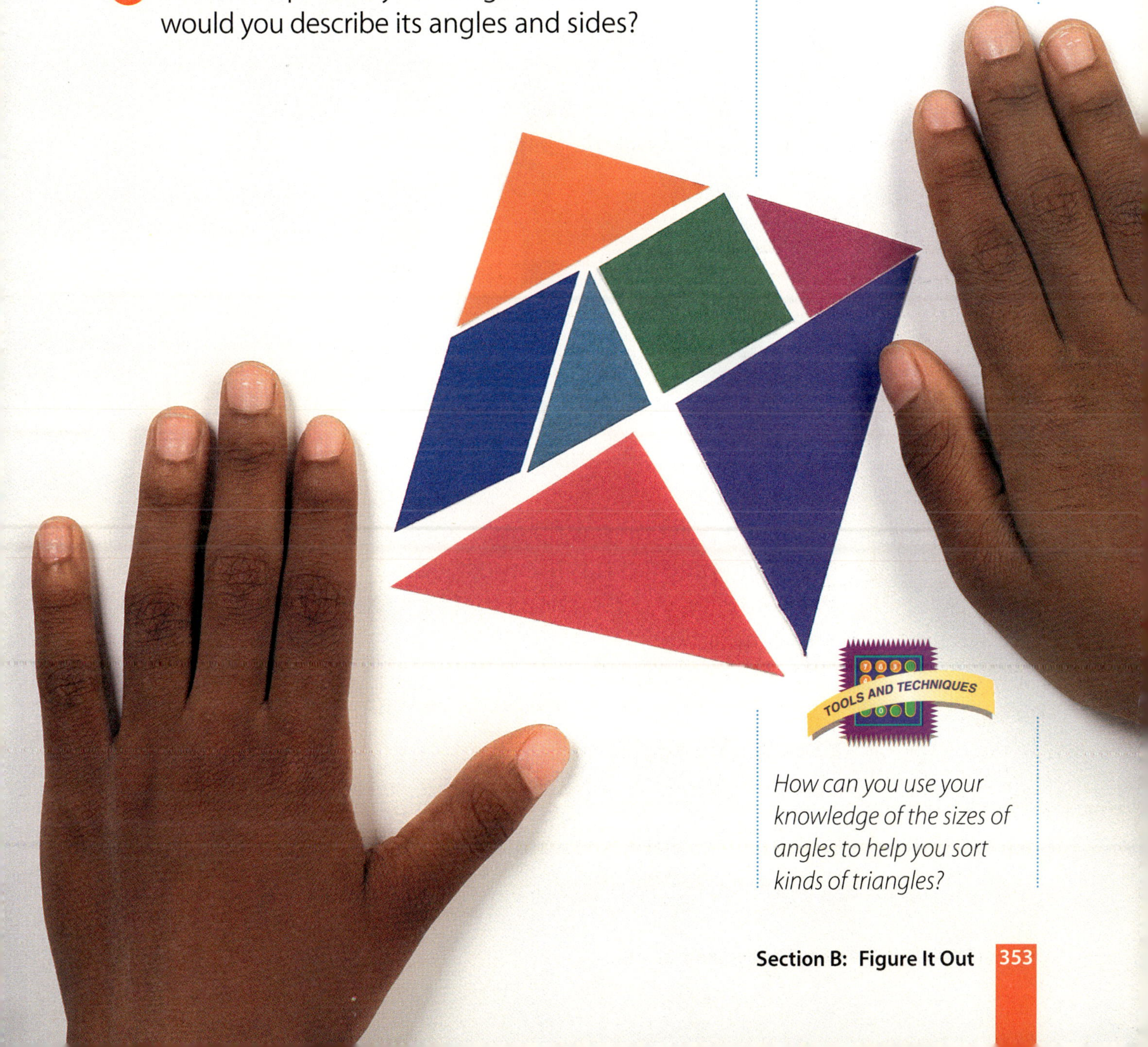

TOOLS AND TECHNIQUES

How can you use your knowledge of the sizes of angles to help you sort kinds of triangles?

DRAWING TO LEARN

How can you use the corner of a piece of paper to help you draw rectangles?

7 Draw some rectangles. What kinds of angles do they have? Which sides are alike?

8 Draw some squares. Discuss with your partner whether you think a square is a rectangle. How will you share your work with the class?

Do You Remember?

Try It!

Write the letter for the shape.

a.  **b.** 

c.  **d.** 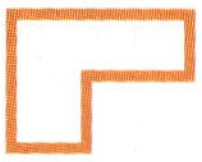

1. square **2.** triangle

3. rectangle

4. Which polygon has no right angles?

5. Which polygon has the most sides?

6 through 10. Add fractions that have the same denominator.

$\frac{3}{8}$, $\frac{3}{4}$, $\frac{4}{6}$, $\frac{6}{10}$, $\frac{1}{3}$, $\frac{1}{3}$, $\frac{1}{6}$, $\frac{3}{10}$, $\frac{7}{8}$, $\frac{3}{4}$

Think About It

11. Four sides of a polygon have the same length. Can you be sure the polygon is a square? Explain.

Investigation

Tangram Tryout

Either Exercise 1 or Exercise 2 will help you explore your tangram. Choose one exercise.

1. Can you make a triangle out of 2 pieces of your tangram? of 3 pieces? of 7 pieces? How about a square or a rectangle? Use a chart like the one below to keep track of your results.

Use this many pieces	square	rectangle	triangle
2			
3			
4			

2. Try making some of the shapes shown here. You can make up shapes of your own, too. Use as many pieces as you want.

Ask Yourself

- ☐ Am I familiar with the tangram shapes?
- ☐ Which kind of shape will I start with?
- ☐ Will I begin with small pieces or large ones?
- ☐ Can I draw the shapes I made?
- ☐ Can I write to explain how to build one shape?

LESSON 5 Getting Around

ACTIVITY 1 In the Circle

With Your Group A marbles game starts with marbles inside a circle. Then players shoot another marble to knock marbles out of the circle.

1. Which marbles are inside the circle? Which are outside? Explain how you can tell.
2. Make a rule about when a marble is inside the circle and when it is outside the circle.

The player who knocks the most marbles out of the circle wins.

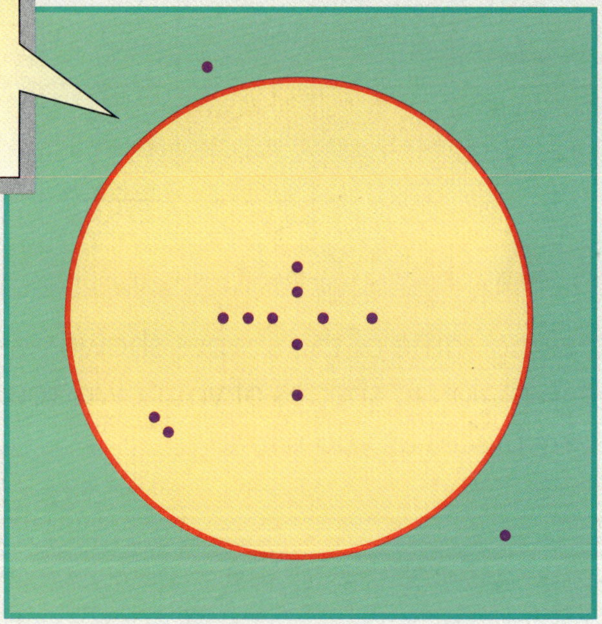

REASONING AND PROBLEM SOLVING

Why do you think a wheel rolls?

3. A wheel is shaped like a circle. What else can you think of that is shaped like a circle? Sketch some of your circle objects.
4. Is a circle a polygon? Explain.

ACTIVITY 2 Halfway Across

On Your Own Learn about special parts of circles.

1 **Trace a circle. Cut it out, fold it in half, and unfold it.**

2 **Fold it in half a different way. Unfold and mark both of the fold lines.**

3 Each fold line is a **diameter.** Can you fold to find more diameters? Explain what a diameter is.

4 Describe the **center** of the circle. Is there only one center? Explain how you know.

What You'll Need

- *Fraction Tool or circle shapes*
- *scissors*
- *ruler*

Do You Remember?

Try It!

Use letters from the circle to name each of these.

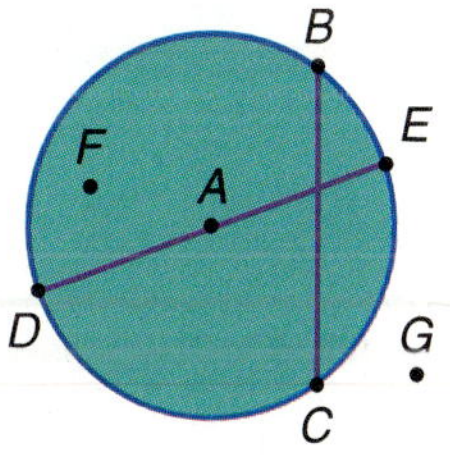

1. the center
2. a diameter
3. a point inside the circle
4. a point outside the circle
5. a point on the circle

Divide. Answer only questions with quotients less than 7.

6. $4\overline{)12}$ 7. $4\overline{)17}$ 8. $7\overline{)21}$ 9. $5\overline{)15}$ 10. $4\overline{)32}$

Think About It

11. Write how you can find the center of a circle.

Do You Remember? Cumulative Review

Field of Shapes

Look at the baseball diamond. What figures do you see? Look for line segments and rays, too.

Use the baseball diamond to answer Exercises 1 through 5.

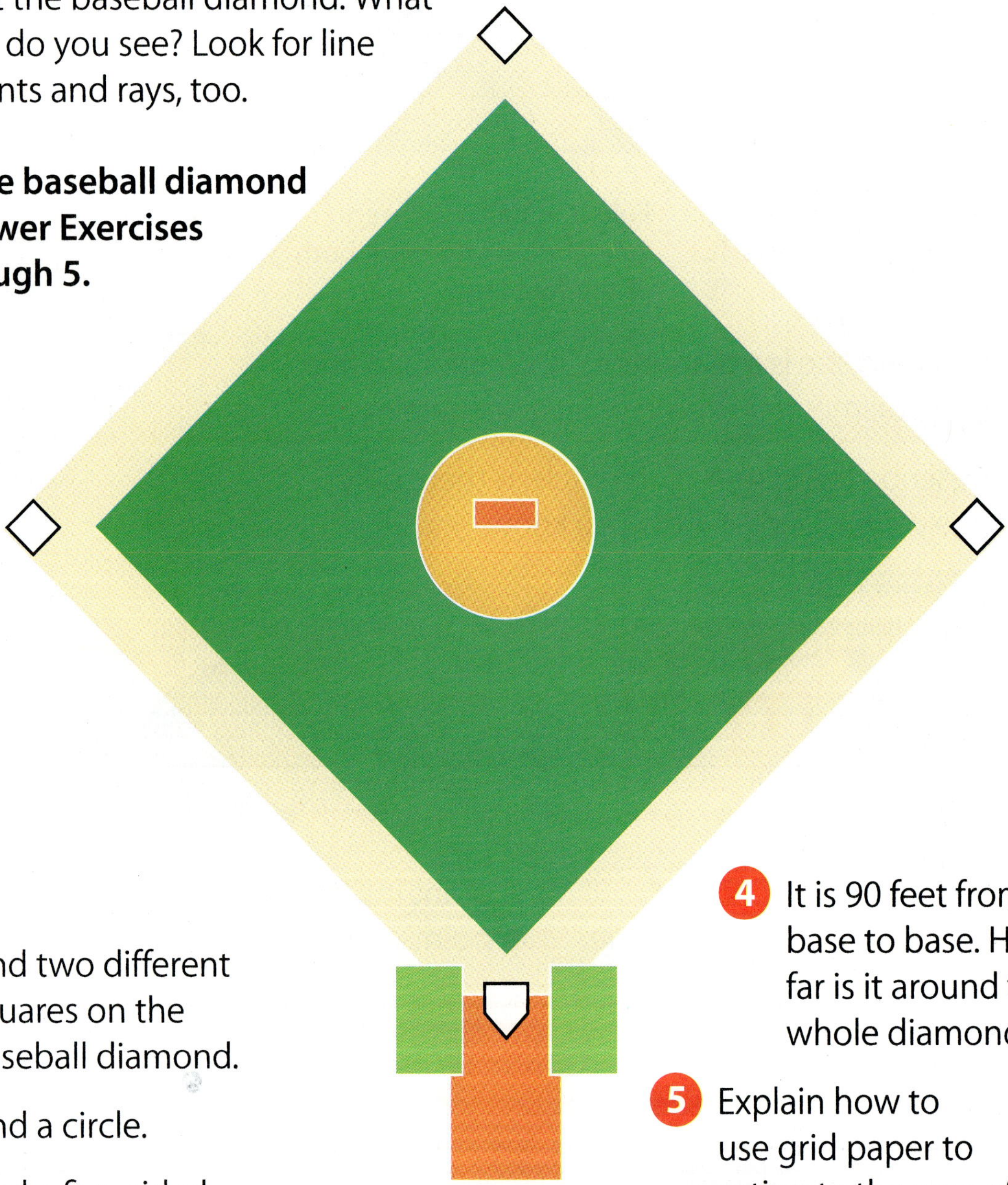

1 Find two different squares on the baseball diamond.

2 Find a circle.

3 Find a five-sided polygon.

4 It is 90 feet from base to base. How far is it around the whole diamond?

5 Explain how to use grid paper to estimate the area of the diamond.

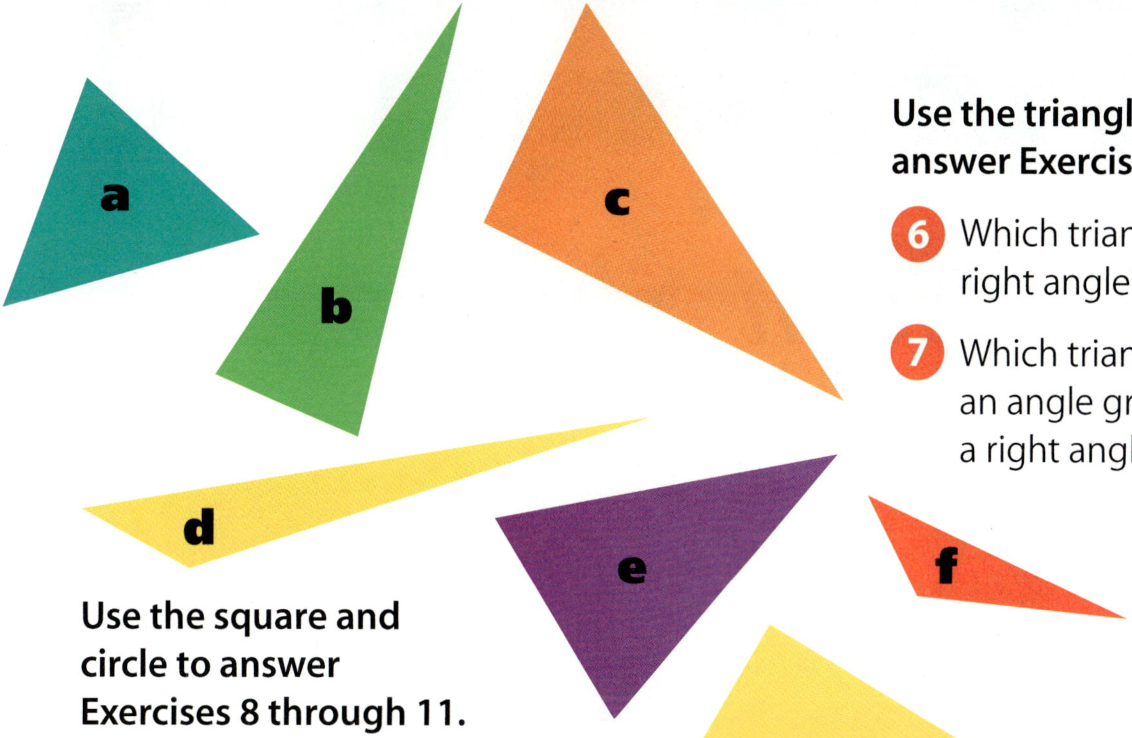

Use the triangles to answer Exercises 6 and 7.

6 Which triangle has a right angle?

7 Which triangles have an angle greater than a right angle?

Use the square and circle to answer Exercises 8 through 11.

8 Which line segment is a diameter?

9 What fraction of the circle is red?

10 Which point is the center of the circle? outside the circle?

11 Suppose the side of this square is 4 inches long. How long are all 4 sides together?

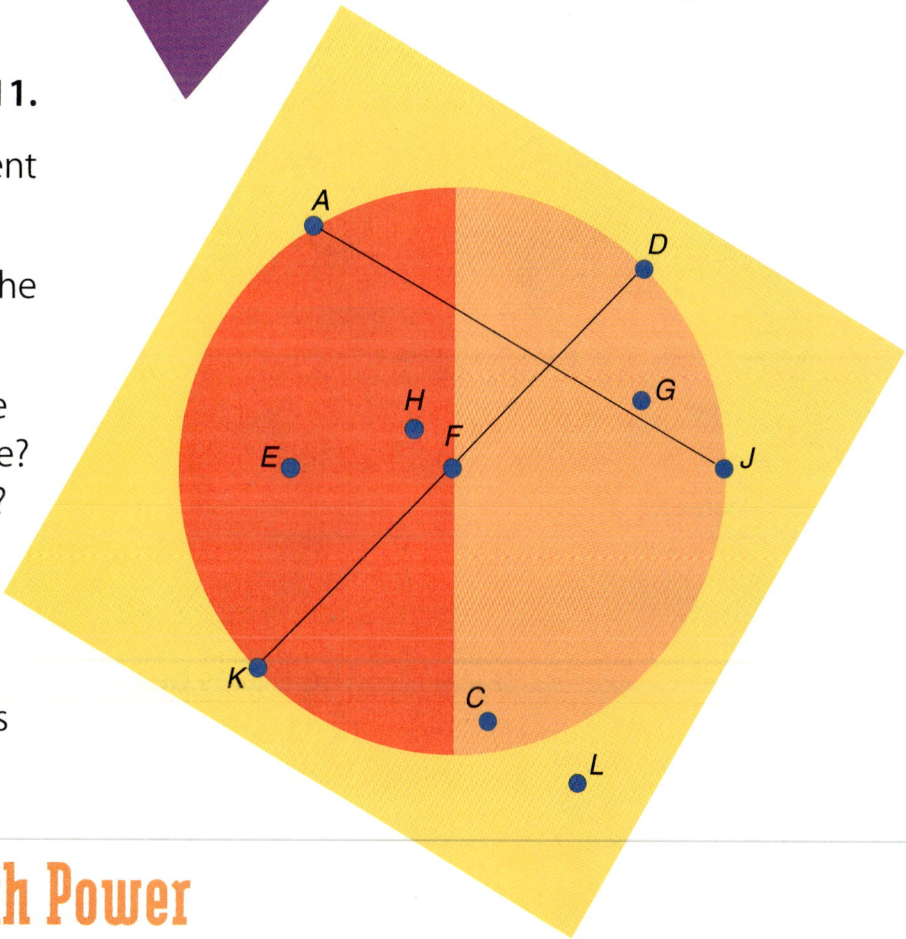

Check Your Math Power

12 Shapes and polygons are all around you. Use shapes you find around the classroom to show a classmate examples of polygons and shapes that are not polygons.

SECTION C Division Is Sharing

LESSON 6

Even Shares

ACTIVITY 1 Divide It Up

What You'll Need
- *base ten blocks*

With Your Group These students are planning an amazing game called Future Ball. Use base ten blocks to help you divide up the equipment.

1 There are 58 flags to share evenly among 4 players. How many flags will each player get? Will there be any flags left over?

Divide a sheet of paper into six areas. Use the paper to keep your base ten blocks in order as you make equal groups.

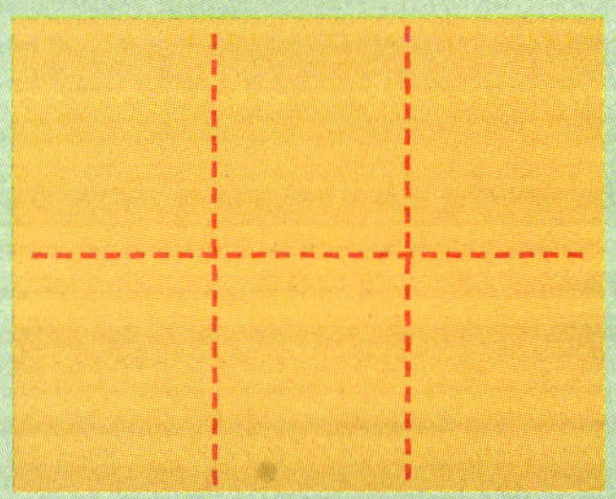

2 The boxes below hold a total of 30 flying disks. Three teams share the disks evenly. How many disks does each team get?

3 Can 6 teams share 77 hoops evenly? How many hoops does each team get?

4 Forty-three players want to form 6 equal teams. How many players are on each team?

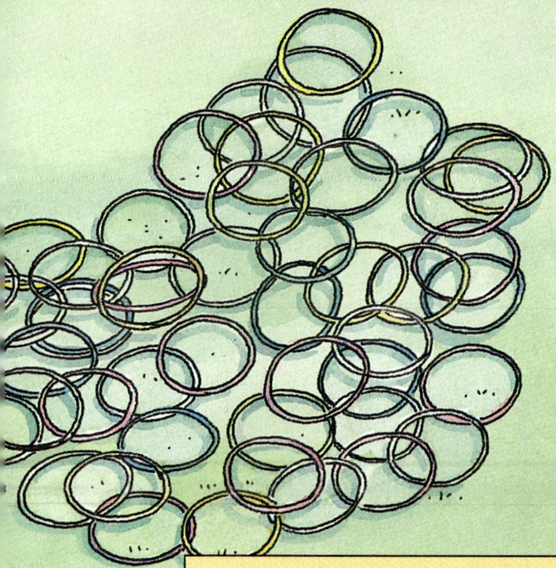

5 Share 14 sticks evenly among 5 players. How many sticks does each player get?

6 There are 46 kick balls to share evenly among 4 teams. How many do you give to each team?

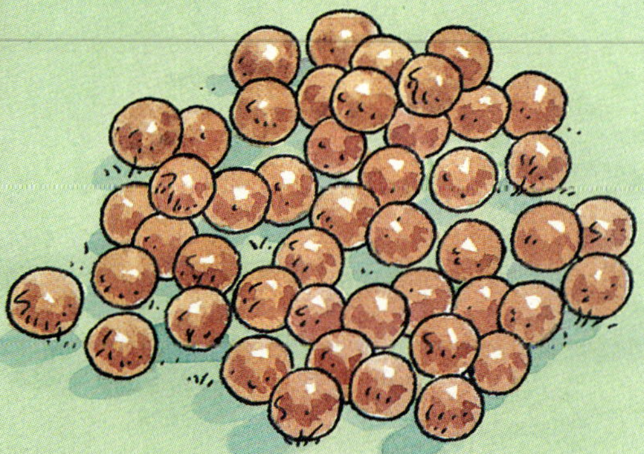

REASONING AND PROBLEM SOLVING

Think before you decide what to do with a remainder. For example, would you divide a kick ball in half to share a remainder of one among two groups? Explain.

ACTIVITY 2

What's Left?

With Your Class The sharing questions in Activity 1 left you with lots of extra things—1 player, 2 flags, 5 hoops, 4 sticks, and 2 kick balls. What do you do with the leftover things?

1. Suppose you share 6 snack bars equally among 4 people. What is a fair way to share the extra bars?
2. Twelve students are going to a basketball game together. A car holds 5 students. How many cars are needed?
3. Explain how you decide what to do with a remainder when you divide.

ACTIVITY 3 How Did You Do It?

On Your Own How can you figure out how to share 43 pick-up sticks among 3 players? Here is one method. Explain each step shown below.

What You'll Need
- *base ten blocks*

1. Each ones' cube stands for a pick-up stick. Each tens' rod stands for 10 pick-up sticks.

2. How many sticks have the 3 players shared so far?

3. Why isn't there a tens' rod here?

4. What will you do with the extra pick-up stick?
5. How did you divide? Explain your way to the class.

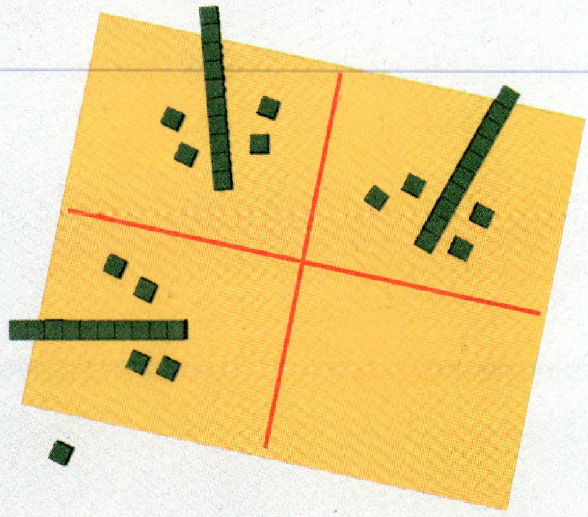

CONNECT AND COMMUNICATE

In Your Journal Explain to a friend how to use base ten blocks to divide. Use pictures to make your ideas clear.

ACTIVITY 4 Estimate!

With Your Group Estimating can help you check your work.

DRAWING TO LEARN

When you don't have base ten blocks, you can use a sketch to help you divide and estimate.

1. Share 62 marbles among 5 people. Will each person get more than 10 marbles? How do you know?
2. You have 28 balls to put in 3 cans. Will more than 10 balls go in each can? Explain.
3. You have 78 caps to put in 6 boxes. Will more than 10 caps go in each box?
4. Describe your thinking for Exercises 1, 2, and 3. How did you decide whether your answer was less than or greater than 10?

Do You Remember? Try It!

Use base ten blocks. Find out how many each student will get and whether there are any left over.

1. 45 baseball cards for 3 students
2. 6 bowling balls for 4 students
3. 72 marbles for 6 students
4. 62 hoops for 5 students
5. 84 rubber balls for 7 students

6 through 8. Name each figure at the right.

9 through 11. Find the perimeter of each figure above.

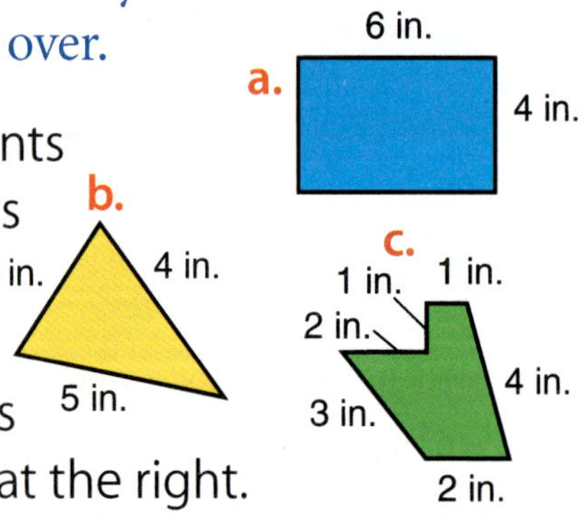

Think About It

12. Explain in writing how estimation can help you divide.

Write It!

LESSON 7

ACTIVITY 1 Make a Record

With Your Group Here are three ways to record how to share 46 marbles evenly among 3 students. How does each method show the following facts.

- One tens' rod is left after you share 3.
- You have 16 ones' cubes to share.

Do these base ten blocks show the division correctly?

Brenda's way

15 R1
3)46
-3 16
1 -15
1

Keiko's way

15 R1
3)46
-3
16
-15
1

Eduard's way

15 R1
3)4¹6

Do you use a different method of recording division? Use your favorite method to record how to share 71 marbles evenly among 3 players.

Divide-a-Maze

What You'll Need
- *gameboard*
- *spinner*
- *game pieces*
  - *base ten blocks*

ACTIVITY 2 Maze Race

With Your Group Use your division skills to win this game.

1 Play in teams of two. Spin the spinner. Divide the number you start on by the number you spin. Drop any remainder.

2 One player divides with base ten blocks. The other player records the process. Use your favorite method of recording.

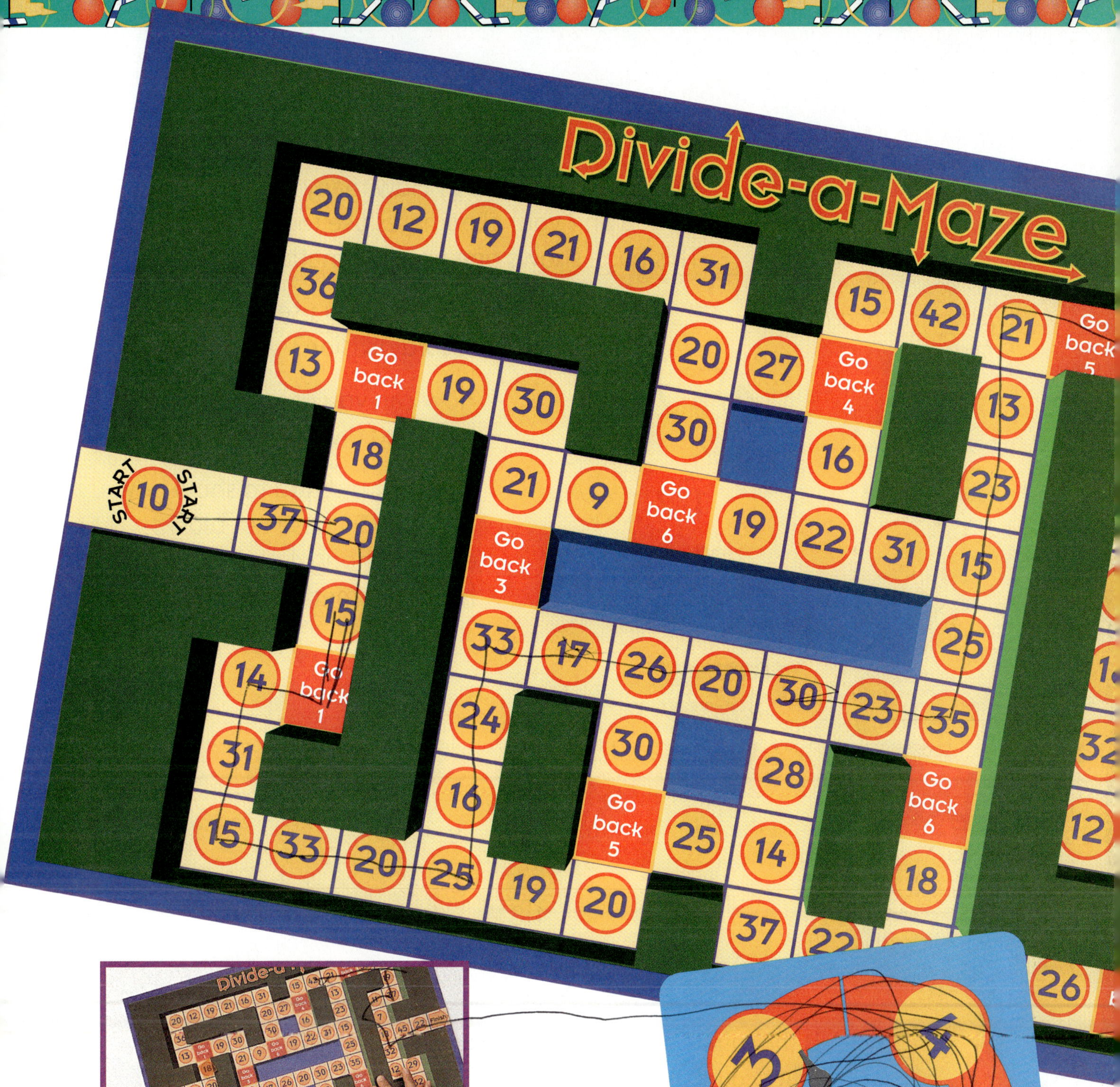

3

If you divide correctly with the base ten blocks, move that number of spaces. If you record correctly, move the same number of spaces again.

What You'll Need

- *base ten blocks*

Self-Check *Ask yourself, "Can I record division problems so my partner can understand my process?"*

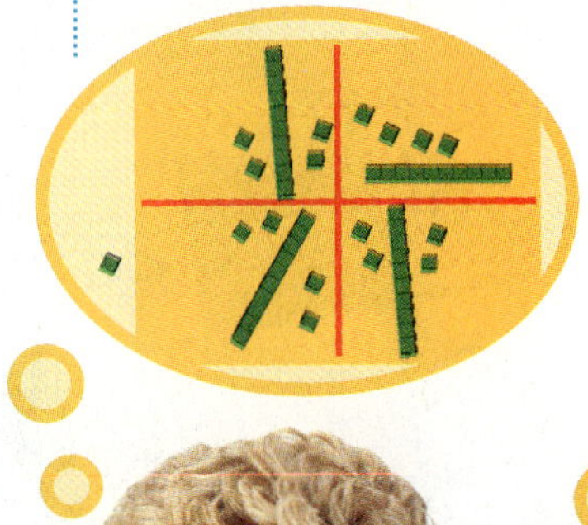

ACTIVITY 3 Talk It Over

With Your Class How many different ways do you and your classmates use to record division? This page shows one possible method.

```
   1 4 R1
4)5 7
 -4
  1 7
 -1 6
     1
```

1. How can you use subtraction to record division?
2. How can you use multiplication to record division?
3. Use your method to show how to divide 94 base ten blocks evenly among 4 players. Explain how your method works.

Do You Remember? Try It!

Find the missing number.

1. $4\overline{)\blacksquare\,\blacksquare}$ = 5 R1
2. $4\overline{)8\,\blacksquare}$ = ■1 R1
3. $4\overline{)\blacksquare\,7}$ = 1 1R3
4. $6\overline{)\blacksquare\,\blacksquare}$ = 1 2
5. $\blacksquare\overline{)39}$ = 9 R3
6. $4\overline{)\blacksquare\,\blacksquare}$ = 1 6R3

Is the spinner equally likely to land on red as to land on any other color? Answer yes or no for each spinner below.

7. 
8. 
9. 
10. 
11. 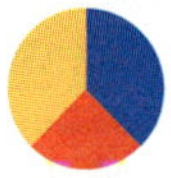

Think About It

12. Are you more likely to have a remainder when you divide by 2 or when you divide by 9? Explain why.

Investigation

The Lost Key

You have a calculator with one small problem—the division key is broken. Figure out ways to solve division exercises anyway. Remember, all the other keys work normally.

Ask Yourself

- ☐ What keys *do* work on your calculator?
- ☐ Is there more than one answer?
- ☐ Will you work with easy problems first?
- ☐ Have you talked about your method with a classmate?
- ☐ Would you like to save this work for your portfolio?

LESSON 8 Shapes That Match

Fold your paper like this. Cut along the folds to make cards. Trace one figure from below onto each card.

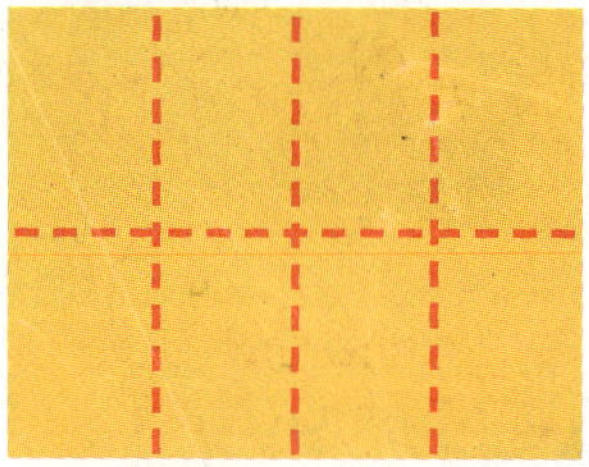

ACTIVITY 1 Match the Figures

With Your Group Play Match the Figures with 2, 4, or 6 players.

1. **Look** at the Tools and Techniques to find out how to make 8 playing cards for each player.
2. **Mix** the group's cards. Hand out eight cards to each player face down. Players look at their cards. Lay down any matching pairs.
3. **Start** by one player taking one card from the player to his or her right. Do not look before you pick. If the card matches one you already have, lay the pair down. Then the player to your left takes a turn.
4. **Play** until one player is out of cards. That player wins.

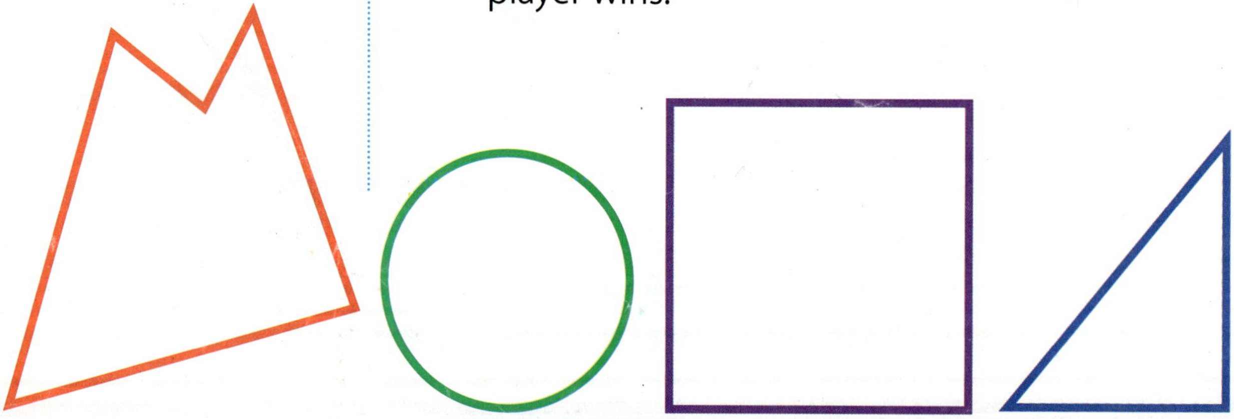

ACTIVITY 2 Congruent Shapes

On Your Own Can you tell whether two figures match?

1. Cut out four different shapes from the cards you used to play the game.
2. Compare the cut-out figures with the figures on the page. Can you tell when two figures have the same size and shape? Explain.
3. Figures that are the same size and shape are called **congruent** figures. Are any of your figures congruent?

REASONING AND PROBLEM SOLVING

Are squares always congruent? How can you tell whether squares are always congruent? Share with your class.

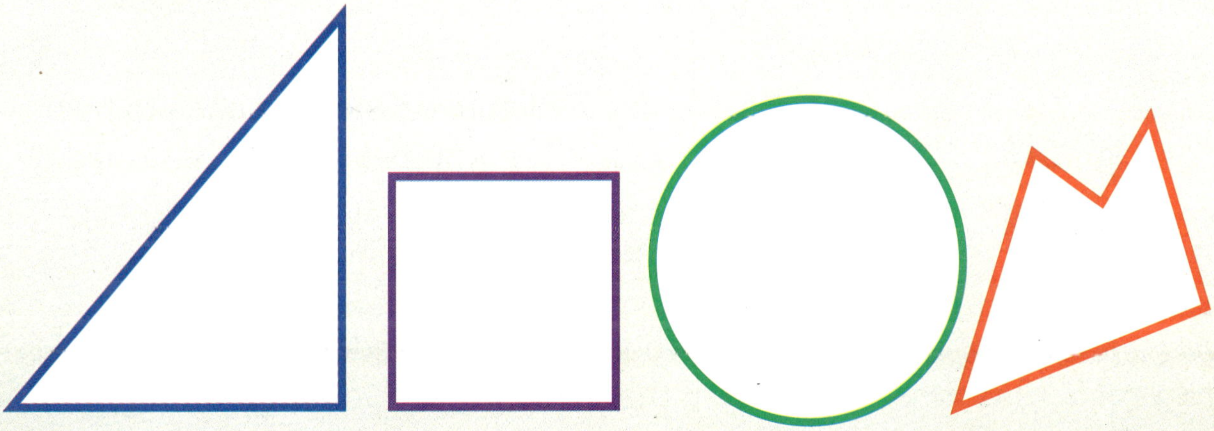

What You'll Need
- *Tracing Tool or tracing paper*

ACTIVITY 3 Slides, Flips, Turns

On Your Own Slides, flips, and turns are ways of moving figures.

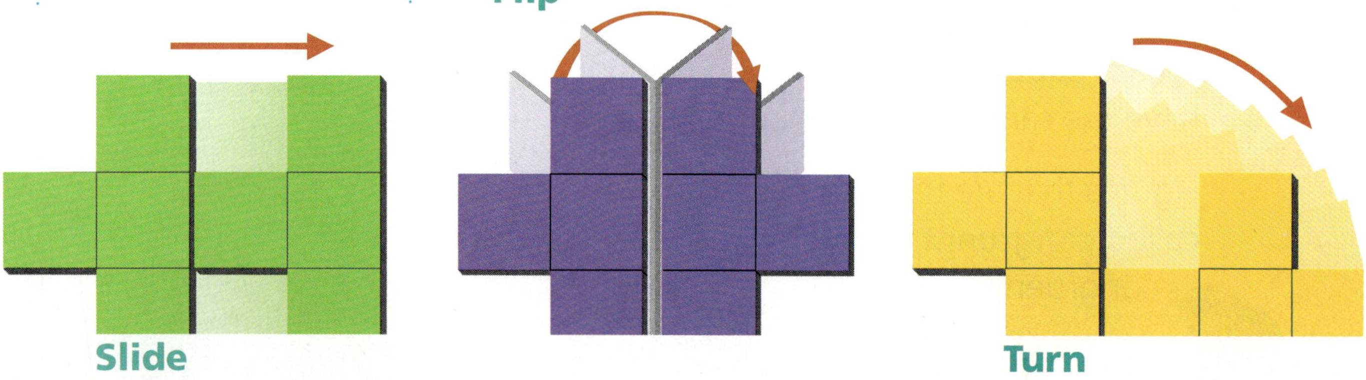

Use your Tracing Tool. Copy the  above. Move your Tracing Tool to see what flips, slides, and turns look like. The turn pictured is a quarter turn. What would a half turn look like?

What You'll Need
- *spinner*
- *grid paper*
- *scissors*

ACTIVITY 4 Move Your Figure

With Your Partner Choose one of the figures on the next page. Copy the figure using grid paper. Use it to trace slides, flips, and turns on the grid.

1. **Look** at the picture on the next page to help you. Spin to see whether your move should be a slide, a flip, or a turn. The first player to get to the other side of the grid paper wins.

2. **Put** your figure at one edge of your paper. Spin the spinner. Move your figure.

TOOLS AND TECHNIQUES

Practicc sliding, flipping, and turning your figure before starting this game.

3 **Map** your route. Trace your figure after each move. Label moves as flips, slides, or turns.

Do You Remember?

Try It!

Use these figures to answer Exercises 1 through 4.

a. b. c. d. e.

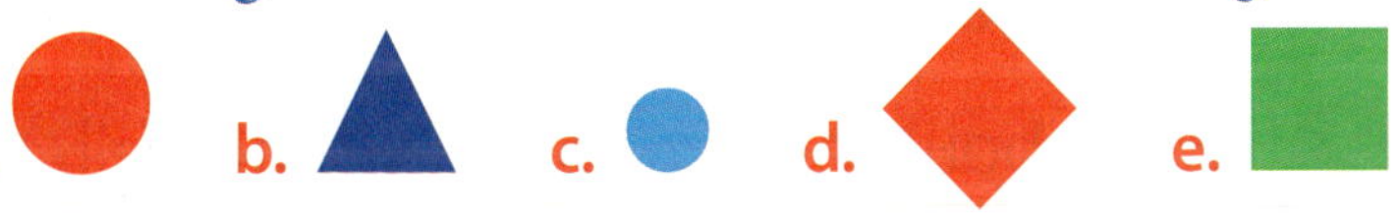

Explain why the shapes in each pair are or are not congruent.

1. a and e
2. d and e
3. c and b
4. c and a

Draw a picture that shows each fraction.

5. $\frac{2}{4}$
6. $\frac{2}{6}$
7. $\frac{3}{6}$
8. $\frac{2}{8}$
9. Draw two congruent triangles.
10. Draw two congruent line segments.

Think About It

11. Explain why the figures you drew for Exercises 9 and 10 are congruent.

LESSON 9 Parts That Match

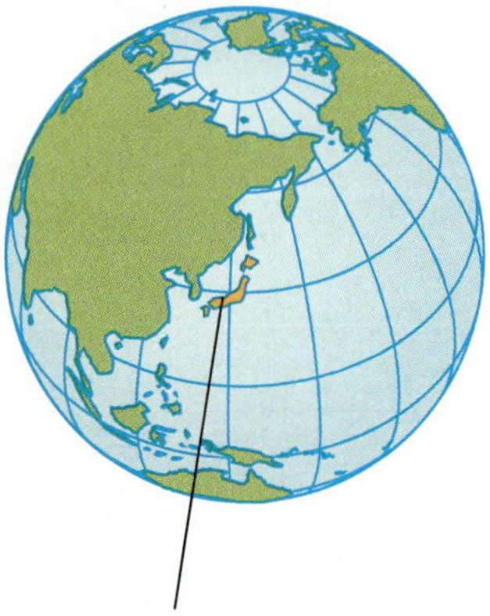

Japan

ACTIVITY 1 Kite Symmetry

On Your Own Kites in Japan are used for more than just fun. Kites are also used for festivals and celebrations.

Look at the diagram. Figures with parts that match when you fold them have **symmetry.**

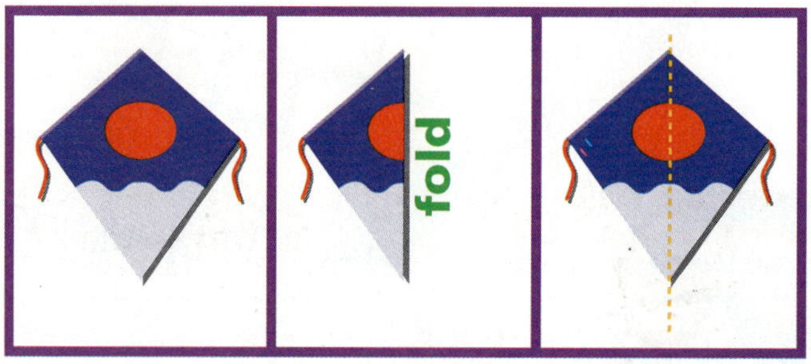

The line that splits the figure into matching halves is called a **line of symmetry.**

1. Write about the kites on this page. Tell whether the kites have lines of symmetry.
2. Find other figures with symmetry in your classroom.

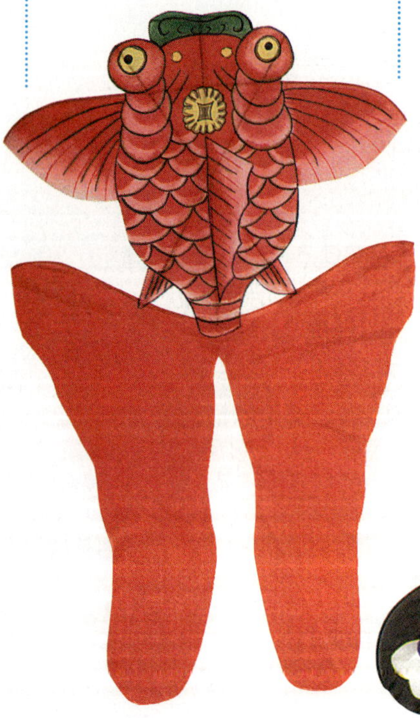

ACTIVITY 2 Make Your Own!

On Your Own Make a kite pattern like the one in the picture below. Use symmetry to help you.

What You'll Need

- *construction paper*
- *markers*
- *scissors*

1. **Fold paper and cut out a shape as shown. Will the fold be a line of symmetry?**

2. **Paste or color congruent shapes onto your kite. Where will you put figures so that the pattern on your kite has symmetry?**

3. **Share your kite with your class.**

4. **How many lines of symmetry does the kite in the picture have? Do the shapes on this kite have symmetry?**

ACTIVITY 3

Game Symmetry

On Your Own Shapes on playing fields sometimes have lines of symmetry.

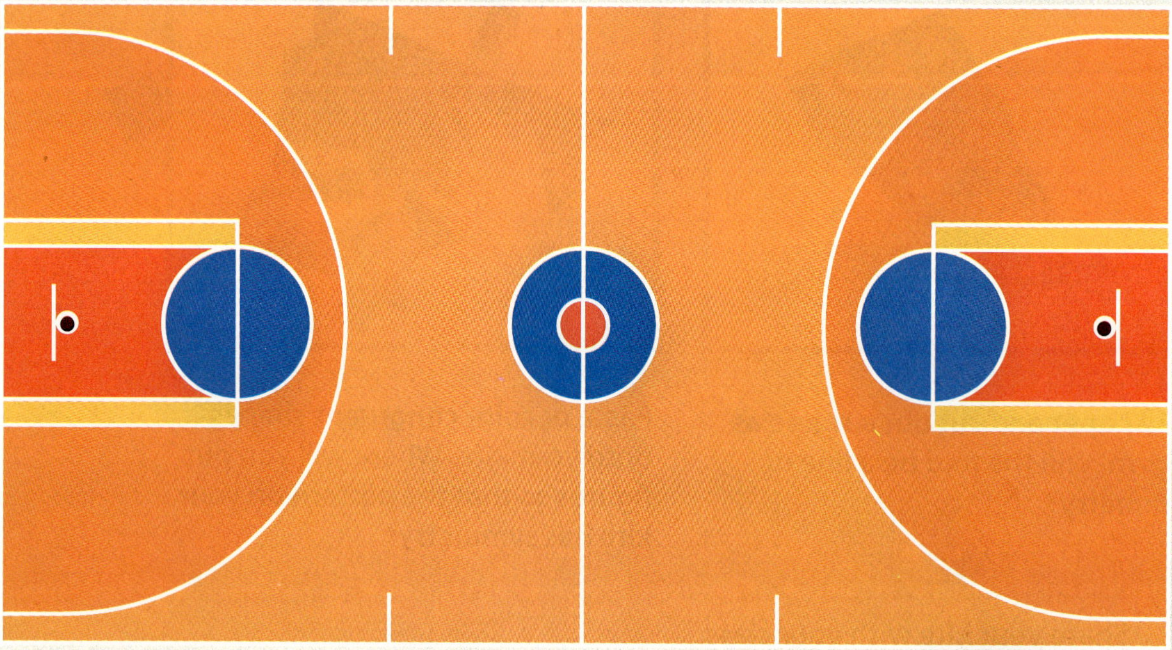

1. How many lines of symmetry can you find on this basketball court? Describe them.

2. List the different types of geometric figures on the basketball court.

Write out the alphabet in capital letters. Which letters have symmetry? Draw the lines of symmetry and share with the class.

3 To play shuffleboard you have to push your disk into a figure to get points. How many lines of symmetry can you find on the shuffleboard court shown above? Describe any that you find.

4 To play hopscotch you have to jump in each box from 1 through 9 and then HOME. Is there a line of symmetry? If yes, describe it.

5 Are all of the shapes that make up the hopscotch pattern congruent? Explain.

6 Think of other types of playing fields. Can you think of any that have more than one line of symmetry? no lines of symmetry?

DRAWING TO LEARN

You cannot always fold things to see whether they have symmetry. Make a drawing. See whether what you drew has parts that match when you fold them.

Exercises and Problems

Tiles and Designs

Use your Tracing Tool to help you answer the questions.

Games and sports fields aren't the only places to find symmetry and congruent figures. Look at these old Italian tiles and Arabic patterns.

Italian

1. Which figures in this tile pattern have one line of symmetry? two? three? four?
2. Find five line segments in the design. Find three lines of symmetry in the design. Can you find more?
3. Find two congruent squares in the pattern. Do you think all the squares are congruent? Why?

Italian

Arabic

4. Find three different kinds of figures in the design above. If you do not know the names of the figures, tell the number of sides.

5. Which figures are congruent? Explain.

6. Find right angles in the pattern. Do you see angles smaller than right angles? larger? Where?

7. List all of the shapes in the pattern above.

8. Are the black and orange figures above congruent? How do you know?

9. Would you use a flip, slide, or turn to place figure *A* on top of figure *B*? How would you move figure *A* on top of figure *C*?

10. How many lines of symmetry do the blue and orange figures have? Find one line of symmetry for the entire pattern. Describe it.

Do You Remember?

Cumulative Review

Looking Back

Choose the right answer. Write *a, b, c,* or *d* for each question.

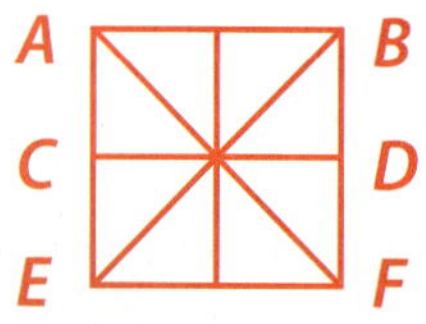

1. Which line segment does not mark a line of symmetry?

   a. *AB* b. *CD*
   c. *AF* d. *BE*

$$\begin{array}{r} 2\ \ 2\text{R3} \\ 4\overline{)\blacksquare\ \blacksquare} \end{array}$$

2. What number goes in the gray boxes above?

   a. 88 b. 81
   c. 48 d. 91

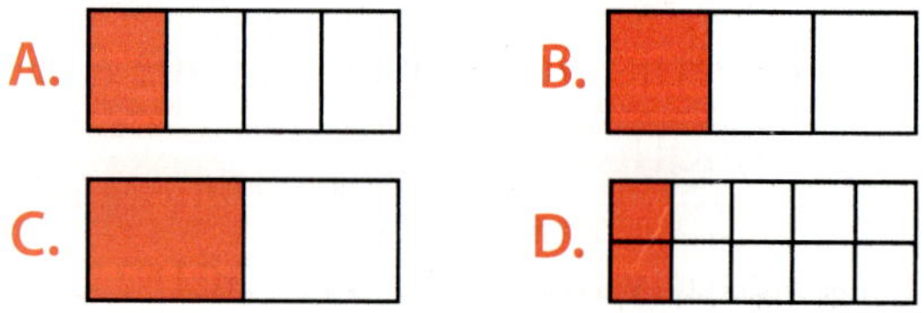

3. Arrange the fractions shown by the pictures in order from smallest to greatest.

   a. A, C, B, D b. A, B, C, D
   c. D, B, C, A d. D, A, B, C

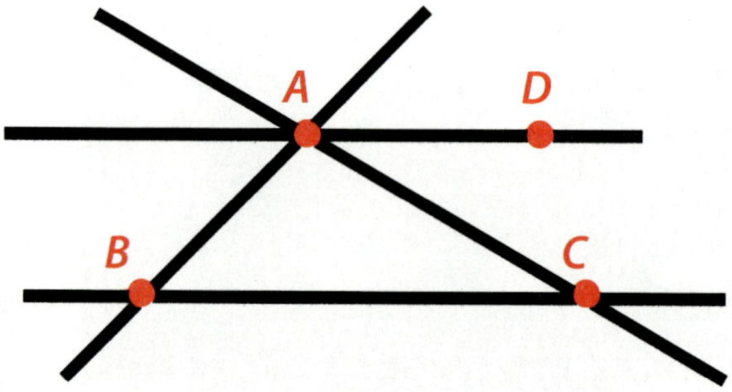

4. Which point is on the greatest number of line segments?

   a. *A* b. *B*
   c. *C* d. *D*

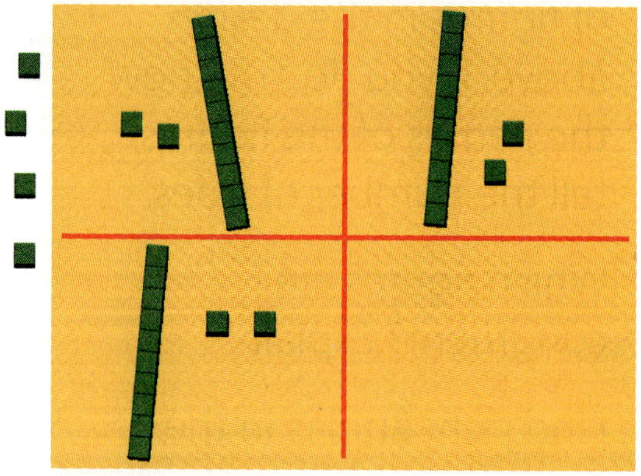

5. Which division do the base ten blocks show?

   a. $4\overline{)30}$ b. $3\overline{)36}$
   c. $3\overline{)40}$ d. $6\overline{)40}$

6. Which figure is congruent to the figure shown here? 

a. 
b. 
c. 
d. 

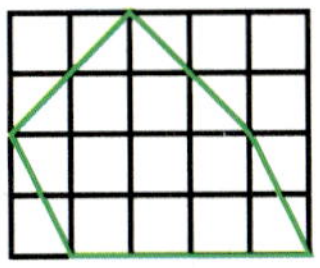

7. How many square units is the polygon on the grid?

a. 15
b. 10
c. 8
d. 12

Use these polygons to answer Exercises 8 through 10.

a. 
b. 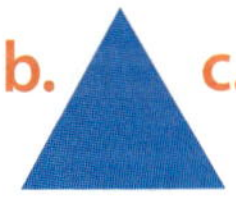
c. 
d. 

8. Which polygon does not have all equal sides?

a. a
b. b
c. c
d. d

9. Which polygon does not have equal angles?

a. a
b. b
c. c
d. d

10. Which polygon has angles greater than a right angle?

a. a
b. b
c. c
d. d

Check Your Math Power

11. Which has more lines of symmetry, a square or a rectangle that is not a square? Explain with words and diagrams.

12. Think of the hour from noon to 1:00 P.M. At what times is the angle between the hands of the clock less than a right angle? greater than a right angle? equal to a right angle?

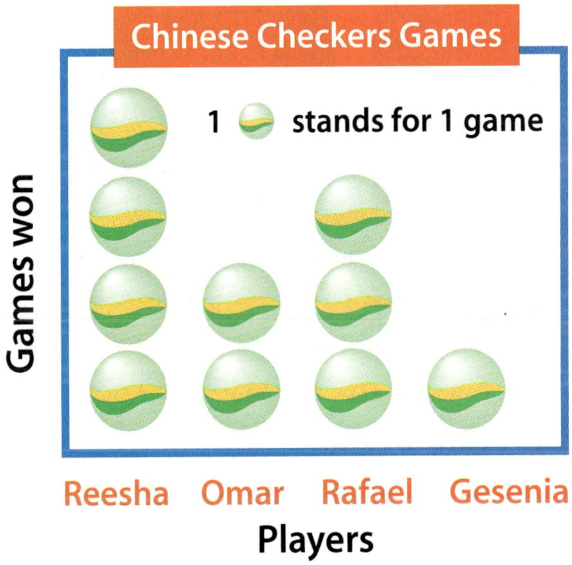

13. Write three number sentences using information from the picture graph.

14. Describe your method of dividing things into equal groups. How do you use multiplication ideas to divide?

Module 8 Investigations

Puzzle Pictures

Here is a chance to make your own puzzle!

Investigation A The Polygon Puzzle

1 Use a grid like the one above. Draw polygons shaped like the ones shown in the pictures. Use two, three, or four squares.

2 Color your polygons with different colors. Then make a record of what your puzzle looks like. Now cut out your puzzle pieces and trade with a partner.

3 Solve your partner's puzzle. Are any of the shapes congruent? Do any of the shapes have a line of symmetry? How will you know when you have solved the puzzle?

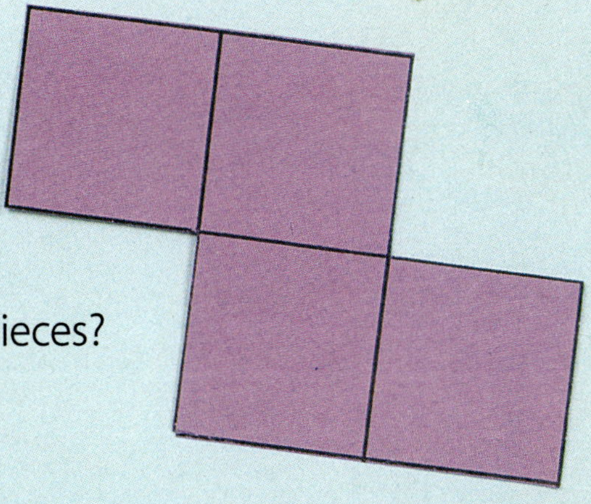

4 Check your work using the record your partner made. Are there any other shapes you can make with the puzzle pieces?

5 Trade puzzles with other classmates.

Computer Option If you have a computer, you can use a drawing program to make a polygon puzzle.

Keep in Mind

Your work will be judged on the following:

- ☐ Did you use a variety of polygons in your puzzle?
- ☐ Did your record prove that the puzzle was put back together correctly?
- ☐ Did you use what you know about congruent figures and symmetry to make and solve puzzles?

Investigation B: Line Segment Puzzle

Use four toothpicks to make as many figures as you can out of four line segments.

Here are the rules:

- You can only place your toothpicks at right angles or end to end in a straight line.
- Each toothpick must touch the end of at least one other toothpick.

1. How could you record the figures you made?
2. Could you make the same figure twice? How could you keep from repeating figures?
3. How many figures did you make? Share and compare the figures you made with the class.

Ongoing Investigation: Wrapping up "How Do We Grow?"

Get ready to check your growth predictions. Compare your final data with your predictions from the beginning of the year. How close were you? Did the class grow more or less than you expected? Write a report to describe what you found. Be sure to include graphs or charts to show your data.

Tool Kit

Contents

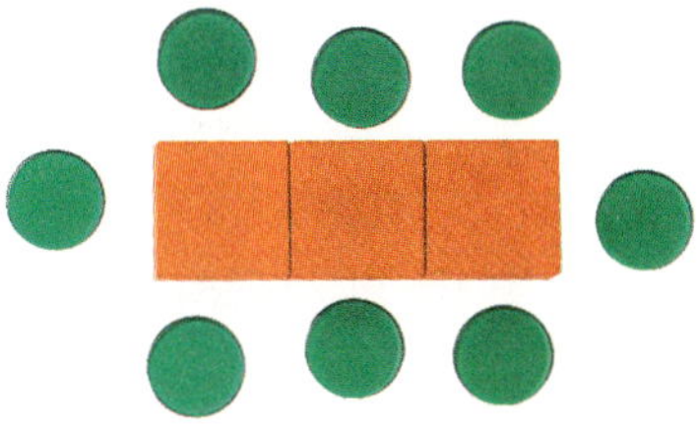

Problem Solving Strategies

Draw a Picture or a Diagram 386
Build a Model or Act It Out 387
Use a Pattern 387
Organize Information 388
Use a Simpler or Related Problem 390
Guess and Check 391

Computation Tools

Paper and Pencil 392
Mental Math 396
Estimation 398

Technology

Computer 400
Calculator 402

Data Collection

Eight Steps to Good Data Collection 404

Drawing to Learn

Drawing to Discover 406
Drawing to Understand 407
Drawing to Share 407

Measurement

Length • Capacity • Mass/ Weight • Temperature • Time 408

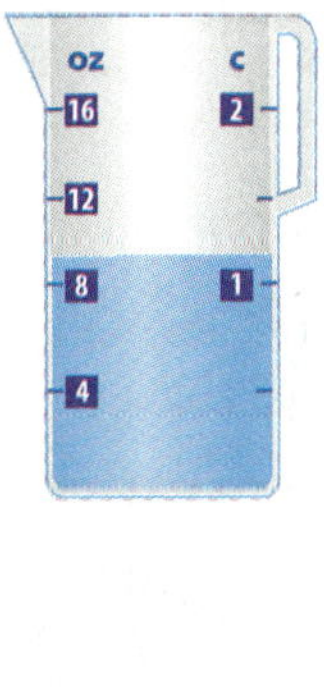

Tool Kit

Problem Solving Strategies

Ways to Solve Problems

On the next few pages, you'll find different strategies, or ways, for solving math problems. Learning these strategies will give you a powerful set of problem solving tools.

Problem

You have square tables for a party. Only one person can sit comfortably on each side. What is the greatest number of people you can seat at 1, 2, 3, 4, 5, and 6 tables if you want the tables to touch on at least one side?

Draw a Picture or a Diagram

Drawing a picture or diagram can help you solve many problems. You will probably find it helpful to draw a picture when a problem asks you to arrange objects, work with shapes, or compare varying measurements in a space. (See Drawing to Learn on pages 406–407.)

Build a Model or Act It Out

Making a model with objects is another way to find solutions to a problem about arrangements. In this case, you could use blocks to show tables and counters to show chairs. You could move the blocks and counters all sorts of ways to find the best arrangements.

Use a Pattern

You may find a pattern when you are trying to solve some problems. If you do, use the pattern to predict numbers without doing extra calculations. Drawing a picture or making a table can also help you discover the pattern.

Steps

1. **Work through the first several steps of the problem. Drawing a picture often helps.**
2. **Write the numbers in a table and look for a pattern.**

Tables	1	2	3	4	5	6
Chairs	4	6	8	10		

Pattern: Add 2 chairs for each table.

3. **Use the pattern to complete the table.**

Tables	1	2	3	4	5	6
Chairs	4	6	8	10	12	14

Tool Kit

Problem Solving Strategies

Problem

What is the least number of coins you can use to make 35 cents? What is the greatest number of coins you can use? How many different ways can you make 35 cents?

Organize Information

Some problems require you to make combinations or arrange data. In these cases, it helps to organize your information in a list, table, chart, or graph. On the next two pages, you'll see ways to make a list and a table. For an example of a graph, see Data Collection on pages 404–405.

First I'll list all the ways to make 35¢ using just one quarter. Then I'll write all the ways to make 35¢ using 3 dimes.

Write a List Making a list is one way to organize your information. Write down all the possibilities.

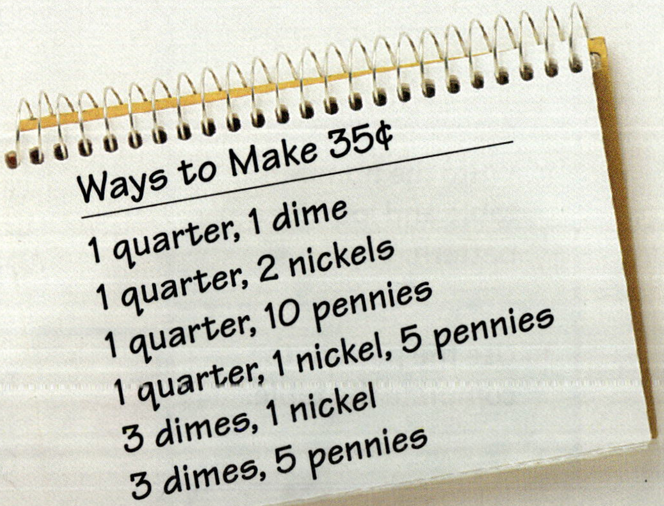

Make a Table or Chart If you find yourself writing the same words again and again, organize your information into a table. Making a table will save you time and space. The categories in your table will be the words you are repeating. Writing a title for the table helps make your purpose clear.

You can use a table to quickly answer questions like these:

- Which combination uses the most coins?
- Which combination uses the most nickels?

Quarters	Dimes	Nickels	Pennies
1	1		
1		2	
1			10
1		1	5
	3	1	
	3		5

Tool Kit

Problem Solving Strategies

Problem

A sporting goods store usually sells bats for $8.95. Now they're on sale for $6.98. If balls cost $4.95, how many bat-and-ball sets can you buy with $120?

Use a Simpler or Related Problem

Some problems seem hard because they involve lots of data or large numbers. Unnecessary data also makes problems difficult to solve. In such cases, working a simpler or related problem can show you how to work through the original problem.

Steps

1. **Cut out words and numbers you don't need. (In this case, it doesn't matter that bats *used* to sell for $8.95.)**
2. **Create a simpler problem using "easy" numbers.**
3. **Solve the simpler problem.**
4. **Use that method to work through the first problem.**

Simpler Problem:
Bats cost $3; balls cost $2. How many sets can I get for $15?

$3
+$2
$5

5) $15
3 sets for $15

First Problem:

$6.98
+$4.95
$11.93

about $12 for one set

12) $120
10 sets for $120

Subtracting Fractions: Same Denominators

1. See if the denominators are the same.

$$\frac{4}{5} - \frac{1}{5}$$

Both denominators are the same.

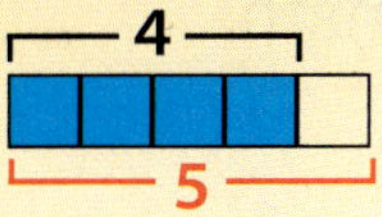

2. Subtract the numerators.

$$\frac{4}{5} - \frac{1}{5}$$

4 − 1

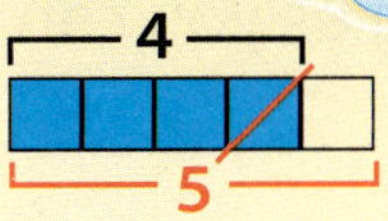

3. Write the difference over the common denominator.

$$\frac{4}{5} - \frac{1}{5} = \frac{3}{5}$$

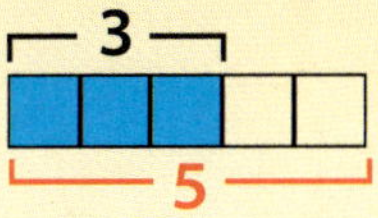

Addition: Decimals

1. Line up the decimal points so you will be adding "like" quantities.

$$\begin{array}{r} 0.4 \\ +\ 0.3 \\ \hline \end{array}$$

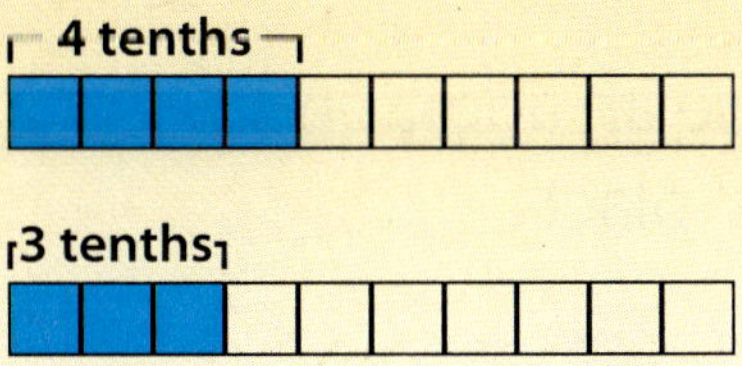

2. Add the tenths. Put the decimal point in the answer.

$$\begin{array}{r} 0.4 \\ +\ 0.3 \\ \hline 0.7 \end{array}$$

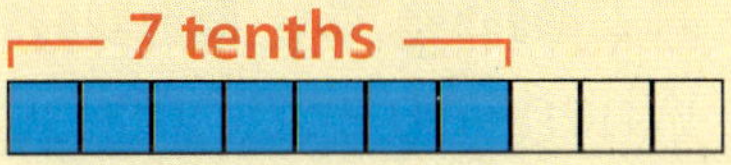

Tool Kit

Computation Tools

Mental Math

Doing computation mentally can be faster than writing numbers down. Here are some strategies you can use for mental math.

Counting On or Counting Back

When you add or subtract with small numbers, you can count ahead or count back to find the answer mentally.

Add: 48 + 3

Start with 48 and count on.

Think:
48 . . . 49, 50, 51

Subtract: 59 − 3

Think:
59 . . . 58, 57, 56

Adding by Endings

When you add numbers mentally, use an addition fact with the same digits in the ones' place.

38 + 7 = ?

8 + 7 = 15
This sum ends in a 5.

38 + 7 must end in a 5 too.

Grouping for Tens

When you have several numbers to add, make groups of tens first.

$$\begin{array}{r} {}^{2}\\ 16 \\ 9 \\ 1 \\ +\ 34 \\ \hline 60 \end{array}$$

10 10

First group for tens in the ones' place. Then add all of the tens.

Compensation

When you add or subtract, changing one number to a rounded number can make solving easier. Then change your answer to compensate.

$22 + 59 = n$

$22 + 60 = 82$

$82 - 1 = 81$

$22 + 59 = 81$

Add 1 to 59 to get 60. **Subtract 1** from the answer to compensate.

Breaking Apart Numbers

You can break apart numbers so that they are easier to use mentally.

Add

$64 + 23$

$64 + (20 + 3)$ Break apart 23.

$(64 + 20) + 3$

$84 + 3 = 87$

Think: 20 + 3

Tool Kit

Computation Tools

Estimation

Estimation is using mental math to get an answer that's close to the actual answer but not exact. When is it helpful to estimate?

- When an exact answer isn't necessary
- When you want to know if your answer is reasonable
- When there is no way of getting an exact number

Here are four estimation strategies.

Rounding

You can make a number simpler to work with mentally by rounding it.

Rounding to nearest 100		*Rounding to nearest 10*	
122 →	100	42 →	40
375 →	400	87 →	90
889 →	900	35 →	40

Rounding to Estimate Products

To get a quick multiplication estimate, round the factors.

$$4 \times 385$$

$$\downarrow \quad \downarrow$$

$$4 \times 400 = 1{,}600$$

Front-End Estimation

Use front-end estimation to quickly add money amounts.

First group dollars. You get $6.

$$\begin{array}{r} \$2.10 \\ 1.95 \\ 1.50 \\ 1.25 \\ +\ 1.30 \\ \hline \end{array}$$

\$2.10 + 1.95: about \$1

1.50 + 1.25 + 1.30: about \$1

Then group the cents by dollars. You get about $2.

\$6.00 + about \$2.00 = about \$8.00

Compatible Numbers

Compatible numbers are numbers that are easy to compute. You can use compatible numbers to estimate division.

$3\overline{)95}$

Think: $3\overline{)90}$

Quotient: about 30

Electronic Tools

Computers and calculators can help you solve problems, calculate numbers, and present work. The trick is in knowing how and when to use them.

Computer

Computers can help you collect, organize, and analyze large amounts of data. With different kinds of software, you can create diagrams, charts, tables, graphs, and pictures.

Software Software programs are the instructions that tell a computer what to do. Drawing programs, spreadsheets, word processing packages, and computer games are all software.

Drawing Programs Pictures can help you solve a problem or explain an idea. Using drawing software is a fun and easy way to make all kinds of pictures. And on the computer you can always change your picture.

Drawing Software Uses:

- draw pictures
- make patterns
- illustrate stories
- create floor plans

Spreadsheets/Graphs Spreadsheet programs are very useful when you are working with lots of numbers. Spreadsheets have columns and rows, like a table. You can enter your own numbers or have the computer calculate them for you. Then you can sort, rearrange, and even graph your information.

Spreadsheet Uses:

- organize budgets
- make tables
- draw graphs

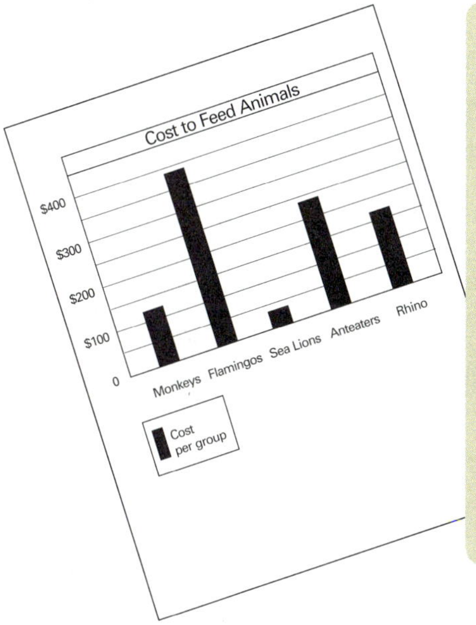

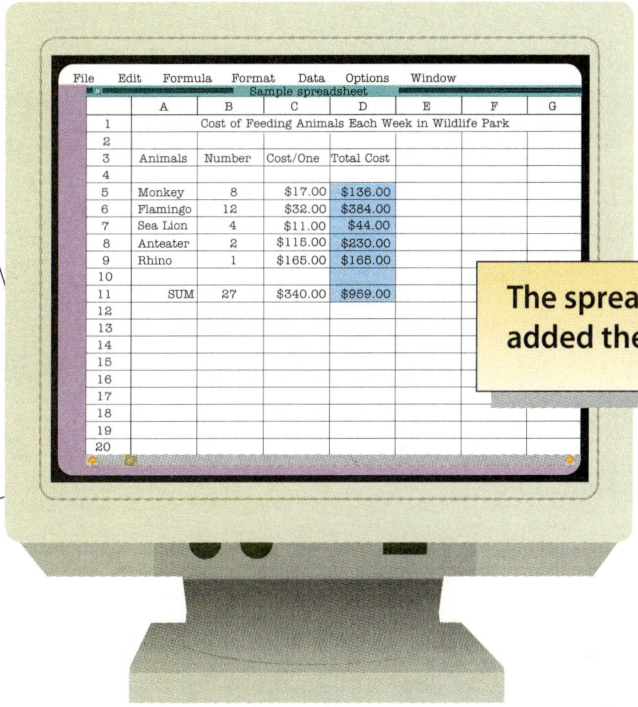

	A	B	C	D	E	F	G
1	Cost of Feeding Animals Each Week in Wildlife Park						
2							
3	Animals	Number	Cost/One	Total Cost			
4							
5	Monkey	8	$17.00	$136.00			
6	Flamingo	12	$32.00	$384.00			
7	Sea Lion	4	$11.00	$44.00			
8	Anteater	2	$115.00	$230.00			
9	Rhino	1	$165.00	$165.00			
10							
11	SUM	27	$340.00	$959.00			
12							
13							
14							
15							
16							
17							
18							
19							
20							

The spreadsheet added the total cost.

Databases With database software you can organize large amounts of data, including words, dates, and numbers. A database is a great place to put survey results because it can sort through all the answers in the survey. For example, for this survey, the database can search for how many boys have pet hamsters or what kind of pet is owned by the most students.

Database Uses:

- record survey data
- group data into categories

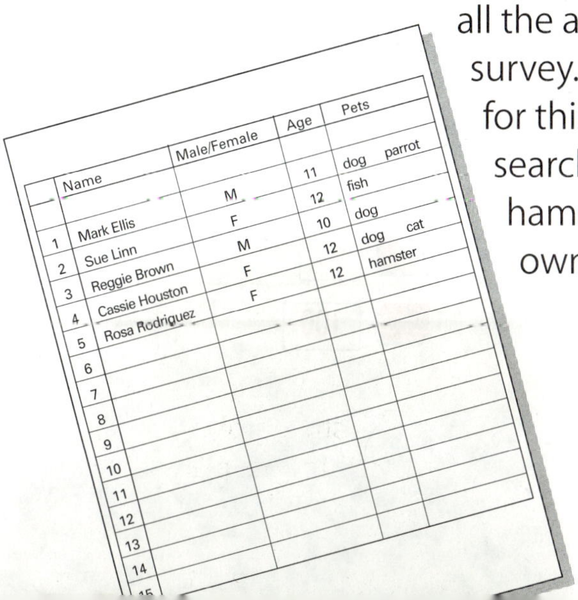

	Name	Male/Female	Age	Pets
1	Mark Ellis	M	11	dog parrot
2	Sue Linn	F	12	fish
3	Reggie Brown	M	10	dog
4	Cassie Houston	F	12	dog cat
5	Rosa Rodriguez	F	12	hamster
6				
7				
8				
9				
10				
11				
12				
13				
14				

Tool Kit

Technology

Calculator

These pages show several things that a calculator can do. Each calculator is a little different. Read the instructions that come with your calculator to learn how to use it.

	Examples:
Memory This calculator will store numbers and operations in memory.	**10 + 20 + 10 + 10 + 10** 10 [M+] [+] 20 [=] 30 [+] [MRC] [=] 40 [+] [MRC] [=] 50 [+] [MRC] [=] 60
Decimals This calculator will calculate decimals.	**1.25 + 3.72** 1 [.] 25 [+] 3 [.] 72 [=] 4.97
Repeat This calculator will repeat any operation if you press the [=] key.	**25 + 25+ 25 + 25** 25 [+] [=] 25 [=] 50 [=] 75 [=] 100

1 Display

Look at the display to see your work.

2 Memory Keys

M+ Press this key to put the number on the display into memory.

M- Press this key to subtract the number on your display from memory.

MRC Press this key when you want to use the number you stored in memory.

3 Arithmetic Keys

Use these keys to divide, multiply, subtract, and add.

4 Equals Key

Press the equals key = to find the answer. Also use it to repeat an operation.

5 Decimal Point

Use the decimal point when you key in money amounts.

6 On and Clear Key

Press the ON/C key to begin work. Also use it to clear your work on a problem and start over.

Tool Kit

Data Collection

Working with Data

Data refers to facts of all kinds. Numbers, statistics, dates, and responses to interviews are all examples of data. Here are some steps to help you plan and organize data at several stages.

Eight Steps to Good Data Collection

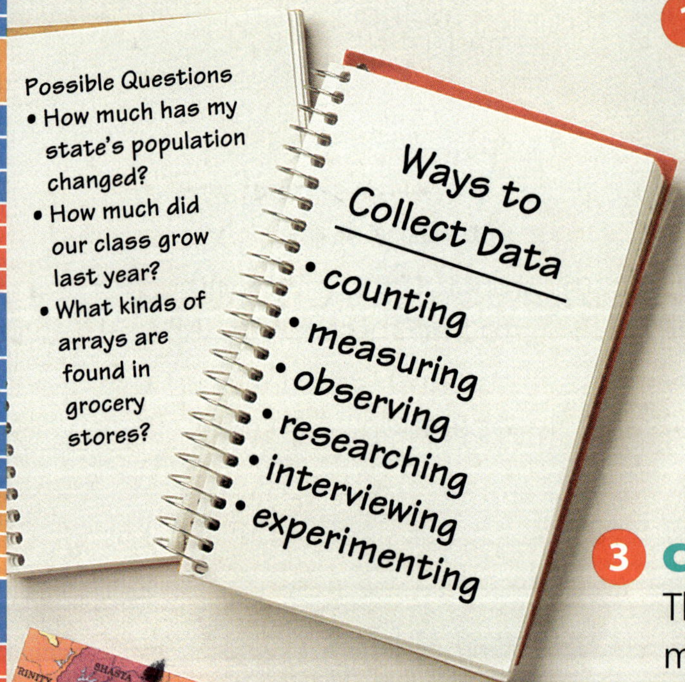

1 Begin with a Question

Choose a question that you can answer by collecting data from several people or sources.

2 Plan Your Strategy

Choose a way to collect data. Where will you go for information? What kind of data are you likely to collect? How can you share it?

3 Collect and Record the Data

This could be as simple as a few tally marks in response to a question or as complex as making several graphs.

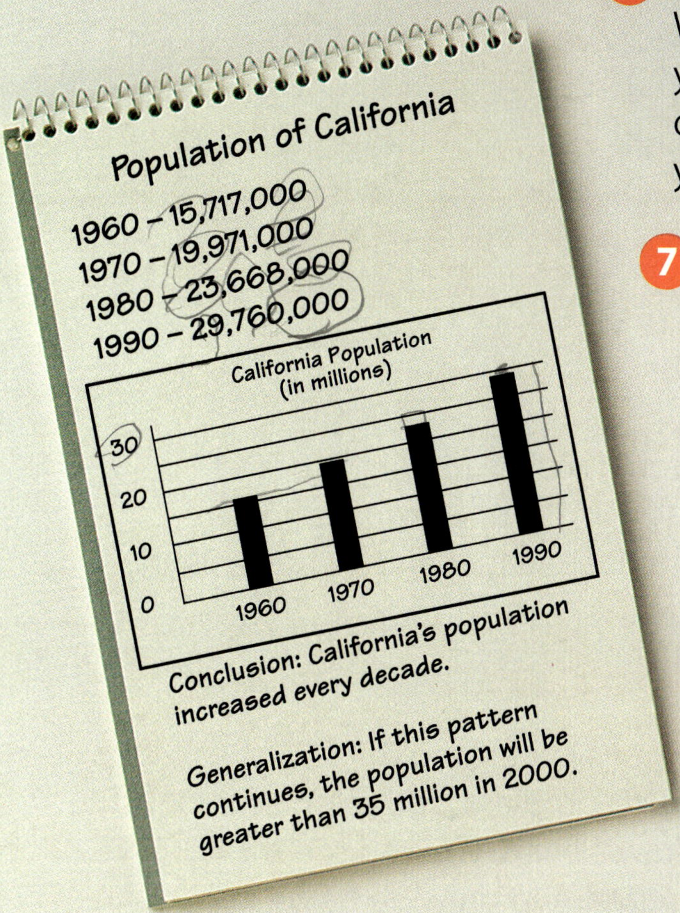

6 Draw a Conclusion

What does the data tell you about your original question? Does it describe something? Does it allow you to make comparisons?

7 Use Your Conclusion

You may be able to use your conclusion as a basis for a prediction, generalization, or decision.

8 Look Back/Look Ahead

As you look over the results of your data collection, you may want to begin the process again with a related or refined question. Or you may wish to test the theory you developed.

4 Organize the Data

Review and arrange your data. What's the best way to categorize your data?

5 Represent Your Data

What's the best way to display your data? A table? A chart? A graph? Now you're ready to share your results.

Drawing as a Math Tool

Drawing can help you discover, understand, and share key concepts in math. Use your Drawing to Learn tools to make a variety of precise shapes and measurements.

Drawing to Discover

Drawing can lead to discovery. For example, if you draw what you know about a problem, you often find the solution. If you draw a chart, you can see how groups of numbers relate. And drawing helps you discover your own creative ideas about math.

As you draw, patterns appear that you might not have noticed otherwise.

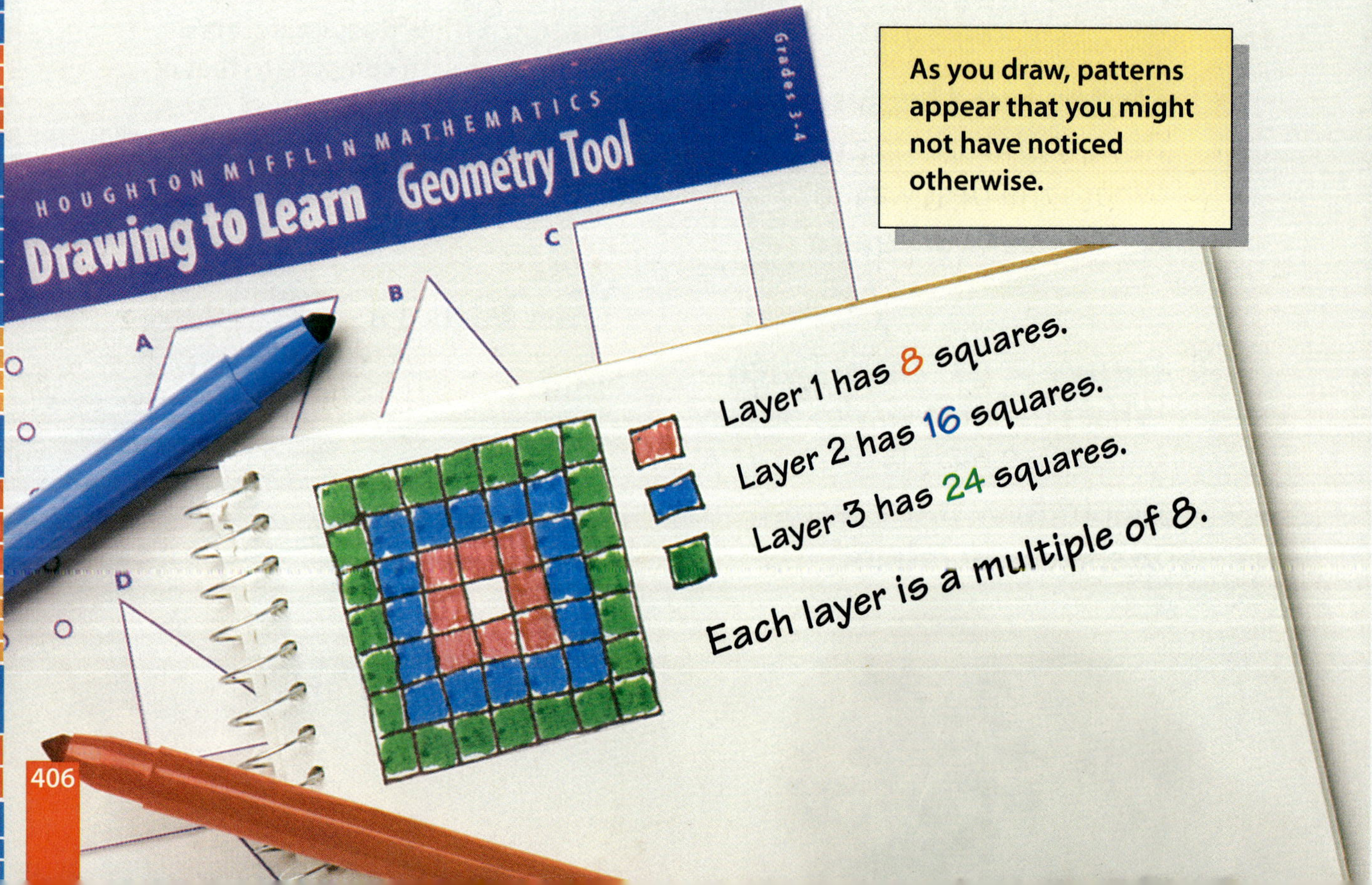

Drawing to Understand

To simplify the steps of a process, pick up a pencil and start to draw. Drawing can also help you understand key concepts in math, including the basic computations of adding, subtracting, multiplying, and dividing.

You can use drawing to create your own system for understanding a key math concept.

Drawing to Share

Pictures, diagrams, graphs—all these are visual ways to share information. You can pack a great deal of data into a drawing.

People can point to your graph and ask questions or give feedback.

Tool Kit
Measurement

Measurement Tools

The charts on this page identify common measures. Check the glossary and index for more information on specific terms.

	Customary	Metric
Length	1 foot (ft) = 12 inches (in.) 1 yard (yd) = 3 feet (ft) or 36 inches (in.) 1 mile (mi) = 5,280 feet (ft)	1 centimeter (cm) = 10 millimeters (mm) 1 decimeter (dm) = 10 centimeters (cm) 1 meter (m) = 10 decimeters (dm) 1 kilometer (km) = 1,000 meters (m)
Capacity	1 cup (c) = 8 fluid ounces (fl oz) 1 pint (pt) = 2 cups (c) 1 quart (qt) = 2 pints (pt) 1 gallon (gal) = 4 quarts (qt)	1 liter (L) = 1,000 milliliters (mL) 1 kiloliter (kL) = 1,000 liters (L)
Mass/ Weight	1 pound (lb) = 16 ounces (oz) 1 ton (t) = 2,000 pounds (lb)	1 gram (g) = 1,000 milligrams (mg) 1 kilogram (kg) = 1,000 grams (g)
Temperature	*Fahrenheit* freezing point = 32° F boiling point = 212° F	*Celsius* freezing point = 0° C boiling point = 100° C

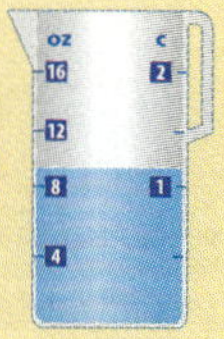

Time
1 minute (min) = 60 seconds (s)
1 hour (h) = 60 minutes (min)
1 day = 24 hours (h)
1 week = 7 days
1 year = 52 weeks

Module 3.1 Section A

a For use with Lesson 1 (pages 4–7)

Fill in the blanks.

1. The first month of the year is ■.
2. The shortest month is ■.
3. There are ■ days in a week.
4. The first day of the week is ■.
5. The last day of each week is ■.
6. The day after Tuesday is ■.
7. The month after May is ■.
8. There are ■ days in a year.
9. There are ■ days in June.
10. There are ■ weeks in each month.

b For use with Lesson 2 (pages 8–11)

Draw a clock to show each time.

11. 8:15
12. 12:30
13. 3:55
14. 6:00
15. 9:30
16. 11:45

For each time, write the time before the hour.

17. 8:45
18. 7:30
19. 3:55
20. 12:25
21. 2:50
22. 2:10
23. 9:40
24. 9:20
25. 10:47

c For use with Lesson 3 (pages 12–13)

Choose the temperature that matches best.

26. making snowmen — a. 75° F — b. 30° F
27. playing baseball — a. 0° F — b. 85° F
28. swimming — a. 102° F — b. 45° F
29. ice skating — a. 25° F — b. 90° F

Module 3.1 Section B

a For use with Lesson 4 (pages 14–19)

Make the greatest possible number with these digits.

1. 1, 2, 3, 4
2. 1, 5, 3, 0
3. 1, 4, 4, 4
4. 0, 9, 8, 4
5. 2, 7, 6, 4
6. 9, 9, 4, 4
7. 6, 0, 2, 0
8. 1, 6, 9, 2
9. 9, 2, 1, 4
10. 1, 9, 9, 5
11. 6, 2, 5, 4
12. 8, 2, 5, 4

Tell the place value of the underlined digit.

13. 2<u>4</u>5
14. 2,<u>4</u>53
15. 6,75<u>1</u>
16. <u>7</u>,778
17. 6,9<u>8</u>7
18. <u>7</u>45
19. 8,<u>7</u>69
20. 1,23<u>4</u>
21. 6,7<u>5</u>4
22. <u>7</u>,896
23. 5,<u>6</u>43
24. 8,5<u>1</u>0
25. 2,<u>4</u>57
26. 8,<u>4</u>53
27. 6,<u>7</u>51
28. <u>7</u>,898
29. 6,3<u>8</u>7
30. <u>7</u>4
31. 9,<u>7</u>69
32. 2,93<u>4</u>
33. 2,7<u>5</u>4
34. <u>7</u>,496
35. 3,<u>5</u>43
36. 8,7<u>1</u>0

b For use with Lesson 5 (pages 20–23)

Use the number line. Write > or < for each.

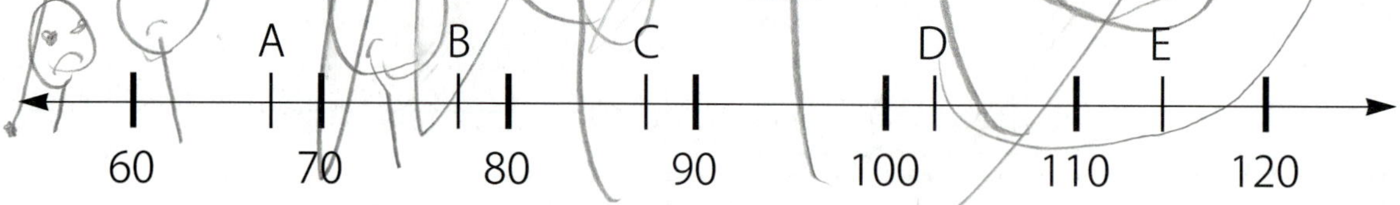

37. A ● B
38. D ● B
39. E ● D
40. 85 ● B
41. C ● 85
42. D ● 100
43. E ● 200
44. A ● 60
45. C ● 100
46. 65 ● 70
47. 87 ● 97
48. 100 ● 105

Module 3.1 Section C

a For use with Lesson 6 (pages 26–28)

Name the number that goes in the blank.

1. 120, 130, ____, 150, 160
2. ____, 210, 220, 230, 240
3. 470, 480, 490, ____, 510
4. ____; 1,130; 1,140; 1,150
5. 1,200; 1,300; 1,400; ____
6. 7,000; 8,000; 9,000; ____

Write a number for each set of tally marks.

7. 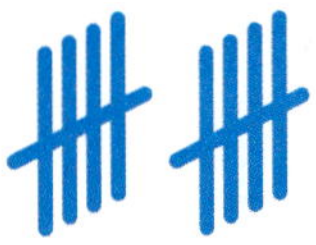

8. 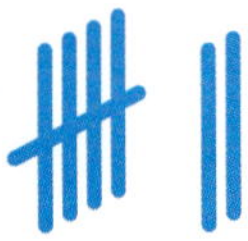

9. 

10. 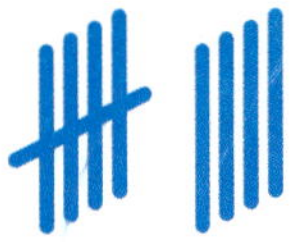

11. 

12. 

b For use with Lesson 7 (pages 29–33)

Add or subtract.

13. $12 - 5$
14. $5 + 7$
15. $11 - 3$
16. $6 + 9$
17. $16 - 7$
18. $3 + 7$
19. $13 - 7$
20. $6 + 8$
21. $9 - 5$
22. $9 + 1$
23. $10 - 8$
24. $7 + 7$
25. $\begin{array}{r} 6 \\ -6 \\ \hline \end{array}$
26. $\begin{array}{r} 4 \\ +4 \\ \hline \end{array}$
27. $\begin{array}{r} 9 \\ -4 \\ \hline \end{array}$
28. $\begin{array}{r} 5 \\ +9 \\ \hline \end{array}$
29. $\begin{array}{r} 14 \\ -8 \\ \hline \end{array}$
30. $\begin{array}{r} 8 \\ +7 \end{array}$
31. $\begin{array}{r} 13 \\ -6 \\ \hline \end{array}$
32. $\begin{array}{r} 6 \\ +7 \\ \hline \end{array}$
33. $\begin{array}{r} 15 \\ -5 \\ \hline \end{array}$
34. $\begin{array}{r} 9 \\ +9 \\ \hline \end{array}$
35. $\begin{array}{r} 15 \\ -9 \\ \hline \end{array}$
36. $\begin{array}{r} 6 \\ +3 \\ \hline \end{array}$

Module 3.1 Section D

a For use with Lesson 8 (pages 34–38)

Use number words to tell the position.

First Last

1.  is________.

2.  is________.

3.  is________.

4.  is________.

5.  is________.

6.  is________.

Use this list to answer these questions.

22, 23, 24, 25, 26, 27, 28, 29, 30, 31, 32, 33, 34, 35, 36, 37, 38, 39

7. What number is third to the right of 31?
8. What number is fourth to the left of 31?
9. What is the sixth number to the right of 24?
10. What is the tenth number to the left of 38?
11. What is the seventh number to the right of 23?
12. What is the twelfth number to the left of 39?

b For use with Lesson 9 (pages 39–43)

Make your own estimate for each.

13. How many lima beans are in a handful?
14. How many pieces of chalk are in a full box?
15. How many paper clips are in a box?
16. How many leaves are on a tree?
17. How many jellybeans are in a jar?

Module 3.2 Section A

a For use with Lesson 1 (pages 52–54)

Compare the numbers. Write > or <.

1. 5 ● 9	2. 8 ● 7	3. 6 ● 9	4. 4 ● 6
5. 9 ● 4	6. 7 ● 5	7. 3 ● 2	8. 6 ● 1
9. 12 ● 15	10. 7 ● 4	11. 8 ● 4	12. 17 ● 12

b For use with Lesson 2 (pages 55–58)

Find the sum. Count on, make a ten, or use doubles to help you.

13. 6 + 4	14. 5 + 8	15. 4 + 4	16. 7 + 5
17. 9 + 9	18. 7 + 5	19. 7+ 3	20. 8 + 8
21. 3 + 3	22. 5 + 9	23. 8 + 4	24. 7 + 7
25. 9 + 2	26. 4 + 5	27. 8 + 3	28. 8 + 6
29. 7 + 5	30. 6 + 9	31. 5 + 5	32. 8 + 3
33. 9 + 7	34. 8 + 6	35. 7 + 2	36. 8 + 7
37. 9 + 3	38. 6 + 9	39. 8 + 8	40. 3 + 7
41. 9 + 5	42. 7 + 5	43. 5 + 6	44. 9 + 9

c For use with Lesson 3 (pages 59–63)

Add. Use sums of ten to help you.

45. 4 + 6 + 2	46. 8 + 5+ 2	47. 7 + 3 + 4
48. 9 + 1 + 3	49. 5 + 5 + 2	50. 9 + 1 + 8
51. 8 + 2 + 2	52. 3 + 7 + 1	53. 8 + 1 + 9

54. $\begin{array}{r}2\\8\\+2\\\hline\end{array}$ 55. $\begin{array}{r}5\\5\\+3\\\hline\end{array}$ 56. $\begin{array}{r}1\\3\\+9\\\hline\end{array}$ 57. $\begin{array}{r}6\\4\\+7\\\hline\end{array}$ 58. $\begin{array}{r}5\\5\\+6\\\hline\end{array}$ 59. $\begin{array}{r}6\\5\\+4\\\hline\end{array}$ 60. $\begin{array}{r}6\\4\\+8\\\hline\end{array}$ 61. $\begin{array}{r}2\\3\\+7\\\hline\end{array}$

Module 3.2 Section B

a For use with Lesson 4 (pages 64–67)

Choose the best unit of measure. Write *inches, feet,* or *yards.*

1. your book
2. football field
3. boot
4. classroom
5. notebook paper
6. corn field
7. finger
8. car
9. airplane

b For use with Lesson 5 (pages 68–73)

Find the sum or difference.

10. 12 − 8
11. 6 + 8
12. 8 − 5
13. 6 + 7
14. 4 + 6
15. 11 − 8
16. 10 − 8
17. 9 − 4
18. 14 − 5
19. 4 + 5
20. 10 − 7
21. 5 + 8
22. 6 + 9
23. 11 − 5
24. 9 + 6
25. 15 − 8

Find the sum.

26. 2 + 6
27. 4 + 8
28. 4 + 5
29. 2 + 9
30. 4 + 7
31. 7 + 6
32. 2+ 6
33. 9 + 7
34. 1 + 8
35. 4 + 9
36. 5 + 7
37. 1 + 6
38. 4 + 9
39. 4 + 6
40. 9 + 6
41. 5 + 6

Find the difference.

42. 6 − 2
43. 8 − 2
44. 10 − 5
45. 6 − 3
46. 11 − 3
47. 9 − 2
48. 6 − 5
49. 8 − 2
50. 6 − 4
51. 6 − 5
52. 8 − 1
53. 9 − 6
54. 9 − 5
55. 8 − 2
56. 10 − 3
57. 7 − 2

Module 3.2 Section C

a For use with Lesson 6 (pages 76–77)

Tell whether the object weighs more or less than 1 oz.

1. table tennis ball
2. bowling ball
3. nickel
4. chicken egg
5. sheet of paper
6. mouse

Use > or < to show which weighs more.

7. table tennis ball ● bowling ball
8. penny ● quarter
9. mouse ● cat
10. elephant ● horse
11. cow ● sheep
12. bus ● taxicab

b For use with Lesson 7 (pages 78–80)

Find the missing addend.

13. 5 + ■ = 11
14. 6 + ■ = 8
15. 3 + ■ = 11
16. 12 + ■ = 13
17. 7 + ■ = 14
18. 9 + ■ = 16
19. 8 + ■ = 16
20. 3 + ■ = 12
21. 5 + ■ = 10

Add. Use sums of ten to help you.

22. $\begin{array}{r}4\\6\\+2\\\hline\end{array}$
23. $\begin{array}{r}7\\5\\+3\\\hline\end{array}$
24. $\begin{array}{r}5\\3\\+5\\\hline\end{array}$
25. $\begin{array}{r}6\\4\\+7\\\hline\end{array}$
26. $\begin{array}{r}2\\8\\+6\\\hline\end{array}$
27. $\begin{array}{r}6\\5\\+4\\\hline\end{array}$
28. $\begin{array}{r}1\\9\\+8\\\hline\end{array}$
29. $\begin{array}{r}3\\4\\+7\\\hline\end{array}$

c For use with Lesson 8 (pages 81–83)

How many more ounces do you need to make a pound?

30. 6 oz
31. 8 oz
32. 10 oz
33. 14 oz

Put these weights in order from lightest to heaviest.

34. 15 oz, 18 oz, 1 lb, 13 oz
35. 1 lb, 2 lbs, 14 oz, 6 oz, 18 oz
36. 2 lbs, 2 oz, 18 oz, 14 lbs
37. 12 oz, 1 lb, 20 oz, 2 lb, 24 oz

Module 3.2 Section D

a For use with Lesson 9 (pages 84–87)

Subtract. Include the units of measure in your answers.

1. 9 c − 4 c
2. 10 gal − 4 gal
3. 5 pt − 2 pt
4. 7 qt − 2 qt
5. 8 gal − 5 gal
6. 12 pt − 8 pt
7. 14 c − 12 c
8. 11 qt − 9 qt

Find the missing numbers.

9. 1 pt = ■ c
10. 2 pt = ■ c
11. 1 qt = ■ c
12. 1 qt = ■ pt
13. 2 qt = ■ pt
14. 2 qt = ■ c
15. 1 gal = ■ qt
16. 2 gal = ■ qt
17. 3 gal = ■ qt

b For use with Lesson 10 (pages 88–91)

Find the missing number. Then rewrite as subtraction sentences.

18. 4 + ■ = 7
19. ■ + 5 = 7
20. 7 + 8 = ■
21. 8 + 9 = ■
22. 10 + ■ = 15
23. 6 + ■ = 12
24. 7 + ■ = 14
25. 14 + ■ = 15
26. ■ + 9 = 18

Complete each chart.

27. Rule: add 5

Before	1	2	3	4
After				

28. Rule: subtract 3

Before	10	8	6	5	4
After					

29. Rule: add 7

Before	3	6		
After			8	10

30. Rule: subtract 9

Before	12	16		
After			1	5

Module 3.3 Section A

a For use with Lesson 1 (pages 100–104)

Draw two groups of base ten blocks for each.

1. 256
2. 190
3. 544
4. 125
5. 675
6. 159
7. 111
8. 863
9. 358

b For use with Lesson 2 (pages 105–109)

Use these numbers to answer the questions.

345 149 120 555 263

10. Which two numbers have a sum of 900?
11. Which two numbers have a sum less than 300?
12. Which two numbers have a sum of 383?
13. Which two numbers have the greatest sum?
14. Which pair of numbers have a sum of 465?
15. Which pair of numbers will give an even sum?

Find the sum of each pair of numbers.

16. 142 + 253
17. 250 + 238
18. 747 + 253
19. 172 + 223
20. 145 + 213
21. 148 + 253
22. 242 + 253
23. 652 + 283
24. 140 + 133
25. 140 + 353
26. 503 + 157
27. 416 + 377
28. 442 + 273
29. 115 + 253
30. 146 + 383
31. 142 + 259
32. 642 + 283
33. 182 + 253
34. 742 + 853
35. 142 + 253
36. 147 + 133
37. 150 + 353
38. 442 + 573
39. 615 + 256

Extra Practice

Module 3.3 Section B

a For use with Lesson 3 (pages 110–113)

Subtract. Use base ten blocks or mental math.

1. 321 − 10
2. 452 − 15
3. 246 − 18
4. 89 − 20
5. 575 − 75
6. 215 − 20
7. 162 − 81
8. 246 − 35
9. 732 − 40
10. 421 − 20
11. 562 − 25
12. 346 − 28
13. 99 − 30
14. 685 − 75
15. 515 − 35
16. 562 − 63
17. 256 − 45
18. 332 − 42

b For use with Lesson 4 (pages 114–121)

Subtract. Use paper and pencil, mental math, or base ten blocks.

19. 123 − 21
20. 152 − 53
21. 742 − 521
22. 142 − 80
23. 147 − 38
24. 150 − 43
25. 480 − 76
26. 200 − 85
27. 215 − 200
28. 356 − 253
29. 767 − 352
30. 432 − 118
31. 147 − 133
32. 134 − 73
33. 423 − 111
34. 255 − 133
35. 367 − 156
36. 345 − 125
37. 243 − 134
38. 528 − 253

Module 3.3 Section C

a For use with Lesson 5 (pages 124–127)

Estimate the length of each object in centimeters or meters.

1. textbook
2. desk
3. new pencil
4. notebook
5. paper clip
6. telephone
7. car
8. quarter
9. picture frame
10. table
11. yardstick
12. door

Estimate the length of each object in inches or feet.

13. truck
14. broom
15. calculator
16. map
17. mug
18. table
19. classroom
20. box
21. stove
22. refrigerator
23. garage
24. door

b For use with Lesson 6 (pages 128–131)

Estimate the number of grams or kilograms for each.

25. cup of water
26. nickel
27. calculator
28. this book
29. empty mug
30. table
31. ice cube
32. apple
33. a grape
34. banana
35. can of soup
36. car

Estimate Celsius temperature.

37. frozen food
38. hot water
39. warm water
40. ice water
41. warm day
42. cold day
43. classroom
44. oven
45. shower

Module 3.3 Section D

a For use with Lesson 7 (pages 132–134)

Write the number.

1. two thousand, three hundred
2. one thousand, two hundred six
3. four hundred ninety-five
4. seven thousand, five hundred
5. ten thousand
6. one thousand, forty-five
7. twenty thousand, eight
8. nine thousand, three hundred seventy-five
9. thirty thousand, three hundred thirty-three
10. six thousand, nine
11. thirteen thousand, five hundred thirty-five
12. twenty-five thousand, six hundred nineteen
13. ninety-nine thousand, seventy-five
14. twelve thousand, eight hundred forty-two
15. fifty-five thousand, two hundred twenty-nine
16. eighty thousand, four hundred nine

b For use with Lesson 8 (pages 135–139)

Write the number you would subtract to change the underlined digit to a zero. You cannot change any other numbers.

17. 5<u>3</u>2	18. 9,<u>6</u>52	19. 8<u>5</u>,436	20. <u>3</u>,869	21. 10,4<u>8</u>6
22. 57,<u>8</u>79	23. 14,<u>3</u>78	24. 6<u>7</u>8	25. 3<u>5</u>,687	26. 4,8<u>7</u>9
27. <u>7</u>6,525	28. <u>7</u>6,832	29. 409,8<u>2</u>1	30. 87<u>6</u>	31. 97,0<u>6</u>3

Write the number you would add to change the digit underlined to a zero.

32. 7,5<u>1</u>2	33. 10,<u>6</u>54	34. 6<u>5</u>,432	35. <u>5</u>3,869	36. 9<u>3</u>,465
37. 13,<u>8</u>79	38. 1<u>4</u>,274	39. <u>4</u>,678	40. 5,<u>6</u>87	41. <u>4</u>,879
42. 6,<u>5</u>25	43. <u>5</u>6,832	44. 8<u>2</u>1	45. <u>9</u>,876	46. <u>9</u>7,000

Module 3.4 Section A

a For use with Lesson 1 (pages 148–151)

Tell how many. Then tell which has the greatest number.

1. socks in 4 pairs
2. legs on 5 frogs
3. days in two weeks
4. legs on 5 spiders
5. legs on 3 cats
6. legs on 7 frogs
7. shoes in 9 pairs
8. legs on 4 chairs
9. days in 4 weeks
10. wheels on 4 cars

Name a group that the number reminds you of.

11. 50
12. 10
13. 7
14. 4
15. 5
16. 365
17. 60
18. 24

b For use with Lesson 2 (pages 152–157)

How many items in each group? Draw a picture if necessary.

19. 3 groups of 2
20. 4 groups of 3
21. 5 groups of 2
22. 2 groups of 4
23. 6 groups of 2
24. 5 groups of 3
25. 7 groups of 3
26. 8 groups of 3

Describe each array.

27. 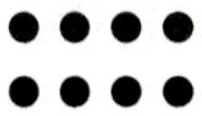

28. 

29. 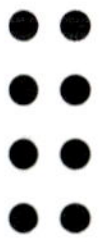

30. 

31. 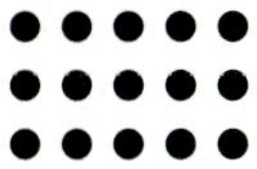

32. 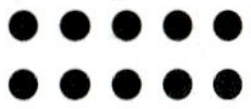

Module 3.4 Section B

(a) For use with Lesson 3 (pages 158–159)

Draw an array for each. Which have the product 12?

1. 3 x 4
2. 6 x 3
3. 4 x 3
4. 2 x 6

Is 4 a factor? Draw arrays for help. Write *yes* or *no*.

5. ■ × ▲ = 12
6. ▲ × ▲ = 9
7. ■ × ▲ = 8
8. ■ × ▲ = 7
9. ■ × ■ = 16
10. ■ × ▲ = 15
11. ■ × ▲ = 14
12. ■ × ▲ = 20
13. ■ × ▲ = 13

(b) For use with Lesson 4 (pages 160–162)

Find a pair of factors for each product. Draw arrays for help.

14. 14
15. 10
16. 12
17. 21
18. 24
19. 20
20. 15
21. 16
22. 18

(c) For use with Lesson 5 (pages 163–165)

Draw one array for each product. Write a multiplication sentence. Use your multiplication table for help.

23. 8
24. 9
25. 14
26. 18
27. 20
28. 28
29. 30
30. 36

Module 3.4 Section C

a For use with Lesson 6 (pages 168–172)

Write a multiplication sentence for each.

1. $2 + 2$
2. $6 + 6$
3. $4 + 4$
4. $5 + 5$
5. $3 + 3$
6. $9 + 9$

Write the products.

7. 2×9
8. 2×5
9. 7×2
10. 6×2
11. 2×8
12. 2×4

Use your multiplication table. Write two number sentences for the product.

13. 12
14. 16
15. 24
16. 18
17. 28
18. 20
19. 32
20. 14

b For use with Lesson 7 (pages 173–175)

21. Skip count by 5's up to 50.
22. Skip count by 3's up to 30.
23. Skip count by 2's up to 20.

Write the number of cents for each.

24. 5 nickels
25. 8 nickels
26. 3 nickels

c For use with Lesson 8 (pages 176–177)

x stands for 4 people. Write a multiplication sentence.

27. xx
28. xxxx
29. xxx
30. xxxxx

y stands for 5 people. Write a multiplication sentence.

31. yyy
32. yyyyy
33. yyyyyy
34. yy

Module 3.4 Section D

a For use with Lesson 9 (pages 178–181)

Which products are odd? Which are even?
Guess before you multiply.

1. 3×5
2. 4×3
3. 6×3
4. 3×9
5. 7×3
6. 8×3
7. 5×3
8. 9×3
9. 3×7

Make the number sentence true.

10. $3 \times 5 = \blacksquare$
11. $3 \times \blacksquare = 21$
12. $\blacksquare \times 3 = 12$
13. $5 \times 3 = \blacksquare$
14. $3 + 8 = \blacksquare$
15. $\blacksquare \times 3 = 6$
16. $6 \times \blacksquare = 18$
17. $8 - 2 = \blacksquare$
18. $8 \times \blacksquare = 24$
19. $4 \times \blacksquare = 24$
20. $\blacksquare \times 5 = 15$
21. $\blacksquare + 6 = 12$

b For use with Lesson 10 (pages 182–183)

Find the number of combinations for each if you only use one bread and one filling.

22. 3 breads, 3 fillings
23. 5 breads, 3 fillings
24. 4 breads, 5 fillings
25. 6 breads, 4 fillings
26. 5 breads, 5 fillings
27. 3 breads, 7 fillings

c For use with Lesson 11 (pages 184–187)

Use the following number sentence. $\blacksquare \times \blacktriangle + \bullet = \cdot$
Arrange the numbers in each exercise to get the greatest total. Use a calculator if you need it.

28. 2, 3, 4
29. 5, 4, 6
30. 4, 1, 2
31. 7, 5, 4
32. 4, 3, 5
33. 3, 2, 5
34. 1, 4, 3
35. 6, 5, 4

Module 3.5 Section A

a For use with Lesson 1 (pages 196–199)

Write the product.

1. $3 \times 8 = \blacksquare$
2. $6 \times 3 = \blacksquare$
3. $5 \times 7 = \blacksquare$
4. $5 \times 4 = \blacksquare$
5. $6 \times 4 = \blacksquare$
6. $5 \times 3 = \blacksquare$
7. $7 \times 7 = \blacksquare$
8. $5 \times 6 = \blacksquare$
9. $4 \times 8 = \blacksquare$
10. $8 \times 5 = \blacksquare$
11. $2 \times 9 = \blacksquare$
12. $4 \times 5 = \blacksquare$

Use the Commutative Property to rewrite each fact.

13. $4 \times 7 = 28$
14. $3 \times 6 = 18$
15. $4 \times 9 = 36$
16. $5 \times 6 = 30$
17. $2 \times 7 = 14$
18. $3 \times 8 = 24$

b For use with Lesson 2 (pages 200–205)

Find the products.

19. $6 \times 8 = \blacksquare$
20. $6 \times 9 = \blacksquare$
21. $9 \times 9 = \blacksquare$
22. $9 \times 7 = \blacksquare$
23. $8 \times 8 = \blacksquare$
24. $4 \times 9 = \blacksquare$
25. $8 \times 7 = \blacksquare$
26. $5 \times 9 = \blacksquare$
27. $9 \times 8 = \blacksquare$
28. $6 \times 6 = \blacksquare$
29. $7 \times 7 = \blacksquare$
30. $5 \times 8 = \blacksquare$

What rule has been used to get from the factor to the product?

31.

Factor	4	5	6	7
Product	20	25	30	35

32.

Factor	7	8	9	10
Product	49	56	63	70

33.

Factor	6	7	8	9
Product	48	56	64	72

34.

Factor	5	6	7	8
Product	45	54	63	72

Module 3.5 Section B

a For use with Lesson 3 (pages 208–211)

Add or multiply to find the total. Draw a model to show how you found the answer.

1. A pet parade has 10 dogs, 5 cats, 3 birds. How many pets?
2. One wagon had 3 cages with 2 birds in each cage. How many birds?
3. Another wagon had 4 fish bowls. One bowl had 2 fish, another had 3 fish, and the third had 1 fish. How many fish in all?
4. Three families each had 3 dogs. How many dogs?

Write a problem for each model. Show how you would find the answer.

5.

12			whole
4	3	5	parts

6.

16				whole
[illegible]	[illegible]	[illegible]	[illegible]	parts

7.

20		whole
10	10	parts

8.

				whole
6	6	6	6	parts

9.

					whole
[illegible]	3	2	2	2	parts

10.

			whole
7	7	7	parts

b For use with Lesson 4 (pages 212–215)

Write *rectangular prism*, *cube*, *both* or *neither* for each clue.

11. has 8 faces
12. all faces are squares
13. faces are all same size
14. two faces are triangles
15. has 6 square faces
16. has 8 rectangular faces
17. has square corners
18. has 6 rectangular faces

Module 3.5 Section C

a For use with Lesson 5 (pages 218–223)

Solve. Write a related multiplication fact.

1. $54 \div 6 =$ ■
2. $18 \div 6 =$ ■
3. $32 \div 4 =$ ■
4. $4\overline{)24}$
5. $7\overline{)35}$
6. $8\overline{)40}$
7. $27 \div 3 =$ ■
8. $42 \div 7 =$ ■
9. $63 \div 9 =$ ■
10. $64 \div 8 =$ ■
11. $48 \div 6 =$ ■
12. $72 \div 8 =$ ■
13. $8\overline{)56}$
14. $9\overline{)36}$
15. $5\overline{)30}$
16. $16 \div 4 =$ ■
17. $81 \div 9 =$ ■
18. $45 \div 5 =$ ■

b For use with Lesson 6 (pages 224–227)

Make the number sentence true.

19. $24 \div 6 =$ ■
20. ■ $\div 7 = 6$
21. $28 \div$ ■ $= 4$
22. $6 \times$ ■ $= 36$
23. ■ $\times 9 = 72$
24. $8 \times 7 =$ ■
25. $32 \div 4 =$ ■
26. ■ $\div 7 = 7$
27. $40 \div 5 =$ ■
28. $18 \div 9 =$ ■
29. $16 \div$ ■ $= 8$
30. $14 \div 2 =$ ■
31. $9 \times$ ■ $= 63$
32. ■ $\times 9 = 27$
33. $9 \times 2 =$ ■
34. $49 \div$ ■ $= 7$
35. $36 \div$ ■ $= 6$
36. $24 \div 3 =$ ■
37. ■ $\times 8 = 32$
38. $5 \times$ ■ $= 25$
39. $9 \times 4 =$ ■
40. $20 \div$ ■ $= 4$
41. $45 \div$ ■ $= 5$
42. $64 \div 8 =$ ■
43. $6 \times$ ■ $= 54$
44. ■ $\times 8 = 40$
45. $9 \times 9 =$ ■

Module 3.5 Section D

a For use with Lesson 7 (pages 228–231)

Solve to find the answer. What is the remainder?

1. $4\overline{)13}$
2. $2\overline{)15}$
3. $8\overline{)23}$
4. $9\overline{)20}$
5. $7\overline{)24}$
6. $7\overline{)15}$
7. $42 \div 8 = y$
8. $39 \div 6 = y$
9. $30 \div 9 = y$
10. $47 \div 9 = y$
11. $35 \div 8 = y$
12. $44 \div 6 = y$
13. $60 \div 7 = y$
14. $42 \div 5 = y$
15. $66 \div 9 = y$
16. $27 \div 4 = y$
17. $74 \div 9 = y$
18. $55 \div 7 = y$

Write a division example. Use the given number as the remainder.

19. 3
20. 2
21. 4
22. 6
23. 5
24. 8
25. 1
26. 7

b For use with Lesson 8 (pages 232–235)

What shape does each object have? Write *rectangular prism, cylinder, sphere.*

27. cereal box
28. globe
29. a notebook
30. soup can
31. game box
32. orange
33. a door
34. basketball
35. video deck
36. paper towel roll

Module 3.6 Section A

a For use with Lesson 1 (pages 244–247)

Write a name for the shaded part of the shape.

1.

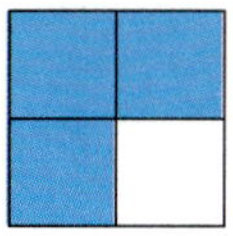

2.

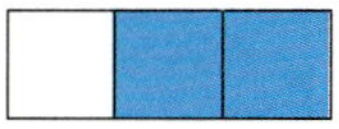

3.

4.

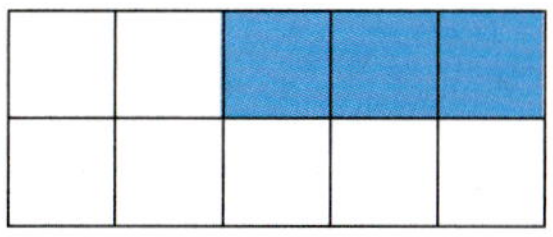

5.

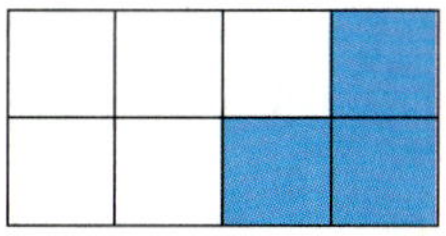

6.

b For use with Lesson 2 (pages 248–253)

Write the fraction for the shaded parts.
Then write the mixed number.

7.

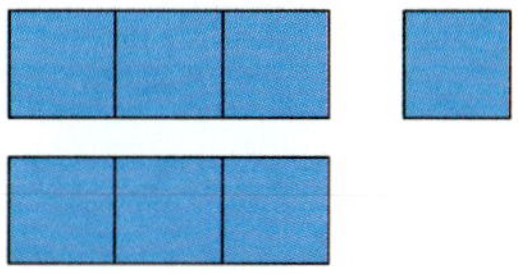

8.

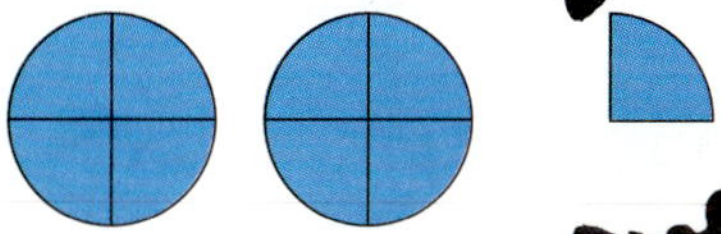

9.

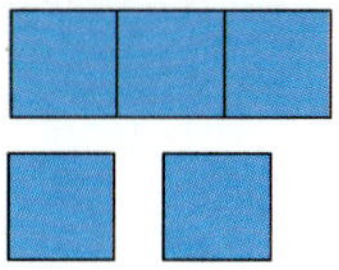

10.

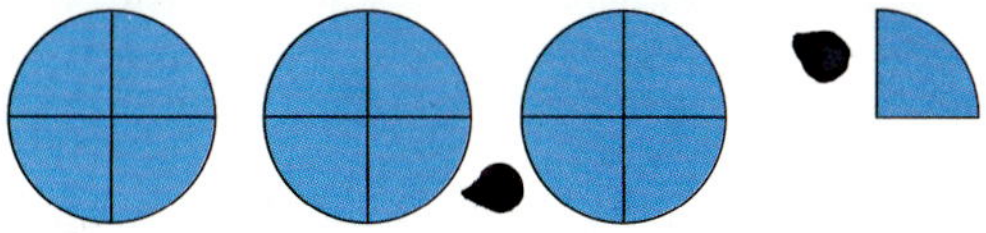

11.

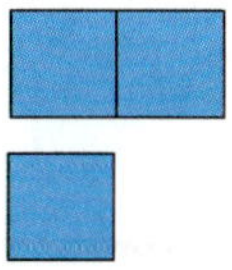

12.

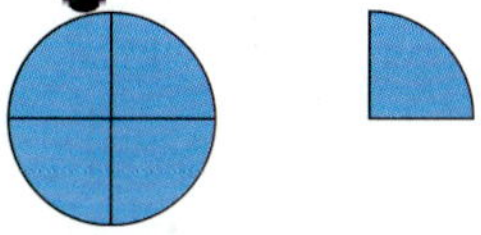

Draw a picture for each mixed number.

13. $2\frac{1}{2}$ 14. $1\frac{1}{3}$ 15. $3\frac{3}{4}$ 16. $4\frac{1}{5}$

Module 3.6 Section B

a For use with Lesson 3 (pages 254–259)

Draw a picture to show an equivalent fraction.

1. $\frac{2}{4}$
2. $\frac{4}{6}$
3. $\frac{2}{10}$
4. $\frac{4}{12}$
5. $\frac{6}{10}$
6. $\frac{3}{3}$
7. $\frac{4}{8}$
8. $\frac{8}{1}$

Order the fractions from least to greatest.

9. $\frac{1}{2}, \frac{1}{4}, \frac{1}{6}$
10. $\frac{1}{3}, \frac{1}{6}, \frac{1}{8}$
11. $\frac{1}{5}, \frac{2}{3}, \frac{1}{2}$
12. $\frac{8}{1}, \frac{1}{2}, \frac{2}{3}$
13. $\frac{1}{2}, \frac{1}{10}, \frac{3}{1}$
14. $\frac{7}{8}, \frac{1}{4}, \frac{1}{2}$

b For use with Lesson 4 (pages 260–263)

Measure the length of each segment to the nearest quarter inch.

15.
16.
17.
18.

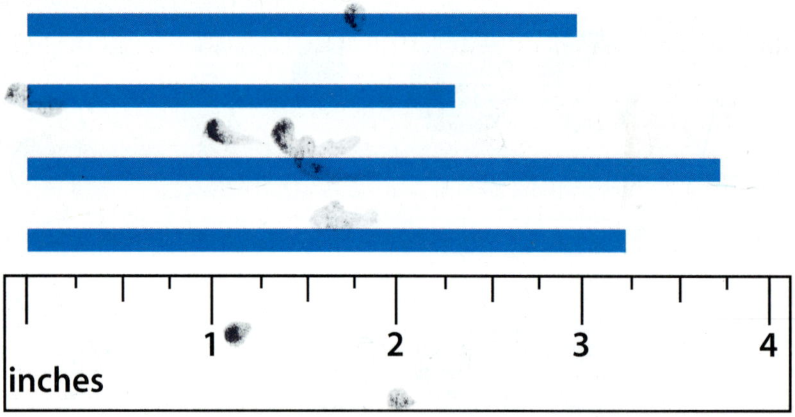

Choose a measurement between the given measurements. On your paper, draw a line and write the length for each of your segments.

19. between 1 inch and 2 inches
20. between 2 in. and 3 in.
21. between 2 in. and $2\frac{1}{2}$ in.
22. between $1\frac{1}{2}$ in. and $2\frac{1}{2}$ in.
23. between $\frac{1}{2}$ in. and 1 in.
24. between 0 in. and $\frac{3}{4}$ in.

Module 3.6 Section C

a For use with Lesson 5 (pages 266–267)

Name two fractions that give each sum below.
Write the number sentence.

1. 5 thirds
2. 8 fifths
3. 9 eighths
4. 12 tenths
5. 5 halves
6. 5 fourths
7. 7 fifths
8. 8 eighths
9. 9 sixths

b For use with Lesson 6 (pages 268–275)

Name one fraction for each figure. Write an addition sentence for the figure.

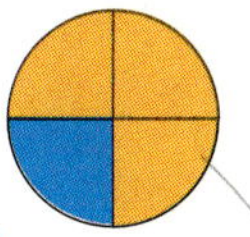
10.

11.

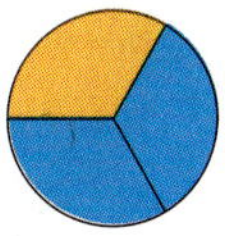
12.

13.

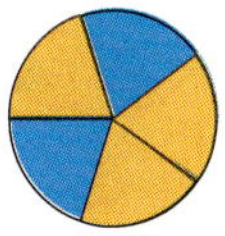
14.

Name the fraction that is shaded. Write a subtraction sentence for the figure.

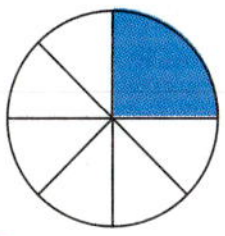
15.

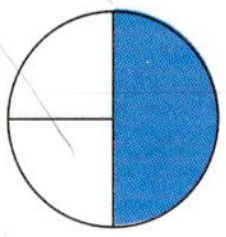
16.

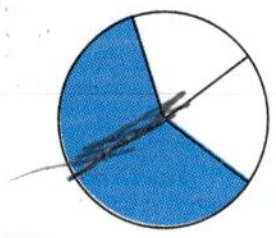
17.

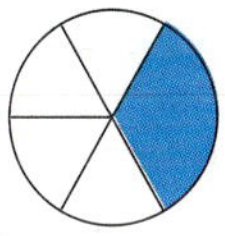
18.

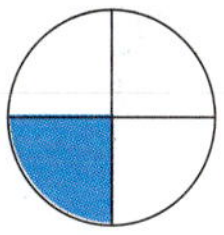
19.

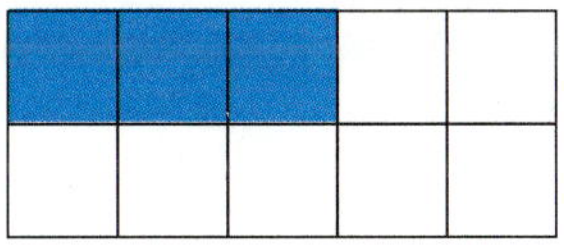
20.

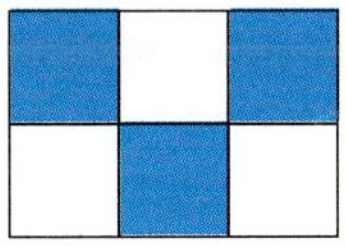
21.

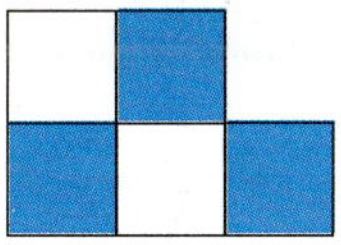
22.

Find the sum or difference.

23. $\frac{1}{3} + \frac{1}{3} =$
24. $\frac{3}{4} - \frac{1}{4} =$
25. $\frac{6}{8} - \frac{2}{8} =$
26. $\frac{1}{4} + \frac{3}{4} =$
27. $\frac{1}{2} - \frac{1}{2} =$
28. $\frac{2}{5} + \frac{1}{5} =$

Module 3.6 Section D

a For use with Lesson 7 (pages 276–279)

Draw a picture to show how each set can be divided into 3 equal parts. Write the fraction for one part.

1. 

2. 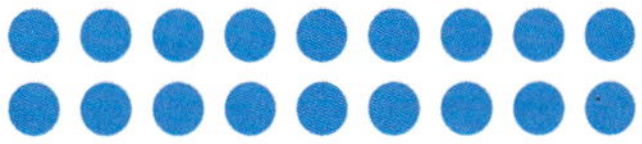

3. 

Write a fraction for the part of the set that is blue.

4. 

5. 

6. A B C D E F G
H I J

7. 

b For use with Lesson 8 (pages 280–283)

Tell which color the spinner outcome is most likely.

8. 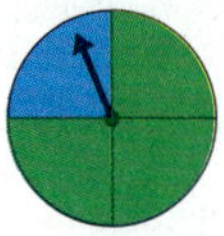

9. 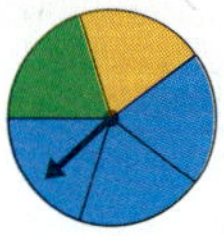

10. 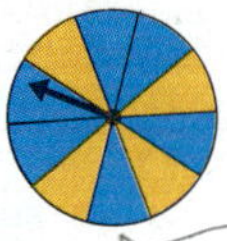

11. 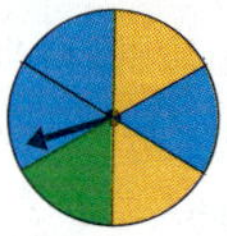

Use the clues to draw a spinner for each.

12. 4 equal parts; greater chance of spinning red than yellow or blue

13. less than 6 equal parts; same chance of spinning red and blue

14. two equal parts; no chance of spinning red

15. 5 equal parts; less chance of spinning blue than red or yellow; same chance of spinning red as yellow

Module 3.7 Section A

a For use with Lesson 1 (pages 292–295)

Complete each number sentence.

1. 3 × 40 = ■	2. 2 × 20 = ■	3. 3 × 30 = ■
4. 4 × 20 = ■	5. 5 × 30 = ■	6. 6 × 40 = ■
7. 2 × 80 = ■	8. 3 × 50 = ■	9. 8 × 20 = ■
10. 3 × 70 = ■	11. 2 × 90 = ■	12. 5 × 50 = ■
13. 7 × 20 = ■	14. 6 × 60 = ■	15. 6 × 80 = ■
16. 7 × 80 = ■	17. 9 × 50 = ■	18. 8 × 70 = ■

b For use with Lesson 2 (pages 296–301)

Estimate whether the product is greater or less than 100.

19. 3 × 30	20. 5 × 23	21. 3 × 40
22. 4 × 21	23. 5 × 25	24. 6 × 20
25. 2 × 81	26. 3 × 54	27. 8 × 12
28. 3 × 25	29. 9 × 90	30. 5 × 16
31. 7 × 23	32. 6 × 60	33. 4 × 80
34. 7 × 14	35. 2 × 56	36. 8 × 20

Find the product. Use counters to help you.

37. 3 × 12 = ■	38. 2 × 23 = ■	39. 3 × 33 = ■
40. 4 × 21 = ■	41. 5 × 15 = ■	42. 6 × 23 = ■
43. 2 × 81 = ■	44. 3 × 54 = ■	45. 8 × 28 = ■
46. 3 × 71 = ■	47. 3 × 90 = ■	48. 5 × 53 = ■
49. 7 × 23 = ■	50. 6 × 65 = ■	51. 4 × 80 = ■
52. 7 × 83 = ■	53. 9 × 56 = ■	54. 8 × 75 = ■

Module 3.7 Section B

a For use with Lesson 3 (pages 302–307)

Estimate to choose an answer. Then multiply to see if you are correct.

1. 23 × 4 — 82 or 92
2. 46 × 3 — 138 or 148
3. 35 × 2 — 70 or 80
4. 54 × 4 — 216 or 206
5. 46 × 7 — 322 or 282
6. 65 × 2 — 140 or 130

Find these products.

7. 53 × 4
8. 54 × 3
9. 72 × 3
10. 64 × 4
11. 78 × 5
12. 26 × 9

b For use with Lesson 4 (pages 308–311)

Estimate to choose an answer. Then multiply to see if you are correct.

13. 200 × 4 — 800 or 80
14. 300 × 5 — 1,500 or 150
15. 203 × 9 — 1,827 or 18,027
16. 305 × 4 — 1,220 or 12,020
17. 120 × 4 — 480 or 48
18. 123 × 3 — 3,609 or 369

Find these products.

19. 300 × 4
20. 703 × 5
21. 206 × 9
22. 403 × 4
23. 115 × 5
24. 243 × 4

Complete each number sentence. Use these factors: 3, 65, 5, 29, 8, 33.

25. △ × □ = 325
26. △ × □ = 264
27. △ × □ = 87

Module 3.7 Section C

a For use with Lesson 5 (pages 314–321)

Write the decimals, then find the sum or difference.

1. 2 tenths + 5 tenths
2. 9 tenths − 3 tenths
3. 8 tenths + 1 tenth
4. 7 tenths − 5 tenths
5. 3 tenths − 3 tenths
6. 4 tenths + 4 tenths

Find the sum or difference.

7. $2.1 + 3.2$
8. $4.5 + 0.9$
9. $7.3 + 1.8$
10. $0.6 + 4.5$
11. $8.7 - 3.2$
12. $4.1 - 2.1$
13. $6.9 - 5.4$
14. $9.0 - 3.4$

Find the answers that are equal to or less than 1.

15. 0.3 + 0.4
16. 0.7 + 0.8
17. 0.2 + 0.5
18. 0.9 + 0.5
19. 0.6 + 0.4
20. 0.1 + 0.4
21. 0.8 + 0.6
22. 0.2 + 0.5
23. 0.5 + 0.5

b For use with Lesson 6 (pages 322–323)

Write a decimal for each fraction.

24. $\frac{3}{10}$
25. $\frac{3}{100}$
26. $\frac{9}{10}$
27. $\frac{9}{100}$
28. $\frac{67}{100}$
29. $\frac{5}{10}$
30. $\frac{25}{100}$
31. $\frac{46}{100}$
32. $\frac{4}{100}$
33. $\frac{87}{100}$
34. $\frac{20}{100}$
35. $\frac{40}{10}$

Write a fraction for each decimal.

36. 0.6
37. 0.32
38. 0.02
39. 0.09
40. 0.87
41. 0.1
42. 0.22
43. 0.50
44. 0.39
45. 0.04
46. 2.1
47. 5.08

Module 3.7 Section D

a For use with Lesson 7 (pages 324–327)

Find the total cost for those amounts that are more than \$10.

1. \$1.25 × 3
2. \$1.10 × 5
3. \$2.00 × 6
4. \$7.20 × 2
5. \$3.50 × 4
6. \$5.35 × 8
7. \$.25 × 6
8. \$9.00 × 3
9. \$4.03 × 5
10. \$.98 × 2
11. \$ 1.75 × 6
12. \$1.45 × 9

b For use with Lesson 8 (pages 328–331)

If you use a \$1.00 bill for each item, what is your change ?

13. 45¢
14. 20¢
15. 95¢
16. 50¢
17. 15¢
18. 34¢
19. 87¢
20. 65¢
21. 8¢
22. 61¢
23. 56¢
24. 79¢

Use these grocery prices to answer the questions:

box of cereal	\$2.25
quart of milk	\$1.15
oranges	\$.75 each
bananas	\$.49 a pound

25. How much will three boxes of cereal cost?
26. If you buy a box of cereal and a quart of milk and pay with a \$5.00 bill what is your change?
27. If you buy 3 oranges, how many quarters do you need?
28. What is the cost of 2 pounds of bananas and a quart of milk?
29. Will \$7.00 buy 6 oranges and 3 pounds of bananas?
30. Will 15 dimes buy cereal? How much more money do you need?
31. If each orange weighs about a pound, are they more or less expensive than the bananas?

Module 3.8 Section A

a For use with Lesson 1 (pages 340–345)

Draw a picture that shows each of these.

1. a line segment
2. a line
3. a point
4. a curve
5. a circle
6. a cube

Use a word to describe each of these.

7. a straight path that goes on forever
8. a group of points that connects two points
9. a position

What do these models remind you of?

10. a length of string
11. beads on a thread
12. a long, long rope
13. a winding road
14. a floor in a room
15. a cardboard box

b For use with Lesson 2 (pages 346–347)

Match the angles with the clues.

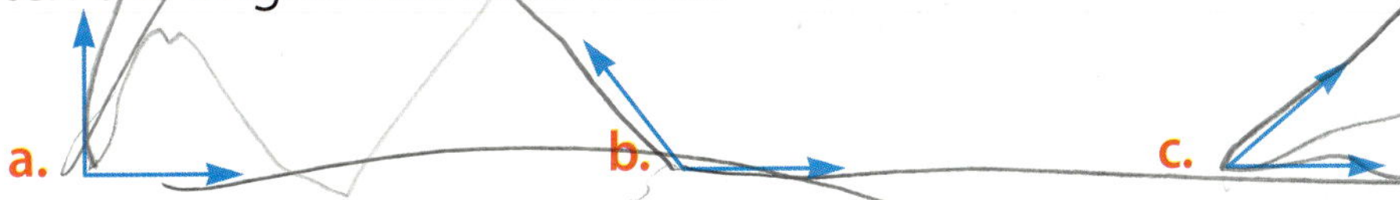

16. a right angle
17. less than a right angle
18. greater than a right angle

Copy the figure and draw a segment that follows the instructions for each.

19. Divide the rectangle into two equal parts.

20. Divide the rectangle into 3 equal parts.

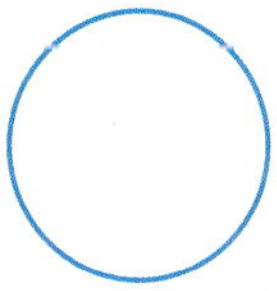

21. Divide the circle into 2 equal parts.

Module 3.8 Section B

a For use with Lesson 3 (pages 348–349)

Which of these figures are open and which are closed?

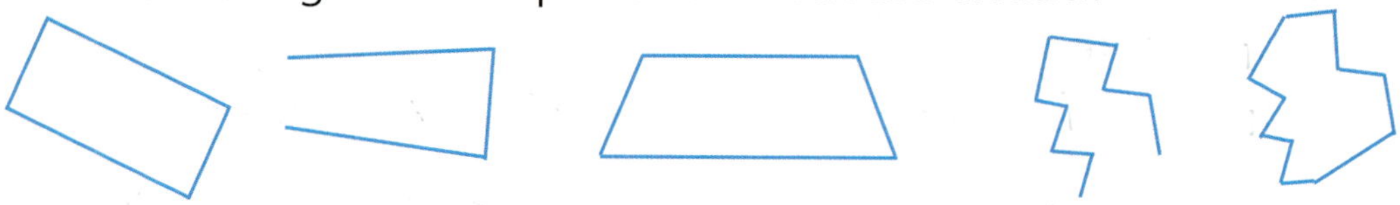

1. 2. 3. 4. 5.

Make an open figure with each number of segments.

6. 6 segments
7. 4 segments
8. 9 segments

Make a closed figure with each number of segments.

9. 5 segments
10. 7 segments
11. 4 segments

Make a closed figure that has the following:

12. two right angles
13. 1 right angle
14. 6 angles

b For use with Lesson 4 (pages 350–355)

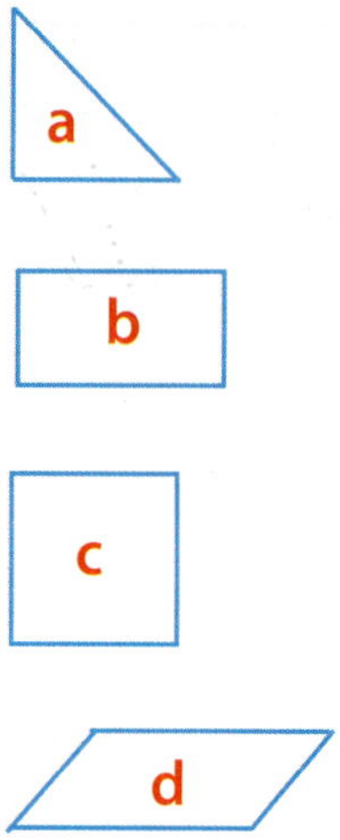

Use shapes a, b, c, and d to answer the questions.

15. Which shapes are rectangles?
16. Which figures have four sides?
17. Which figures are squares?
18. Which figures have at least one right angle?
19. Which figures are triangles?
20. Which shapes have angles greater than right angles?
21. Which shapes have no right angles?
22. Which shapes have angles less than right angles?

c For use with Lesson 5 (pages 356–357)

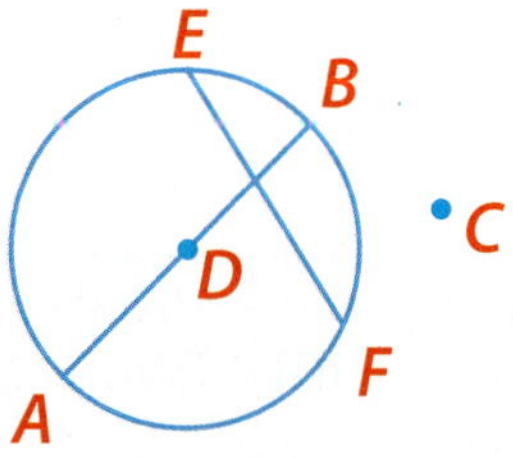

Use letters from the drawing to name each of these.

23. diameter
24. center of circle
25. point outside circle
26. point inside circle

Module 3.8 Section C

a For use with Lesson 6 (pages 360–364)

Use base ten blocks. Find out how many each student will get and whether there are any left over.

1. 35 note cards for 5 students
2. 54 paper clips for 6 students
3. 45 marbles for 8 students
4. 36 crayons for 4 students
5. 60 stamps for 5 students
6. 6 eggs for 4 students
7. 10 ride tickets for 7 students
8. 8 books for 5 students
9. 25 markers for 6 students
10. 19 hoops for 3 students

b For use with Lesson 7 (pages 365–369)

Find the missing number.

11. $\begin{array}{r} 4 \text{ R2} \\ 9\overline{)\square\square} \end{array}$

12. $\begin{array}{r} 6 \text{ R3} \\ 5\overline{)\square\square} \end{array}$

13. $\begin{array}{r} 13 \text{ R1} \\ 2\overline{)\square\square} \end{array}$

14. $\begin{array}{r} 7 \text{ R}\square \\ 7\overline{)50} \end{array}$

15. $\begin{array}{r} 6 \text{ R2} \\ 5\overline{)\square 2} \end{array}$

16. $\begin{array}{r} 8 \text{ R6} \\ 4\overline{)\square\square} \end{array}$

17. $\begin{array}{r} 9 \text{ R3} \\ 6\overline{)\square\square} \end{array}$

18. $\begin{array}{r} 10 \text{ R3} \\ 8\overline{)\square\square} \end{array}$

19. $\begin{array}{r} 11 \text{ R2} \\ 4\overline{)\square\square} \end{array}$

20. $\begin{array}{r} \square \text{ R2} \\ 4\overline{)26} \end{array}$

21. $\begin{array}{r} \square \text{ R2} \\ 6\overline{)50} \end{array}$

22. $\begin{array}{r} \square\square \\ 5\overline{)55} \end{array}$

23. $\begin{array}{r} \square\square \\ 2\overline{)28} \end{array}$

24. $\begin{array}{r} \square \text{ R}\square \\ 5\overline{)28} \end{array}$

25. $\begin{array}{r} \square \text{ R}\square \\ 8\overline{)44} \end{array}$

Module 3.8 Section D

a For use with Lesson 8 (pages 370–373)

Use these figures to answer the questions.

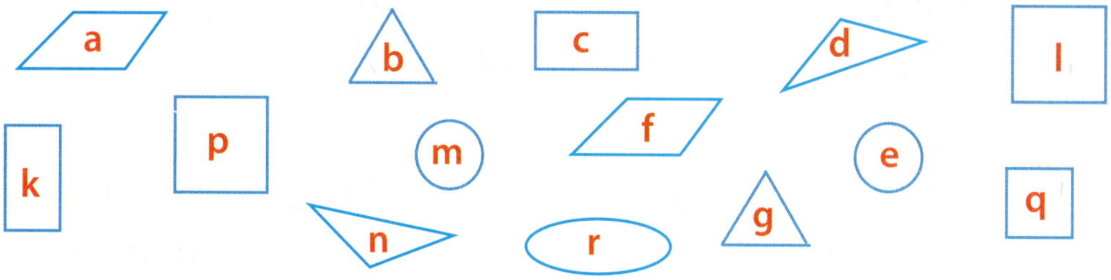

1. Which figure is congruent to figure a?
2. Which figure is congruent to b?
3. Is figure n a flip, slide, or turn of figure d?
4. Is figure k a flip, slide, or turn of figure c?
5. Are figures k and l congruent? Explain why or why not.

b For use with Lesson 9 (pages 374–379)

Use these figures to answer each question.

6. Which figures have more than one line of symmetry?
7. Which have right angles?
8. Which are polygons?
9. Which are rectangles?

Draw these figures and color them so they have two lines of symmetry.

10. 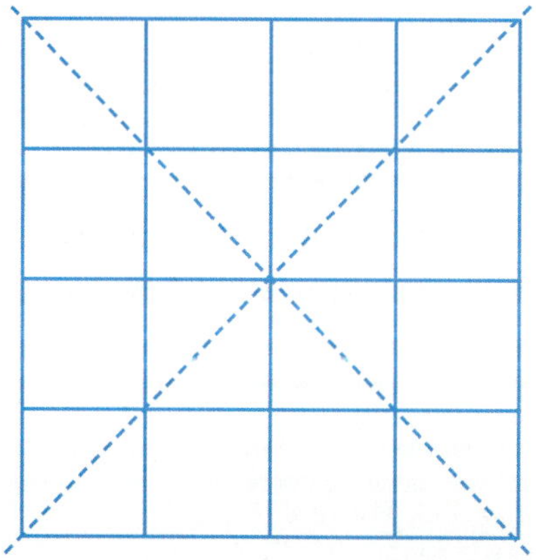

11. 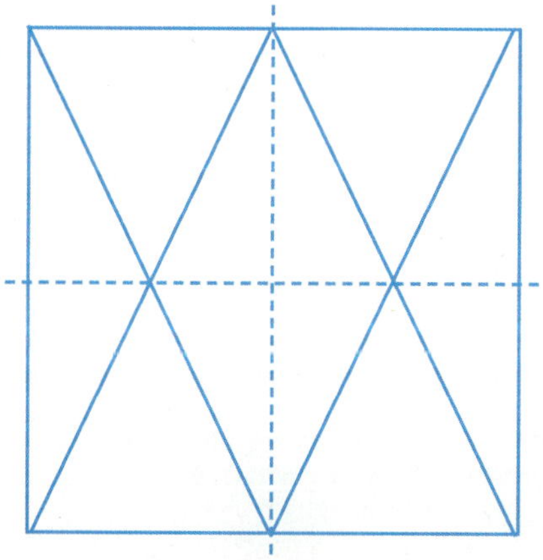

Glossary

A

A.M. (p. 10) An abbreviation for the time from midnight to noon.

abacus (p. 24) A tool that helps you add and subtract by using beads in a frame.

addends (p. 55) Numbers being added in addition.

angle (p. 346) Two rays with the same endpoint.

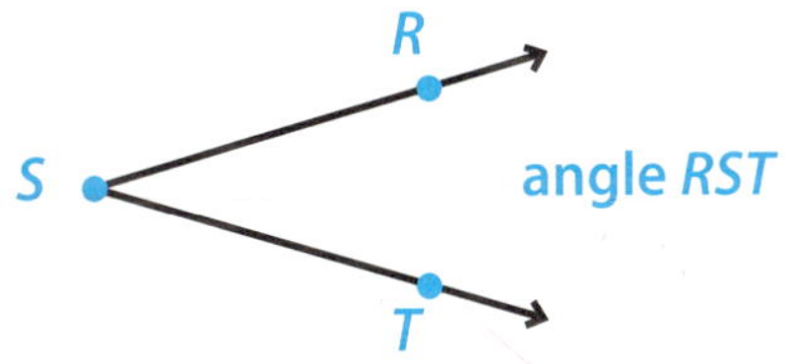

area (p. 203) The number of square units inside of a shape.

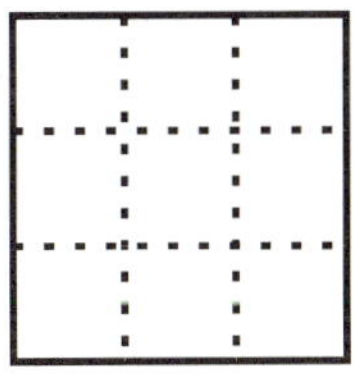

Area is 9 square units.

array (p. 152) An arrangement of rows. An egg carton is an example of an array.

Associative Property of Addition (p. 59) Changing the grouping of the addends does not change the sum. Example:

$(4 + 3) + 7 = 14$

$4 + (3 + 7) = 14$

so $(4 + 3) + 7 = 4 + (3 + 7)$

B

bar graph (p. 27) A graph that uses bars to compare data.

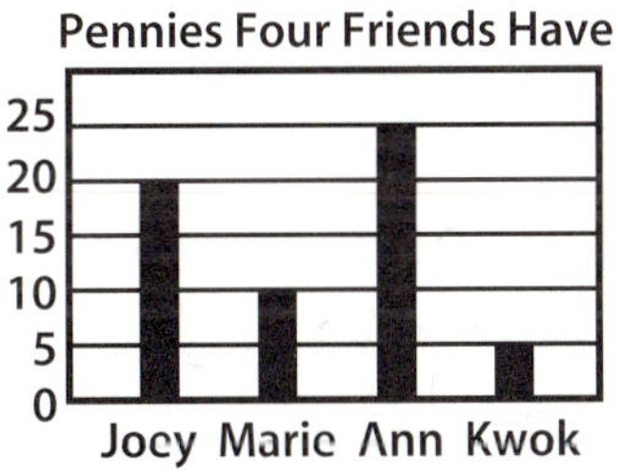

C

Celsius (p. 130) The metric temperature scale that has 0 degrees as the freezing point of water and 100 degrees as the boiling point.

Glossary

center of a circle (p. 357) The point that is the same distance from all points on the circle.

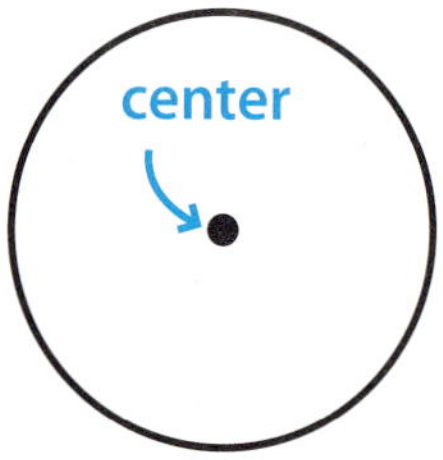

centimeter (cm) (p. 124) A metric unit for measuring length.
100 cm = 1 meter

closed figure (p. 349) Figures that have an inside and an outside.

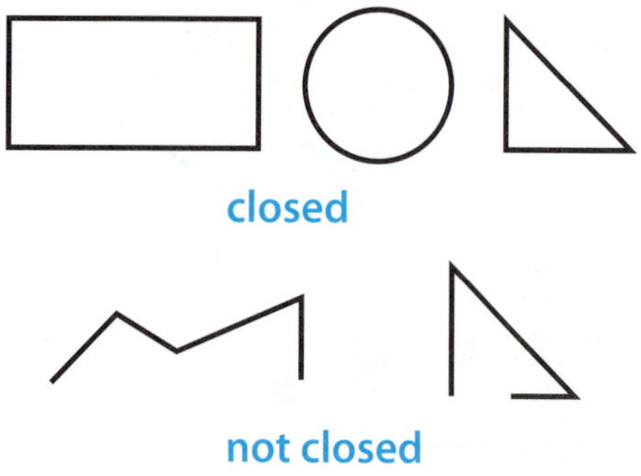

Commutative Property of Addition (p. 55) Changing the order of the addends does not change the sum. Example:

$7 + 4 = 11$

$4 + 7 = 11$

so $7 + 4 = 4 + 7$

Commutative Property of Multiplication (p. 171) Changing the order of the factors does not change the product. Example:

$5 \times 8 = 40$

$8 \times 5 = 40$

so $5 \times 8 = 8 \times 5$

cone (p. 233) A solid with one flat face that is a circle and one surface that meets in a point.

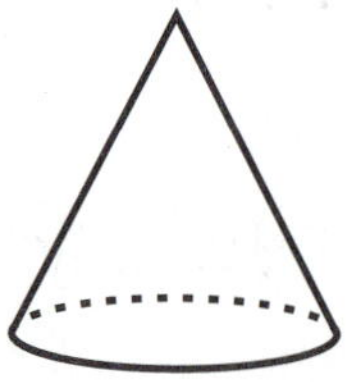

congruent (p. 371) Having the same size and shape.

consecutive numbers (p. 62) Numbers that have a difference of one. Example: 1, 2, 3, 4

cube (p. 213) A solid with six square faces, all the same size.

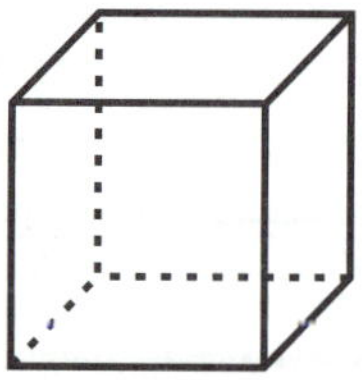

cubic unit (p. 213) A unit used to measure the volume of a solid. A cubic centimeter is the volume of a cube with every edge measuring 1 centimeter.

cup (c) (p. 85) A unit for measuring capacity. 2 c = 1 pint

cylinder (p. 233) A solid with circles for bases and no corners.

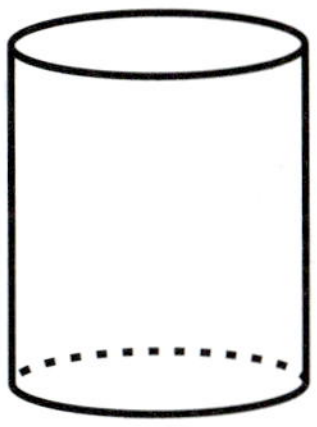

D

data (p. 180) Numbers that give information.

day (p. 4) The time it takes Earth to make one complete turn. 1 day = 24 hours

decimal (p. 315) A number that uses a decimal point to show tenths and hundredths. Another way to write fractions with denominators of 10, 100, and so on. Examples: 0.2 and 1.76

decimal point (p. 315) The point that separates the whole number from the fractional part of a decimal number.

degree (p. 13) A unit for measuring temperature.

denominator (p. 248) The bottom number of a fraction. It shows the total number of equal parts.

$$\frac{2}{3}$$ ← denominator

diagonal (p. 197) A line segment that joins two opposite corners.

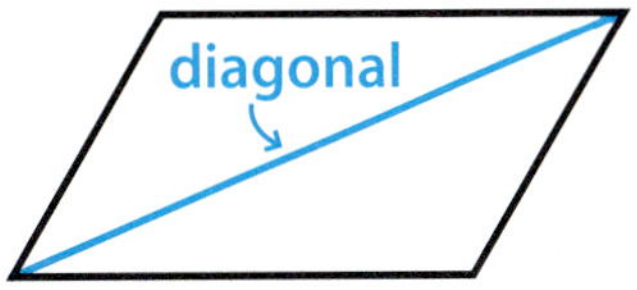

diameter (p. 357) A line segment that passes through the center of a circle and has its endpoints on the circle.

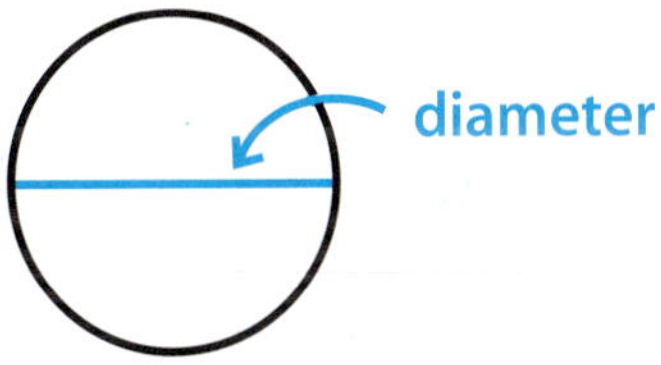

difference (p. 69) The answer in subtraction. In the number sentence 10 – 3 = 7, the difference is 7.

digit (p. 46) A symbol used to name a number. There are ten digits: 0, 1, 2, 3, 4, 5, 6, 7, 8, 9. In the number 47, 4 and 7 are digits.

doubling (p. 169) Adding a number to itself or multiplying by 2. Doubling 6 gives 12.

Glossary

E

equivalent fractions (p. 257) Fractions that name the same number. $\frac{1}{2}$, $\frac{2}{4}$, and $\frac{3}{6}$ are equivalent fractions.

estimate (p. 39) A number that is not exact.

even number (p. 202) A number that ends in 0, 2, 4, 6, or 8.

F

face (p. 212) A flat surface of a solid.

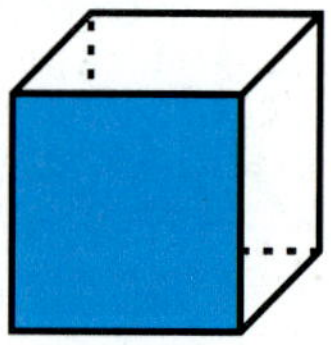

factor (p. 159) A number being multiplied to obtain a product. In the number sentence $4 \times 6 = 24$, the factors are 4 and 6.

Fahrenheit (p. 13) The temperature scale that has 32 degrees as the freezing point of water and 212 degrees as the boiling point.

flip (p. 372) Reflecting a figure about a line.

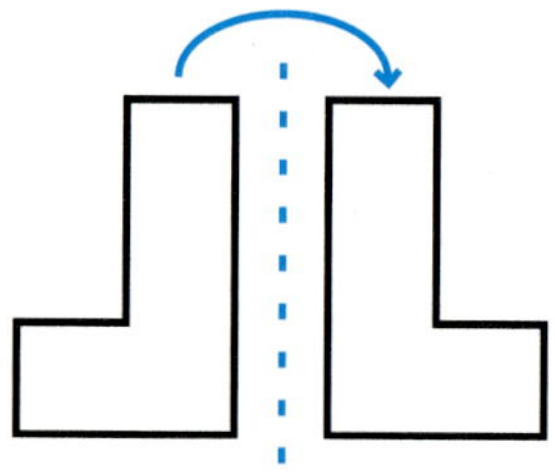

foot (ft) (p. 66) A unit of length. 1 ft = 12 inches

fraction (p. 244) A number that shows part of a whole unit. Examples: $\frac{1}{2}$, $\frac{4}{5}$, $\frac{5}{7}$

G

gallon (gal) (p. 87) A unit for measuring liquids. 1 gal = 4 quarts

gram (g) (p. 130) A metric unit for measuring mass. 1,000 g = 1 kilogram

greater than (>) (p. 184) A term used to compare numbers. 8 > 5, or "8 is greater than 5."

grid (p. 126) Parallel and perpendicular line segments on which points are plotted.

H

hundredth (p. 322) One of 100 equal parts. In the decimal 0.86, the digit 6 is in the hundredths' place.

I

inch (in.) (p. 64) A unit of length. 12 in. = 1 foot

K

kilogram (kg) (p. 129) A metric unit for measuring mass. 1 kg = 1,000 grams

L

less than (<) (p. 184) A term used to compare numbers. 3 < 7, or "3 is less than 7."

line (p. 344) A path that goes on and on in both directions.

line of symmetry (p. 374) The line that divides a figure into two matching parts.

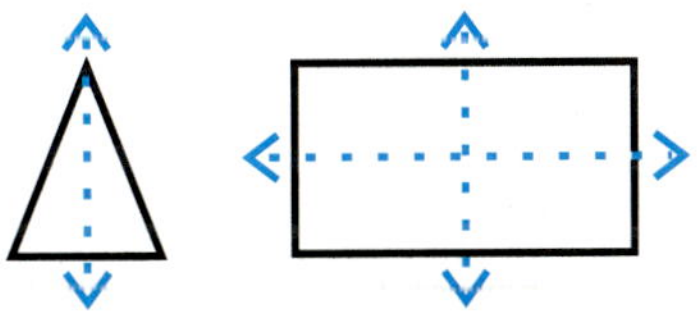

line segment (p. 343) A part of a line with two endpoints, named with two letters. The line segment below is named line segment *AB*.

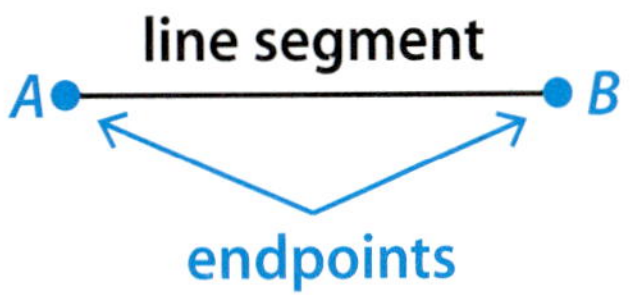

liter (L) (p. 128) A metric unit for measuring capacity. 1 L = 1,000 milliliters

M

meter (m) (p. 126) A metric unit for measuring length. 1 m = 100 centimeters

mixed number (p. 251) A number that has a whole number part and a fraction part, such as $1\frac{1}{2}$.

multiplication (p. 159) The operation of repeated addition. For example, $5 + 5 + 5 = 5 \times 3$.

N

number sentence (p. 158) A sentence that shows how numbers are related. Examples: $6 + 2 = 8$, $5 + 3 > 6$

Glossary

numerator (p. 248) The top number of a fraction. It shows the number of parts chosen.

$\frac{2}{3}$ ← numerator

O

odd number (p. 202) A number that ends in 1, 3, 5, 7, or 9.

open figure (p. 349) A figure that is not closed. These figures are open.

ounce (oz) (p. 76) A unit for measuring weight. 16 oz = 1 pound

P

P.M. (p. 10) An abbreviation for the time from noon to midnight.

perimeter (p. 125) The distance around any figure.

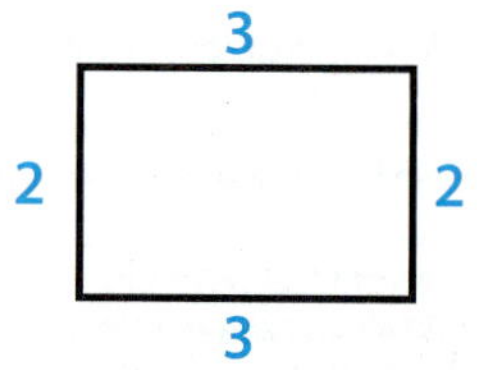

The perimeter is 10 units.

pictograph (p. 177) A graph that shows data by using pictures. Each picture stands for a certain number of items.

pint (pt) (p. 87) A unit for measuring capacity. 1 pt = 2 cups

place value (p. 18) A value assigned to a position in a number. The place values for a three-digit number are shown below.

Hundreds	Tens	Ones
3	7	6

point (p. 342) An exact location. Points are usually named with capital letters.

polygon (p. 350) A closed shape formed by line segments. Squares and triangles are types of polygons.

pound (lb) (p. 78) A unit for measuring weight. 1 lb = 16 ounces

prediction (p. 282) A guess about a future event based on facts known in the present.

product (p. 159) The answer in multiplication. In the number sentence $8 \times 6 = 48$, the product is 48.

pyramid (p. 233) A solid with a polygon for a base and triangles for the other faces.

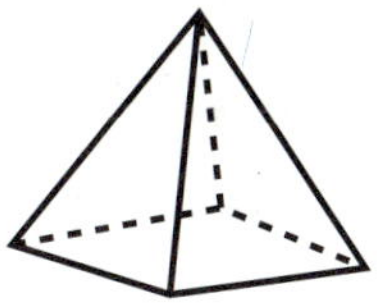

Q

quart (qt) (p. 86) A unit for measuring capacity. 1 qt = 2 pints

quotient (p. 222) The answer in division. In the number sentence 8 ÷ 4 = 2, the quotient is 2.

R

ray (p. 346) A part of a line with one endpoint. A ray goes on and on in one direction.

rectangle (p. 352) A special kind of parallelogram with all angles right angles.

rectangular prism (p. 212) A solid that has six faces with opposite faces congruent.

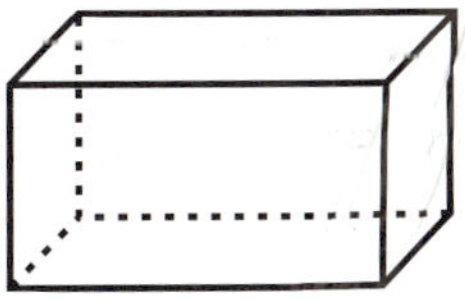

remainder (p. 228) The number left over when division is complete.

right angle (p. 346) An angle that measures 90° and makes a square corner.

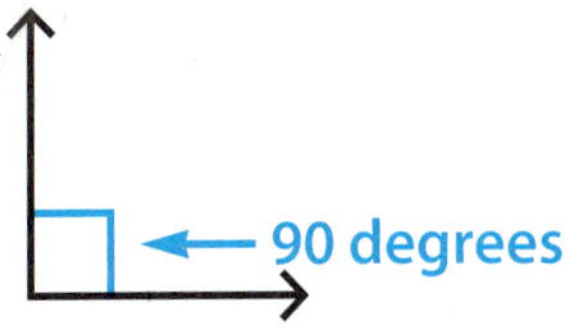

rounding (p. 22) Changing a number to the nearest ten or hundred to make it easier to use. 67 rounded to the nearest ten is 70.

S

set (p. 276) A collection or group of objects or numbers.

slide (p. 372) Moving a figure in one direction.

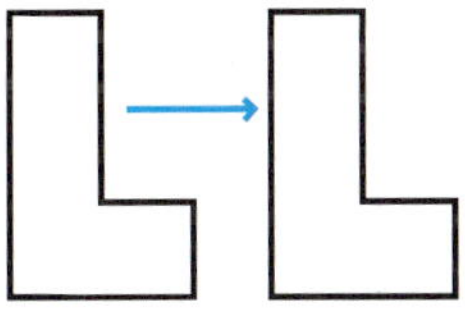

sphere (p. 233) A solid that has no flat faces and no corners. A ball is a model of a sphere.

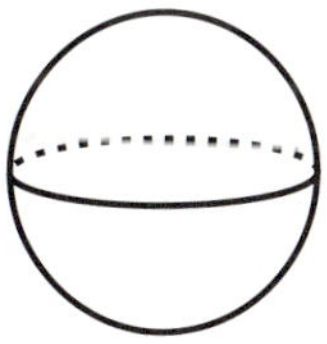

square (p. 278) A rectangle with four sides the same length.

sum (p. 55) The answer in addition. In $2 + 5 = 7$, the sum is 7.

survey (p. 26) Information gathered by asking questions and writing down answers.

symmetry (p. 374) What a shape has when it can be folded into two parts that match exactly.

T

tenth (p. 314) One of 10 equal parts. In the decimal 0.86, the digit 8 is in the tenths' place.

trade (p. 17) Exchanging units of 10, 100, 1,000, and so on in computation. In the example below, 10 was traded to the ones' place so that 8 could be subtracted from 5.

$$\begin{array}{r} {\scriptstyle 5\ 15} \\ \not{6}\,\not{5} \\ -\ 1\,8 \\ \hline 4\,7 \end{array}$$

triangle (p. 278) A polygon with three sides.

turn (p. 372) Rotating a figure about a point.

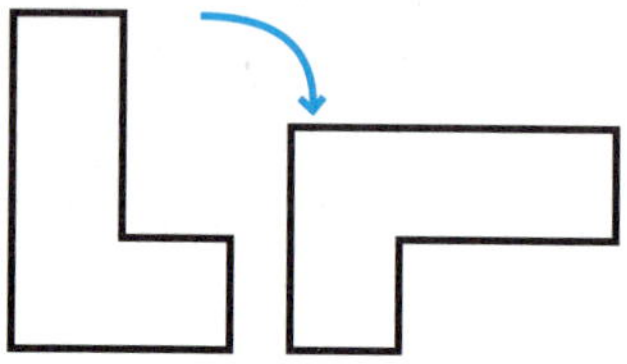

V

volume (p. 213) The amount of space inside a solid shape.

W

whole number (p. 251) A number that has no fraction part. Examples: 1, 2, 3, 4

Y

yard (yd) (p. 66) A unit for measuring length. 1 yd = 3 feet

year (p. 4) The time it takes Earth to revolve around the sun.

Index

A

Abacus, 24–25
Addend, defined, 55
Addition
  addends
    defined, 55
    grouping of, 59, 60–61, 107
    missing, 78, 79, 80, 104, 107
    odd and even, 62–63
    three or more, 59, 60–61, 62–63
  Associative Property of, 59
  column, 59
  Commutative Property of, 55, 171
  of consecutive numbers, 62–63
  of decimals, 317–318, 319, 320–321, 395
  estimating with, 98–99, 108–109, 134, 399
  finding perimeter, 125
  of fractions, 266–267, 268–269, 270–271, 394
  investigations, 62–63, 122–123
  mental math and, 57–58, 59, 104, 107, 396–397
  methods summarized, 390–391, 392–393, 394–395, 396–397, 399
  modeling
    using base ten blocks and hundreds' board, 100–101, 102–103, 104, 105
    using play money, 108–109
    using tiles, 62–63
  of money, 175, 326–327, 329
  multiplication and, 159, 184–185, 208–209
  patterns based on, 62–63, 88, 89, 90–91
  problem solving and, 57–58, 59–60, 61, 100–101, 102–103, 104, 105, 106, 107, 108–109, 122–123, 125, 126–127, 138–139, 390, 391
  recording, 105–107, 108–109
  related to subtraction, 111
  strategies
    adding doubles, 57–58
    adding by endings, 396
    breaking apart numbers, 397
    compensation, 397
    counting on, 57–58, 396
    grouping addends to make ten, 57–58, 59, 107, 397
    paper and pencil, 392–393
  sum, defined, 55
  trading ones or tens, 392–393
  of units of measure, 125, 126–127, 128
  of whole numbers,
    four-digit, 137–138
    three-digit, 102–103, 104, 105, 106, 107, 108–109
    two-digit, 100–101, 122–123, 392–393
  zero in, 104, 107
Algebra. *See also* Equations, writing.
  addition and, 54, 58, 59, 60, 61, 62–63, 77, 80, 91, 92–93, 104, 109, 134, 183, 199, 223, 236–237, 317–318, 319, 320–321, 354, 397
  decimals and, 317–318, 319, 320–321
  division and, 223, 227, 236–237, 247, 368
  fractions and, 254–255, 268–269, 318, 354
  missing factors, 263, 307, 331
  multiplication and, 159, 165, 169, 172, 181, 188, 199, 205, 236–237, 263, 294–295, 299, 307, 331
  subtraction and, 32, 44–45, 69, 70–71, 72–73, 91, 92–93, 113, 134, 183, 199, 205
  using variables in, 397
  writing equations from patterns, 62–63, 94–96, 300–301
  zero in, 104, 107
A.M. and P.M., 10
Analyzing. *See* Logical reasoning, analyzing and synthesizing.
Angle
  classifying, 346, 347
  defined, 346
  right, 346
Area, modeling using array, 203
Arithmetic operations. *See also* Addition; Division; Multiplication; Subtraction.
  creating alternative algorithms for, 105, 106, 110–111, 116, 302–303, 304–305, 308–309, 311, 362, 363, 365, 368
Array
  defined, 152
  described in table, 158, 163
  investigations based on, 190–193, 238–240
  modeling, 147, 150, 152, 153, 158–159
  patterns in, 151, 163, 164, 165
  problem solving and, 152–153, 154–155, 156–157, 163–165, 166–167
  rows in, 146–147, 238–240
  writing equations from, 159, 160–161, 165, 169
Assessment. *See also* Investigations; Review.
  student self-assessment, 6, 11, 28, 61, 72, 80, 87, 112, 128, 138, 152, 159, 173, 185, 209, 227, 229, 253, 256, 271, 280, 293, 303, 315, 345, 349, 368
  tasks, 25, 45, 75, 93, 167, 189, 217, 237, 265, 313, 333, 359, 381
Associative Property of Addition, 59

B

Bar graph, 27, 28, 36–37, 38, 296–297

Index

C

Calculator
how to use, 294–295, 402–403
Calculator activities
addition, 104, 137
checking answers, 30, 310
comparing with mental math, 104
dividing by multiples of ten, 314
dividing without using division key, 369
multiplication, 180, 187, 294, 310
multiplying by ten, 48
patterns, 48, 104
subtraction, 137
Calendar, 4–5, 6, 7, 292–293, 295
Capacity
metric units of, 128, 408
U.S. customary units of, 85, 86–87, 408
Celsius scale, 130, 408
Centimeter, 124, 125, 126–127, 408
Charts and tables
making, 65, 76, 90–91, 94–95, 96, 109, 112, 124, 149, 151, 158, 163, 173, 178–179, 198–199, 200–201, 206–207, 268–269, 282–283, 299, 300–301, 355, 388, 389, 401
reading and interpreting, 61, 69, 71, 81, 82–83, 88, 94–95, 96, 135, 138–139, 151, 158, 180, 206–207, 210–211, 282–283, 292–293, 295, 296–297, 299, 305, 309, 315, 401
Circle
diameter, 357
review, 356
tracing, 319
Classification. *See* Data.
Closed figure, 349
Combinations, 183
Communication. *See also* Co-operative learning; Journals.
creating problems or puzzles, 6, 10, 32, 70–71, 112, 150–151, 171, 225, 226–227, 308–309
sharing, 2, 6, 15, 17, 34, 35, 36–37, 38, 40, 54, 62–63, 77, 94–95, 96, 101–102, 103–104, 106, 112, 113, 116, 117, 126, 131, 133, 148, 152, 156–157, 190–191, 192, 207, 210–211, 225, 226–227, 232–233, 234, 238–239, 240, 242–243, 248–249, 256, 260–261, 262–263, 278–279, 280–281, 288, 292–293, 294, 297–299, 308–309, 310, 315, 317, 319, 324–325, 328, 329, 330–331, 334–335, 336, 340, 341, 345, 349, 350, 352–354, 357, 360–361, 364, 376–377, 407
writing, 17, 39, 46–47, 54, 62–63, 94–95, 105, 106, 108, 109, 112, 116, 122–123, 127, 128, 131, 135, 141, 142–143, 148, 152, 156–157, 190–191, 192, 207, 210–211, 225, 226–227, 232, 233, 234, 238–239, 240, 248–249, 251, 253, 260–261, 266, 274–275, 281, 286–287, 288, 295, 308–309, 311, 315, 318, 322, 334–335, 336, 355, 357, 364, 365, 373
Commutative Property
of Addition, 55, 171
of Multiplication, 55, 171, 172, 198–199, 200, 301
Comparing
addends, 107
addition and multiplication, 184–185, 208–209
angles, 346, 347
Commutative Properties of Addition and Multiplication, 171
containers, 84–85
data, 177, 180, 210–211
decimals and fractions, 314–315, 316–317, 317–318, 319, 322–323
equations, 79
estimates and results, 39, 65, 111, 134, 297–299, 308–309, 311
fractions, 254–255, 258–259, 260–261
lengths, 52–54, 65, 70–71
line and line segment, 345
number sentences, 63
numbers in table, 163
open and closed figures, 348, 349
perimeters, 125
place value, 18
polygons, 351, 352–354
relative sizes of objects, 50–51
results to predictions, 282–283
rounded and actual numbers, 22–23
ruler to number line, 262–263
shapes, 212–213, 232–233, 234, 235, 278–279, 351, 352–354, 358–359, 371, 372–373
sums and products, 184–185
units of measure, 66–67, 78, 94–95, 126–127, 130, 408
ways to multiply, 179
weight, 76, 77, 78, 96, 129–130
whole numbers, 22–23, 54, 58
Compatible numbers, 57–58, 107, 399
Computer activities
drawing
lines, shapes, or patterns, 144, 158, 262, 336, 383, 400
symbols, 48
table to describe array, 158
graphing data, 297, 401
making spreadsheets, 401
organizing information with database, 401
Computer programs
databases, 401
drawing, 144, 158, 262, 336, 383, 400
spreadsheets/graphs, 297, 401
Cone, 233
Congruent figures, 371, 372–373, 377, 378–379, 382–383

Connect and Communicate. *See also* Journals.
comparing, 163, 179
describing patterns, 89
drawing lines of symmetry, 376
drawing pictures, 153, 315, 331
explaining, 81, 137, 153, 182, 267, 292, 315
keeping journals, 6, 18, 19, 55, 71, 105, 116, 131, 169, 187, 222, 231, 246, 281, 309, 323, 325, 363
understanding, 4, 13
writing
comparison, 187
definition, 55, 246
description, 153, 281
directions, 105
explanation, 6, 18, 19, 169, 187, 222, 231, 309, 323, 325, 363,
lists, 34, 116
problems, 171
rules, 163
stories, 131
Connections. *See* Connect and Communicate; Curriculum connections.
Consecutive numbers, defined, 62
Consumer awareness. *See* Money.
Cooperative learning. *See also* Communication, sharing.
in groups, 4–5, 6, 7, 11, 13, 16–17, 20–21, 22, 30–31, 32, 35, 40, 41, 57–58, 60, 72–73, 79, 84–85, 86–87, 88, 90–91, 100–101, 102–103, 105, 106, 107, 108–109, 110–111, 124–125, 130, 131, 133, 135, 136–137, 138–139, 149, 164, 165, 170, 177, 178, 180, 182–183, 197, 230–231, 234, 245, 260–261, 270–271, 277, 292–293, 304–305, 308–309, 310, 316–317, 320–321, 324–325, 329, 350, 351, 352–354, 356, 360–361, 364, 365, 370
with partners, 11, 18, 19, 22–23, 29, 51, 52–54, 56–57, 61, 65, 66–67, 69, 70–71, 76, 77, 89, 104, 112, 113, 129–130, 134, 176, 201, 205, 208–209, 213, 215, 219–220, 224–225, 235, 242–243, 247–249, 252–253, 256, 262–263, 267, 268–269, 279, 282–283, 295, 297–299, 309, 328, 330–331, 340, 341, 343, 345, 346, 347, 368, 382–383
Critical thinking. *See* Logical reasoning.
Cube, 213
Cubic units, 213
Cultural connections
African American cowboys, 224
Apache game, 176
Arabic patterns, 378–379
Ashanti kente cloth, 274
Chinese abacus, 24–25
Chinese and Korean game, 340
Chinese tangrams, 352–354, 355
Egyptian scales, 79
Italian tiles, 378–379
Japanese egg packages, 157
Japanese kites, 374
Juneteenth parade, 194
Mexican quesadilla, 315
umbrellas in Sri Lanka, 68
Cumulative review. *See* Review.
Cup, 85, 408
Curriculum connections
art and design, 274–275
literature. *See* Literature for problem solving.
science, 59, 76
social studies, 24–25, 68, 81, 84, 194, 216–217, 218–219, 224, 340, 352–354, 355, 374
Customary units. *See* Measurement, U.S. customary units.
Cylinder, 233

D

Data. *See also* Graphs; Number sense; Probability; Survey.
collecting and organizing, 14–15, 26–27, 28, 32, 36–37, 38, 52–54, 56–57, 76, 94–95, 96, 149, 182–183, 234, 296–297, 298, 401, 404–405
drawing conclusions from, 14–15, 26–27, 28, 36–37, 38, 52–54, 57, 81, 82–83, 88, 94–95, 96, 138–139, 177, 180, 210–211, 296–297, 298, 401, 404–405
grouping using database, 401
patterns in, 88, 94–95, 96, 151
representing
on spreadsheets, 401
by tallying, 26, 28, 32, 37, 296–297, 404–405
using bar graphs, 27, 28, 36–37, 38, 296–297
using charts, 65, 76, 90–91, 94–95, 96, 109, 112, 124, 149, 151, 158, 163, 173, 178–179, 198–199, 200–201, 206–207, 268–269, 282–283, 299, 300–301, 355, 388, 389, 401
using pictographs, 177
using picture graphs, 14–15
Decimal point, defined, 315
Decimals
adding, 317–318, 319, 320–321, 395
calculator activities with, 314
fractions and, 314–315, 316–318, 319, 322–323
games using, 316–317, 320–321
hundredths, 322–323
mental math with, 320–321
modeling, 323
money and, 324–325, 326–327
multiplying, 324–325, 326–327
place value, 314–315, 316–318, 319, 322–323
problem solving and, 314–315, 316–318, 319, 322–323
reading, 319, 322
subtracting, 317–318, 319, 320–321
tenths, 314–315, 316–317, 319, 395
visualizing, with shapes, 314–315, 316–317, 318, 319, 323
writing fractions as, 317–318, 319, 322–323
Decimeter, 408

Index

Degrees (of temperature)
Celsius, 130, 408
Fahrenheit, 13, 408
Denominator, defined, 248
Diameter, defined, 357
Difference, defined, 69
Discrete mathematics. *See also* Data, representing; Graphs; Numbers, comparing and ordering.
combinations, 183
organized list, 109, 388
tallying, 26, 28, 32, 37, 296–297, 404–405
Division. *See also* Fractions.
arrays and, 219–220, 221–222, 224–225
calculator activities using, 314, 369
estimating with, 364
explaining, 221–222, 360–361, 362, 363, 364, 365, 368
games using, 366–367
interpreting remainders, 228–229, 362
investigations, 334–335, 336, 369
meaning of, 221–222
modeling
with arrays, 219–220, 224–225
with base ten blocks, 360–361, 363, 364, 365, 366–367
with counters, 219–220, 226
by folding paper, 360
by sketching, 251, 252–253, 260–261, 276
of money, 326–327
by multiples of ten, 314–315
multiplication and, 224–225, 368
with one-digit divisors, 221
patterns in, 314–315
problem solving with, 218, 219–220, 221–222, 223, 224–225, 226–227, 228–229, 230–231, 314–315, 360–361, 362, 363, 364
recording, 221–222, 229, 365, 368
remainders and, 228–229, 362
subtraction and, 368
Drawing to Learn. *See also* Problem solving strategies.
9, 15, 37, 53, 65, 77, 90, 103, 126, 133, 150, 179, 203, 249, 255, 258, 269, 279, 294, 317, 331, 343, 354, 364, 377

E

Equations, writing, 54, 56, 60, 61, 62–63, 65, 69, 78, 79, 80, 94–95, 96, 159, 160–161, 165, 169, 174–175, 208–209, 267, 268–269, 300–301
Equivalent fractions
defined, 257
finding, 258–259
Estimation
addition and, 98–99, 108–109, 398–399
of area and perimeter, 125, 351
benchmark, 124
checking work using, 39, 65, 111, 134, 297–299, 308–309, 311, 364
compatible numbers and, 399
deciding when to use, 98–99, 116, 398–399
division and, 399
explaining strategies for, 39, 41, 42–43, 98–99, 351, 398–399
front-end, 399
of length, 52–54, 124, 127
of money, 108–109, 399
multiplication and, 297–298, 302–303, 304, 308–309, 311, 324–325, 398
of number of objects, 39, 41–43
problem solving and, 39, 40, 41–43, 124, 128
of products, 398
of reasonable answers, 39, 40, 41, 42–43, 116
revising estimates, 42–43
by rounding to tens or hundreds, 292–293, 297–299, 302–303, 304, 398
of sums, 399
using calculator to check, 30, 310
of weight, 129–130

F

Face, defined, 212
Factor, defined, 159
Fahrenheit, 13, 408
Fluid ounce, 408
Foot, 66, 408
Fractions. *See also* Division.
adding, 266, 267, 268–269, 270–271, 318, 394
calculator activities using, 314, 369
common denominator, 394
comparing and ordering, 244, 254–255, 256, 260–261
decimals and, 314–315, 316–317, 318, 319, 322–323
defined, 244
denominator, defined, 248
drawing to understand, 251, 252–253, 260–261, 276
equivalent, 257, 258–259
of an inch, 262–263
investigations, 274–275, 286–287, 288
measurement and, 262–263
as mixed numbers, 251
modeling
using counters, 252–253, 266, 268–269
using shapes, 242–243, 245, 246–247, 248–249, 250–251, 254–255, 256, 257, 258–259, 260–261, 266, 268–269
on the number line, 260–261
numerator, defined, 248
as part of a set, 252–253, 276–277, 278–279
as part of a shape or region, 242–243, 244, 245, 246–247, 248–249, 250–251, 254–255, 256, 257, 258–259, 260–261, 266, 267, 268–269, 270–271

problem solving with, 242–243, 244, 245, 246–247, 248–249, 250–251, 252–253, 254–255, 256, 257, 258–259, 260–261, 262–263, 264–265, 266, 267, 268–269, 270–271, 272–273, 274–275, 276–277, 278–279
subtraction of, 318, 395
writing, 244, 248–249, 251, 253, 257, 266, 318
Fraction Tool, 254, 256, 282
Front-end estimation, 399
Functions, 199, 223

G

Games, 7, 18, 20–21, 72–73, 107, 136–137, 160–161, 176, 184–185, 197, 230–231, 270–271, 306–307, 316–317, 320–321, 329, 340, 341, 346, 356, 366–367, 370
Generalizing. *See* Logical reasoning, making generalizations
Geometry
angle, 346, 347
area, modeling using array, 203
classifying and comparing shapes, 212–213, 232–233, 234, 235, 351, 352–354, 358–359, 371, 372–373
congruent figures, 371, 372–373, 377, 378–379, 382–383
describing shapes, 212–213, 232–233, 352–354, 355, 356
drawing or tracing shapes, 212–213, 250–251, 346, 372, 378–379
estimating with, 351
face, 212
investigations based on, 382–383, 384
line, 344
line segment, 343, 384
naming
line, 344
line segment, 343
point, 342
perimeter, 125, 126–127
plane figures
circle, 356, 357
polygon, 350–354, 370, 371
square, 352–354
triangle, 352–354
point, 342
problem solving with, 340, 341, 342, 343, 344, 345, 346, 347, 348, 349, 350, 351, 352–354, 355, 356, 357, 358–359, 370, 371, 372–373, 374, 375, 376–377, 378–379, 380–381
slide, flip, turn, 372–373
space figures
cone, 233
cube, 213
cylinder, 233
pyramid, 233
rectangular prism, 212–213
sphere, 233
symmetry, 374, 375, 376–377, 378–379
three-dimensional objects. *See* space figures.
two-dimensional figures. *See* plane figures.
to visualize fractions, 251, 253, 260–261, 276
volume, 213–214, 215
Geometry Tool, 213, 278
Gram, 129–130, 408
Graphs
bar, 27, 28, 36–37, 38, 210–211
organized list, 109, 388
pictographs, 177
picture graphs, 14–15
tallying, 26, 28, 32, 37, 296–297, 404–405

H

Hundreds, 102–103, 104, 105, 106, 107, 308–309
Hundreds' board. *See* Modeling, with base ten blocks and hundreds' board.
Hundreds' chart, finding patterns in, 206–207
Hundredth, defined, 322
Hundred thousands, 134

I

Inch, 66–67, 262–263, 408
Investigations, xiv–xvi, 33, 46–48, 62–63, 94–96, 120–121, 142–144, 156–157, 190–192, 206–207, 238–240, 274–275, 286–288, 300–301, 334–336, 369, 382–384

J

Journals, 6, 18, 19, 55, 71, 105, 116, 131, 169, 187, 222, 231, 246, 251, 281, 309, 323, 325, 331, 363

K

Kilogram, 129–130, 408
Kiloliter, 408
Kilometer, 408

L

Language. *See* Logical reasoning, generalizing; Journals; Word Bank.
Lattice multiplication, 311
Length
metric units of, 124, 126–127
nonstandard units of, 52–54, 55, 56–57
U.S. customary units of, 66–67
Less than. *See* Numbers, comparing and ordering.
Line, defined, 344
Line segment, defined, 343
Line of symmetry, 374
Liquid measure
metric units of, 128, 408
U. S. customary units of, 86–87, 408
Liter, 128, 408
Literature for problem solving
"The Elephant" by Louis Phillips, 132
How to Count Sheep Without Falling Asleep by Ralph Leighton and Carl Feynman, 16
Jacob Two-Two and the Dinosaur by Mordecai Richler, 168
Justin and the Best Biscuits in the World by Mildred Pitts Walter, 224
The Kingdom of Geometry by Alma Flor Ada, 352

Index

Literature for problem solving (cont.)
"A Mother's Advice" by Ahmed and Zane Zagbul, 250
The Umbrella Thief by Sybil Wettasinghe, 68
What's Cooking, Jenny Archer? by Ellen Conford, 324
Logical reasoning. *See also* Problem solving strategies.
analyzing and synthesizing, 11, 62–63, 81, 94–95, 96, 126–127, 142–143, 144, 171, 180, 210–211, 311, 317–318, 321, 347, 404–405
comparing and classifying, 50–51, 62–63, 76, 94–95, 96, 152, 153, 169, 171, 172, 179, 184–185, 210–211, 212–213, 234, 344, 345, 346, 347, 351, 352–354, 382–383
inductive and deductive reasoning, 178–179, 294, 404–405
making generalizations, 62–63, 64, 81, 122–123, 153, 163, 170, 171, 172, 194–195, 210–211, 294, 297–299, 310, 364, 404–405
observing, 122–123, 142–143, 144, 190–191, 192, 212–213, 234, 314–315, 374, 375
open-ended problems, xiv–xvi, 33, 46–48, 62–63, 94–95, 96, 120–121, 133, 142–143, 144, 156–157, 190–191, 192, 206–207, 238–239, 240, 274–275, 286–287, 288, 300–301, 334–335, 336, 344, 369, 382–383, 384
patterning and sequencing, 4–5, 6, 7, 22–23, 24–25, 34, 38, 62–63, 84, 114, 122–123, 127, 130, 184–185, 200–201, 256, 260–261, 346, 387, 406
predicting and verifying, xiv–xvi, 35, 84–85, 86–87, 88, 89, 111, 165, 184–185, 200, 282–283
reasonable answers, 39, 40, 41, 42–43, 116, 138
spatial visualization, 125, 126–127, 133, 372–373, 374, 375, 376–377, 378–379
visualizing, 4–5, 14–15, 57, 133, 142–143, 144, 190–191, 192, 213, 214, 215, 235, 242–243, 244, 245, 314–315, 316–317, 319, 323, 351, 406–407

M

Making change, 30–31, 32, 174–175, 328, 329, 330–331
Maps, 126–127, 190–191, 192
Mass
metric units of, 129–130, 408
U.S. customary units of, 76, 77, 78, 408
Measurement. *See also* Calendar.
of capacity, 84–85, 128, 408
comparing measurements, 52–54, 65, 76, 84–85, 86–87, 124, 125, 126, 129–130
cubic units, 213
cup, 85
of elapsed time, 4–5, 6, 7, 8–9, 10, 11, 408
equivalent units of
capacity, 86–87, 128, 129–130, 408
length, 66–67, 126–127, 408
mass (weight), 78, 79, 129–130
temperature, 13, 130, 408
time, 8–9, 10, 11
estimating and, xiv–xvi, 52–54, 65, 66–67, 84, 85, 124
fractions in, 262–263
investigations, 355, 382–383, 384
length, 52–54, 56–57, 66–67, 124, 126–127, 262–263, 408
mass (weight), 76, 77, 78, 129–130, 408
metric units
of capacity, 124, 408
equivalent, 126, 130, 408
of length, 125, 126–127, 408
of mass (weight), 129–130, 408
nonstandard units, 52–54, 55, 56–57
problem solving and, 4–5, 6, 7, 8–9, 10, 11, 12, 13, 52–54, 55, 56–57, 78–80, 84–87, 124, 125, 126–127, 128, 129–130
process of, xiv–xvi, 52–54, 56–57, 77, 124, 125, 126–127, 128, 129–130, 192, 262–263, 288, 384
temperature, 12–13, 130, 131, 408
time, 8–9, 10, 11
U.S. customary units
abbreviations for, 408
capacity, 85, 86–87, 408
equivalent, 66–67, 86–87, 408
length, 66–67, 408
mass (weight), 76, 77, 78, 408
temperature, 408
using ruler, 64, 65, 66–67, 262–263,
Mental math. *See also* Estimation.
addition, 57–58, 104, 107, 128, 392–393, 394–395, 396–397, 399
division, 399
multiplication, 169, 292–293, 297–299, 308–309, 398
strategies
adding by endings, 396
breaking apart numbers, 202–203, 397
compatible numbers, 57–58, 107, 399
compensation, 397
counting on or back, 57–58, 396
doubling, 169
grouping for tens, 59, 70–71, 107, 397
rounding, 398
using multiples of ten, 19, 104, 201
using properties, 198, 205
subtraction, 114–115, 117, 396

visualizing. *See* Charts and tables; Data, representing; Problem solving strategies.
when to use, 117, 396–397
Meter, 126, 408
Metric system. *See* Measurement.
Mile, 408
Milliliter, 408
Million, 180
Missing addends, 78, 79, 80
Missing factors, 263, 307, 331
Mixed numbers, defined, 251
Modeling
with base ten blocks and hundreds' board, 17, 100–101, 102–103, 104, 105, 110–111, 112, 113, 114–115, 302–303, 304–305, 308–309, 311, 323, 360–361, 363, 364, 365, 366–367
with counters, 16–17, 62–63, 152, 153, 171, 219–220, 292–293, 297–299, 387
decimals, 323
by folding paper, 14, 243, 245, 252–253, 257, 258–259, 266, 360, 370
fractions, 242–243, 245, 246–247, 252–253, 257, 258–259, 260–261, 266, 268–269
hands-on activities, 8–9, 24–25, 62–63, 64, 65, 76, 78, 84–85, 86–87, 190–191, 192, 242–243, 244, 245, 260–261, 340, 341, 348, 350, 370, 371
making models, 8–9, 125, 213, 214, 215, 242–243, 245, 246–247, 248–249, 250–251, 254–255, 256, 257, 258–259, 260–261, 266, 268–269, 345, 387
making representations, 12, 62–63, 108–109, 125, 126–127, 147, 150, 158–159, 162–163, 164, 170, 171, 172, 208–209, 210–211, 224–225, 226, 246–247, 251, 252–253, 257, 260–261, 276–277, 315, 317, 318, 319, 331, 342, 343, 345, 348, 350, 351, 352–354, 356, 364
with play money, 108–109, 300–301, 324–325, 328, 329
with ten-frame, 57
Money
addition with, 108–109, 326–327, 329, 399
cents sign, 324–325
comparing values of, 29, 30–31, 32
counting, 29, 30–31, 32
division with, 326–327
estimating with, 108–109, 399
investigation based on, 33, 334–335, 336
making change, 30–31, 32, 174–175, 328, 329, 330–331
mental math with, 399
multiplication of, 174–175, 324–325, 326–327
place value and, 117
recognizing, 29, 30–31
subtraction with, 30–31, 32, 117, 326–327
writing value of, 325
More than. *See* Numbers, comparing and ordering.
Multicultural connections. *See* Cultural connections.
Multiplication
addition and, 184–185, 186, 208–209
alternative algorithms for, 302–303, 304–305, 308–309, 311
analyzing data, 180
with arrays, 152–153, 154–155, 156–157, 158–159, 160–161, 162, 163, 164, 165, 169, 170, 171, 186, 190–191, 192, 202–203, 220, 224–225, 300–301
in calculator activities, 48, 180, 187
Commutative Property of, 55, 171, 172, 198–199, 200, 301
division and, 219–220, 224–225
estimating products, 297–299, 308–309, 398
factors, 159, 160–161, 307
facts, strategies for learning
doubling, 169, 170, 186–187
skip counting, 173, 177, 178–179, 186–187
using Commutative Property, 55, 171, 172, 198–199
using other facts, 202–203
using patterns, 200–201
finding factors, 160, 307
games, 230–231, 306–307
investigations based on, 206–207, 300–301, 334–335, 336
lattice, 311
mental math, 169, 292–293, 297–299, 308–309, 398
modeling
using arrays, 152–153, 154–155, 156–157, 158–159, 160–161, 162, 163, 164, 165, 169, 170, 171, 186, 190–191, 192, 202–203, 220, 224–225, 300–301
using counters, 292–293, 297–299
of money, 174–175, 324–325, 326–327
by one, 205
problem solving with, 158–159, 160–161, 169, 172, 173, 174–175, 176–177, 178–179, 180–181, 182–183, 184–185, 186–187, 190–191, 192, 200–201, 202–205, 210–211, 292–293, 294–295, 296–297, 298–299, 300–301, 302–303, 304, 306–307, 308–309, 310, 311, 312–313, 324–325, 326–327, 334–335, 336
product, defined, 159
recording, 302–303, 304, 305, 308–309
table of facts
making, 163, 173, 178–179, 198–199, 200–201
patterns in, 163, 172, 173, 178–179, 185, 198–199, 200–201, 206–207
of tens and hundreds, 292–293, 294–295
two-digit
with no trading, 294–295
with trading, 297–299, 306–307, 308–309, 310

Index

Multiplication (cont,)
writing number sentence from array, 159, 160–161, 165, 170, 186, 294–295, 300–301
by zero, 205

N

Number line, 22–23, 260–261
Numbers, whole. *See also* Decimals; Fractions.
comparing and ordering, 16–17, 18, 19, 34, 54, 58, 107, 314–315
consecutive, 62
even and odd, 62–63
modeling, 16–17, 62–63
ordinal, 34, 35, 38
rounding, 20–21, 22–23, 297–299, 398–399
writing, 17, 18, 19, 316–317, 318, 319, 322–323
Number sense. *See also* Data; Estimation; Logical reasoning, reasonable answers; Proportional reasoning, choosing scale or units.
large numbers and, 84, 133, 134, 135, 136–137, 138–139, 142–143, 144, 180
number relationships, 50–51, 84–85, 126–127, 128, 184–185, 199, 244, 254–255, 256, 260–261, 314–315
operation sense, 112, 117, 136–137, 208–209, 290–291, 304, 326–327
place value and, 18, 310, 322–323
rounding to estimate, 20–21, 22–23, 297–299, 398–399
units of measure and, 8–9, 10, 11, 66–67, 86–87, 124, 125, 126
Numerator, defined, 248

O

One, property of, 205
Ongoing Investigation, xiv–xvi, 96, 192, 288, 384
Open-ended problems, xiv–xvi, 33, 46–47, 48, 62–63, 94–95, 96, 120–121, 133, 142–143, 144, 156–157, 190–191, 192, 206–207, 238–239, 240, 274–275, 286–287, 288, 344
Organized list, making, 109, 388
Ounce, 76, 408

P

Palindrome, 120–121
Patterns
in arrays, 163, 164, 165, 200–201, 206–207, 300–301
charts and, 122–123, 300–301
creating, 89, 90–91, 238–239, 240
describing, 62–63, 88, 89, 90–91, 94–95, 96, 104, 151, 163, 164, 165, 300–301, 314–315
division and, 314–315
finding, 62–63, 88, 89, 90–91, 94–95, 96, 122–123, 259, 292–293, 294–295, 314–315, 406
investigations based on, 62–63, 206–207
multiples of ten and, 292–293, 294–295, 314–315
multiplication tables and, 163, 173, 175, 178–179, 185, 198–199, 200–201, 206–207
in numerators and denominators, 259
predicting, 88, 89, 206–207
problem solving using, 88–89, 90–91, 200–201, 206–207, 300–301, 387
writing expressions based on, 62–63, 94–95, 96
Perimeter, 125, 126–127
Pictographs, 177
Picture graph, 14–15
Pint, 87, 408
Place value
in addition, 100–101, 102–103, 104, 105, 106, 107, 108–109,
calculators and, 19, 310, 314
charts, 17, 18, 134, 305, 315, 322
comparing, 18, 310, 322–323
decimals and, 314–315, 319, 322–323
defined, 18
in division, 360–361
hundreds, 102–103, 104, 105, 106, 107, 308–309
hundred thousands, 134
investigation, 46–48, 142–143, 144
millions, 180
modeling
using abacus, 24–25
using base ten blocks, 17, 100–101, 102–103, 104, 105, 110–111, 112, 113, 114–115
with money, 117
in multiplication, 304–305, 306–307, 308–309, 310
order of digits, 18, 19
problem solving using, 16–17, 18, 19, 24–25, 46–47, 133, 134, 135, 136–137, 138–139
reading large numbers, 17, 133,
in subtraction, 110–111, 112, 113, 114–115, 116
tens and ones, 100–101, 102–103, 104, 105, 106, 107, 114–115, 116, 134, 302–303, 304, 308–309, 314–315, 319
ten thousands, 134
tenths, 314–315, 316–317, 319
thousands, 134, 135, 136–137, 138–139
word form, 133, 134
Plane figures. *See* Geometry.
Point, defined, 342
Polygon, 350, 351, 352–354, 370, 371
Pound, 78, 408
Predicting. *See* Logical reasoning, predicting and verifying; Probability, predicting and recording outcomes.
Prediction, defined, 282
Prism, rectangular, 212–213, 214

Probability
combinations, 183
experimental, 282–283
predicting and recording outcomes, 282–283
problem solving with, 280–281, 282–283
Problem solving activities. *See also* Data, representing; Investigations; Logical reasoning.
Check Your Math Power, 25, 45, 75, 93, 123, 141, 167, 189, 217, 237, 265, 285, 313, 333, 359, 381
designing and, 62–63, 156–157, 190–191, 192, 336
Exercises and Problems, 42-43, 82–83, 118–119, 154–155, 174–175, 210–211, 272–273, 326–327, 378–379
hypothesizing and, 404–405
planning and, 190–191, 192, 334–335, 336, 404–405
Problem solving strategies. *See also* Tools and techniques.
acting it out, 78, 387
choosing operations, 112, 117, 136–137, 208–209, 290–291, 304, 326–327
choosing strategies, 29, 110–111, 117, 137, 169, 179, 196, 294–295, 340, 341, 404–405
drawing pictures or diagrams, 90–91, 147, 190–191, 192, 206–207, 208–209, 214, 251, 252–253, 260–261, 276, 315, 317, 318, 319, 331, 342, 343, 345, 348, 350, 351, 352–354, 356, 364, 386
guessing and checking, 84–86, 391
interpreting pictures, graphs, maps, and diagrams, 61, 69, 71, 81, 82–83, 88, 94–95, 96, 135, 138–139, 151, 158, 180, 206–207, 210–211, 282–283, 292–293, 295, 296–297, 299, 305, 309, 315, 322–323, 401
making lists, charts, or tables, 14–15, 32, 34, 109, 112, 122–123, 268–269, 280–281, 282, 296–297, 300–301, 334–335, 336, 343, 355, 387, 388, 389, 404–405
making models, 8–9, 125, 213, 214, 215, 242–243, 245, 246–247, 248–249, 250–251, 254–255, 256, 257, 258–259, 260–261, 266, 268–269, 345, 387
using compatible numbers, 57–58, 107, 399
using estimation, 39, 40, 41, 42–43, 98–99, 108–109, 110–111, 124, 128, 129
using patterns, 62–63, 88, 89, 90–91, 104, 122–123, 151, 163, 164, 165, 200–201, 206–207, 300–301, 387, 406
using simpler or related problem, 390
writing equations or expressions, 54, 57, 60, 61, 62–63, 65, 69, 78, 79, 80, 94–95, 96, 159, 160–161, 165, 169, 174–175, 208–209, 267, 268–269
writing rules, 89, 90–91, 295
Product, defined, 159
Properties
Associative of Addition, 59
Commutative of Addition, 55, 171
Commutative of Multiplication, 55, 171, 172, 198–199, 200, 301
Identity of Multiplication, 205
Zero of Multiplication, 205
Proportional reasoning, choosing scale or units, 66–67, 78, 126
Pyramid, 233

Q

Quart, 86–87, 408

R

Reasonable answers, 39, 40, 41, 42–43, 116, 138
Reasoning. *See* Journals; Logical reasoning; Problem solving strategies.
Reasoning and Problem Solving, 10, 12, 16, 35, 60, 70, 79, 87, 107, 110–111, 125, 139, 151, 165, 169, 170, 180, 199, 251, 255, 268, 283, 295, 304, 310, 318, 340, 356, 362
Rectangular prism, 212–213, 214
Remainder, 228–229, 362
Representing. *See also* Computer activities; Geometry; Graphs; Modeling; Visualizing.
data
on spreadsheets, 401
by tallying, 26, 28, 32, 37, 296–297, 404–405
using bar graphs, 27, 28, 36–37, 38, 296–297
using charts, 65, 76, 90–91, 94–95, 96, 109, 112, 124, 149, 151, 158, 163, 173, 178–179, 198–199, 200–201, 206–207, 268–269, 282–283, 299, 300–301, 355, 388, 389, 401
using pictographs, 177
using picture graphs, 14–15
decimals, 314–315, 316–317, 317–318, 319, 322–323
drawing pictures or diagrams, 9, 15, 33, 37, 53, 65, 77, 90, 103, 126, 133, 150, 179, 203, 249, 255, 258, 269, 279, 294, 317, 331, 343, 354, 364, 377
fractions
using counters, 252–253, 266, 268–269
using shapes, 242–243, 245, 246–247, 248–249, 250–251, 254–255, 256, 257, 258–259, 260–261, 266, 268–269
shapes, 203, 212–213, 250–251, 346, 355, 372, 378–379, 382–383, 384
whole-number operations
by drawing pictures, 251, 252–253, 260–261, 276
using arrays and, 152–153, 154–155, 156–157, 158–159, 160–161, 162, 163, 164, 165, 169, 170, 171, 186, 190–191, 192, 202–203, 219–220, 221–222, 224–225

Index

Representing (cont.)
using base ten blocks and hundreds' board, 100–101, 102–103, 104, 105, 110–111, 112, 113, 114–115, 360–361, 363, 364, 365, 366–367
using counters, 219–220, 226, 292–293, 297–299
using play money, 108–109
Review. *See also* Assessment.
cumulative, 24–25, 44–45, 74–75, 92–93, 122–123, 140–141, 166–167, 188–189, 216–217, 236–237, 264–265, 284–285, 312–313, 332–333, 358–359, 380–381
Try It!, 7, 11, 13, 19, 32, 38, 54, 58, 61, 67, 73, 77, 80, 87, 91, 104, 109, 113, 131, 134, 139, 151, 159, 165, 172, 177, 179, 181, 183, 185, 199, 205, 215, 223, 227, 231, 253, 259, 267, 279, 283, 295, 299, 318, 321, 323, 331, 345, 349, 357, 368
Right angle, 346
Rounding
money, 399
problem solving and, 20–21, 22–23, 297–299, 398–399
rounded numbers, defined, 22
to tens or hundreds, 20–23, 292–293, 297–299, 398–399
when to round, 398–399
whole numbers, 20–21, 22–23, 292–293, 297–299, 398–399
Rules. *See* Games; Problem solving strategies, writing rules.

S

Segment, 343
Shapes. *See* Geometry, plane figures, space figures.
Similar figures, 372–373
Skip counting, 173–175, 177, 178–179, 186–187
Slides, flips, turns, 372–373
Space figures. *See* Geometry.
Sphere, 233
Spreadsheet, 401
Square, 352–354
Subtraction
calculator activities using, 137, 369
checking, 111
with decimals, 317–318, 319, 320–321
difference, defined, 69
division and, 369
estimating with, 386
with fractions, 395
modeling using base ten blocks, 110–111, 112, 113, 114–115
of money, 30–31, 117, 320–321, 326–327, 328, 329, 330–331
problem solving with, 69, 70–71, 72–73, 110–111, 112, 113, 114–115, 116, 117, 118–119, 139, 328, 330–331, 393, 394–395
recording, 110–111, 112, 113, 114–115, 116, 393, 394–395
renaming digits and, 393, 394–395
strategies
counting back, 69, 70–71
counting up, 70–71
making ten, 70–71
of whole numbers
four- and five-digit, 137–138
three-digit, 110–111, 112, 113, 114–115, 116, 117, 118–119, 394
two-digit, 114–115, 393
zero in, 113, 114–115
Sum, defined, 55
Survey. *See also* Data.
designing, 404–405
recording data
with database, 401
tallying, 26, 28, 32, 36, 404–405
using bar graph, 27, 28, 36–37, 38, 296–297
Symmetry, lines of, 374, 375, 376–377, 378–379, 382–383

T

Table of measures, 408
Tallying, 26, 28, 32, 37, 296–297, 404–405
Tangram, 352–354, 355
Technology. *See* Calculator activities; Computer activities.
Telling time, 8–9, 10, 11
Temperature
Celsius, 130, 408
Fahrenheit, 13, 408
reading thermometer, 131
telling stories about, 131
Tens, grouping for, 59, 70–71, 107, 292–295, 302–303, 304, 397
Tenth
as decimal, 315
defined, 314
Tests. *See* Assessment.
Three-dimensional figures. *See* Geometry, space figures.
Time
A.M. and P.M., 10
calendar, 4–5, 6, 7, 292–293, 295
clock, 8–9, 10, 11
days in month, 5
minutes
on clock, 8–9, 10, 11
converting to hours, 8–9, 408
writing dates, 4–7, 292–293, 295
Ton, 408
Tools and Techniques. *See also* Drawing to Learn; Problem solving strategies.
5, 14, 20, 22, 30, 39, 57, 73, 85, 100–101, 109, 117, 130, 135, 149, 158, 175, 198, 214, 229, 244, 262, 282, 297, 305, 319, 328, 342, 353, 360, 370
Tracing Tool, 250–251, 346, 372, 378–379
Triangle, 352–354
Two-dimensional figures. *See* Geometry, plane figures.

U

U.S. customary units. *See* Measurement, U.S. customary units.

V

Variable, 397
Visualizing. *See* Logical reasoning, visualizing; Modeling; Problem solving strategies; Representing.
Volume
  defined, 213
  exploring with models, 213–215

W

Weight, measuring. *See* Measurement, mass (weight).
Whole number. *See* Addition, of whole numbers; Comparing, whole numbers; Division, with one-digit divisors; Multiplication, two-digit; Numbers, whole; Subtraction, of whole numbers.
Word Bank, 3, 51, 99, 147, 194, 242, 290, 338
Writing about math. *See* Communication, writing; Connect and Communicate; Journals.

Y

Yard, 66–67

Z

Zero, 205
  in addition, 104, 107
  in subtraction, 113, 114–115
Zero Property of Multiplication, 205

Acknowledgments

Text *(continued from page iv)*

Copyright © 1976. Used by permission of the publisher, Prentice Hall/a division of Simon & Schuster. **68** From *The Umbrella Thief,* by Sybil Wettasinghe, first American edition published in 1987 by Kane/Miller Book Publishers. Copyright © by Sybil Wettasinghe. Originally published in 1986 as *Kasa Doroboh* by Fukutake Publishing Co., Ltd., Tokyo, Japan. Reprinted by permission of Kane/Miller Book Publishers. **132** "The Elephant" by Louis Phillips, published in *A Zooful of Animals,* selected by William Cole and illustrated by Lynn Munsinger. New York: Houghton Mifflin Company, 1992. Reprinted by permission of the author. **168** From *Jacob Two-Two and the Dinosaur,* by Mordecai Richler, illustrated by Norman Eyolfson. Text copyright © 1987 by Mordecai Richler. Illustrations copyright © 1987 by Norman Eyolfson. Reprinted by permission Alfred A. Knopf, Inc. **224** From "Rodeo Time" from *Justin and the Best Biscuits in the World,* by Mildred Pitts Walter. New York: Lothrop, Lee & Shepard Books, a Division of William Morrow & Company, Inc., 1986. **250** From "A Mother's Advice" in *The Black Prince and Other Egyptian Folk Tales,* told by Ahmed and Zane Zagloul. New York: Doubleday & Company, Inc., 1971. **324** From *What's Cooking, Jenny Archer,* by Ellen Conford. Boston: Little, Brown and Company, 1989. **352** From *The Kingdom of Geometry,* originally published as *El reino de la geometría,* written by Alma Flor Ada, illustrated by José Ramón Sánchez. Copyright © 1993 by Alma Flor Ada. Reprinted by permission of Laredo Publishing Company, Torrance, California.

Illustrations

2–3 Steven Mach. **31** Patty O'Friel. **52–53** Paul Mirocha. **76** Margaret Bruns. **102–3** David Csicsko. **232–33** Chris Reed. **360–61** Randy Chewning.

Photography

Front cover Allan Landau. **Back cover** Sharon Hoogstraten. **i** Allan Landau. **ii–iii** Allan Landau. **vi–vii** Sharon Hoogstraten. **viii** Allan Landau (b). **viii–ix** Sharon Hoogstraten. **x** Allan Landau (b); Sharon Hoogstraten (r). **xi** Sharon Hoogstraten (t, c, bl); Allan Landau (br). **xii–xiii** Allan Landau. **xiv** Sharon Hoogstraten. **xv** Allan Landau. **xvi** Sharon Hoogstraten.**1** Sharon Hoogstraten. **4–5** Allan Landau. **5** Aric Attas. **6** Allan Landau. **7** Allan Landau (l, lc, rc), Sharon Hoogstraten (r). **8** Sharon Hoogstraten (b, insets tl, tr). **9** Sharon Hoogstraten (b, insets tl, tr). **10** Sharon Hoogstraten. **14–15** Sharon Hoogstraten. **15** Sharon Hoogstraten (t), Allan Landau (b). **16** Sharon Hoogstraten (t), Allan Landau (b). **18** Allan Landau. **19** Allan Landau. **20** Susan Andrews. **20–21** Sharon Hoogstraten. **21** Susan Andrews (insets l, r). **22** Sharon Hoogstraten. **24–25** Sharon Hoogstraten. **26–27** Sharon Hoogstraten. **28** Sharon Hoogstraten. **29** Sharon Hoogstraten. **30** Sharon Hoogstraten. **32** Allan Landau. **33** Sharon Hoogstraten. **34–35** Allan Landau. **35** Allan Landau (l, c), Sharon Hoogstraten (r). **36–37** Allan Landau. **38** Sharon Hoogstraten. **39** Sharon Hoogstraten (l, r). **40** Allan Landau. **41** Allan Landau. **42–43** Sharon Hoogstraten. **44** Sharon Hoogstraten. **45** Sharon Hoogstraten (t, b). **46–47** Aric Attas. **48** Sharon Hoogstraten. **49** Sharon Hoogstraten. **50–51** Aric Attas. **54–55** Sharon Hoogstraten. **56** Allan Landau (b, insets tl, tc, tr). **57** Allan Landau. **59** © Betty K. Bruce/Animals Animals. **60** Sharon Hoogstraten. **61** Aric Attas. **62** Sharon Hoogstraten. **63** Art Wise. **64** Aric Attas. **64–65** Sharon Hoogstraten. **66** Allan Landau. **68–69** Sharon Hoogstraten. **70–71** Sharon Hoogstraten. **72** Allan Landau. **74** © Hideo Kurihara/Tony Stone Images. **76** Allan Landau. **77** Allan Landau. **78** Allan Landau. **79** Michael Holford (t), Sharon Hoogstraten (b). **81** © Fritz Prenzel/Animals Animals. **82–83** Aric Attas. **83** © Breck P. Kent/Animals Animals. **84** Devaney Stock Photos. **84–85** Aric Attas. **85** Allan Landau. **86** Sharon Hoogstraten. **89** © Terry Wild Studio. **90** Art Wise (b, insets tl, tr). **91** Art Wise. **94–95** Sharon Hoogstraten. **95** Allan Landau. **96** Aric Attas. **97** Sharon Hoogstraten. **98–99** Allan Landau. **100** Allan Landau. **101** Sharon Hoogstraten. **104** Sharon Hoogstraten (insets l, c, r). **105** Sharon Hoogstraten.**106** Allan Landau. **107** Sharon Hoogstraten. **108–9** Sharon Hoogstraten. **110–11** Sharon Hoogstraten. **112** Sharon Hoogstraten. **113** Allan Landau. **114–15** Sharon Hoogstraten. **116** Allan Landau. **117** Allan Landau. **118–19** Sharon Hoogstraten. **120** Allan Landau. **120–21** Sharon Hoogstraten. **122** © L.L.T. Rhodes/Tony Stone Images (clown). **122–23** Allan Landau. **124–25** Sharon Hoogstraten. **126** Allan Landau. **127** Sharon Hoogstraten. **128** Allan Landau. **129** Allan Landau. **131** Sharon Hoogstraten. **132** Sharon Hoogstraten. **133** Allan Landau. **134** © Anthony Bannister/Animals Animals (t), © E.R. Degginger/ Animals Animals (b). **135** Sharon Hoogstraten. **136** Allan Landau. **136–37** Sharon

Hoogstraten. **138–39** Sharon Hoogstraten. **142–43** Sharon Hoogstraten. **144** Sharon Hoogstraten.**145** Allan Landau. **146** © Michel Viard/Peter Arnold. **146–47** Allan Landau. **147** Aric Attas. **148** Sharon Hoogstraten (tl, tr, bl, br). **149** Ralph J. Brunke (t), Allan Landau (b). **150** © Animals Animals (r), Sharon Hoogstraten (l). **151** Sharon Hoogstraten. **152** Aric Attas. **153** Aric Attas. **154** Ralph J. Brunke (l, c, r). **155** Sharon Hoogstraten (l, c, r). **156** Sharon Hoogstraten. **156–57** Allan Landau. **157** Sharon Hoogstraten (t), courtesy of Weatherhill Inc. (b). **158** Sharon Hoogstraten. **160** Ralph J. Brunke (insets l, c), Allan Landau (r). **161** Allan Landau. **162** Aric Attas (l, r). **163** Ralph J. Brunke. **164** Sharon Hoogstraten (insets t, c), Ralph J. Brunke (b). **165** Sharon Hoogstraten. **166–67** Sharon Hoogstraten. **173** Sharon Hoogstraten. **174–75** Aric Attas. **176–77** Aric Attas. **179** Allan Landau. **180** Sharon Hoogstraten. **181** Ralph J. Brunke. **182–83** Aric Attas. **184** Sharon Hoogstraten. **184–85** Sharon Hoogstraten. **186–87** © Paul Miller. **187** Sharon Hoogstraten. **189** Sharon Hoogstraten. **190–91** Aric Attas. **191** Allan Landau. **192** Aric Attas, © Michael Hart/FPG International (inset l), © Arthur Tilley/FPG International (inset r).**193** Sharon Hoogstraten.**194–95** Sharon Hoogstraten, © Bob Daemmrich/Tony Stone Images (inset). **195** © Bob Daemmrich. **196** Sharon Hoogstraten, © Katie Deits/FPG International (inset). **197** Susan Andrews. **198** Sharon Hoogstraten. **200** Susan Andrews. **201** Aric Attas, © Suzanne Murphy/FPG International (inset). **202–3** Sharon Hoogstraten. **203** Susan Andrews. **204** Sharon Hoogstraten. **205** Sharon Hoogstraten. **206–7** Sharon Hoogstraten. **208** Ellen Balkin (t, b). **209** Ellen Balkin. **210–11** Sharon Hoogstraten. **212** Aric Attas. **213** Sharon Hoogstraten. **214** Sharon Hoogstraten. **215** Sharon Hoogstraten. **216–17** Sharon Hoogstraten. **218–19** Aric Attas, courtesy Twins Day Festival Committee (inset). **220** Sharon Hoogstraten (t, insets bl, bc, br). **221** Allan Landau. **222** Aric Attas. **224** Brown Brothers. **225** Sharon Hoogstraten, © Magayne-Roshak/Third Coast (inset). **226–27** Sharon Hoogstraten. **228** Sharon Hoogstraten (insets l, r). **228–29** Sharon Hoogstraten. **230–31** Sharon Hoogstraten. **234** Susan Andrews. **235** Sharon Hoogstraten. **238** Susan Andrews. **238–39** Sharon Hoogstraten. **239** Susan Andrews. **240** Sharon Hoogstraten. **241** Sharon Hoogstraten. **242–43** Sh
Hoogstraten. **244–45** Sharon Hoogstraten. **24**
Hoogstraten (insets l, r). **246–47** Sharon Hoog
249 Allan Landau. **250** Sharon Hoogstraten. **25**
Sharon Hoogstraten. **252** Sharon Hoogstraten. **252-**
Sharon Hoogstraten. **253** Sharon Hoogstraten. **254–5**
Sharon Hoogstraten. **256–57** Sharon Hoogstraten. **257** Sharon Hoogstraten (insets l, c, r). **258–59** Sharon

Hoogstraten. **260** Sharon Hoogstraten. **261** Sharon Hoogstraten (t, c, b). **262–63** Sharon Hoogstraten. **263** Sharon Hoogstraten (l, c, r). **264–65** Sharon Hoogstraten. **266** Sharon Hoogstraten (r, c, l). **266–67** Sharon Hoogstraten. **268** Sharon Hoogstraten (l, r). **268–69** Sharon Hoogstraten. **269** Sharon Hoogstraten (l, r). **271** Allan Landau. **272–73** Sharon Hoogstraten. **274** Sharon Hoogstraten (l, c, r). **274–75** Sharon Hoogstraten. **276** Sharon Hoogstraten. **277** Sharon Hoogstraten. **278–79** Sharon Hoogstraten. **280** Allan Landau. **281** Sharon Hoogstraten (b, insets l, r). **282–83** Sharon Hoogstraten. **286–87** Sharon Hoogstraten. **288** Sharon Hoogstraten. **289** Sharon Hoogstraten. **290** Allan Landau. **291** Allan Landau. **292** Allan Landau (l, r). **293** Sharon Hoogstraten. **294** Sharon Hoogstraten. **296** Allan Landau. **297** Sharon Hoogstraten. **298** Allan Landau (t, insets bl, br). **299** Sharon Hoogstraten. **300** Allan Landau. **301** Sharon Hoogstraten. **302** Sharon Hoogstraten. **303** Sharon Hoogstraten. **304** Sharon Hoogstraten (t), Allan Landau (insets bl, br). **305** Sharon Hoogstraten. **306** Sharon Hoogstraten. **307** Allan Landau. **308** Allan Landau. **309** Sharon Hoogstraten. **310** Allan Landau. **312–13** Sharon Hoogstraten, © Tony Stone Images (inset). **314–15** Sharon Hoogstraten. **31**
Sharon Hoogstraten. **317** Allan Landau (l, r). **319**
Sharon Hoogstraten. **320–21** Allan Landau. **322**
Sharon Hoogstraten. **324** Sharon Hoogstrate
Allan Landau. **326** Sharon Hoogstraten. **32**
Hoogstraten. **328** Sharon Hoogstraten
Landau. **330** Allan Landau. **331** Shar
334–35 Sharon Hoogstraten. **33**
337 Sharon Hoogstraten. **338-**
341 Allan Landau. **342** Alla
Hoogstraten. **344–45** Al
Hoogstraten (l, r). **34**
tr). **350–51** Sharon
Hoogstraten. **3**
Hoogstraten
Hoogstra
Hoogs
Lan

  9,812
+ 5,054
+ 1,001
+ 9,991
+ 11,111
+ 10,000

38,074

1 2 3 4 5 6 7 8 9 10

+2 3 4 5 6 7 8 9

+3 4 5 6 7 8 9 10 11 12 13 14 15

+4 5 6 7 8 9 10 11 12 13 14 15

+5 6 7 8 9 10 11 12 13 14 15

+6 7 8 9 10 11 12 13 14 15

+6 7 8 9 10 11 12 13 14

+7 8 9 10 11 12 13 14

+8 9 10 11 12 13 14 15 16 17 18 19 20

100$
1000$